HAPPY BUT STRIVING

HAPPY BUT STRIVING

Memoirs of a Buddhist Canadian

Suwanda H. J. Sugunasiri

MOSAIC PRESS

Library and Archives Canada Cataloguing in Publication

Title: Happy but striving: Memoirs of a Buddhist Canadian /
by Suwanda Sugunasiri.

Names: Sugunasiri, Suwanda H. J., author.

Identifiers: Canadiana (print) 20210170735 | Canadiana (ebook) 2021017076X |
ISBN 9781771615761 (softcover) | ISBN 9781771615778 (PDF) |
ISBN 9781771615785 (EPUB) |ISBN 9781771615792 (Kindle)

Subjects: LCSH: Sugunasiri, Suwanda H. J. | LCSH:
Buddhists—Canada—Biography. | LCGFT: Autobiographies.

Classification: LCC BQ988.S84 A3 2021 | DDC 294.3092—dc23

Published by Mosaic Press, Oakville, Ontario, Canada, 2021.

MOSAIC PRESS, Publishers
www.Mosaic-Press.com
Copyright © Suwanda Sugunasiri, 2021

All rights reserved. Without limiting the rights under copyright reserved
here, no part of this publication may be reproduced, stored in or
introduced into any retrieval system, or transmitted in any form or by any
means—electronic, mechanical, by photocopy, recording or otherwise—
without the prior written permission and consent of both the copyright
owners and the Publisher of this book.
All materials in this book are published on a non-exclusive basis.

MOSAIC PRESS
1252 Speers Road, Units 1 & 2, Oakville, Ontario, L6L 5N9
(905) 825-2130 • info@mosaic-press.com • www.mosaic-press.com

DEDICATION

Parents

Mother
Missinona Warnakulasuriya
of Dodanduwa

Father
Kalaguru S. H. Sauris Silva
of Tangalla

GRATITUDE

Dr. Richard Arndt *(USA)*
Chair, Ceylon Fulbright Committee

Sri Lanka; USA; Canada

CONTENTS

FOREWORD ix
PREFACE xv

BOOK I
A US FULBRIGHT CONNECTION, 1964 TO 1973

BOOK II
CANADA - HOME AWAY FROM HOME, 1973 ON

Part 1	*Early years*	53
Part 2	*Watch Out! Social Animal on the Prowl*	82
Part 3	*Planting Buddhist Seeds On Canadian Soil*	155
Part 4	*Sensitizing the Political Heavyweights, Left, Right & Centre* ..	175
Part 5	*Buddhism in the Academy*	199
Part 6	*A Media Presence*	238
Part 7	*A Creative Renaissance - Poetry, Short Fiction and Novel* .	268
Part 8	*Shrinking & Expanding the World*	290

BOOK III
A CREATIVE GRATITUDINAL CLOSING

NEW TERMS 340
POEMS INDEX 341
PLACE INDEX 342
NAME INDEX 345
WORKS BY THE AUTHOR (Selected) 353

THANK YOU

I thank Prof. Lionel Steiman of the University of Manitoba for his extensive Foreword, capturing the diverse dimensions of this Autosociobiography.

I thank Johnny Osorio of CorelPrint for the many hours put in by way of designing this book, as well as incorporating over time many a change in the text and doing the Indexes.

My thanks are due to Rosemarie Levman for her meticulous proofreading.

Without the interest and ongoing support of Howard Aster of Mosaic Press, this Memoir would never have come to see the light of day.

The sensitivity of Rahim Piracha in seeking a calming effect in the cover, capturing the Buddhist sensibility in the book, is much appreciated.

Last but not least goes my gratitude to Swarna who encouraged me to put my life in print! And her suggestions and modifications add much to the quality of the text.

And it is to the readers I finally thank for your interest in this multidimensional saga. Hope you'll enjoy it!

Metta!

Suwanda H J Sugunasiri

FOREWORD

Professor Lionel Steiman

Senior Scholar, Department of History,
University of Manitoba, Canada

Suwanda Sugunasiri's Memoir is more than an autobiography. Written by a man who defies categorization, it is a document of Canadian society transforming itself from what was in many ways still a polyglot British colony into a committed multicultural community. Its protagonist is a Sinhalese Sri Lankan immigrant, carrying his deeply ingrained native culture and religion to his new home in the west.

Although showing little academic promise growing up in Sri Lanka, being more involved in extra-curricular activities, including cricket, cadetting, literary associations and various others, an opportunity in 1964 gained him a Fulbright Fellowship to study at an Ivy League University in the United States. There he quickly acquired impressive academic credentials, earning a Master's Degree in Linguistics, subsequently augmented with two more Master's Degrees and a doctoral degree from the University of Toronto.

His nearly six decades in North America, the last five in Toronto, coincided with that crucial but contentious phase in Canadian history launched in 1970, when the nation embraced the ideals of multiculturalism and set out to build a society that was to inspire admiration and emulation around the globe.

Rather than simply exploiting and enjoying the benefits of this epochal transformation, Suwanda Sugunasiri became an active and committed participant in and contributor to almost every facet of the whole multicultural process. What gave his contributions their unique value was his remaining firmly rooted in the principles and practice of Buddhism, so that whatever he offered in advocacy or criticism was always advanced in a spirit of toleration, with understanding and with friendly good humor.

No doubt it was growing up in Sri Lanka when it was still a very colonial Ceylon that provided him with the emotional armor and intellectual fortitude that served him so well later on. His family life there was certainly solid and tightly-knit, but the real strength of its ties was in the affection that bound them, and in the warmth with which all family members, extended as well as immediate, customarily addressed one another. Music and dance, respect for literacy and education, all had a lasting impact on young Sugunasiri. His participation in theatre and dance, as well as early forays in writing and journalism, absorbed much more of his energies than did academics, in which he distinguished himself only much later, as a young adult in America.

It was in Philadelphia in September 1964 that I met and got to know the friend I still call "Sugi". We were novice graduate students at the University of Pennsylvania, proud to be enrolled in an "Ivy league" college. He was there to study linguistics, and I, history. In our conversations he would point out etymologies and expand on the difference between the aspirate and inaspirate consonant `p´ as pronounced, respectively, by him or me. He was just as enthusiastic about the linguistics as he was about the substance of our discussions. The cheerful, boundless enthusiasm that struck me as the foundation of his character then, remains his most notable feature today. After a year at Penn, Sugi went on to the University of Michigan and before long settled in Toronto to begin the five decades encapsulated in the title of his autobiography, "Happy but Striving."

The striving refers to the years of sacrifice required to gain his Ph.D., followed by the endless searching for employment that was commensurate with his experience and credentials. Though well paid in his employment in schools, his academic skills clearly far exceeded both the capacities of students and the appreciation of administrators.

As if to absorb the creative energies untapped in this professional work, Suwanda plunged into journalism and a variety of cultural and community activities, invariably volunteer. What these activities gave him would prove far more valuable than any financial benefit, for it was in and through these activities that Dr. Sugunasiri nurtured his interest in the issues that were to be debated in coming decades during Canada´s great cultural transformation. Thus, when he did engage the issues of the day in letters to editors or on radio or television, it was always with a sound grasp and nuanced understanding of their elements and complex ramifications.

The "Happy" part in all this derived from a combination of his loving family life and a surprisingly positive outlook, despite seemingly unending frustration in his numerous professional endeavors and community involvements. In this, he was driven by an insatiable curiosity about his new home, and the limitless opportunities available to its citizens. That his wife Swarna and son had been able to join him in the "new world" just a year after he had left the old one gave his personal life a solid and secure foundation, and further energized his efforts outside the home. Soon the birth of their daughter made the family a happy foursome.

While the children and Swarna, herself a professional with a solid income who advanced to become a Departmental Head in the Secondary School System, emerge in Suwanda's story only periodically, as in his descriptions of their family holidays in North America and abroad, their love remains a constant, energizing his efforts and enabling him to surmount countless obstacles and meet new challenges with fresh courage.

Setbacks and disappointments were more than offset by achievements. Dr. Sugunasiri was instrumental in bringing together the growing number of Buddhists into an organization that would eventually culminate in the Buddhist Council of Canada. Further, he was actively involved with an astounding array of educational, interdisciplinary, cultural, cross-cultural and inter-faith conferences, dialogues, institutes, and publications, all of which are documented in detail as a treasure trove for Canadian historians.

Indeed, one of this book's many virtues is its value as an aid to understanding Canada in the process of transforming itself into a multicultural society - and this from the perspective of one who actively participated in that process with a keen understanding of all parties involved. This understanding was honed during years of study and living in novel cultural environments, and was sharpened particularly by his varied teaching situations in Toronto. These included voluntary as well as paid positions, where multiculturalism was not a project but a messy reality. The conception that Sugunasiri ultimately came to embody and communicate was one in which composite cultures were neither mixed, melted, or blended but instead fully affirmed themselves and each other. Their members would not just "tolerate" others but would respect, affirm, and enjoy them, including and especially their differences. His vision also includes a self-critical dimension in which one would willingly discard those aspects of one's native culture that proved not conducive to or supportive of the goals and ideals of Canada's multicultural project.

In all this, Dr. Sugunasiri's commitment to Buddhism never faltered. If anything it grew. The experience of teaching Buddhism at the University of Toronto's School of Continuing Studies during the 1990s expressed his commitment to Buddhist education in particular. This culminated in 2000 in his founding of the Nalanda College of Buddhist Studies, the first

Buddhist academic institution in Canada.

At the same time he continued an energetic engagement in all the issues of multiculturalism. His many forays via appearances before community groups, interviews on radio and television, and provocative newspaper columns - including good-natured responses to readers who took issue with him - culminated in the publication of his book, *Towards Multicultural Growth, A look at Canada from Classical Racism to Neomulticulturalism*, not long after the founding of Nalanda College. This was no expression of a "dual commitment", but was rather the product of a genuinely lived multicultural ideal.

Sugunasiri´s life of striving was a happy one in both the archaic and contemporary meanings of the word `happy´. He is possessed of a unique emotional armor which never allows rejection or criticism to penetrate or ever stall the engine of his engagement with the world. This armor is more than the familiar emotional defense that automatically deflects criticism of the self onto others. For example, when applications for positions for which he clearly qualifies were rejected, he would interpret this as indicative of an inert racism that still persisted in a Canada early on its path to multiculturalism. While he calls it racism, he never takes it personally, but sees it rather as a transitional phase in the evolution of multiculturalism. This kind of insight, combined with his good humor, makes for Sugunasiri´s most endearing quality. Despite a certain intellectual doggedness in matters close to his heart, his humor saves him from his dogmatism: Sugunasiri takes his principles seriously, but not his self. And despite temptations to do so, he never carries a grudge. One illustration will suffice: when a Forest Hill neighbor suffered a tragic, devastating personal loss, Sugunasiri paid the family a visit of condolence- despite the fact that the neighbor had led a racially motivated campaign opposing the city´s approval of a proposed addition to the Sugunasiri family home. The visit to the bereaved neighbor was simply an expression of the compassion that is part of the man´s nature, as well as a cherished principle of his Buddhism.

The other side of the coin of this compassion is Sugunasiri´s optimism, which is amply displayed in the chapter recounting repeated unsuccessful approaches he made to various ministries at both the federal and the provincial levels offering to place his skills and experience at their service as they proceeded with the formulation and implementation of policies based on the principles of multiculturalism. Yet in the end there is never any questioning the value of all these efforts: every little bit helps - that is his philosophy - as is the adage that change never happens overnight. The secret of his persistence lay in his enduring equanimity in the face of success as well as setbacks: success never made him complacent, nor did he ever lose heart in the face of obstacles or setbacks.

Nevertheless it is by no means the case that Sugunasiri is excessively modest or self-effacing, and he certainly doesn't exhibit the ostentatious humility that covers pride. Clearly he is proud of his accomplishments, just as he is of the accomplishments of other members of his family; clearly he takes pride in his academic and professional achievements, in his receiving many invitations to speak, in the publication of his letters, essays, and articles, and in having met so many prominent Canadians on various significant occasions. But at the same time he never hesitates to offer ample evidence of the shortcomings that others see in him, acknowledging their criticism and even quoting their letters in a way other writers would never dare. Some may find his *obiter dicta* infuriating, while others might find their own views confirmed by them. But even the most exasperated reader will be won back by Dr. Sugunasiri's loving, good nature, which occasionally expresses itself in digs at himself that are at least as outrageous as those he levels at society's sacred cows.

Cheerful throughout, this saga of a multi-cultural Canadian is a treasure trove of fascinating information about Canadian and Sri Lankan culture and character during a period of profound transformation, a time when both societies were going through a process of decolonization. Although Sugunasiri himself doesn't use it, the term `decolonization' serves to highlight the commonalities shared by these former members of the British Empire, diverse as they were and are in most other ways.

The feature of this book that should endear itself most to readers is also its underlying theme and leading motif, namely that of Buddhism. Dr. Sugunasiri's deep familiarity with the precepts and ideals of the Buddha enables him to communicate them with an enthusiasm and conviction borne of life-long study and devotion. Moreover, the happiness that suffuses this biography and justifies its title is bound up in the author's love of his family, religion, and culture. It is a happiness that nourishes itself more in the pleasure of others than in itself; it is an other-directed love, much akin to the Christian ideal of agape. Finally, it is the foundation of the peace in his cheerful nature, and the inspiration of his striving. It will also be the reward of his readers.

PREFACE

A young fellow is frolicking in the warm tropical ocean. Getting up on his feet, he sees the wavelets approaching him. He dives, and swimming back gets on to his feet again, only to see the waves getting bigger, the wind getting rougher and the landing louder. So he stretches his two hands as wide as they would go, and tries to contain the rough sea with his bare hands. Try as he might time and again, retreating and advancing, the waves keep pounding.

Then, seeing a hand waving, over the horizon, from far away, he takes to the wings and flies out on Trans World Airlines, hoping to return, better armed, hands wider and bigger, and brain tweaked.

This is the Memoir of that young man. Now you will see him burning the midnight oil on a US Fulbright at the Universities of Pennsylvania and Michigan, writing his Master's Thesis, while also mastering French!

Later on, in Canada, you may be trying to catch your breath trying to get a word in edgewise, the man developing a theory of Development for the Post-Colonial nations in doctoral studies, at University of Toronto, next getting knee deep in the local social waters - running over from one grounding to another to another to another, traveling across the country, meeting myriads of people seeking support or promoting one or another cause, not rarely getting the head banged, providing advice to governments, appearing on radio and TV, one time calling upon all Canadians to celebrate the life of Lord Jesus from their rooftops at Christmas time, watching how Christians were coming to be sidelined. Or it could be writing Columns in the print media, such as at the *Toronto Star*, on Multiculturalism or Buddhism, or writing a Letter to the Editor how the English Canadians who opened the immigrant door have been, in the name of multiculturalism, turned into TWASPs - Tortured White Anglo-Saxon Protestants. Or it would be dancing at Toronto's Harbourfront or doing an invited poetry Reading at the International Reading series, and on on and on....

But why should you be interested? Good question. To begin with, it will take you across two lands of N American vintage, i.e., Canada and the US, with an occasional by the way peek at one Asian, namely Sri Lanka. As you will see, the US of A will only serve as an opener in the unfolding drama. But there will be no less entertainment – swimming in the beaches of Waikiki in Honolulu, taking the rides in Disneyland in LA, or experiencing the astronaut in Cape Canaveral, Florida, buckled up in the rocket ship that took Neil Armstrong to the moon, all this, of course, with the family.

But if you're looking for juicy gossip, you'll be truly disappointed. For what you will read here is the social history rather than a personal story. When it comes to Canada, you will be treated to the unique drama of a monocultural British colony of a hundred years evolving into a multicultural independent Canada, taking you to the nooks and crannies of history of over five decades – to recall, discover, re-discover, learn from, lean against, scream out, reflect upon, build upon or look for your kids to share an ice cream or a mouth burn of their history.

But having given the 'strictly objective here' line, I have to now talk from the other side of the mouth. It was indeed Canada that taught me that if you don't beat your own drum, nobody else will At least not as good as you would! I came from a culture where humility is the marker of quality. Indeed I had written a column at the passing away of a Sinhala monk with the words, 'the heavier the fruits, the lower the branch'. So this Sangha Elder, I wrote, was an epitome of someone who was humble as ever despite his erudition and learnedness. So, up to the time I came to be the Founder of Nalanda College of Buddhist Studies (Canada) (2000), over three decades since arriving in Canada, I had never attached any of my academic qualifications at the end of my name in my public life. I had not shown my five degrees (London, Philadelphia, Toronto (3)) in the signature of my e-mail. Or ever mentioned that I had been a Fulbright Smith-Mundt Scholar in the US. It was enough for the Buddhist community that I had a PhD, not even wanting to know if it was from Timbuktu, to accept my leadership. But Nalanda forced my hand to show the best of me academically, as I was trying to establish its academic credentials. 'Branding' was the name of the game, as I came to be advised by the younger generation around me seeking to promote the College. They would point to Honest Ed as the example *par excellence*: "Only the floor boards are crooked here!"

And it is the same frame of mind then that I had brought to writing the Memoir. Mind you, not that I don't have the nod from the Buddha. Says he, "I don't see anybody who loves myself better than myself." So while in places at least, the Memoir may appear to be a brag book, I like to think of it as a 'Merit Ledger' (*pin pota*), as kept by Sinhala Rulers. So I can think of two reasons why I am writing it:
1. as a history of an era, for posterity; and
2. as a case study of Buddhism in action, i.e., Buddhist praxis.

As for the second, I could not put it better than Professors Hori & McLellan, who writing a short bio of me in *Wild Geese* (2010) – characterize me as "a prism" through which to understand the development of Buddhism in Canada. While my work in the other diverse dimensions find no comprehensive survey, the Memoir will come with a tray full of them, from critiquing History Texts used in Ontario classrooms to providing alternative wording for the Preamble of the Canadian Constitution to being 'nursing mom' to both Canadian multiculturalism and Vision TV.

Sure, there may be any number of historians, sociologists or other scholars who may be able to give a deeper, theoretical understanding of all these terrains, but none of them will come with anywhere near a human touch, providing you an orchestra seat of the participant observer-activist. Nor will they entertain you in a cross-cultural perspective. Which Canadian, e.g.,, would you hear being told, over public airways, "Go back to where you came from" as when I was, invited to host a program on multiculturalism on Radio CFRB? Which *Toronto Star* columnist will come to earn both the ire and the praise of his readers coast to coast? So what you will encounter is that rare combination of the outsider-insider, insider-outsider.

If you find an *Autobiographer* in these pages, you will also find the *Fieldworker*: collecting data, long forgotten. But, you will also not fail to find the *social scientist*, analyzing the material as if I were analyzing somebody else's. Hopefully, I have ended up with sound judgements in my choice of material and my evaluations, if also presentations. Of course, there was no attempt to be well-rounded; rather my analysis was to the extent needed to tell the story. But you may also find the *Reporter* here who wants to make sure no relevant material is left out, the Poet pitching in as well.

Reflecting the academic, you may also on occasion find the Bio sounding more like a term paper than just a narrative. If this is partly because of my own background as a 'multidisciplinologist' (as characterized in *Canadian Who's Who*), it is also because I am faced with having to write for an audience that may not have the background on the early phases of multiculturalism in Canada, or indeed pre-multicultural Canada, but privy to this writer having arrived in 1967. Nor will many a reader come with a background in a diversity of areas and disciplines covered. So I have been compelled to add background material to put my life stories in context. Apologies then for the license taken, but I do sincerely hope that the extra time you may have to put in to enjoy my Bio will be amply rewarded at the end of the day.

I've tried to be as chronological as possible, but there is more than one strand. So to conflate everything that I've been involved in at a given point in time or period would be too confusing. Besides, it needs more of an effort on my part to pull all the strings together. In addition to my laziness of not wanting to take that extra step, it would also turn the Bio into a Doctoral thesis!

It was Swarna – it must have been in her retirement imagination, who originally asked me why I should not be writing my life story. My response was, "Who'd be interested in my story?" Children, of course, and she herself. But was that enough to spend time talking about me?

But then when I began to think a bit about it, it occurred to me that, yes, there indeed was a history, intertwined with my life in Canada in more than one area.

Even more, as I began to write this only would I myself realize how much social history there is in my story. So in a very real sense it is about you, you and you, because this Memoir is not about my personal life, "warts and all". While it has had its ups and downs, it would be of no use to anyone in society. No social good. And it would be no different from the life of any other. But what may be different in my life is that it relates to society. So what you will find in the pages is where and how I interact with you – society. Which is why this Memoir can be said to be about you, you and you, as much as, of course, I, myself and me. I also now know, as I was to discover working on the Memoir, why Prof. David Waterhouse of University of Toronto, had suggested to me a long time ago to write my life story. Apparently, I had not given serious thought to the kind friendly suggestion.

This, then is that story, written up at the original request of my life-long partner, Swarna – wife-wife, mother-wife, sister-wife, friend-wife, critic-wife, and not just the wife behind a successful man, but as you will read, a successful woman in her own right, sitting right on the driver's seat.

So what you will be enjoying in *Happy But Striving* is coming to face to face with a Canadian of Buddhist, and Asian, vintage of five plus decades, pioneering many a trail flying in multiple directions, succeeding and failing, failing and succeeding but both happy and striving and striving and happy and mercifully, living the moment, with a smile on the lips. Hope you will then get a taste of not only an Autobiography, but, to coin a term and concept, an *Autosociobiography*. If it is a personal history, it is also a social history. What more can I give Canada, the land that has cherished me for these many decades and Lanka that nurtured me and the US that provided a scaffold towards the future?

And now to end these words with the initial input of over 20 years ago following Swarna's request (January 1, 2002):

> *When I blurted out my very first mbaaa...ah at the rush of that first breath of fresh air into my lungs in the wee hours of March 10, 1936, in a place called Medaketiya in Tangalla (in Sri Lanka), who could have guessed it will be heard 10,000 miles away from it, across oceans, in a land called Canada, home of our family since 1967? May be the year 1936, when mothers gave birth at home with a midwife at bedside, was one that didn't allow newborns to do more than just cry!*

But the cry it appears has been heard, and on occasion even put on display as on June Callwood's 'National Treasure' on Vision TV, *Canadian Who's Who* and *Canada at the Millennium,* and in more detail in *Wild Geese, Buddhism in Canada* not to mention the several interviews.

Happy But Striving... is long, but it is not as if I was striving to stretch my happiness, and/or boosting my ego, nor to go overboard enjoying the art of writing. First, it covers the life of a Canadian in an immigrant setting. And covered in this Memoir is no short period of time either but, as noted, five decades. Thus, every segment and sub-segment can be said to have evolved naturally, doing justice to the diverse dimensions of my involvement, and the society I was living in America or Canada. Given the length, I hope I will have your understanding for some overlap between and among my activities, and possible repetitions.

While I had come up with a decent draft by 2009, it had come to be pushed to the backburner by many an other involvement. And so it is that it is reaching your hand over a decade later. But happily, the delay has allowed me to bring you up to date on some other ground-breaking dimensions in my life.

I see this Memoir as my small gift to humanity in my Octogenarian years to be inspired by, or learned from, to do or not to do, at an individual level or a social level.

Thank you for your patience.
Metta!
Suwanda H J Sugunasiri
3 Ardmore Road, Forest Hill,
Toronto ON M5P 1V4

BOOK I
A US FULBRIGHT CONNECTION

1 A US FULBRIGHT CONNECTION, 1964 TO 1973
    1.1 Lucky Bloke, this 'First Reserve' 1
    1.2 Entry to Ivy League at Penn, Philadelphia, USA 6
    1.3 Swarna and Son join me in Ann Arbor, Michigan 13
    1.4 At an International Student Camp in San Francisco 18
    1.5 Homeless! Across the US on a Rambling Rambler 23

2 BONJOUR, CANADA!
    2.1 Canada: French for a Son, Teacher Training for Swarna 27
    2.2 Master's Degree in Moral Philosophy 32
    2.3 Ven Prof. Hammalawa Saddhatissa 34
    2.4 An Educational Tour of Western and Eastern Europe 35
    2.5 A Visit to the Holy Sites of India with Dad 39
    2.6 A Return to Sri Lanka 42

3 A LEAVE OF ABSENCE FROM CANADA
    3.1 Adieu, Canada, the True North Strong N' Free! 43
    3.2 Kabuki and a Tea Ceremony in Japan 44
    3.3 A Welcome from Red Guards in China 46
    3.4 A Shopping Spree in Singapore! 51

BOOK II
CANADA, HOME AWAY FROM HOME, 1973 ON

BOOK II, PART 1
EARLY YEARS

4 PROUD TO BE CANADIAN!
    4.1 Settling down in Canada. 53
    4.2 Swarna, the Professional 57
    4.3 Swarna, the Food Connoisseur 59
    4.4 Swarna, the Autobiographer 60
    4.5 Swarna, the Golden One 61

5 IN SEARCH OF LEARNING
    5.1 Humanistic Nationalism: a PhD from OISE 63
    5.2 Life at OISE 69
    5.3 MA in the Scientific Study of Buddhism 70
    5.4 A Degree-loving Family 72
    5.5 No Academic Love-in 74
    5.6 Enjoying a Lemonade 80

BOOK II, PART 2
WATCH OUT! SOCIAL ANIMAL ON THE PROWL

6 WITH THE CANADIAN SRI LANKAN COMMUNITY
    6.1 On Stage 82
        6.1.1 Celebrating Sinhala and Tamil New Year 82
        6.1.2 Directing Sinhala Play Nari Bena 83
        6.1.3 Dance at the Harbourfront 83
    6.2 Founding the Cultural Circle *Samskruti* 83
    6.3 Sri Lankans on TV 84
    6.4 No Sinhala at the Sinhala Buddhist Wesak 86
    6.5 Research and Writing 87
    6.6 Sinhala, Tamil & English Literature Under One Cover 88

7 HELPING SHAPE EDUCATION IN ONTARIO
    7.1 "Smarten Up Indians, & Go Western" 90
    7.2 Multiculturalizing Canadian Literature 91
    7.3 Toronto Board of Education Curriculum Consultant 92
    7.4 School Opening Exercises 94
    7.5 Buddhism, in *Religions of India* 95
    7.6 ESL/D Teacher and Language Across the Curriculum 96
    7.7 Teacher Training in the People's Republic of China 96

8 LIFE IN THE LITERARY LANE
    8.1 "*The Search for Meaning: the Literature of
         the Canadians of South Asian Origins*" 98
    8.2 Joining Moyez Vassanji, Co-Founding
        Toronto South Asian Review 101
    8.3 A Few Pieces of Critical Writing. 106
    8.4 A Brown among Browns: a Marginalization 108

9 HELPING SHAPE MULTICULTURALISM
    9.1 Opening Salvos in Multiculturalism 111
    9.2 An Order-in-Council Appointment: OACMC 114
    9.3 Public Speaking 116
    9.4 Kicking Multiculturalism in Its Teeth! History of a Book 118
    9.5 Who, then, is a 'Canadian'? 126

10. LIFE IN THE INTERFAITH LANE
    10.1 Envisioning Vision TV: a Midwifery Role 128
    10.2 Buddhist-Christian Dialogue 133
    10.3 'Tis no Reason to Steal Lord Jesus! 139
    10.4 Buddhist-Jewish Dialogue 141
    10.5 "Buddhist Protests 'God' in Constitution preamble" 143
    10.6 Multifaith Participation 147
    10.7 Dynamics of Interfaith 150
    10.8 A few Publications 153

BOOK II, PART 3
PLANTING BUDDHIST SEEDS ON CANADIAN SOIL

11. WORLD BUDDHISTS UNDER ONE UMBRELLA
    11.1 An Invitation to Participate 155
    11.2 Buddhists Come together 156
    11.3 Pan-Buddhist WESAK (1981): a North American First 160
    11.4 Buddhist Council of Canada: Traveling to form Chapters 163
    11.5 Growth and Impediments 166
    11.6 Buddhist Literary Festival 169
    11.7 Buddhism on a Wider Screen 170

BOOK II, PART 4
SENSITIZING THE POLITICAL HEAVYWEIGHTS, LEFT, RIGHT & CENTRE

12. POLITICIANS MEET LIVING BUDDHISTS - A NOVEL EXPERIENCE
    12.1 Communicating with the Provincial Heavyweights 175
    12.2 Communicating with the Federal Heavyweights 184
    12.3 Encountering Municipal Politicians 195
    12.4 A Personal Reflection 197

BOOK II, PART 5
BUDDHISM IN THE ACADEMY

13 SCIENCE FOR PEACE: A BUDDHIST CONRIBUTION
13.1 Sci Spi: Science of Spirituality 119
13.2 You're What You Sense 203
13.3 Challenging Cartesian Dualism, Defining Sentience 205

14 UNIVERSITY OF TORONTO COMES A-CALLING
14.1 Trinity Seminars on Buddhism 207
14.2 Teaching Buddhism at the School of Continuing Studies 209
14.3 A Few Publications 212

15 NALANDA COLLEGE OF BUDDHIST STUDIES
15.1 A New Beginning in the New Millennium 214
15.2 An Application to offer B A (Hons.) in Buddhadharma Studies 221
15.3 Nalanda Research Centres of Excellence 225
15.4 One Hundred Years of Buddhism in Canada 227
15.5 A Lecture-Meditation (*suta-bhàvanà*) series 228
15.6 A Few Other Initiatives 228
15.7 A Retirement 229
15.8 A Buddhist Educational Plan for Canada 231
15.9 An Interview 232
15.10 Canadian Journal of Buddhist Studies 232
15.11 A Meeting with Prof. Herbert Guenther 234

BOOK II, PART 6
A MEDIA PRESENCE

16 ON THE HOT SEAT: ON CAMERA AND MICROPHONE
16.1 On the Hot Seat on Radio 238
16.2 Tangoing with CBC TV 239
16.3 Still on TV 242

17 TORONTO STAR COLUMNIST IN READER ENGAGEMENT
17.1 Introducing Multiculturalism to Canadians, Coast to Coast 243
17.2 Anatomy of a word: Rejuvenating a Readership 255

18 A BIOETHICALLY ENGAGED A BUDDHIST COLUMNIST
18.1 A Suggestion to the *Toronto Star* 261
18.2 Digging into Bioethical Issues in Canadian Society 261
18.3 'Blue Book Expert' 266

BOOK II, PART 7
A CREATIVE RENAISSANCE -
POETRY, SHORT FICTION AND NOVEL

19. POEMS WITH DEEP THOUGHTS CLAD IN MUSICAL RHYTHMS
  19.1 Faces of Galle Face Green, 1995 268
  19.2 Celestial Conversations, 2007 272
  19.3 Obama-Ji, 2009 276

20 FICTION: SHORT AND LONG
  20.1 Symbolism Galore in Short Fiction 279
  20.2 A First Novel @ 75 , Untouchable Woman's Odyssey 280

21 WRITING AS ART
  21.1 "You're a Great Writer" 283
  21.2 Featured in 'Precise Writing' 285
  21.3 A Family Bouquet 285
  21.4 Writing Lucidly in Sinhala 286
  21.5 Writing Skills: Genetic? Learned? Both? 287

BOOK II, PART 8
SHRINKING & EXPANDING THE WORLD

22 OUR TRAVELS
  22.1 Travel In Canada: From Sea to High Sea 290
  22.2 Over to Hawai'i & the Caribbean 292
  22.3 Driving One-Eyed Through European Tunnels 294
  22.4 Asia and the Pacific Rim 298
  22.5 A Cruise on the *Sovereign of the Seas* 300

23 A CULTURAL RETURN TO 'GOOD OLE SRI LANKA'
  23.1 A Return After 26 years! 301
  23.2 Two Old Tourists 307

BOOK III
A CREATIVE GRATITUDINAL CLOSING

24. A CRINTFREETH IN THE ACADEMY

24.1 Introduction 312
24.2 Books
    24.2.1 Night of the Buddha's Enlightenment 313
    24.2.2 Dhamma Aboard Evolution:
        Buddha Unfolding the Universe 313
    24.2.3 Triune Mind, Triune Brain: Map of the Mind through
        the Eyes of Buddhianscience and Westernscience 315
    24.2.4 Swarna Sugunasiri: Born Streamentrant,
        Next Life Nibbana (forthcoming) 316
    24.2.5 Sauris Silva... : in the Eyes of Himself and Others 317
24.3 Articles
    24.3.1 Gandhabba, the Celestian Pro-mom Pheromone chaser 318
    24.3.2 Sarabhañña: An Esthetic Buddhist Chanting Style 318
    24.3.3 ESP: Reality Turned Myth in Westernscience
        (forthcoming) 319

25 HAPPY BUT STRIVING

REFLECTIONS AND A FINAL STRIVING

25.1 Minimum Expectations 320
25.2 What's in a Name? A Parental Projection 320
25.3 Buddhadhamma as the Source of Happiness and Striving 327
25.4 Visible Conditioning - Other Sources of Happiness 330
    25.4.1 Family 331
    25.4.2 Three Countries: Sri Lanka, USA, Canada 332
        25.4.2.1 Sri Lanka 332
        25.4.2.2 USA 332
        25.4.2.3 Canada 335
25.5 Invisible Conditioning? 336
    25.5.1 Watch Out! Kamma Policeman on Duty 24/7! 336
25.6 A Final Striving 338
25.7 A Final Bow 339

BOOK I

A US FULBRIGHT CONNECTION

1 A US FULBRIGHT CONNECTION, 1964 TO 1973

1.1 Lucky Bloke, this 'First Reserve'

"So when are you leaving?".

Towards the end of 1963, an Ad in the *Ceylon Daily News* caught my attention. It called for applications for Fulbright Scholarships. On an instinct, but with absolutely no conviction that I would have the slightest chance, I made the application. A degree I had earned alright, but an external degree from London, known, or thought, to be for the not so bright. The brightest, of course, like Swarna and my colleagues at Ananda, would go to the University of Ceylon, established by Sir Ivor Jennings and had the highest academic standards. And the chances were also high that the Scholarship Selection Committee itself would be made up of the home-grown products, who would not likely hold the external degree in high regard. And, of course, I had had no contacts whatsoever with the US Embassy, my cultural contacts being with the Soviet and the Chinese.

But then imagine my surprise when I was called for an interview! I don't remember if I went for the interview in my national dress or tie and coat, although my hunch is the latter, probably reminded of the adage that discretion is the better part of valour. Going for a local job interview in my national attire, as I had done for all the jobs, was only natural, the chances of an interviewing committee rejecting me just for that not being very high, and the risk low. But this was a rare overseas opportunity, and although I am not known to be a pragmatist, I might not have wanted to blow it. How open would the Committee be to one seen to go against the current? Everyone of my generation wore the western attire – certainly to weddings, interviews and other formal occasions. Of course, I already had a western suit, wearing it as bestman for a cousin, and earlier in school photos.

I remember walking into a huge room at the US Cultural Centre just off Galle Road, at the Galle Face Hotel. Around the table sat the committee, but I could recognize no faces. I had, for some reason, applied to do Cultural Anthropology, and asked why I had chosen it, I believe I said something like, "I know nothing of it, and so I wanted to explore it." As far as I knew, there were no courses available in the country. Knee-deep in the local cultural scene, I might have wanted to get an academic handle on it. Perhaps also asked the obvious question, "Why are you interested in the scholarship?", I could have given only one genuine answer: to be able to serve my country better. This was what I was already doing. But one thing

I do remember well - making sure that everyone around the table had something or other, by me or about me, to look at. I had my MA thesis, the three collections of short fiction, the two translations, articles and columns written for magazines and newspapers, etc., radio programs, acting in plays, dancing in ballets and etc.

Hearing nothing back for months, I had completely put the matter out of my mind. Having resigned my job in the meantime, I was merrily going on with my writing and cultural involvement. With no income, pension or savings of my own, Swarna alone provided the bread and butter for the family, teaching at a High School. We had rented an Annex in Mt. Lavinia, and she took the bus to Panadura, her home town, and also where she was now teaching. Transferred to a high school in Malabe, such random transfers being the norm, we had moved to Talahena, renting a house.

Invited to serve on the Arts Council of Ceylon (volunteer), I had come to be a member of the Folk Arts Sub-Committee, puppetry being one area of interest. An American puppet expert, Mrs. McFarlane, was visiting Sri Lanka, and I had gone to the airport to welcome her. Waiting for her was also, as I had come to be alerted, the US Cultural Attache, Dr. Richard Arndt, who apparently recognized me. It was he, to my surprise, who asked me, "So when are you leaving?".

"For where?" I asked. Or may be I just looked at him in surprise. Then he said that I should be looking for a telegram when I got home that day.

Walking back from the Terminal, he had asked me, as I would come to know a sentence or two later, if I was not concerned about going to Philadelpia. As part of the Fulbright application, we had been asked to identify not only the area of study but the educational institution as well. While I had applied for Cultural Anthropology at the time of my initial application, I had changed my mind at the point of applying to a university. Prof. Sugatapala de Silva of the University of Sri Lanka had done some research on the language of the Veddahs, Sri Lanka's aboriginal people, and was looking for some young people to join him in his research. Given my background in languages, I had volunteered. Having himself done graduate work in the US, it was his advice that I study Linguistics on my scholarship. Accordingly, I had applied to the University of Pennsylvania, the *alma mater* of the famous Noam Chomsky. Of course, I could have chosen any university, but as it turned out, I

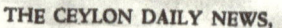

Mrs. Marjorie B. McPharlin, American puppetry expert, met at the airport by Prof. Jayadeva Thilakasiri and the author

had, with no knowledge of the US of A, applied to be at one of the coldest parts of the country when I could have just as easily earned a degree in Linguistics in the warmer climes of California! Foolish perhaps as I was, as indeed now you might add, I hadn't factored in personal comfort or asked the right questions.

Philadelphia was the city where University of Pennsylvania was located, and a murder had just taken place. Barely understanding his American accent, I had said yes when asked if I had no concerns going there, nearly torpedoing my chances. But after a few clarifications I had corrected myself, and said, no, I had no concerns. I was either too excited to be not concerned about some impersonal murder some 10,000 miles away, or if I had thought through the question, I was probably reminded of the Sinhala saying, 'Would you be putting up your house in a cemetery if you were scared of devils?'.

Sure enough, returning home, there it was! A cable. My wife was at the gate, as always, with her usual beaming smile on her lips. But today it came to be as well for an additional reason that would change our lives for ever! Stepping into the house, she handed me the telegram. Lo and behold, I had been offered the scholarship! I was to go to the US Embassy asap.

It was from Dr Ananda Guruge I would hear, meeting him decades later in California, how it all had happened. As I was to understand, he had been the Ministry representative on the Fulbright Committee. So here then is what he writes to me:

> *I am really proud of you and I feel very happy that long years ago I agreed with Dick Arndt to put you as the first reserve in our list of Fulbrighters much against the policy of the Ministry of Education that preference had to be given to Medicine, Engineering, Agriculture and Science. You were one of the rare humanities graduates to be selected and looking back on what you have achieved for Sri Lanka and Buddhism, Dick Arndt's persuasion was most appropriate.* (e-mail of June 15 2014).

So now I knew what he had meant meeting him earlier at the World Parliament of Religions in Chicago in 1993, when he had told me that I was a 'lucky bloke'. Somehow, I had come through by accident, when one of the 8 selectees, this being

Swarna and me meeting Prof. Ananda Guruge at the University of the West, California

the number of scholarships awarded annually, could not make it. And as luck, or is it fate, rather karma, would have it, indeed one of the selectees not being able to accept it, eyes had fallen on me. And enhancing my happiness most recently was the opportunity to pay a gratitudinal visit five decades later (2016), to my alma mater, University of Pennsylvania.

Lucky I may have been, but not without a bit of work on my part. I mean how many young people of age 27 come with more qualifications (see Chart 6 above), and tenacity, could the Selection Committee have encountered in the country? So if I was the 'first reserve', it was only because the criterion was qualifications in science. If they had been looking for the 'brightest on the soil', or some such thing, Yours Truly may have had, if I could say so with all humility, a better than excellent shot at it.

Ecstatic, I am sure, I must have been, when I received the news. It seemed to confirm what a soothsayer had said - that marriage would bring me good luck and foreign travel! And it was also to portend a future for Swarna, as predicted by the soothsayer - that she would spend her life away from the land of birth. How about that! But both of us probably took it all calmly. In any case, unlike UK scholarships, there was no accommodation for the spouse.

This is the background I would have thought would have been conveyed to Prof Victor Hori of McGill University, Montreal when he interviewed me, with Prof Janet McLellan of Wilfred Laurier University, and author of *Many Petals of the Lotus*, for an upcoming publication (*Wild Geese*). Their interest, of course, was my Buddhist leadership role in Canada beginning 1980. Thus it was that I was sort of taken aback to hear him say, "Oh, so it was as an artist that you were selected for the Fulbright Scholarship." I had clearly not come out with all my flags!

At age 22, I already had a BA (2nd class) from the University of London and had completed all but one of the course work requirements for an MA at Vidyalankara University, but had completed the thesis (in Sinhala). As noted, I had translated Bertrand Russel's *Commonsense and Nuclear Warfare*, and later an academic treatment, *Classical Sanskrit literature,* by A B Keith.

But I had never thought of myself as an 'artist', the term conjuring up images of maestros like W D Amaradeva ('father of Sinhala music'), Prof Ediriweera Saracchandra (the foremost dramatist and reviver of folk *Nadagam* drama) or Chitrasena (ballet virtuoso), or writers like Martin Wickramasinghe and the younger Gunadasa Amarasekara, etc. Of course, I had engaged in a few things that would put me under the category 'artist', but I had never thought of myself as an 'artist', but more as a hanger-on in the cultural world. In my own perception, I was not even close to the second or third tier of artists blossoming in society, but merely expressing myself artistically in Sinhala.

Yet, writing this Memoir, I now realize that Victor's comment may not have been entirely off the mark. And the real reason for the Fulbright committee to select me may have been the breadth of my experience, if also the depth. This must have most likely impressed the American on the committee, perhaps surprised to see in an Asian country a 'Renaissance Man'!

It is then with much gratitude that I came to visit him in his Washington DC home in the US, continuing to communicate thereafter. Happy I am also that I would dedicate a recent breakthrough publication of mine, *Arahant Mahinda - Redactor of the Buddhapuava in Sinhala Buddhism* (2012) to Mr.. J. W. Fulbright himself, along with my parents, in gratitude.

On a visit to Dr. Richard Arndt in Washington DC, 2016

Now, resigning from government service meant that no one had a hold on me. It is my resignation, foolish as it may have seen to be, that can be said to have been the critical condition that would allow me to leave the shores on the scholarship. From that point of view, then, my resignation may be seen as living proof of that adage, "If you don't buy a ticket, you can't win the lottery". Buying the ticket here, of course, here means buying up *untethered* time. It could also be seen as an example of another adage (just made up by me) that "The daring shall be rewarded!". I don't have to look far. Prince Siddhartha did it, and was amply rewarded – becoming the Buddha.

But there was still a little hitch. While the 'Fulbright' part of the scholarship was the academic component, the 'Smith Mundt' part was for travel. By now, the Marxist Dr N M Perera was the Minister of Finance under the Mrs. Sirimavo Bandaranaike government. The first woman Prime Minister in the world, she had assumed office following the assassination of her husband, S. W. R. D. Bandaranaike. With the economy in bad shape, exchange control restrictions had been put in place. Although the Smith-Mundt travel component was part of the US Scholarship, the money was to come from our of PL 480 funds, meaning funds owed to the US by Sri Lanka for the rice and wheat provided. But the Minister was not releasing any funds. Period. Now suddenly it looked as if the scholarship door was shut on me.

Luckily, with some swift leg work, putting friends in high places to work, word came that the Prime Minister had authorized the release of PL 480 funds! Getting a passport didn't take much time at all, with my colleague from Ananda, C W Siriwardhana, now in a senior position at Immigration. And it allowed travel to any country in the world. The US Visa was automatic, and I had also been given US $ 35.00 as travel money for the trip. Thomas Cooks Travel would handle the travel arrangements. I would travel on TWA (Trans World Airline), via Bombay, Paris and London, to JFK in the US, before flying over to Philadelphia.

University registration beginning on September 8, I left Sri Lanka on August 25, 1964, leaving a 3 week old son in the care of Swarna. I was confident that she could well manage things in my absence. As she would tell me later, I had walked to the airplane, down the tarmac (as was the system at that time), as if I were just going to a store! That is to say that it appears that there had been no emotional scene. As far as I was concerned, I was going to be returning in 10 months, the period of my scholarship, and that was it. And so I would be seeing my family soon.

1.2 Entry to Ivy League at Penn, Philadelphia, USA

Attired in my national dress – which by now was the norm for me, I was traveling by TWA. It had a cute little motto: 'Time flies, so does TWA'! My first stop was Paris. Stepping out of the hotel after checking in, I had my first view of the Seine, walking along the brickstone and cobbled paving. A note on the ticket dust jacket tells me that I spent 20 Francs in Paris, out of the US $ 35.00, given for travel, exchanged into 3.10 British pounds. In London I would spend 2 Shillings and 4 Pence. Wow, I seem to have gone on a spending spree alright!

Padmini, my cousin was happy to welcome me in London, England, my next stop. I had carried their luggage to the ship when she left then Ceylon, after getting married to Dr Douglas de Almeida. I had been fairly close to Padmini, having met her only as a teenager when, my uncle, Sugathadasa by name but whom we called *baala maama* 'younger uncle', had returned from a life time of work in Africa in the postal service under the British Administration. His older brother, Sirisena, whom we called *ratu mama* 'Uncle Fair' had worked there, too. Although it was Uncle Fair who had sent me some money while in Africa, Padmini was my age, while her brother, Jayanta, and *ratu mama's* children, Shanti and Lalitha, were younger.

While the Almeidas were happy to see me in London after some time, they were not thrilled that I had come in my Ariya Sinhala attire. Indeed, upon getting the news back in Lanka, my uncle had exploded. Making it a point to visit Swarna, he had expressed the opinion that I was a fool to have been so attired. After all, Britain was mother colonial, and my uncles, like any other English-speaking Sinhalaya, wore the western attire. Succumbing to pressure, I agree to have a suit made in London, reimbursing the cost from Philadelphia. Padmini and Dougie were kind to show me around London – the Big Ben, the Thames, Parliament, Buckingham Palace, Trafalgar Square and just about everything else we had read, heard or talked about in our student days.

Having left UK from 'Airways Terminal Buckingham Palace Road, Victoria', as handwritten in my ticket, I was happy to be met by Alice Dodge of the International Student Service at the JFK in New York, who warmly welcomed me It was probably arranged by the Fulbright folks. I knew that I was in secure hands in this new land about which I knew practically nothing. I had had probably less than a month to leave Sri Lanka, and things had moved fast and furious. There had been no time for the usual orientation Fulbright scholars are given. Not even time to study a map. But Alice assured me that there would be someone at the Airport in Philadelphia to meet me.

Soon, I was on my merry way to Philadelphia. But, upon my arrival, I found no one waiting for me. Now what? I was stranded. I didn't know where to go or how to get to wherever that I was going. Arriving past 3 pm, the Airport banks were closed, and unable to cash whatever was left of the British money I had been given. Just then, luckily, I noticed a lady at a desk with a sign that read Travel Assistance, or something to that effect. But she was getting ready to leave. Tugging the piece of luggage I had with me, and in my national, I must have run in time to catch her. Listening to my story, she called somebody, who I found later was at the International House (IH hereafter). Giving me a round piece of metal of silver colour, she said, "Here, take this." I took it in hand, though thoroughly confused. What? No money needed to travel in the US? Explaining that it was a *token*, she gave me direction to take the subway. Subway? What was that? Sensing my consternation, she explained to me that it was an underground train, and that it would take me to the University.

It was with trepidation that I followed her directions to get to the IH. Happily, I was able to find my way, tugging along my suitcase which in those days were not on wheels.

Upon arriving at the International House, at 140 N. 15th Street as I would come to know later, I was, to my great relief, warmly welcomed by Suzanne (whose last name escapes me). Phew, I must have said, that was close! On the road now for a few days, and tired enough, I must have had a good night's sleep on that first day in the United States of America. Never mind that I didn't know that I was at an Ivy League School; I didn't even have the vaguest notion of an Ivy League! A select group of universities, they were said to be the very best in the US.

Lining up along with other students, I registered for my courses on the due date, Sept 8, 1964. As an Ivy League Private University, tuition fees at Penn, as it was called, would have gone through the roof. But then, I didn't have to worry. The Scholarship was taking care of it all – tuition, board and books allowance. The terms of the Scholarship also allowed working up to 10 hours a week for additional income.

But the Registration I enjoyed more was another semester when, seeking a little extra cash, or as part of an Assistantship, I was to sit on the other side, registering students for their courses. This is when I took pleasure in almost always identifying the ethnolinguistic background of a student, judging by his / her name. Most were surprised how good I was at it. A semester of Linguistics had given me enough of a sophistication apparently to be sensitive to different languages.

Prior to registering, I had met with the Graduate Chairman of the Linguistics Department, Prof Henry Hiz "who helped me to tide over a difficult period of my studies", as I would write in my Thesis Preface. The reference must be to the fact that I had come with no background in Linguistics at all, and had to begin from scratch.

I remember that it was love at first sight with Linguistics. It was the study of language, any language, and it was with great interest that I came to discover that the International Phonetic Alphabet (IPA), developed by scholars to transcribe a language, any language indeed in the world, was modeled after the Indian Grammarian Panini. English, following a Greek model, was not even on the horizon. Let me explain.

The English 'alphabet', as the label suggests, begins with the Greek 'alpha', 'beta', English A and B. But already, as you can see, there is a vowel and a consonant, as also in the sequence C, D, E, and thereafter. In Sanskrit, and following it, in Sinhala, however, the alphabet begins with the *vowels*, and go into consonants only after the vowels have been exhausted.

And again, while in English, the letters don't seem to follow a logical pattern, the IPA, like Sanskrit and Sinhala, is systematic. When we speak, the first part in the mouth that stops the air flowing from the lungs is the velum, way at the back of the mouth. This is how we get the initial sounds such as of 'king' or 'go' (/k/, /g/ respectively). At the tip of the mouth, it is the lips that have the function of stopping the air flow, producing the sounds such as /p/, /b/, /m/. It seems all so logical. So the IPA organizes the sounds of a language, following the point of contact, from back of the mouth to the front - velar, palatal, alveolar, labiodental and labial

It was all so logical, and so much fun to be able to get into the formal study of language. Thank you, Prof. Lisker, my Professor in Phonetics. Though I had studied Sinhala, Pali and Sanskrit, as language, that is, as a tool of communication, this was the first time I had looked at language academically and analytically.

Tracing the history of languages in the course on Historical Linguistics was a lot of fun, too. This is when I came to learn that Sinhala, though so far fetched in culture and distance, is in fact, related to English, both having branched off from a reconstructed language called 'Proto-Indo European'. Two of its ten branches are Germanic and Indo-Iranian, English branching off from the former, and Sinhala from the latter, through Indic. Does it not surprise you that *'three'* in English, as a quick example, is *'tri'* (with the same pronunciation, except for the short final vowel /i/) in (Sanskrit, and) Sinhala? Extending it, English 'tricon' (also spelt 'tricorn(e)') means triangle (note the meaning of /tri/ here again), but literally, 'three corners', noting also Sanskrit –*kona* paralleling 'corner'!

Here is the English word 'daughter' to help us get a glimpse of the connection with Sinhala at the same vocabulary level:

Proto IE	*dughāter*	-*ter* 'the one who does' *dugha* 'milking'
English	*daughter*	still showing the '-*ter*' ending, although our daughters don't any more milk cows!
Sanskrit	*duhitru*	-*tru* 'the one who does' *duh*- 'milking'
Sinhala	*dū*	seemingly distancing the girls from a difficult chore, even linguistically!

'Daughter' in Proto-Indo European, English, Sanskrit and Sinhala

Establishing Sinhala to be of Indo-Aryan origin, as early German scholars of Sinhala, Professors Wilhelm Geiger and Herbert Guenther also point out, is the similarity or word order as well. Verb following a noun (e.g., *The cat purred*), and adjective preceding a noun (*The fat cat purred*), unlike, say in French when the adjective *follows* the Noun. *Les peuples Canadiens* 'the Canadian people'. Of course, a language is not just words, and sentences, with each language having its own peculiarities and nuances and rules and regulations, but it was to open my eyes to both the genealogy of a language as well as the wider unity of the human community, something studies in DNA are beginning to show even more conclusively.

In addition to the required courses, I also had the choice of learning a South Asian language. I was tempted to take Tamil, partly honouring my father's wish that I learn Tamil, but given that I could pick it up once back in Sri Lanka, I opted for an Indian language. Marathi, taught by Prof. Franklin Southworth was probably not been offered that year, and so I chose Gujerati, taught by this brilliant linguist, Prof. George Cardona, an expert on the Indian linguist of the 4th to 3rd c. BCE, Panini.

Our textbook for Gujerati was the one our Professor was working on. Although it was an intensive course, all what has stuck in my memory is a couple of sentences.

Kem cho? 'How are you."
Majaamaa. 'Fine'
Ame gaadiyama jaawun chun. 'I'm going by train'.

Hmmm! So much for my memory! Did I say I failed exams?

However, it was not just learning the language that was contributive to my growth in Linguistics. It was that it gave me an understanding of the pattern of yet another language, in addition to Sinhala, Pali and Sanskrit, and the Latin I had learned in junior school. Helping us with this new linguistic eye-opener and new eye to the world was another course taken with Prof. Lisker, 'Informant Work', as a 'field study'. This was to train us to decipher an unknown language spoken by a people, merely by listening to it being spoken. Indeed one of my colleagues in the class was a Christian Evangelist who was in the program precisely for that – so the Bible could be eventually translated into the language. Typically while field work is done in the real world, we were simulating it in the classroom, with a student at the university playing the role of informant. And the language was Swahili. Our challenge was to listen to him, and try to decipher the phonemes – the minimum meaningful sounds of the language, and over time, its grammar. And it was a lot of fun to be told by the informant how wrong we often were!

Another interesting course was Articulatory Phonetics when we could watch the sounds produced by us on an oscillograph, in terms of its timbre and quality of sound. I saw how the initial /p/ in 'pin' (pronounced as /ph/ with more air, called aspirate) is so different in its intensity of pronunciation from /p/ in 'spin', the Professor showing a further weakening in 'potatoes' where the /p/ is barely audible. It would not blow out the matchstick light that was used to show the difference.

It was the course, 'Avestan and Old Persian', under the guidance of Prof. Dresden, that actually helped me see the workings of the Indo-Iranian as a branch of Indo-European. The parallels between Vedic Sanskrit and Old Persian were enough to show how they had branched out from a common Indo-Iranian.

Attending the class in the Philadelphia winter morning at 8 am was not anybody's cup of tea, but it gave me my first cup of black coffee. Yeck! At break time, the American students started walking towards what they called a vending machine. What? A machine that sells? Cute, I thought, and how efficient. Plus one for mechanization. Following them, I put in a dime and got my own cup. Known to be tea-drinkers, coffee was a rarity as we grew up, us kids looking forward to the ice-coffee served at weddings and such other special occasions. So it was with great expectation I kept the cup to my lips, only to nearly throw out. It was bitter as bitter can be! As kids, it was not with enthusiasm we looked forward to the time of the year when we had to take the 'opening dose', the concoction to get rid of ringworms and other stomach devils. And it was to this yeckie taste the American black coffee drove my mind back to! And that perhaps was the first and last time I had a black coffee. Today I have graduated from my Tim Horton's double double, to regular minus sugar, coming closest to the Philadelphia experience. A 40-year evolution!

At the Registration line-up, I was to meet a Pakistani student, Ahmad Sarwana. Both trying to save money, we decided to share an apartment, not too far from the university. Being a spoilt brat when it came to cooking, by mom first and then by Swarna, Ahmad was a saviour. An army officer, he knew how to turn out a spicy dish. But I wasn't the only one to savour the tastes. I had befriended, in the line up or at orientation, a Canadian on a scholarship himself from Winnipeg. And so a regular visitor to our apartment was Lionel Steiman. And so, with a taste for food, it was with no surprise that I was to find him, after retirement from the university, the resident chef at his home in Winnipeg! My contribution was as dishwasher, a task I carry out even today, when not called upon by Swarna to be *sous-chef*. The second semester, Sarwana moving out, I was joined by Dr Fernando, a veterinarian from Sri Lanka, who, having returned to Sri Lanka, would visit us in Canada with his wife.

One afternoon early in the Fall, it was a clear blue sky I saw through my window. The sun shining bright, I was reminded of the tropics I had left behind. Armed with my books, I walked out, in my Ariya Sinhala Aenduma – a cotton verti wrap-around and a long-sleeve top over it falling just above the knee, only to beat a hasty retreat. It was cold! Even that early in the Fall. It was in pants and shirt, I was next heading back to class. But if this was an experience of cold weather for this warm-blooded tropical animal, little would I know what I would experience a few three months later, when one January morning, Lionel came to visit me, wearing a Russian fur cap. "Let's go for a walk, Suji", calling me with a name he had minted for me. A walk? Why would you want to suffer in that blustery cold? 'C'mon, Suji", he urged. Cajoled, I join him, when we trudge through the snow. He was ready with his winter boots, whereas my barely clad feet nearly froze. However, getting warmer gear, I would later go on walks with him routinely. Later on in Ann Arbor, Michigan, I would laugh at myself getting into a bulky suit, just to take the garbage out of the house! But all this prepared me better for my job later at the University of Michigan Library when as part of my assistantship, I had to pick up books dropped off by students in a bin, away from the library. It was with great cheer that, a few months later, I watched a young girl do a handstand and a cart-wheel as if to roll in the spring, giving a kick to the Philly cold.

The Department Chair of the strong Linguistics faculty at Penn was Prof. M. Hoenigswald, whom I would thank later in the Preface to my Thesis, for being "always a source of inspiration" and for his "paternal interest in my progress". In admitting me, the University of Pennsylvania, Philadelphia had been cautious. Given that I had had no specific background in Linguistics, I had been offered only a 'Program of Study' for 10 months, likely taking into consideration my background in languages at the BA level – Sinhala, Pali and Sanskrit. Happily, my transcript at the end of the 10 months seemed to show that, burning the midnight oil at the Library had paid off. With no cricket practice, cadeting, debates and flowers to be picked for devotees to deflect my studies as at Ananda, and keeping my nose to the grind, I had managed to earn 2 A's and 2 B's in my first semester itself. On the basis of my performance, and after four more credits in the second semester, my status had been upgraded from 'Special Student' to MA student!

Successful completion of the degree, however, called for two other requirements: earning pass grades in courses at the Summer School at Ann Arbor and writing a Thesis. And I was happy that I had not let down the Fulbright Committee in Sri Lanka, the Linguistics department of this Ivy League university which had admitted me on trust, just based on my Second Class pass in my BA but with zilch background in Linguistics, and Swarna, who had cheerily agreed to look after a 3 week old baby and the home allowing me to pursue my academic interests.

Though burning the midnight oil,... ow okay, electricity, in Philadelphia, my extra-curricular interests had not gone into total hibernation. The International Festival Ball was "probably the biggest and certainly the most colourful of all Philadelphia parties....", noted Reporter Blanche Krause, writing in *The Sunday Bulletin* of Feb. 14, 1965. It was sponsored by the "International House, the 'home away from home' for some 3000 young men and women from foreign countries who are currently studying in Philadelphia." Continuing, it said, "Many of the students attending this March 5th event .. will come in their own national dress." If the Fall chill had forced me out my Ariya Sinhala Aenduma, here was the Ball inviting me back into it. The picture shows me in my National, "warm[ing] up". But on stage, I was to perform the Bahuboota Dance, which I had performed as a 'pre-performance' in the Operative Play Maname. With face painted to show

Doing a dance step in the presence of International students at U of Pennsylvania in preparation for the Annual Ball, 1965

a distorted mouth, the dance was to be bare-bodied waist up. The performance called for "some spirited dancing", the Bulletin reported. The vibrant fast beat dance a hit, the audience went into a long applause after the performance. Yet, there was to be someone in the audience who thought otherwise. As I would be told later, dancing bare-bodied was not giving the country a good name. This was Vasheeharan, son of the well known Sri Lanka Tamil politician. He must have been relieved to see me in the picture that appeared in the Bulletin fully dressed! But I was to let him down again when he saw me wearing socks with holes in them!

But Prof. Sathasivam, another Tamil Fulbright scholar from Sri Lanka, had no such issues with me as we walked into the Waldorf Astoria Hotel in New York, attending a Linguistics Conference. While I was attending as a student participant, he, on the faculty of the University of Ceylon, was presenting a paper, seeking to establish that the as-yet-undeciphered script in Mohenjadaro Harappa was indeed the Tamil script. I was to hear later that the evidence had not been convincing. But what was convincing was that I should become a vegetarian. Taking our seats at the Restaurant table, I was more than surprised to hear him order a vegetarian lunch. This is New York, Professor, not Sri Lanka, I must have said to myself. But I was surprised again when our order was served. His lunch certainly looked more appetizing and attractive than my own, which must have been the standard fare. Is that – i.e., catering to the every need of the every client, that makes for a grand hotel?

There was one other activity I had been invited to be part of at the University. And that was to speak on (then) Ceylon. With the national flag planted on a table flag post, I was to speak in my national dress again. Mr.. William Carr, Asst. Director, Office of International Services, writes (Feb. 11, 1966),

While at the University of Pennsylvania.... Mr.. Sugunasiri made an excellent social adjustment to our campus, and through his frequent appearance in shows and in programs, was an excellent representative of his country and culture....As a performer of his country's dances, Mr.. Sugunasiiri gave excellent performances both on and off campus. In this connection, his photograph was recently used in city-wide publicity by the International House of Philadelphia...

With academic studies well under my belt, I used some spare time to visit the historic Liberty Bell, the site where the Fathers of Confederation of the United States of America had first sealed the first union - of New Jersey and the adjoining Pennsylvania State in Dec., 1787. I also had the opportunity to visit the famous Rodin Museum, displaying the many works of the renowned sculptor. But there had been no opportunity, or interest on my part, to visit the Black neighbourhoods about which Dr Arndt had talked at the Airport in Sri Lanka.

Making a presentation on Ceylon by invitation of the Office of International Services.

1.3 Swarna and Son Join me in Ann Arbor, Michigan

It was at the encouragement by Prof. Hiz, Chair of the Linguistics Department at Penn that took me to the Summer School of Linguistics at the University of Michigan in Ann Arbor, spending two more months to allow me to complete the course requirements. I would be registered as student Number 6932255 at the Horace H. Rackham School of Graduate Studies for the Summer of 1965. My intention had been to return home upon completion of it, because writing a Thesis to meet the final requirement for an MA would retain me in the US longer. I had left a 3-week old baby in Swarna's hands, and I just had to get back to the family. But, then, there came to be advice, from all quarters. For academic reasons, and possibly impressed by my progress, my Professors would encourage me to complete the degree by meeting the final requirement. There never possibly had been a Sinhala scholar from Sri Lanka at the university, and the university would want to add one to its roster of international students who have earned degrees. Friends in Sri Lanka encouraged me towards the same goal, but for a reason less than academic. They rightly judged that returning home without formal qualifications in hand would not only be a waste of time as far as Sri Lanka was concerned, but not help me in my further advancement in the country either. US qualifications were already suspect, in a colonial climate when higher degrees had prestige only if British. And having no formal qualifications would provide an additional basis for ignoring me, or not recognizing the expertise I had gained in Linguistics.

Hm! Now what? A dilemma alright it was. Indeed I could now see the value of completing my MA before returning, and of course, I would still be eligible for funding under the Scholarship, as my faculty adviser would assure me. However, there was no way that I would be willing to be away for another year if not two without Swarna and son.

Swarna helped me in making the decision. Even though I had booked my return flight several times, she, too, was in favour of me completing my degree. But I would agree on one condition - that both she and baby would join me on a no pay leave. Decision made, she would come on a 3-month leave. Upon hearing about Swarna going overseas, a friend is supposed to have asked, "On a Fulbright?" A good buddy, as I was to be told later, had quipped, to roaring laughter, "No, half-bright ", adding, "You know..., Sugune was only half-bright"!

But when it came to be evident that it would be two years before we could return, she would eventually resign her job, having got a couple of extensions earlier.

The arrival of Swarna and Puta, our son, however, meant that there was an additional cost, not borne under the scholarship. This financial burden meant that now I could not work on my thesis full time. Having a family also meant that I wouldn't be able to go 6 am to 12 midnight with the nose to the grind in my studies as I had done the past year. The two conditions were enough to delay earning my Master's.

The conditions of the scholarship not requiring me to return to Philadelphia, Swarna arrived in Ann Arbor, sometime in early September, 1965. I had saved up some money over the year for the ticket; and my friend from Philadelphia, Lionel Steiman, had lent some money to make up for the shortfall.

Desperate to take in my arms the treasure of our life for the first time in a year, I reach out to the baby in Swarna's hands at the airport. Puta wanted to have nothing of it! Or of me. He bawled, as if to say, "Huh, didn't you leave me behind when I needed you most?". It should hardly be surprising that I was to him nothing more than a total stranger trying to grab him. Served me right alright for abandoning! Laid down in the crib just beside our bed, he would fall into sleep to the sounds of his own words - hand, hand, hand, looking for Swarna's comforting hand. But before long, he would be getting shoulder rides from the best dad in the world, as I also carried the grocery bags. Swarna in her sari could not be of much help.

Swarna's first impressions of the US came from the residence of a fairly well to do host family, who put us up for the first few days. The dinner, with dishes of meat and all, was far richer than what I had come to be used in student life, but .. wait a minute, a disaster, would you believe, for Swarna who went practically hungry that night. An otherwise jet lag after traveling over 24 hours might have come as a welcome in managing the hunger! Having not touched meat in Sri Lanka, not for any particular religious reason, but perhaps pampered as the only girl in the family, she could not stomach the main items on the menu. She ended up with veggies, and potato chips for dinner, breakfast and lunch!

The arrangement was thanks primarily to Mrs. McIvor who was a most gracious and friendly Quaker, living in her own house. She would be host to other visiting students as well.

The continuing Scholarship did not require that I be a full time student either, only that I be enrolled as an MA student under a supervisor. With Prof. Southworth agreeing to supervise me from a distance, I was also allowed to work up to 10 hours a week. And, arriving under a spousal Visa, Swarna was also allowed to work the same number of hours. Even with scholarship money added, we barely managed.

Ann Arbor, being a university city, is among the most expensive cities, if perhaps not the most, in the US. In addition to that, Swarna and baby had arrived in September when occupancy was the highest. Even though she had applied for her leave, it would be a few months of uncertainty before she finally got it. Jealousy perhaps showing up in full regalia? Not many a spouse would be leaving for overseas. For any reason.

With no cheaper apartments available, we were lucky even to to get a house, with garden and all, on rent. It was on South Forest Street, as if a foreboding of things to come, when in Toronto, we end up in Forest Hill! It was a lovely street, specially in the Fall as leaves of different hues – brown, red, rust, orange and yellow, began to pile up along the sidewalks, making it look pretty and fun to wade through and roll in, along with Puta. And I remember having a good laugh in the winter when I had to put on piles of garments and wear boots just to put out the garbage! A running joke in AA: If you don't like the weather, just wait a minute! What it was seeking to capture was how quickly the AA weather changed. Located at the foot of Lakes Eerie and St Clair, the wind pattern changed so drastically that the temperature could fluctuate at the height of winter by as much as 10 degrees within a given day. But that was hardly much comfort to us who had come from a country where the weather was always a balmy 80 plus!

That didn't, of course, stop us from taking up the challenge of going to the closest northernmost point of the State, Bay City, a place I would now know to be into 'Canadian' territory, judging by the lateral. A family had invited us to come along for the ride, and we were not ones to turn down the kind offer. What a surprise it was to see a whole lake frozen solid! It was the height of winter. It must also have been the height of folly on my part to have agreed to be in the car, not just by myself but including Swarna and son, too, to go for the rare thrill of being spun on ice, each time our friend slammed on the brakes having revved up the engine! But it was re-assuring to hear that car racing on the frozen lake was a favourite local sport. Another was ice fishing, through a hole carved out of the ice, as a fisherman would set up a heated tent waiting for a catch. Fishing for fun not being a Sinhala Buddhist practice, I had perhaps found no interest in it.

But there was no fish on our dinner table either, not easy to find perhaps, Puta and I managing on meat, Swarna still not into it. The discovery of a small boutique that carried a spice or two was a surprise. Not that it made much of a difference, however, given that putting a meal of rice and curry on the table was a challenge for Swarna. As a pampered only girl among seven boys, and the 'brainy one' in the family, she was spared the woman's job of cooking. She had never stepped into the family kitchen except when hungry! After getting married, she only had to decide the menu. The servant woman would do the cooking to her requirement. So she had to now learn from scratch. Who would have imagined that those halting steps would produce a first rate chef four decades later, accomplished enough to have her own book published, *Cooking from My Heart: Loving Spoonfuls from a Sri Lankan Family Kitchen* (2008).

The rental too much to carry, we were lucky to find two students from India to rent a room. I can still hear the melodic voice of one of them resonating as I bring to mind the first words, and the tune, of a Bengali song: *nuraa jusay...* It was the first time we had heard an Indian song live in an Indian language sung by Indians! Whatever we had heard back in Sri Lanka - popular film hits sung by Lata Mangeshkar, was over the radio.

The next year, we were lucky to have got 'married student' accommodation on campus, or very near, at 327-1456 University Terrace.

This was the time when the hippie movement was in full swing, and student protest against the war in Vietnam was peaking across the universities. University of Michigan was no exception. But, being a foreign student, I had to be careful to keep my left leanings in check as I joined, or watched, the students on the Diag, the paved pathway that went through the centre of the campus facing the library. Late returning home from the library one day, Swarna nearly called the police, afraid that I might have been arrested by the CIA!

Doing my 10-hours a week at the library, much of the work entailed ensuring that books returned were returned to the shelves, making sure they were in the right place. A book misplaced is a book lost, I seem to remember the slogan. One of the main Return Book locations being outside of the library, another job was to simply collect them and hauling them back to the library in the bitter AA winter weather. But luckily, the supervisor, an Egyptian student named Gundehi, if I remember his name right, assigned me the chore only if another student was not around.

Having completed a winter in Philadelphia, I was at least ready with appropriate Winter wear. I was no longer wearing my national attire either. But, fresh from Sri Lanka, Swarna was still in her sari. And what a toil it was for her to trudge through the slush in boots and a cotton sari! She had found work as a secretary at the university, having successfully completed a speed typing course.

Swarna in Sari in Ann Arbor, Michigan

The spring was equally, if not more, beautiful in AA. The downhill near our unit was a popular playground for our now two-year old son to enjoy. An enlargement of a photo that had been taken at the time, given to us in later years by our son, recovering it from the family slide collection, perhaps speaks to our *joie de vivre* of the time. We would keep looking back and back at our son. Was something wrong? Perhaps it was that, as Uncle Lionel, our Canadian friend, would often tell, "Your eyes are bigger than your tummy!" So was it the brown eyes and black hair that had been the attraction for the passers by who may never have seen a brown cutie?

Completing the course requirements for the MA, I had taken three courses - *Caucasian Linguistics*; *Semantics* and *General Grammar*, in AA, earning an A, A- and B. I was happy I had not let down my Penn Professors who had upgraded me from special student to Master's level. I had also sat in on *Linguistics and Society*, now getting some handle on the sociological dimensions of language.

My thesis, *Morphological Analysis of the Finite Verb in Spoken Sinhala*, was a study of my mother tongue, Sinhala, but little known in linguistic circles. Accepted on Dec. 2, 1966, it is possibly the very first linguistic study of Sinhala in North America. Prof. Sugathapala de Silva, under whose encouragement I had applied to study Linguistics, had done his own studies in the UK. My colleague, J B Dissananyaka, who would become the leading scholar in the country on Sinhala Linguistics after Prof. de Silva, and now Professor Emeritus, had indeed come on a Fulbright Scholarship to the US the year before me, studying in California (1963 – 65), but he had earned no formal qualifications, though he would spend some time at the U of London. When I was eventually awarded my MA degree, on Dec. 21, 1966, the Sinhala newspaper *Dawasa* reported it on Jan. 5, 1967.

There was one more requirement I had to complete, and that was to pass a French Exam at the Master's Level. Wauw wauw! Luckily I had registered for a course in Reading French at Michigan, and to my own surprise, I was able to read and translate from a Linguistics text by the end of the year.

Invited to the "Two Hundred and Eleventh Public Commencement" by Penn President Gaylord P Harnwell, we – Swarna, Puta and me, had left Ann Arbor to be on our way to be present at the Municipal Auditorium on May 22, 1967 to receive my Master's Diploma in person. Arriving in Pittsburgh, not far from Philadelphia, we had stopped over for the night at a Sri Lankan friend's house.

Getting up early morning, we headed for Philadelphia by car, when, somehow, I felt that we were going in the wrong direction. Sure enough! Taking the next exit, as directed by the helping person we had talked to, and driving for some time, I again found myself not heading towards Philadelphia. Stopping to ask again, we were given directions. But, we were not getting anywhere. We had got into the loop around the city! By the time we arrived at the university, people were coming out of the Convocation Hall. But, having recovered the Certificate, I had my picture taken, in the Ariya Sinhala Aenduma and the Master's head gear.

Master's now completed in December, and Visa valid until the end of the Academic Year, I had enrolled in a Teacher Education Program at the English Language Institute, in the Winter of 1967. Even though I had no intention of being in the field of English as a Second Language, that appeared to allow the closest practical application of my training and background in Linguistics in a Sri Lankan context upon the intended return.

Given my background in Linguistics, I had been allowed a special program tailored to my interests. Thus, in addition to the standard courses like '*Methodology in EFL Teaching*' and *Audiovisual Methods,* I had also taken a course on '*Psychology as a Social Science*'. Allowed to make up for a poor exam with a paper, I wrote on *Tovil, Ceylonese Exorcistic Ceremonies, as Psychotherapy*, where I seek to establish (a) that *Tovil* is a form of folk psychotherapy, and (b) that it is indeed *more efficacious than western psychotherapy*! I note four parallel elements in the two practices: 1. a healer, 2. a patient, 3. patient's confidence in both the healer and the efficacy of the practice, and 4. an intended healing being through a transformation of consciousness in the patient. Regarding efficacy, I was to argue that, unlike the lonesome experience in an isolated room in western psychotherapy, *Tovil* was executed in an environment facilitative of healing – masks, drumming, chanting and an entire supportive village. The Professor was impressed, the paper earning a B +. During the brief return to Sri Lanka, I was to give a talk at the Ceylon Museum on the topic. And it was to my delight that I would discover recently that other researchers, such as Christine Harbaugh, and Mark S. Bailey & H. Janaka de Silva had come to make the same general point of the healing efficacy of *Tovil* some four decades later.

I had also taken *Children's Literature*, as an observer, for no particular reason, except perhaps my interest in literature, now in relation to a generation I had not written for. And it would be forty years before I would write my first children's book, *Two Palm Bow*, inspired by our first granddaughter.

Course work completed, I was awarded the Certificate in EFL at the end of the semester. And so within three years, I had earned, this busy-body in high school who had failed to make it to the university, three qualifications – one academic, one professional, one learning a European language.

1.4 At an International Student Camp in San Francisco

Swarna had resigned from her jobs, and it would be a job search that she would immediately have to plunge into upon returning to Lanka. I had, of course, given up on jobs, and was not seeking employment, my expectation being to continue writing. And particularly if Swarna was to get back to teaching, it would be advantageous to have the additional qualification of Teacher Training. The practice in the country was for university graduates to go into teaching at the secondary school level, with those without a degree becoming 'Trained teachers' and teach at the Primary school level. Graduates looking for teacher training would go on to do a Diploma.

So it was with teacher training for Swarna primarily in mind that we had decided to go to Canada before returning. Killing two birds with one stone ... oops, sorry! un-Buddhist expression – 'abstaining from killing' being the first Training Principle for a Buddhist ... so, taking it metaphorically, we were also hoping that perchance our son, too, could get some benefit from our stay, by learning a little French. Not that a 3 year old would be a French scholar. But it would be at least a start, we had hoped, just as we would enroll him in a *violin* class, not long after arriving in Canada when an opportunity arose. It was the Suzuki method, specifically developed for tiny ones. May be I, too, was hoping to develop my French speaking skills, having passed reading French. Putting my newly acquired linguistic analytical skills, I had begun to carefully record our son's developing English speaking skills. So I may even have had an additional theoretical justification – to likewise record the stages of learning French by a Sinhala kid!

Because of this interest in French, we had applied for a Canadian Landed Immigrant Visa at a Montreal office. This meant, as we were to understand later, more delay than applying to an English-speaking Province. The Official Languages Act, that brought in French as an official language alongside English, was introduced in 1969, two years after our arrival. The delay in processing had an interesting side outcome – rendering us literally homeless! Our US VISA was expiring at the end of the term, i.e., June 1967, but we hadn't heard from Canada. And so we had to make our reservations to return to Sri Lanka, also giving notice to vacate university housing.

Just then, Lady Luck seems to have paid one of her visits to us. Swarna and I were invited to participate in an International Student Camp in California. It must have been through the International Student Centre or the Host Family system. This gave us breathing space, since arrangements were made to have our Visas extended till the end of Summer, ending on August 31.

Each of us given US $ 250.00 for our train ticket to and from San Francisco, we thought we had a better idea. How about if were to pool it and buy a car! I had my International Driver's Licence, and the American Highways would be a piece of cake to drive on compared to the 18 elbow bends I had negotiated driving up to Kandy!

How did I know? As part of a summer job, I had been hired to work at a construction work site, at a driving distance from AA, when my ego got a beating upon discovering that the construction workers I was supposed to be supervising in terms of their pay were earning way, way more than the pittance I was being paid. Anyhow, it was a job. It was better than my two unsuccessful attempts at being salesman. One was selling the *World Book Encyclopedia*, the American answer to the *Encyclopedia Britannica*. The other was selling vacuum cleaners, mostly to African Americans.

At the construction sight, self-pity turned shock when one day, my boss threw the keys to his car at me, asking me to bring it over to the worksite, from where it was. Gosh!. Licence aside, I had never driven on a US road, never mind a highway. But, having no choice – and not being one to run away from a challenge, I was now at the car when my heart began to beat. It was a boat – that old fashioned American Chrysler, long, and wide, of the type belonging to an Executive. The Peugeot I had driven appeared in my mind as being half the size. And, if the size wasn't threatening enough, it was an automatic, too. And I had no idea how it operated.

Once in the car, key in hand, I remember that it was with difficulty the moron found the keyhole. Perhaps it was on the steering wheel itself, at the base, and not on the dashboard as I had expected. Happy to find it finally, I try to start the engine. Now my heart thumped. The engine wouldn't turn on. Oh no! Had I busted the engine? With no one around, I must have tried for several minutes. And then, either with someone appearing by chance, or me monkeying around with it, the problem was discovered. My boss had carelessly left the gear on Drive. Moved to the Park position, the engine roared to life when I carefully managed to drive it out of the parking place to wherever it was that I was supposed to take it. But suddenly it felt odd. I was driving on the 'wrong side'! In Sri Lanka, driving is on the left, sitting on the right side in the car. But now I was sitting on the left, and driving on the right. Or whatever!

Five hundred dollars was not much we knew, but with Swarna agreeing, we spread the word around. Luckily, we didn't have to go far. A gentleman from Ceylon, Mr.. Rabel, who was in Ann Arbor for some reason, was willing to sell his car for the money we had. Wow! Even though I would confess to having taken an auto maintenance course at the Technical College in Maradana in my fanciful teenage years before I owned a car, all I could do was to go around the car before deciding to buy it. Even before the Green Revolution, we seemed to have been taken up by the green body of the car!

The camp being mid-July, we had about two weeks to get there by car. Giving up our home at the end of the month, we had packed the few worldly belongings we had into the car, and *whaddaya know*, we were on the road for what would be an exciting exploration of the vast land called the United States of America. I could also confess that my knowledge of running a car was limited to putting in the gas and pressing and slamming on the break pedal and shifting the gears. Oh yes, an occasional look in the side mirror! But as we traveled, gas was not the problem. It was the oil. Our little Rambler was a ravenous oil guzzler; its oil thirst had to be quenched every 100 miles or so! But, of course, we were well prepared for it. We had simply packed the trunk with oil.

Puta was an excellent little traveler. We had made a bed for him at the back seat with his crib mattress. Once fed and made comfortable, he would be playing with his toys for hours on end. In fact, having to stop every 100 miles might have helped. One of his favourite past-times was as back seat driver, making all the turns diligently on the *straight* highway with his Frisbee!

The highway, with its straight long stretches, and flat land around, was beginning to be monotonous, particularly driving through Midwest. But not for Swarna. She was having her first driving lessons! On the highway, at a comfortable 100 mph. And with no licence to boot! Unlike the divided front seats of modern day cars, our darling Rambler, like most cars of the time, had a single front seat. Moving as close to me as possible, I would first let her keep her hands on the steering wheel. Movement was when, on a stretch with no vehicles, she would very carefully change lanes, left and right, left and right, weaving in and out. Then, after a while, her left foot would, for experimental seconds, and then minutes, gradually replace my right foot on the accelerator pedal, feeling her way to press just the right amount to maintain the driving speed. The excellent student that she was, by the time we reached San Francisco after a few days, I would have the confidence to let her sit in the driver's seat, not on the highway, but when we got to a smaller rural road, looking for a park to stop for the night. And, of course, I would be sitting right beside her.

As assured by Mrs. McIvor, there was no shortage of parks for the highway traveler, many of them with a hot shower, not to mention washroom facilities. This was the time when US Executives were saving on travel by living in a mobile home, equipped with all the amenities of the home - fridge, stove, laundry, toilet, shower, bedroom, dining table, etc., all crammed into it. And it may be months before they would move to a new city. There were also other users of park facilities, like ourselves – simply driving through the country, on business or pleasure.

Our first night at a park was memorable. Mrs. McIvor had taken us to K-Mart where we would buy what she called a pup tent. This was one of the few things we had packed into the trunk, in addition to the oil. For our first night on the road, we had pulled into a park, found a parking spot where there was enough room for us to put up our home for the night. As I struggled to set up the tent, carefully following the instructions in the printed sheet that was in the package, someone taking sympathy on this clueless clutz, helped me hammer in the long spikes into the ground at the four corners. Then, opening up the tent, he anchored each end to the spikes as I watched with interest. Anchored to a ridgepole, the centre of the tent stood at a maximum height of about three feet as I waited for it to go up. Probably reading what was in my mind, my newly found American friend said, "There it is". What? That's how high? Then he laughed and explained that it was meant only to sleep, giving enough height to crawl in!

Which is in fact what we did. And to our surprise, there was enough room for the three of us to sleep comfortably. In fact, as we would come to know the next morning, it had rained the night before. But the ground canvas, perhaps rubber, was enough to keep any water out.

But it was Swarna's turn to be surprised and frustrated before we got into the tent. Hoping to prepare a meal of rice and curry, we had brought a stove with us. But try as she would, she could not get the rice cooked. And again, it must have been a kind camp neighbour that might have saved us from hunger that night. Puta was luckier. He had his ready-made bottled food.

Upon arriving in San Francisco, we were welcomed by Uncle Cy and Aunt Edna, the elderly couple behind the idea, and also the camp Directors. While most of the students at the camp were American, there was a student from Sierra Leone, Donyol from Korea and a third, Sarah, from Japan who literally thought that the streets of the US were paved in gold! Such must have been the propaganda.

As part of the program, we would go to a suburb of San Francisco, to visit Black homesteads where the disadvantaged children were on a Headstart educational program. Our experience thus far being in White American homes, our visits to Black homes were an eye-opener, to our American colleagues than even for us. Many a home had barely any furniture at all. But at least, there was a program intended to give the next generation better opportunities, and Uncle Cy and Aunt Edna had a keen interest in it. The International camp was as much an opportunity for white America to see the plight of Black America under friendly conditions.

The camp being also an opportunity for young Americans to meet with international students, the rest of the time was mostly spent enjoying the American culture. It was an enjoyable experience for Swarna and me, too. We were getting a glimpse of real American culture, as we sang children's songs like *E I E I O*, *Michael row the boat ashore - alelujah*, *Home on the Range...*, and many an American folksong. Many an evening would be spent at the top of a hillock around a bonfire.

The one unpleasant experience was when an American girl refused to participate in some activity, the student from Sierra Leone also participating. In protest, I would refuse to participate in an activity at a later time. Uncle Cy was surprised at my stance, because he had seen me as being 'mature'. And I suppose protesting in principle for a perceived wrong must have been seen as immature, or not a way of keeping friendships.

Puta, with his rounded big eyes, as many would comment, had become the darling of the campers. Walking into a girl's room one day, he had asked, "Are you *applying* lipstick?" Leslie was taken aback, sort of, as she would tell Swarna later. She had been impressed by his vocabulary. Not 'putting on' lipstick, but 'applying'. An early reader, starting at age 2 plus, Puta was a blotting paper when it came to language. Even before he could read, he had a terrific memory for language. Listening to a record of the story being re-told, after it had been read out by Swarna or me, he would turn the page exactly at the right time, even before the instruction, "Turn the page" would be heard on the record. A voracious reader, he would read book after book, again and again. Puta's 3rd birthday falling while we were at the camp, there was to be a party. Our gift was a toy car in which he would spend hours as I played a round of amateur tennis. The last time, and the first, I had played tennis had been about twelve years earlier, as a student at Ananda, but at Tangalla. Tennis was a 'cultur' (pronounced *kul-toor*) game of the westernized class, it being the favourite sport of our Principal at Christ Church College, Mr.. Samuel. Neither at Ananda nor Nalanda was tennis an extracurricular activity. The tennis club at Tangalla was by membership, and limited to the elite class. I had a friend at Ananda, Indra Kulatilaka, whose father had been posted to Tangalla as the Judge. So when Indra would come to Tangalla during the school holidays, I would go along with him. So the only experience at tennis was the few times I was on the courts with him.

While in San Francisco, we had the pleasure of crossing the Bay Bridge, which would later appear on the cover of my publication, *Multiculturalism, Peace and Development*, decades later (2007).

1.5 Homeless! Across the US on a Rambling Rambler

Camp over, and not yet hearing from Canada, we decided to see the US by car. Our first destination was Los Angeles, the la la land as it had come to be fondly called, still in the State of California. While there was an Interstate Highway that would have taken us there faster, we had opted for the scenic route along the Pacific Coast. And if you were not careful, you could end up rolling down a precipice. While left terrain was hilly, to the right was a deep drop leading to the ocean. All the way down was where we would have ended with a just a little wrong move! But the scenery was terrific. And, having only seen flat land for three years, and 10000 miles away from an island surrounded by the ocean, the attraction of the waters was even more. So much so that I decided to take a dip, the weather being, in the height of summer, more than balmy.

It didn't matter that there was nobody else at that patch of the beach. Changing into my swimming trunks, I dashed towards the water as Swarna and Puta looked on. But only to beat a hasty retreat. Ouch. The water was icy! This was the Pacific Ocean, as somebody would point out to me, later. To me, an ocean was an ocean was an ocean. And hot weather equals warm water. Not so, as it turned out to be to my great disappointment. But I was at least able to know that the Pacific water was not so salty, unlike the warm Indian waters.

In LA, a Sinhala family resident there welcomed us warmly to their house. And it was an excited Puta that would take many a ride at Disneyland, the original one before it spread to Florida and other parts of the world. Hollywood was our excitement as the tour guide pointed to the sets and the locations of many a film I had seen back home, and the background to the comics I had read, sharing with friends. All this was new to Swarna, of course. As the apple of the eye of the family, this only girl was not to be corrupted by western culture, the brothers ensured even as they took in the films! Getting off the bus, she would enjoy taking the tourist favourite, the Hollywood Walk of Fame, where the palm and footprints of famous film stars lay bare, imprinted on the slabs we would walk over.

Another attraction was the Haight-Ashbury, the Mecca of the hippies. There we would see young men and women, in different stages of stupor, docile or conscious followers of Timothy Leary, Guru of the turn on, drop out Culture. These were the young people of America whose dope-taking and free sex had horrified an American public. As I would read, they were protesting the hypocrisy of the parental generation who were asking that the children walk straight while they themselves were walking crooked. If drinking to excess of the parental generation was one of the crooked ways that the younger generation was protesting by even going further – in testing non-standard varieties like Marijuana, sexual excesses was another. Making the rounds was the story of a common practice of couples coming to parties, and then the man throwing the keys on the table, going to bed with the woman picking it up, while the husband would be indulging with another's wife in the meantime. If this was all done in the privacy of a dance venue, or a hotel, the younger generation saw no need to have any place more than a street to engage in their sexual exhibitionism.

Little would I know that I would encounter them later personally in my Buddhist work. As a roster of American Buddhist leaders would show, the spiritual search for many of them – men and women, had begun right here at the Haight-Ashbury. Having tried out the dope, yoga had attracted them as an alternative spiritual path, leading them to meditation. And it is in the process of experimenting with meditation that they ultimately ended up with Buddhism. Not that, of course, Buddhism was new to America. Academic exchange in particular between the US and Japan had gone on for a hundred years between 1850 and 1950, particularly after Hawai'i, with its Japanese population, became the 51st State. Anagarika Dharmapala of Ceylon, with his Jesus-like appearance, had mesmerized scholars and Christian leaders, not to mention the American female community in particular, at the World Parliament of Religions in Chicago in 1883. And Prof. William James, the foremost Psychologist of Religion had declared in his psychology class that Buddhism was the future of psychology, having invited Dharmapala to the front, seeing him seated at the back, and asked to take the class. But it was none of that academic or religious stuff that had brought these young people to Buddhism. It was their personal experience, true to the spirit of the Buddha's invitation to 'Come and See' (*ehi-passika*).

Anagarika Dharmapala at the World Parliament of Religions, Chicago, USA, 1893

Heading out of Los Angeles, we would have another life experience, going past Salt Lake City. A sign at the gas station read, "Desert. No gas for the next

100 miles." My heart went thump. And Swarna's probably, too. It was already getting to be unbearably hot. Our Rambler was cheap enough not to have Air Conditioning. What the sign did was worse - bring memories of stories in the Buddhist Jataka (Birth) Tales of caravans doing the grueling crossing of desserts! Here we were, with a three year old kid, and a trunk full of oil to feed the engine monster. And what if, for some reason, we were to run out of gas? Except for an odd vehicle or two, it was lonely country. But, didn't we want to see the US of A? So, we filled the tank and headed into the desert.

For the next 100 miles, it was heat and more heat and more heat, easily passing the 100 degree mark. Neither Swarna nor I had the luxury of owning sunglasses. Luckily, Puta was taking it in stride, once stripped to his undies. Driving for miles with nothing but sand as far as eye could see, we stopped, just intrigued by what was around us. Touching the sand, ouch, it was hot. And tasting it, it was salty. And we realized how Salt Lake City had earned its name honestly!

The next memorable landmark on our journey was the Painted Desert. Getting off, we treated our eyes to a panorama of colour as we had never seen before. Painted it looked alright, the Painted Desert. But it was no desert. It was a highly colourful foliage that festooned the land.

Not soon after, getting closer to Colorado, was the Grand Canyon. And it was reflecting on the story of how it had been bombarded a long time ago by a crater that we went down to the valley, taking us quite some time. It was the size of the bowl, the canyon, that gave it the name. Living in a flat land in Ceylon, we had never seen, or been to, a canyon.

So it was with nostalgia that recently I got a chance to look at them, but this time from a different vantage point - flying over them. But there was nothing like being at the real thing.

Passing many an other scene along the way, we ultimately returned to Ann Arbor. After traveling over 10,000 miles across the US, we were happy that all three of us were in continuing good health. But not without the help of Puta's back seat driving. The Frisbee was now an interstate-seasoned veteran, ready to roar again. Swarna, still in her Sari, was by now a veteran driver, too. All she needed was to pass a driving test before she could sit behind the wheel legally. Save for a minor hiccup one morning when it refused to start, our Rambler had held its own as well. Not bad, we thought, for 500 bucks.

Back in Ann Arbor, we were happy that our former neighbours, an Indian couple, were willing to put us up. The Canadian VISA had not still arrived. This was when, making use of the opportunity, we made another road trip, this time to Eastern US, stopping first in New York and Washington DC, and ending up in Florida.

But it was a later visit to Florida that I remember better. On our return trip, checking into a hotel at Cocoa Beach, I had gone for a swim towards the evening, in the warm Atlantic water, a few yards from the hotel. There was perhaps no one else in the water or the beach, as I took a dip. But soon, one by one more and more people came to be at the beach, though not in their swim suits. Since no one else was in the water, I began to wonder what was it that I had done to attract them. Had I done anything wrong? But then as I directed my own eyes in the direction of theirs, I knew that it was not my water charisma that had brought them there. In the distance, a space craft was taking off from Cape Canavarel, setting off a vast cloud of red smoke and gradually disappearing into the space. It was exciting to me all the more, because we had just been at the spacecraft site ourselves. In the area open to the public, I had gazed in amazement for many moments at the tall rocket booster, standing upright, that had sent the first moon lander to space, taking Neil Armstrong and Buzz Aldrin to the moon. I had written about it from Canada to a Sinhala newspaper. Puta was more interested in taking in the experience of actual space travel, sitting inside a cabin replica of the real thing. We visited the control room and spent a long time looking at the many other scientific equipment, reading the data and making mental notes of the history of US Space Travel.

My interest in space travel had begun when I had written a piece, in Sinhala, on the Soviet scientist Tsiolkovsky, the father of space travel, before I had ever left the shores of Lanka. Drawing designs of what a spacecraft would look like, he had calculated the required escape velocity for a spaceship to successfully leave the earth's orbit. It had turned out to be accurate, as we came to know from the successful launch of Yuri Gagarin, becoming the first man to walk in space. In Canada, I had come to write a first hand report of the moon landing by Neil Armstrong, watching it on TV (no TV in Sri Lanka at the time). It was headlined, 'A Sinhala Writer sees stepping on to the moon' (Aug. 7, 1969). I end the article philosophically: "What a pity! While man is traversing the moon, we on earth fight each other, trying to destroy ourselves".

2. BONJOUR, CANADA

2.1 Canada: French for a Son, Teacher Training for Swarna

U-haul? What's that? This was the advice given to us by our American friends. Upon returning to Ann Arbor from our Eastern US trip, we were thankful to our Indian friends, who again put us up, as we waited our Canadian documents, biting our nails. The US VISA was expiring at the end of the month (August). Overstaying our stay in the US would have meant swift deportation. Just, then, luckily, the papers arrived, allowing us only a few days to pack up and leave. But happily, there was not much to pack – our son's crib (his mattress being his bed throughout our travels), his play car, his third year birthday gift in San Francisco, during the student camp, some kitchen utensils given to us by Mrs. McIvor and a couple of suitcases of clothing. Then there were my books, purchased over three years, thanks to my general practice of buying the books I needed rather than beg, borrow or steal. In Sri Lanka, I had seen how books didn't sell much, partly perhaps because of the cultural habit of passing on books from hand to hand. I was not going to contribute to a practice that would take the health away from the dissemination of knowledge.

So it was that we bid good-bye to our Indian friends at the crack of dawn on September 1, 1967, and left Ann Arbor. Hauling a U-Haul was a new experience. Not towing it per se but taking bends, and lordy lordy, reversing. Passing Detroit, we came to the Canadian border at Windsor. Our first experience of Canada was a pleasant one. Checking our documentation, we were allowed to enter the country.

Item

My first impressions as recorded in my book *Towards Multicultural Growth, A look at Canada from Classical Racism to Neo- Multiculturalism,* 2001 (p. 4).

> *Entry to a Brand New World*
> *Nineteen Sixty seven marked, like for Canada, a momentous year for our family. My wife Swarna and I crossed the border at Windsor, along with our son, in our 'Rambling Rambler' (as our friends would call it), pulling all our worldly belongings in a U-Haul. As a finishing university student in the US, it wasn't much.*
>
> *The pleasant experience of crossing the border, the fresh air we breathed in our new country as early beneficiaries of the new system of immigration selection, the beauty of the vast landscapes that caught our eye as we drove through past Windsor to Kingston past Toronto ... None of this gave us any indication of entering a target zone!*

Target? Yes, the target of a practice then called 'discrimination'.

Our dealings being with the Montreal Immigration office, it was to Montreal we were headed after entering Canada. Going past Toronto, which to us was just another city, huh!, we stopped by in Kingston. A Sri Lankan, Sirisena Tilakaratne, later Professor back in the country, was doing his doctoral studies at Queen's, and he and his friendly wife, Malini, were kind enough to welcome us to their home. But it was his advice that, given my training in Linguistics, and teaching *English* as a Foreign Language, my chances would be better in Toronto. Now suddenly, Toronto came to be not just a city we had bypassed along 401, but a pivotal one to our future success.

Soon I was in Toronto, staying at the YMCA and scouting around, pretty much in the dark. Returning to Kingston though without any particular leads, we decided that Toronto indeed was the better venue to hang our hat in. Returning to Toronto with Swarna and our son, leaving our worldly goods at our friend's, we were put up at Anndore Hotel on Charles St East, at government cost (Sept 18 to 25) I must have got in touch with the Immigration office in Toronto when I came scouting.

The next day or so, I parked our Rambler in front of the 6 storey building of what was then the Toronto Board of Education just west of Avenue on College Street. Leaving Swarna and son in the car, I went up to the Research Department where I was met by Dr Seymour Trieger. The Department was about to launch a project on English as a Second Language in the City, and my background in Linguistics caught the attention of the Asst. Director. At the end of our interview, he said, "You know, until you showed up we thought we had hired the people we needed. But now with your background, we may change our mind." Dr Trieger, an American, could not have failed to be impressed by a fresh graduate from the US. But, he continued, he had to get the Director's approval when he was back. The project falling under the purview of the Asst Director, I was confident that his recommendation would carry the day.

Back at the car, Swarna was elated. Getting a job on the first day in Toronto? Wow! But, not leaving anything to chance, as I awaited final word, I kept looking around for work. Applying to a trucking company to be a loader of things into the truck, I had, in all my naïve honesty, listed all my academic qualifications, BA, MA and all. It was later that I was to be advised that there was no chance in hell that I would even be considered. The company would have been foolish not to know that I would bolt at the first chance of an academic opening.

The Project team at he Board consisted of Susan Mowat and Ian Craig, a statistician. My responsibility was to develop a Test of English Language Skills, which was given to the ESL students in the system to help determine their level of proficiency, details of which was to be published as a Research Report of the Board after my departure. While my methodology made sense to all of us at the time, I am happy to see better testing instruments developed thereafter, both at the Board and elsewhere.

While the primary reason for coming to Canada was for Swarna to get her teacher training, by the time we arrived in September, it was too late to gain admission for the 1967-68 academic year. So she would get a job at Carleton Cards, on the basis of her experience at the University of Michigan as a secretary. Still in her sari, this was when somebody expressed the concern that her sari would get entangled in the typewriter or the elevator! How far we have come from those heady days when Brown earned a frown, and the sari made some weary if not bring fury. Luckily, we were not faced with what Blacks faced at the time, when being Black meant the door came to be shut on them at rental units.

We were, in fact, lucky to find accommodation very quickly. At the Board, I was to be introduced to a fellow Ceylonese who was by then working for the Metropolitan School Board. The Rajanayagams, Solomon and Rosalind, a kind Christian Tamil family welcomed us in their home. Going on a picnic, our son had great fun playing with their two little daughters. They would also introduce us to the Ekanayakas, a Buddhist Sinhala couple, Stanley and Sita. Living in an apartment building on Bergamot Avenue, off Islington, just north of the 401, he was able to use his charms on the Superintendent to get us an apartment in the subsidized housing scheme, in rapid fire time. We were glad that we were no longer a burden to the government, nay people, of Canada, putting us up at a hotel.

With the subway line ending at Keele, getting downtown called for three transfers, two buses and two subway lines. The bus near the house would take me to Weston, the next bus taking me to the Keele station. Taking the subway going east, I would get off at St George, and take the University line, getting off at Queen's Park, all this taking an hour or more, depending on the connections. It was on one of those travels that I offered my seat to a woman who was standing, something that I, and many a Sri Lanka male, would do routinely, as also for someone handicapped. When she declined, I was surprised. Did I do something wrong? But today I am happy to see a 'courtesy seat' in public transportation assigned to the elderly and the disabled, with a request to accommodate them.

It was later that I would reflect that the woman turning down my offer may have had something to do with an emerging feminism. I don't know if anything was said by her to this effect, or it is me thinking out loud. Perhaps accepting my offer would have been tantamount to a concession that she was inferior to me, that she was indeed the 'weaker sex'. A term for women in Sinhala, *obalat*, in fact, captures such a sympathetic sentiment, even as it does the sense of beauty as in the close sounding *babalat*. Was it an early Germaine Greer I was seeing in the woman's stance? She must have seen my offer as condescending. How is an ignoramus to know?

It was to be expressed as much a decade or so later teaching Teacher Trainees at the Faculty of Education at U of T. I had gone around asking the class for a suggestion for something or the other, and finally, when I did hear something suitable, I had accepted it. Only to be objected to by a woman student, that it was only because it came from a male student! What more could I expect from the female student who would have seen none but a perceived patriarchy-ingrained Brown man? The class of men and women looked taken aback. But the mood was far different when I would, fifteen more years later, organize a 2-day Conference at Trinity under the Seminars on Buddhism series, on *Buddhism after Patriarchy*, inviting the author Rita Gross for the keynote. These were scholars in the academy, not students.

Living in the Bergamot apartment, with little income, our treat was a hamburger at McDonalds, while for our son, it was an Ice cream at the Dairy Queen! Just north of the building, about three traffic lights up the street at Islington and Albion Road, we would also outfit him with clothes bought at the Byway. He also began to babble in Arabic when he came home in the evening from the baby-sitter down the same street, Swarna and I both having daytime jobs. It was also the time Puta was beginning to write. It would trigger from me an article, "Why Write, Why not type?" that appeared in *The British Columbia Teacher*. Little would I imagine that I was unconsciously predicting the future, when today, penmanship is no longer in style for a computer-savvy generation who would rather type in text messages.

Driving downtown in our spare time, the Royal York Hotel stood in its grandeur facing the Union Station, and going along King Street, there was just one tower, the tall TD Bank skyscraper, all out of proportion then for the street, and pitch black. The New City Hall on Queen at Bay looked artistic while the Old City Hall looked majestic. Eatons and Simpsons faced each other a bit to the East.

It was during one of these outings that I felt my first Canadian insult. Seeing a pedestrian while driving, I had stopped at a Crosswalk, but once the pedestrian had gone past our car, I had driven through, only to be pulled over by a waiting cop. The charge: not waiting behind the line until the pedestrian had reached the curb. Not only did I feel that I had not compromised any safety, I felt insulted. Back in Sri Lanka, only the scum of society gets accosted by the Police. I was not sure what to do with the suggestion that it may have something to do with racism.

Arriving in Canada in the Centenary year, we made it a point to visit the Expo 67 in Montreal, visiting it again for the Olympics and many an academic conference. As President of Buddhist Council of Canada, I would also make visits later, two decades later, to help establish a Branch.

Applying in time, Swarna came to be admitted to the University of Toronto Faculty of Education on Bloor Street at Spadina Avenue, beginning in the Fall of 1968. As part of teacher training, she was also required to do 'practice teaching', observed by teachers of the given school as well as faculty members. "You think on your feet", it had been observed of her creative teaching style. Although she had majored in History at the Peradeniya university, she had now switched to English as a Second Language. And she had also returned to the western dress which she had worn at the university back in Sri Lanka.

While there was now no question of the dress getting trapped in the elevator, Swarna was nevertheless getting trapped – in the conveyor belt of racism. Now the 'target zone' of discrimination I had not seen upon entering Canada was coming to be visible. It was the practice of the Boards of Education to set up shop at the FEUT itself in the Spring of each year to look for new recruits. And, with teaching experience in Sri Lanka, teacher training in Toronto, and with commendations of thinking on her feet, it was with great expectations, and full confidence in herself, that Swarna would walk into one of the Board outfits. But was she in for a rude surprise, when she was to be told, even as she handed in the application, that there were better applicants, this without even going through the application. Swarna knew that many an other who got interviews, and eventually got hired, were recent university graduates, with hardly any teaching experience. They were in her class. But they had one qualification Swarna could never match. White skin colour.

There seemed to be another. And that was *not being* Christian. This came as a shocker when a Sinhala Christian from Sri Lanka comes to be hired by the Catholic Board, with neither a degree, nor training. Having however been a teacher of the junior grades, she was to be trained *after* being hired, at Board cost. But Swarna's two BA's, teacher training, and teaching experience were not even in the race.

But Swarna was not the only one to pay the price for being Buddhist. To our great disappointment, admission was denied to our son as well. This was by the Toronto French School, the only one of its kind in Toronto at the time. Only Catholics, we were told, need apply! French for our son was one of the reasons for our being in Canada. The TFS wanted nothing of it. Luckily today, taking French through High School, and with private tutoring, he holds a job which calls for fluency in both official languages.

The first summer, in 1968, ended being a busy one for me. Working on the Project at the Board, I had come to realize the importance of Statistics for research. This was what prompted me to take a course in Statistics at OISE in the summer of 1968. But there was another academic thrill - getting an opportunity to teach Linguistics to Teacher Trainees at the Faculty of Education, University of Toronto. Under a newly developed policy, and curriculum, for ESL Teacher Trainees, Linguistics came to be compulsory, to the chagrin of the trainees themselves. Why Linguistics, when we are only teaching English, was the great objection. But that the course was Linguistics with application to the teaching of English didn't seem to convince them all. So it was to some grumbling adult students that York University Linguistics Professor Ed Burstinzky and I had to teach. But if there had been any doubts, it had all vanished by the end of the course, the students seeing the value of it in their teaching. The course has continued to be part of the curriculum since then, with the Faculty coming to hire permanent faculty to teach it. However, in later years, I was to face a different kind of hostility, when I was hired to teach Linguistics to another batch of English as a Second Language teacher-trainees. Still in the early years of Multiculturalism, they seemed to have difficulty adjusting to a Brown teaching English Linguistics to them! The nerve, they seem to be saying, teaching them about their own language by one whose native language was not English? Little did they know, of course, that I had been a speaker of English since age 10.

Upon completion of my one-year assignment at the Toronto Board of Education, I had come to be hired to the newly formed Department of English as a Second Language at Humber College of Arts & Technology. Mrs. Rankin, who still pronounced 'which' with an /h/ at the front – *Hwhich*, in the good old British style., was Head. Jake Yeramian was another colleague. When hired, my salary would jump by as much as 50%. I knew I was the only MA holder in my department, but it was only later that I would know that I was one of a handful on the entire Humber faculty.

Established at Humber, I was to speak to the Dean, Tom Norton, a jovial but efficient administrator with a Master's Degree, who called Swarna for an interview, hiring her instantly. She worked at a different campus from where I taught. This was the time when we got many refugees from Hungary, and that was the class Swarna had been assigned. And the men in the class in particular seem to have a hard time getting used to being taught by a Brown woman. However, by the end of the course, Swarna was their favourite teacher, appreciation shown with a European made crystal vase given as a class gift. As a matter of fact, the several crystal vases we still have at home are such gifts to her from her grateful Humber students upon their graduation.

2.2 Master's Degree in Moral Philosophy

The Statistics course, taken at OISE, also had the effect of making me interested in Education. I must have seen in it some usefulness when I returned back to Lanka. And so, as Swarna pursued her teacher training, I registered for an M Ed, in the knowledge it could be completed before we would depart. Luckily, given that I already had an MA, I had a lesser course load than the average Master's student. This meant that I could complete the degree in one academic year plus two summers, ending in 1969. It would be the end of the 1970-71 academic year when Swarna would be able to complete her requirements needed to get a permanent Teaching Certificate, also entitling her to a second Bachelor's, this in Education.

I had chosen Philosophy of Education, focusing on Moral Philosophy. My interest in moral issues, of course, dated back to the time of my writing to the media in Sri Lanka. I had expressed my disapproval of showing off at rituals, and of Sinhala brides wearing a veil, adopted the practice of 'giving the pleasure of the company of (Yours Truly)' but no gifts at weddings, and resigned my job unhappy that getting a prestigious job had brought unjustified added literary respectability. I had picked up street tickets strewn on the ground, as my friend Dr. Punchihewa would remind me, and I had urged an end to quarrelling between English-speaking and Sinhala-only speaking middle class Sinhala, proposed that schoolgirls wear the half-sari to school. And so on. So moral philosophy was a natural. It may have been considered an opportunity to test my own philosophical outlook on social mores.

The Department Chair, Prof. Clive Beck, an Australian Canadian who still spoke with a thick 'stralian accent, was my academic counselor. It was with fascination that I read up on Western Philosophy. I was fascinated by Kohlberg's Stages of Moral Development in Prof. Beck's course, as I was with Maslow's hierarchical needs. In all this, I could not help begin to note the parallels with Buddhism. Of particular value for me in this connection was a chapter by Brown and Engler, in *Transformation of Consciousness* (ed. by Ken Wilbur) where Kohlberg's stages come to be compared to the stages of spirituality achieved in meditation in Buddhism.

My comparative stance came to be cogently expressed in a course taken with Prof. Wilfred Wees. But a new area of learning was the course I took with Prof. David Wilson – in Educational Planning. Returning to Ceylon soon at the back of the mind, I decided to develop an *Educational Plan for Ceylon* as my paper. Assigning me an A grade, Professor David Wilson comments:

> *Your Great Proletarian Cultural Revolution is a bit better planned than was Chairman Mao's – but not much. The upheaval implied in your "plan" is staggering! Your phasing seems to me to be overly ambitious and – contrary to what you wrote, costly to implement.*
>
> *This is impressive <u>because</u> it is a panacea, but I often am critical – very critical – of panaceas because I prefer <u>manageable</u> change and what you propose is, I am afraid, far from manageable.*
>
> *I am, however, impressed at the amount of thought – and work – which you have put into this document. A bit more careful integration of tables, charts and data with the text would have given you a much better grade!* [underline in original].

Both Swarna and I earning, we had soon moved out of subsidized housing, when our home came to be at Crown Hill Place, closer to the Lakeshore Blvd where the Humber campus where Swarna taught was. It was a three storied building, and we were on the second floor. Another Sinhala family lived on the third floor. Watching kids play from our balcony, Puta was often found saying, "I wish I had a sister." So it was that in 1970 that Chutti was born. Luckily, this time I was not meeting the Prime Minister of the country, in a different town, as when our son was born. I was right there, no, not in the labour room – fathers still not allowed at the time to be present at delivery, but just outside. Puta got a glimpse of mom and sister from up a low-lying willow-tree, luckily, just beside the maternity ward! And to this day, brother and sister continue to be great buddies, along with their families. Allowed a maternity leave of only three months, Swarna was, however, soon back at work, finding a baby-sitter for Chutti in the building itself.

Just across from our building was another apartment building where two other Sinhala bachelors lived. One was Palita Collure. The other was Edward de Silva where, a great party animal. Many a day, it would be the wee hours when we would head home, with Puta on my shoulder, and Swarna carrying Chutti, dragging them out of their beds at our friends' where they were as we had had a wonderful time with good food and great cheer. Other frequent visitors were newcomers Ari Dassanayaka and Doyne Seneviratna, bachelors for whom Swarna would pack a lunch as well on many an occasion as they went job-hunting. Of the middle class, just about every Sinhalese coming to Canada spoke English, even if poorly. Swarna would also sponsor her younger brother, Maithree, during this time. It fell on me to teach him driving.

Following the year of study at the Faculty of Education, it was a requirement that teacher trainee should get the practical experience of teaching, before a Certificate would be awarded. Swarna had completed that requirement teaching at Humber.

So now that Swarna had earned what she had come to Canada for. I had also completed my M Ed. Mission accomplished, by 1971, it was time to pack up and return home, as had always been the plan.

But, we had both resigned, and neither had jobs to go back to in Sri Lanka. So, no longer able to be rash as in my bachelor years, it was thought wise for me to go alone first, to check out the lay of the land before hauling the family back.

When I resigned my job at Humber, and flew out of the Pearson Airport, Swarna was again left to be the sole breadwinner, and the sole caregiver to our two children!

2.3 Ven Prof. Hammalawa Saddhatissa

Buddhism had been never a strong component of the Department of Religious Studies at the University of Toronto. It was partly to fill this hiatus perhaps that the Department had come to invite Venerable H. Saddhatissa, a Sinhala monk with a PhD in the UK, and author of *Buddhist Ethics,* for a two year appointment as Professor. Prof. A K Warder, specialist in Early Buddhism, also originally from the UK must have provided the connection, and with support of the only other Buddhologist, Leonard Priestley.

Although I had not known him, I had been familiar with his work, and so it was an honour to be able to associate him in Toronto, though in no official capacity, but as a Sinhala Buddhist. He made it a practice to come to the university very early, before the university would spring to life in the morning, and leave after dark, long after the classes were over. He would tell me that, in those pre-multicultural days, it was basically not wanting to take any chances at being taunted by an ignorant public who may never have seen a Buddhist monk in robes. He didn't want to be mistaken for a member of a Hindu cult. So when he would go in public wearing a brownish overcoat in the summer, it would raise some eyebrows.

With not much contact with the community, I would be one of the few who would maintain regular contact with him at his rented room on Baldwin Avenue in Chinatown. With all his contacts being with the university community, he had seen no need to have a phone installed either. So the only communication I would have with him was through personal visit. One Christmas holiday, perhaps busy with the family and the festive occasion, I had failed to visit him for a few days. And when I finally did find the time to visit him, I was in a panic. He had developed a temperature, and seen no doctor, not having OHIP coverage either. Opening the fridge, I found it practically empty as well. This was partly due to the custom that a Buddhist monk is provided for by the community, and therefore going grocery shopping would not be part of his daily living. While Swarna would provide him alms from time to time, I don't believe there was a committed arrangement within the Sinhala Buddhist community, Spartan still at this time, to ensure that he would receive his alms. As the price paid by a monk living in the west, where such an arrangement would not materialize unlike in a home setting, he would do his grocery shopping if no one was around to do it for him. But that would be rare, since during university sessions, food would be no issue, since a Buddhist monk takes no meals after the turn of the sun. Lunch would be on campus, and a breakfast could well be cereal and some milk. But being sick, with no phone and no visitors, no supplies in the fridge, and not getting to a doctor, he was in a very serious health condition. Luckily, a few friends getting together, we were able to collect enough funds to take him to a doctor. And the fridge would have sufficient food as well.

While Swarna and I would benefit immensely from his Dharma teachings whenever we met, I was registered for no program of studies to benefit on a formal level, although I would draw upon his *Buddhist Ethics* again and again both in my personal life, and later when serving as a Buddhist resource person.

Prof Jotiya Dhirasekara would take the place of Ven Saddhatissa upon his departure. But I was to have not much communication with him, he being with his wife in an apartment not far from the university. He would himself enter the robes some years after his return to Sri Lanka, under the name Dhammavihari.

2.4 An Educational Tour of Western and Eastern Europe

As part of my course work for the MEd, we had come to study several overseas innovative educational programs. One of them was a primary school program in the UK. Another was at the other end of the spectrum, the Folk High School, in Denmark primarily, but also in Norway, intended to serve those who could not, for some reason, make it through High School. A third was the kibbutz experiment in Israel.

So it was that I took the opportunity to study them in person, before heading back home. Now that I was academically qualified in Education as well, the country could perhaps benefit from a little innovation. Or so I thought.

In the UK, I was welcomed by the Principal of the Primary School I had visited, and shown around.

In Denmark, I would be given accommodation at the Folk High School, but for a fee. In turn, I was invited to give a few talks to the students – on Sinhala music, e.g., for which I was paid enough to pay for the board and lodging during the few days I was there.

With a day or so to spare, I took the opportunity to take a boat ride from Denmark to Norway, for a bare couple of hours, in what I characterize as 'international waters separated by a 'b''. While on the Denmark side, the place was called Helsingor, on the Norway side, there was a 'b' adding, making it Helsing**b**or. It was later I realized why the boat was packed. The booze was cheap, having to pay no taxes. What ingenious ways human beings devise to get around the law, and to save a few shekels, I thought. But it was to my great surprise that I found the Norwegian newspaper *Helsingborgs Dagblad* interested in featuring me in their front page, photo and all. Quaint I must have appeared, probably the first educator from Sri Lanka they had met, but with a twist - qualifications gained from North America. But to date, I don't even know what was said in the story.

It was due to lack of time that I could not get my visa to Israel. But, unknown to me then, that may have helped avoid a difficult situation for me. On my itinerary following the visits to the West European countries was a tour of

Making a quick visit to Norway, across the river from Denmark, interviewed on Helsingborgs Dagblad, Oct 25, 1971

Eastern European Soviet Bloc countries. Had I been to Israel before that, I might have been taken to be a western spy. If, on the other hand, were I to visit Israel after the East European tour, I may have been taken for a communist spy. So it was a lucky stroke that time ran out on me getting the Israel documents.

As a member of the Puppetry committee of the Arts Council of Ceylon, I had met the Czechoslovakian puppeteer specialist, Dr. Vajitkova in Sri Lanka. If this was a reason I had wanted to go to Czechoslovakia, I had another general reason. And that was to get a handle on Marxist-run countries.

Mr. Bandaranaike's 1956 coalition included Marxist parties, no less than three, in fact. Marxism had been introduced to the country as far back as the 1930's, by Phillip Gunawardhana who was now the Leader of one of the coalition partners, the Revolutionary Lanka Equalitarian Party (VLSSP). Another was the

Lanka Equalitarian Party (LSSP), headed by Dr N M Perera, an economist of the London School of Economics who had studied under Harold Laski. Ironically, he was also a Mill owner, a point generally ignored by the public and the Trade Union he led. He would also happen to be the Minister of Finance under Mrs. Bandaranaike, his policy of freezing all foreign exchange being the one that nearly scuttled my Fulbright scholarship. The third was the Communist Party, jointly headed by Mr. Peiter Keuneman and Dr S A Wickramasingha, a physician. Even though each of the the leaders were members of the Bandaranaike Cabinet, each of the three Trade Unions led by them individually would go on strike against the Bandaranaike government! Only in Ceylon, you would say. Would a Minister in a Canadian cabinet launch a campaign against the government of which s/he would be part?

May 1st, the International Labour Day had been declared a holiday by the new government. And the Marxists were on a roll. And there was no end to the claims of the wonderful, and egalitarian, life under Marxism, and showcasing countries of the Soviet bloc as a model for Sri Lanka. Many a person in leadership positions as well in the rank and file might have been disappointed that I had not been impressed enough to become a member of their party (for no fee), even though I had continued my close contacts with the cultural wings of the Soviet and the Chinese Embassies.

So the general interest I had in going to the Soviet Bloc countries was to be able to look in the eye of my Marxist friends back in Sri Lanka and say, "I've seen your Utopia". While I would not deny my left leanings, I wasn't buying the rosy picture that was portrayed. I knew that the artists behind the Iron Curtain were well paid and looked after, unlike in Ceylon where they would be poor by any standard. But I wasn't convinced that the average masses were well to do. Having lived in the West now for three years, I was even less convinced that Marxism was the way to go for Ceylon. But I wanted to see for myself.

But before starting the Eastern European tour, I had a stop in Greece. Of course, I had read some Greek plays, and the Iliad and the Odyssey in my youth. Then there was the Greek connection with Buddhism in India when it was invaded by Alexander the Great. In the early period of Buddhism, Buddha was not shown in human form, but represented only symbolically, as e.g., by Wheel of Dhamma or the Bodhi Tree or a footprint. And it has been theorized that the first *statues* of the Buddha were the product of Greek influence. Indeed it was with interest that I attended a recent lecture at the ROM, by Prof. Bopearacchi of Sorbonne, a numismatist, where he would show the parallels between a portrayal of Alexander the Great, as found in ancient coins, and the Mahayana god Avalokiteshvara. But even more important was the famous Dialogue between King Menander, shown in Buddhist literature as Milinda, and Bhikkhu Nagasena where the critical issue of the Buddha's teaching of 'asoulity' – absence of a soul as taught in other religions, come to be discussed.

In Greece, even though the ruins of Acropolis were of historical interest, my favourite was the Odeon, the Open Air Theatre. While the Sinhalas in Sri Lanka had flocked to watch folk plays performed in temporary open air theatres, this was a terraced theatre of antiquity where many a classic play had been performed. And it was with delight, then, that, one of our three visits to Sri Lanka, Swarna and I would discover a formally named 'Open Air Theatre' in honour of Prof. Saracchandra on the campus of the Peradeniya university.

Travelling by Aeroflot and arriving in Moscow, I was happy to be welcomed by a Representative of the Soviet Writers' Association, and whisked through customs and immigration. A letter I had with me confirmed that I was an Asst Secretary of the Ceylon Writers' Union, a position I had taken up after resigning my job. Mr. K M Sirisena, who, a stranger to me then, had reviewed my translation of Bertrand Russell under the pseudonym Jayadeva, had written it in his capacity as Secretary, to introduce me to his Soviet counterparts. I was happy to see a subway system, something I hadn't seen in any of the other Eastern European countries. The Soviet friend took me to all the usual tourist attractions, including the Kremlin.

My travels would take me to Czechoslovakia, Bulgaria and Roumania as well.

In Yugoslavia, visiting the War Museum, I was saddened at the thought, "Was it worth all the suffering?" What I had in mind was the successful attempt by President Tito at bringing together the many countries to form a single political entity called Yugoslavia. Its disintegration after his death would only make me sadder.

I only have two memories of my visit. One is how surprised I was to see a woman janitor clean the men's washroom even as we used it. The other is what makes this description of my travel rather scanty, as I recall after forty odd years. On the very last leg of my Eastern European tour, my traveling bag was stolen at a train station in Belgrade. My clothes in it were not the worry, but it was my Notebook, containing details of my travel, carefully recorded, and my camera, though inexpensive was invaluable for what it had captured.

In Belgrade, I had met two young Sinhala men on their way to Turkey, by train, and literally penniless. Keeping my bag in their care, I had gone to the small supermarket at the train station, to buy them some food for their long (overnight?) ride, and until they reached their destination. By the time I got back, I found the young men missing, as was my bag. Looking around, I saw the two of them at the far end of the station, and walking towards them, found no bag. Apparently, in my absence, a stranger had befriended them. Seeing them away from their hand luggage, he had cautioned them not to leave their personal belongings unattended, and to always have their passport in the personal possession. Confidence won, he had advised them to be at the other end of the station to be able to catch the best seats in the train for their long ride, and that he would look after my bag. And our naïve young friends had taken the bait. Now to think that compassion has its rewards! Reporting to a Policeman, his response was, "Oh, I'm sure the thief's around ...You'll find the bag."

Despite the experience, I got what I wanted from the tour - an overall, if only cursory, impression of life under Communism. It wasn't good, to say the least, particularly after living in two capitalist countries. Compared to an earlier historical stage, exploitation may be less, and society more orderly. There appeared to be more gender parity, and an egalitarianism. The arts and culture seemed to be flourishing, but, when it came to material life, scarcity seem to be the order of the day. And, as at that time in the US and Canada as well, heavy drinking, and heavy public smoking were plainly to be seen. Driving was chaotic, although none could beat Sri Lanka in that department, as I was to find out upon arriving there later. The heavy hand of officialdom came to manifest itself crossing a border by train from one country to another. Boarding the train on a cold night, e.g., officials in uniform ordered every single passenger to get off the train, taking all their bag and baggage with them! It was around midnight. And possibly with a light snow fall. However, every single one of my hosts were extremely helpful, as translators and interpreters of the culture, and kind to me. They would often go out of their way to show their country and introduce me to aspects of culture.

By the end of the tour I was confirmed in my hunch, one that I had had before ever leaving the soil of Sri Lanka - that life under Communism wasn't as rosy as the Marxist leaders and their hangers-on sought to portray, seeking to wrest power to create a Utopia of the Undying Revolution.

2.5 A Visit to Holy Sites in India with Dad

Leaving the Soviet Union by Aeroflot, I landed in New Delhi. I had sent a ticket to my father to join me there. Even though there was now no Buddhism in the land of its birth, India still remained the Buddhist 'holy land', and it was my father's wish to visit it at his advanced age of 73 (he was born in 1898). I myself had never been to India, our impression of it, growing up in Sri Lanka, not being very high. For us, it was a poor country, and home to the Tamil estate coolie labourers who sent their money back 'home', with no allegiance to Sri Lanka even after several generations. And then it was the land where Hindus and Muslims were at each other, quite in contrast to the integrated amicable living among the Buddhist, Hindu and Muslim peoples in Lanka. And symbolic of the animosity was, of course, the very killing of Gandhi.

Through the study of Sanskrit, I was somewhat familiar with Vedic religion, but that was in ancient times. Pali, the language of Buddhism in Sri Lanka, also had arrived from India, but now Buddhism was of a homegrown variety with no religious, or psychological, connection to India. I was also somewhat familiar with Kalidasa, India's answer to Shakespeare, preceding by a few centuries. We were familiar with Indian esthetics, through the critical studies on Sinhala literature by scholars such as Martin Wickramasinghe and Prof Saracchandra. Ajanta and Ellora were part of our cultural vocabulary, but only in association with the frescoes of Sigiriya, the rock capital of King Kassapa, identified to be in the same esthetic tradition. But none of us young people, nor anyone of the older generation, had seen the living India. That is, none but a handful of *sangha* members who had been to the holy places – Buddhgaya, Saranath, Savatthi and Kusinara. Unlike now, when direct flights take devotees from Mihintale to Budhgaya, and holy site tours are a booming business, rarely did anyone even dream of visiting the holy cities.

So it was a great event in father's life to be able to visit them. Unlike in the modern world of Skypes and webcams, he and I were also seeing each other after a full seven years. In true Sinhala Buddhist style, meeting him at the airport, I duly went down on my knees and paid obeisance to him, as I was to do as well when he visited Toronto some years later (1980).

Our first stop, taking the train (dusty as it was even in First Class), was Varanasi (anglicized Benarese) where the Buddha is recorded to have 'set the wheel in motion', an euphemism for his first public discourse, called the 'Turning of the Wheel', at the Deer Park in Isipatana. We were indeed happy to see that in the temple were monks from Sri Lanka who kindly gave us accommodation for the night. It was wonderful to be able to personally live history. As the story goes, after attaining Enlightenment, the Buddha looked for his two former teachers, Alara Kalama and Uddaka Ramaputra to share his discovery, only to find that they had passed away. It is then that he goes in search of the Group of Five in whose company he had practiced severe austerities in search of liberation prior to leaving them to go it alone. And it is at the Deer Park he encounters them. Although we saw no deer, the dear scene was carved into an edifice.

Budhgaya was next. This was both more holy and dramatic in our minds. As kids we had read the drama of a Prince Siddhartha sneaking out in the night, having taken a peek at wife Yasodhara and day old baby Rahula deep in sleep, summoning his attendant Channa and leaving on horseback, horse Kanthaka taking a leap across the wide waters of the Anoma River, Siddhartha cutting off his hair and departing, leaving the royal regalia, and the hair with a weeping Channa. It was later, during my academic studies, that I would learn, from one of the few biographical notes we have from the Buddha himself, in the *Tipitaka* 'Three Basket' containing his Teachings, that he had left the Palace, not in the stealth of darkness, but leaving behind a father King Suddhodana in tears, his nursing-mom mother, Mahapajapati Gotami, his mom Queen Mahamaya having died when he was 7 days old.

Six years following renunciation, after failing all other attempts, Samana Gotama 'Wanderer Gotama', the future Buddha, had arrived at River Neranjara, and sat under a Pipal Tree near it, attaining Enlightenment. The place called Gaya, it had come to be christened (okay, **Buddhianized** (new term)) Budhgaya, the tree also coming to be called the Bodhi Tree later. It was this historical tree, even as it stands today after 2500 years, that we were now approaching. It need not have taken much imagination in me to envision that my father would have been moved, the tree having a special significance for Sinhala Buddhists. It was a southern branch of this very tree that Arahant Sanghamitta, daughter of King Asoka, had taken to Sri Lanka some 2300 years ago, in establishing the Buddhadhamma in the island, along with her brother, Arahant Mahinda.

Coming closer, we see a Buddha figure sitting in a cross-legged meditative posture, with Buddhist scenes sculpted below. Around the tree is a golden gate, and standing outside of it, I would catch a falling leaf, yellow in colour, that I would take with me. There were a few devotees, almost all Indian, doing various prostrations at the different times at the tree, including Hindus who consider the place their own holy site, although for no historical reason, except on the stretched claim that the Buddha is nothing but an avatar, incarnation, of their god, Vishnu. Later Buddhist visitors would complain about Hindu devotees desecrating the place by climbing up a part of the structure around the tree to do a prayer dance.

Again, it was at the Sinhala temple at Budhgaya, one of only two or three at the time, that we spent the night, sleeping on the floor.

Spending the next night at the Train station, as First Class passengers, our next destination was Saheth Maheth, when we waited for the bus for almost a full 8 hours, just on the roadside, in boiling hot weather. Better known in Buddhist literature as Savatthi, this is where the Buddha would spend the last 26 years of his life, made memorable in the Discourses, many a discourse in the Tipitaka beginning with the line 'Thus have I heard when, at one time, the Blessed One was living in Savatthi, in the Jeta Grove of the Temple of Anathapindika'.

Dropped off about half a mile away, where there was no sign of habitation, and, with tall grass all around, we would push ourselves through, as dusk was beginning to set in. And it was with much relish that we were to now see an only building, small as it was, with a clearing around it. We were greeted by, again, a smiling Sinhala monk who welcomed us to the temple.

The next day, he would take us through the shrubbery, past a barbed wire fence. Standing beside the foundation of a building, my father started sobbing. This was the *budu kutiya*, as we would say in Sinhala – Buddha's own room, a 20 by 30, going from memory. This is where, after a day's outing – begging for food, meeting with his disciples, or householders or groups who seek him out, he would retire to. The night would be spent engaged in dialogue with the devas (invisible figures highly prominent in the literature), meditate, or sleep, in his preferred posture, as is often depicted in temples, of head resting on his bent right arm, with left arm resting along the body. It was also here that he would wake up in the early hours of the next morning, survey the world with his 'divine eye' (*dibba cakkhu*) to see in whose service he could be that day, go on his alms rounds, partake of it, walk out of and return. It must have been this total persona that my father might have been moved by.

Next to the budu kutiya was the ananda kutiya, the room occupied by his personal attendant Ananda, the 'Treasurer of Dhamma' and thus the speaker of the opening line in the Discourses.

A few hundred feet away, we now come to another historical place: the foundations only, again, of the Assembly Hall where the Buddha would give his sermons to his male and female disciples, also finding mention in the discourses, one of the standard ones being, "Before I came here, oh Bhikkhus, what talk was going on amongst you?", and then answered, the Buddha would use it as an occasion to deliver an appropriate Teaching.

Not too far away was the well at which the Buddha bathed, still with water, although at the deep bottom.

But looking around, it was clear the place was in a dilapidated condition. Returning to the temple, and sleeping on the floor, and covering with a blanket, I was surprised that I, having lived in the cold climes of Canada, was shivering in the cold of the night. And I don't know how my father spent the night, having lived in the hot climate of Sri Lanka all his life. Next morning, washing ourselves at a tap, with water drawn from a well, we used the outback as our toilet. I was to write about it upon arriving in Sri Lanka.

It was clear that Hindu India, or even the secular India under Javaharlal Nehru who speaks highly of the Buddha, had taken no interest in places of Buddhist worship. And it is thanks to the yeoman efforts of Anagarika Dharmapala that there existed even the few facilities that were available to the devotee. He had set up the Mahabodhi Society.

Our last stop was Kusinagar, or Kusinara in Buddhist literature, where Buddha passed away, between two trees, which made me make a mental note how at all critical stages of his life - Birth, Enlightenment and Parinibbana, he was with nature. His mother is said to have given birth to him, while holding a branch at a Park on way to her mother's home for delivery as was the custom, and one still in vogue in rural Sri Lanka in my time. His Enlightenment was under a tree, and his first Discourse at Deer Park. And the Final Demise, or Parinibbana, was between two trees.

It was a pity that we had to miss out on Lumbini, Buddha's birthplace, I had not realized that it was in Nepal, and needed a visa. It was also the time of a war between Pakistan and India, which is also what kept us from visiting Bengal, the home of Rabindranath Tagore, or Thakur as would be known in India, the Nobel Prize winning poet.

It was on this trip again that I would feel the grave loss of the camera. What a pity we would end up having no pictures of our visit.

2.6 A Return to Sri Lanka

Arriving at the Katunayaka Airport after 7 years, I found it, to the extent that I could remember, more modern, spacious and cleaner than when I left. [pix: me and dad] While, when leaving Sri Lanka, I had *walked* to the plane from the Terminal along the tarmac ground, now I came out of the plane through a tunnel directly to the building. And the airport had been named the Bandaranaike International Airport in memory of the late Socialist PM. As if my social consciousness had never left me those many years, I would write about 'Vandalism at Katunayaka' pleading that we look after the place.

My brother in law, the late Ariyaratna Bellana we called *Loku Ayya* 'older brother', was at the airport to pick us up, and take me to their family home in

Panadura. The ride was smooth, and the road was wide. And I was pleased to find that we were taking the 'Canada Highway', a road built with Canadian funds. With taxes paid for four years while in Canada, so what percentage was my contribution – ha ha ha… At least I was getting a return by way of a smooth ride!

Going past Colombo, the capital city, and Moratuwa, we came to an intersection showing the figure of a monk in a debating posture, with a finger pointing up from a bent hand. This was, I came to remember, Migettuwatte Gunananda, who had defeated a Christian Missionary in debate in the 1880's. Indeed it was reading about it that both Col. Henry Steele Olcott and Madame Helena Blavatsky, co-Founders of the American Theosophical Society had been attracted to Buddhism, self-converting themselves while still in the US, and becoming Buddhist formally upon arrival in SL later. Col. Olcott was to eventually play a critical role in helping Buddhism recover from the 500 year old colonial and Christian clutches.

Upon arriving at Swarna's ancestral home, I couldn't wait to carry our daughter Chutti in my arms. In expectation of our return to Lanka next year, she had been sent to Lanka ahead of us, with Swarna's younger brother, Maitri, was going home on vacation. If son Puta, in Ann Arbor, had, at one year old, wanted nothing to do with the man who had abandoned him at three weeks, it was now our daughter Chutti's turn, at one and a bit. Getting out of the car, as I reach out to her, she was to run away! She would hold on tight to her favourite uncle, Swarna's other younger brother, Karu, who was looking after her in the home front. But in later years in Toronto, Chutti would be my work partner until the wee hours of the morning on our home projects while Swarna and Puta would be fast asleep.

3. A LEAVE OF ABSENCE FROM CANADA

3.1 Adieu, Canada, the True North Strong N' Free!

While in Lanka it is true that I had resigned my job to take to writing, my life had taken a twist when I got the Scholarship. And now with two Master's Degrees, in two different subjects, Linguistics and Education, University teaching looked attractive. I hoped there was a contribution to be made with the knowledge I had gained. It would also, of course, allow me to do my writing.

So, having got in the door at the Vidyodaya University on a temporary basis, I had returned to Canada, in the confidence that we were going to be able to re-establish ourselves, now as a family, in the land of our birth. And, as had been planned, allowing the academic year to pass to allow our son to complete his Grade 2 as well, I returned to Canada the summer of next year. I was finally happy that I was now going to be walking the talk! Whenever we got together with Sri Lankan friends in Toronto, the talk of everyone would turn to 'going back home'. But while I knew of no one who would actually go beyond a wish, we were now finally packing up and going. Of course, unlike many others, who had indeed come in search of work, and the good life, we had come to Canada for pragmatic reasons - teacher training and French language, and with no thoughts of permanent residence.

We had now more than met our primary goal of coming to Canada – getting teacher training for Swarna. She had also earned a bonus in the form of an additional degree – B.Ed. I had myself earned an M.Ed.. Both had gained a wider perspective of the world, seen life in North America, earned valuable Canadian work experience, made wonderful new friends, both within the Sri Lankan community and the wider population, made some savings, and had the family as we would have ideally wanted – son and daughter to replace each of us, as our small contribution to the orderly march of the course of human evolution. No flooding, nor draining, of the gene pool. Is that why we had not rarely come to be called the million dollar family? We could now leave Canada with contentment.

During the year I was traveling and scouting around back home, Swarna had continued to teach at Humber College of Applied Arts and Technology. During the four years in Toronto, though we were living in a rented apartment, we had invested in rental property. Now, leaving Canada, I did not want to have a Rahula, i.e., a manacle, on our hands. In other words, we did not want to leave behind a financial incentive that could attract us back. So it was that we sold the investment property. But, merely as a precautionary measure, just in case a little cash would be needed for something or the other, we left $ 500.00 of our return from the proceeds in a bank account. We would use the proceeds of the sale primarily for travel and for the shopping spree in Singapore.

And so it was that we bid goodbye to Canada, never to return – or so we thought, one early September day of 1972, just when we came to be qualified for permanent residence and a Canadian passport. As we took our seats on the Japanese Airlines plane, I took a last look at the Canadian sky, taking in the scene. The Autumn sun was bright, as the ground staff were working around several planes – loading unloading, directing. And then I watched a plane take off, gliding upward smoothly, easing its way up and up and up, gathering enough momentum to reach the sky.

We were looking forward and up to a new phase of our life!

3.2 Kabuki and a Tea Ceremony in Japan

Having done the Eastern European tour, my curiosity about life under Marxism had been satiated. However, neither of us had had the chance to see a part of the world that was closer to us culturally if also religiously. Getting an opportunity to see them once back in Sri Lanka was highly unlikely, if not also expensive. So it was that we, our son with us, decided to visit Japan and China, taking the uncommon Pacific route back to Lanka than the more traditional, and cheaper, Atlantic one cutting through Europe.

If there was one thing we wanted to see in Japan, it was the *Kabuki* theatre. My involvement in Maname had planted enough interest in me. Indeed at one of the Maname stagings, Prof Saracchandra had, borrowing from Kabuki, a *hanamichi*, an extended stage, constructed, cutting through the auditorium to bring the actors closer to the audience. The Japanese string instrument *koto* had came to be used as well as part of the musical ensemble. I also remember watching a documentary on Kabuki (as well as *Noh*, mask dance) during my time as a student at Penn. But, of course, there was nothing like the real thing. So it was that we made it a point to go for a Kabuki show as one of the very first things arriving in Tokyo.

The show was as we had expected – all movement and dialogue stylized, but the music came from behind the curtain. Now I realized that having the orchestra and the chorus in full view on the stage in Maname was an innovation of the oh so creative mind of Prof. Saracchandra. And we were to note another difference. The success of Maname was that it attracted all ages. The young and the educated certainly flocked to the theatre wherever it went, big city or small city, and just as much as the older and the uneducated. By contrast, there was in the Kabuki audience practically no young bone. To our great sadness, there was every sign that Kabuki was a dying art in Japan. Years of Americanization following WWII had possibly had had the effect of turning the young people away from tradition. This, in fact, was a reality, as I would see later, faced by the (Japanese) Toronto Buddhist Church, trying to keep the young flock interested in Buddhism. This, of course, was not limited to, in the Canadian context, Japanese Buddhism. Every temple was faced with the same challenge.

But, if we left the theatre on a sad note, we had entered on a high note. Buying our tickets ahead of time, just to make sure we would get a seat, I had left my camera on the counter, jutting out practically on to the street. It was only some time later it even occurred to me that the camera was not with me. Rushing back with no hope of ever finding it, guess what, it was exactly in the place I had left, untouched! It was a remarkable sign of the honesty of the Japanese people, and the Buddhistness, 'abstaining from taking what is not given' being the second Training Principle of the Buddhist daily guideline.

Added to the honesty of the people was a gentleness we would witness at the Tea Ceremony we attended. It was our first exposure to Japanese Buddhism. The process of having a cup of tea was more than satisfying the palate. Taking over an hour or more, it was art embracing religion embracing art, bringing a serene joy. But, if only you had the patience!

It is more our respect than patience that had to be tapped into as we stood at the famous Kamakura Buddha figure, seated in cross-legged meditation posture, but several metres high. Unlike the Indic features we would see in Buddha statues in India and Sri Lanka, it was a Japanese Buddha we were seeing, reflecting the reality of Buddhism taking on the cultural trappings of the land it comes to be in.

Boiling eggs in small sulphur wells was what intrigued us climbing up some hill. There were such 'wells' – really bowl size openings on the ground from which we could see smoke rising. It was a ride in the Bullet train, however, that must have left us in a dizzy. Not that in fact we were dizzy at all, but the speed was not something we had ever experienced in the advanced North America.

By the third day, we found ourselves dashing towards the Golden Arches of the only McDonald's in the vicinity for a hamburger! How North Americanized we had come to be, we laughed at ourselves, as we thrust our teeth for a bite. A slice of bread costing as much as a dollar, to our surprise, eating Japanese food, on a small budget, wasn't something that worked out well. Luckily, our accommodation didn't cost us an arm and a leg. Swarna's brother, Chandraratana, had given us an introduction to the place he himself had stayed when he had spent some time there as an Izusu trainee some years earlier.

3.3 A Welcome from Red Guards in China

One Sunday, back earlier in Toronto, I was pleasantly surprised to receive a phone call from the Chinese Embassy. "Your visitor's VISA is ready for pick up", the speaker from Ottawa told me. It had been quite a while since we had applied for the Visa, and not hearing back, we thought that our application had ended up in the dustbin. At the peak of the Cultural Revolution, there was hardly a visitor to China. It was later that I would learn that Jan Wong, Canadian-born daughter of a Montreal millionaire, was one of those rare Canadian visitors, a tad after our time, making us probably the very first unofficial Canadians to see China, even though granted we were still only landed immigrants. Enthusiastic about discovering her roots, she had gone to be part of the Cultural Revolution, only to be disappointed. And so would later be critical of the country, book size, in *Red China Blues*.

Indeed it was our good fortune to meet the members of the very first US delegation to visit China, headed by John Kenneth Galbraith, Canadian and then advisor to US President John F. Kennedy. This is how he would record our meeting in *A China Passage* (p. 28).

> *The train from the border to Canton is fast, air-conditioned, with lace-curtained windows and a cosmopolitan passenger list which today included a Counsellor at the Canadian Embassy with his beautiful Japanese wife, three gentlemen of Indian extraction from the Mauritious on their way to Peking (also to arrange athletic affairs) and a Professor and his wife from Sri Lanka (nee Ceylon), formerly of Toronto, Ontario. They are not arranging anything, merely curious. All stopped for a chat.*

As he said, we were just curious. How had Marxism affected an Eastern society? What was the Cultural Revolution all about and how had it manifested itself? China had always been a friendly country to Sri Lanka. Indeed, it was with sadness, and not without a little anger, that we had watched the US withdraw export of rice to the country. The little I was big enough to know. It was China who had stepped in to help.

Then there was the Buddhist connection, when Chinese scholars had come to India and, becoming Buddhist, had taken the scriptures, *Tripitaka*, translating them to Chinese to begin an Agama Literature.

As a culture vulture prior to leaving for the US, I had also had personal contact with the Chinese Embassy at a cultural level. I would receive their latest literature, and attend their socials. As a member of the Arts Council, I had the pleasure of meeting the artistes on a Peking Opera tour, and receiving a mask from one of them.

I don't know to what extent any of these had gone into the favourable decision regarding our application, but what is more likely is that my academic work in Education as well as Swarna's would have worked in our favour as well. As part of my course work, just as I had been exposed to British and Danish models of education, I had also done some little study of Chinese education. *Each One, Teach One* had occurred to me as a marvelous education model. Faced with the challenge of educating a vast population, Chairman Mao had come up with this simple, but brilliant, idea. Providing a basic education for all primary school children was one policy that would constitute a sea of change in this vastly illiterate country under former regimes. The idea, then, was that each child would teach an adult, presumably parents, who would have had no opportunity in their generation. While this might have been a useful propaganda method as well to get the Communist message to the masses, it also had its literacy merits. It would be a cost-effective way of elevating the literacy level, if only a tad in a given generation. And so it was that I, as a member of a university Education faculty, had indicated our interest in getting an understanding of the Chinese education system.

The success story of Chairman's Mao's vision for the country was one we would see first hand just about everywhere we went, keeping in mind that the measurement may not be by some abstract, or statistical international standard, but by comparison to what it had been prior to the Revolution.

One of the first things we would be impressed by was gender equity. It was women Immigration Officers that had checked our documents at the Hong Kong border. Perhaps it was this memory, along with my memories and observations of women in other countries, including, Canada, that may have triggered my poem, *Livin' W'm'n* (*The Faces of Galle Face Green* (1985, pp. 10-11):

LIVIN' W'M'N

Walking
    the mile under the weight of the hoe
Splashing
    a smile at the customs desk
Keeping
    the records through the factory din –
        the woman
        in China.
Owning
    taxis signing cheques
Feeding
    hungry tanks at the gas bar
Hustling
    the mechanics on intercom
        the woman
        in Austria.
Womanning
    men's toilets glum glued to the face
Swiveling
    on a chair for visitor queries
Directing
    traffic at the central square –
        the woman
        in Yugoslavia.
Elfing
    the best silks in Spadina's backlanes
Cleaning
    the floors beating the night streets
Wrapping
    bologna at the Kensington market –
        the chinese
        black
        portuguese
        white
        woman of Toronto.
Nipping
    no bud before it grows
Allowing
    their men to sip scotch at home
Looking
    away as kids run amok
Inviting
    governments to turn a blind eye,
        women
          livin'
          the
          best
          they can.

Today we could have flown to Beijing directly from Tokyo, saving us a long train journey, but at the time, the only entry to China was Hong Kong. Traveling by train in its luxury compartment as Galbraith succinctly describes, I also noted a significant example of government frugality. Getting off at one of the stations, we had been ushered into a well-lit room, and then to an adjoining lunch room. Coming back to the earlier lounging room, I noted that the lights were off. They had been turned off as soon as we left. This practice is something I still remember, and the impact obvious on me, I follow it to this day in our own home, sometimes to the chagrin of other home stakeholders.

Reaching Quang Dung by train, it was by air to Beijing, when one of our first impressions was how well worth Mao's Long March and the associated suffering had been. Judging by the people we encountered on the street, what a difference between generations, we thought. While the elderly looked very much emaciated and undernourished, the next generation looked only a bit better. But the robust looking younger generation was simply.... well, robust looking and healthy. Just like the fruits we saw lined up along the streets.

One of our inevitable visits, of course, was to the Great Wall of China. If it was impressive in its width, it was majestic in its view of a long winding wall, wondering how in those ancient times such a mammoth undertaking was executed. But then, my memories ran back to the Pyramids, and the great big Thupas in ancient Sri Lanka, the biggest one, Ruwanwaelisaeya, of no smaller dimensions (see later).

Another was the Ming tombs where the road leading to it was lined up with figures of ancient royalty. A replica of the tomb, as I would also see at the Royal Ontario Museum in Toronto later, showed how royalty was buried with all their treasures, including horses. May be in the hope of a fast gallop to the wished-for heavenly territory? Then there were also the nobility receiving only a bit less royal treatment.

We also had the occasion to visit a farm.

It was also the year of 'ping-pong diplomacy' when the Asian tournament was held in a huge hall with probably about 20 or 40 ping pong tables, the competitors hammering away at and spinning out the opponent. Visiting a ping-pong factory, we were amazed to see how world class ping-pong balls were being manufactured in what looked like a ramshackle machine, tied in places with wire!

At our request, we had also been taken to the house of a one-time beggar of the Kuomintang period when it was reported that people dying on the road out of hunger was an oh so common event. But this house had electricity, a small plot of land where some vegetables grew, and a couple of pigs roaming around.

One day at the hotel, I woke up to a whirring sound outside our hotel - one of only a few, where we had had our first experience using chopsticks. As I looked out, it was the sound of thousands of cyclists going past us. A similar scene I would witness decades later more recently in Taiwan from my hotel room when hundreds of motorcyclists came in all shapes and varieties – some even carrying an entire family, with a smallest one crushed between mom or dad in front, and the older one holding on to mom/dad in the back seat. We were to find out that in Beijing the bicycle was as ubiquitous as the people.

But it was at the Tien Mien Square, with a portrait of Chairman Mao right in the Centre, that I had the scariest experience. As if we were royalty, Swarna and son were being chauffeured in one limousine, with lace-curtained windows as in the train compartment. I was chauffeured in another, equally luxurious. The separation, then, was our first anxiety. But as it turned out, there was nothing we could detect that told us that it had been anything more than an exercise in treating us visitors royally. But the real scare came next. Driving in the laneless Square, with barely a 4-wheeled vehicle other than the occasional truck carrying soldiers, our two cars nearly collided! It was as if the two drivers were beyond exhilaration at being chosen to drive one of the very few cars on the road. I capture the event in my poem, The Knight at the Square.

Speaking of Red Guards, our first personal encounter with them was a welcome with a huge "Our Friends from Ceylon" banner held by a large number of students in Red Guard uniform with its trade mark red tie, breaking into song as we were led in processional to the school. Although we were coming from Canada, it is the credentials I had as a member of the faculty at Vidyodaya University that had apparently made us 'friends from Ceylon'.

Visiting a school being our primary request, all arrangements had been made to take us to a typical school, each of them run by a joint triumvirate leadership – of a Principal, Army Cadre and Party Rep. Sitting for several hours at a desk as the educational system was explained to us, and with questions from us, we were to be served Green tea by the ever-smiling Red Guards while our son came to be a hit with the younger kids who were playing with him. I was to capture our experience later, in a series of four articles in the *Ceylon Daily News* under 'My China Diary', a friend quipping that I had forgotten my diary at Lake House, the publisher.

Again at our request, we were also taken to a farm, and a hospital. The vast farm stretched for what looked like miles, and the crop seemed lush and ready to be harvested. The hospital was a two large roomed building, more like a Walk-in clinic. But what was unique about it was that while in one room was Chinese medicine, in the other was Western medicine. The equipment looked rather basic, but obviously meeting the basic needs of the people. With all the qualified doctors abandoning the people with Mao's army walking in victoriously, a successful social experiment of the first years of Communist rule was to send 'bare foot doctors' to the hills and valleys with no more than a First Aid Kit and basic medicine. As I would read later, during my doctoral work, doing a comparative study of Chinese and Cuban medicine, this was the period when China was looking strictly within its own resources, living by a self-reliant principle. But 25 years later, they would catch up to the latest western medical research and technology.

Of course, a mandatory visit in Beijing was the Department Store where we bought some nice Chinese silk, bed linen and Chinaware. I still cherish, and preserve carefully, the Mao Tunic I bought, particularly at a time when in China itself, the western suit is replacing it. Would it bring me a fortune as an antique?

Earlier, to begin our visit, we had picked up our ticket, as directed, in Hong Kong, at a Chinese government outfit, and were told we would be informed of the cost of travel and accommodation later. My hunch was that we were being tested for our Communist sympathies, given that a first visit by probably the first non-official Sri Lankan visitors could well have been a good PR exercise. But at the end of our trip, indeed we were billed! I had possibly not measured up, in the eyes of the translator / handler, to an expected unending showering of laudatory adjectives about the system. Little would they know how much we appreciated the revolutionary changes that had taken place in the country. The sceptic in North America, including Chinese ex-pats, and the present generations in particular, in China or elsewhere, would only see Human Rights violations, and lament not enough Capitalism, but what they fail to consider is the context - conditions in pre-Revolutionary China. And we may be critical of the excesses of the Cultural Revolution, but it needs to be seen as a way of re-introducing a post-Revolution second generation to the dynamism of the Revolution.

So my overall impression of China, in the seventies, was that it was taking the difficult steps of transforming a populous society into a self-reliant, and prosperous one. Indeed what Swarna and I saw in this example of Asian Marxism was a smiling, and a happier, people, in contrast to the more morose-looking and unhappier people under European Marxism.

Covering much ground and hopping from place to place in the short duration of a week, our Chinese tour was a brief one, generating a caustic comment from Galbraith on the train. Told we were going to be in China only for a week, he quipped, "Oh, so you have been bitten by the North America bug of replacing thought with motion," or something to that effect. He would also to share another gem – it is perhaps somewhere in his writings, too, that while Capitalism has fine-tuned wealth-making, Communism talks of only wealth-distribution. What is needed is a system that allows for both. My knowledge of Buddhism was not sophisticated enough at the time, or it hadn't come to me to tell him that there indeed was such a system. In the Buddha's Teachings, having, and making wealth is called a 'happiness', providing guidelines in both making wealth – with industry and without harming. And enjoying the wealth justly earned, also sharing with others is also a happiness. In a 4-way distribution, a quarter is to be used for one's upkeep, 50% to be re-invested in the business, but also to save 25% for a rainy day. This is a point I would make later in my own writings.

3.4 A Shopping Spree in Singapore!

There was one more stop to be made before finally getting back to Sri Lanka – in Singapore, to buy some items that would help us retain a life style that our children in particular had gotten used to, and we all had found comforting. Seven years in North America was enough to 'spoil' us, it looked. These were the items that are basic in the West, though would be considered luxuries in Sri Lanka - fridge, laundry machine, dishwasher and kitchen gadgets in particular. But, it was well before leaving for overseas that I had seen the usefulness of a fridge in a country which had a temperature hovering around 80 degrees day in day out throughout the year. It was at the houses of my two uncles who had retired from Africa. It was thus that we made a stopover. A most memorable item I was to buy was no luxury item, but a small watch at a small shop. While the quoted price was US $ 90.00, it came to adorn my wrist for a shade of that, a mere $ 10.00, lasting me a good 10 years! But it was also the variety of foods available in an open bazaar that our Sinhala friend had taken us to, kind enough to not only take us around, but accommodate us as well. Visiting Singapore briefly recently (2006), what I saw was a much more modernized country, with no more cheap prices or open air eating places. Or did I miss them?

BOOK II
CANADA, HOME AWAY FROM HOME, 1973 ON

BOOK II, PART 1: EARLY YEARS

4 PROUD TO BE CANADIAN!
4.1 Settling Down in Canada

"Oh, you're here", said a surprised secretary when I showed up at the Language Studies Centre at the Ontario Institute for Studies in Education at University of Toronto upon returning to Canada. Upon return to Lanka, having left Canada 'never to return', it didn't take long for us to return to Canada as if 'never to return to Lanka'! Within the year in Lanka, we had come to see the writing on the wall - that we were being handed a 're-entry casualty' Award. So, writing to the Chair of the Curriculum Department, I had been offered a Doctoral Fellowship. But the paper work had not been finalized by the time I showed up.

But leaving my studies for later, let us see how we began to settle down in Canada, this time for good.

Taking the cheapest flight, on Aeroflot, we would break journey in Moscow, overnight. Traveling with us were Swarna's brother and two of his children, the only daughter and the second son, the mother still in Sri Lanka with the oldest and the two youngest sons. But little would we know that breaking journey in Moscow would be enough reason for us to be imprisoned in a windowless room when we landed at the La Guardia airport in New York! We were completely taken by surprise when we were rounded up by US security agents upon landing, and kept there literally for the entire duration of the hours until we were put back on the flight to Canada. Only later would it occur to me that perhaps our routing via Moscow was suspicious enough to make us a security threat! If that is not bad enough, we had also been in China, as the Passports would show, on our way back to Sri Lanka a year earlier. So it may have been this double dose of Communism that may have put the US on red alert.

After four years in Canada, we had, on the very day we had left for Sri Lanka a year earlier, qualified for Canadian citizenship. So now that we had made up our minds to settle down in Canada, one of the first things upon returning was to get our Citizenship immediately. Unlike now, when dual citizenship is available, we had to surrender the Sri Lankan passport upon becoming Canadian citizens. And it is with a great amount of happiness that I can say how much of an asset the Canadian Passport came to be during our extensive international travel in the subsequent years. It was always a pleasure to see the face of the relaxed passport control officer at the various international airports checking the documentation. The look of respectable welcome could hardly be missed.

And so, now in Canada, we were going to begin a new stage of our lives.

With Swarna's brother and family with us, and with no income of their own, our first home came to be a 4 storied house, at 300 Woodbine Avenue. The second and the third floors serving as bedrooms for the two families respectively, the first floor, with the kitchen, dining and sitting rooms, came to be the common area. And, the basement having a separate entrance had been rented out, giving us the only other income in those early months, to supplement my Scholarship money from the University of Toronto. But before long, Swarna would get temporary work at Humber College of Arts & Technology, teaching English as a Second Language, a position she had left when leaving Canada for Sri Lanka.

The Woodbine Beach and Ashbridges Bay, on the East end of the city, is today one of our favourite haunts during the hot humid summers. Often I take walks along the Boardwalk, by myself, or with my friend, Prof. Helmut Burkhardt, with Swarna joining me on occasion. At other times, she would be sitting on a bench, sometimes with Helmut's wife Renate, watching Beach Ball in the many courts. But thinking back, while all this excitement that we were to enjoy in our later years was just a walking distance from our home on Woodbine, the Beach was hardly part of our consciousness in those early years. It was perhaps for most others as well, I suspect, given that the present Boardwalk itself is relatively newly laid, as are the Beach Ball tournaments that are so much part of the peoplescape on the Beach.

Our next move was to Mississauga, living at 1550 Boxwood Way (1975-1980), in an enclave like area called Orchard Heights. The road leading to it ran off from the Dixie Plaza, the largest Plaza around in the GTA at the time, until Yorkdale Plaza appeared. Three houses from the end of the no exit street, the location neatly provided a *cul-de-sac* security for our children playing hockey on our driveway. Chutti, our daughter, always found it easy to round up the kids. Doing the paper route, with me behind, she was so well-known that we would be known to many a neighbour simply as 'Chutti's parents'.

Born in Canada, she came to be academically ahead at her Orchard Heights Public School, located in the same neighbourhood. But when a request was made that she be moved up a grade, because she was finding the work too easy, there was much reluctance on the part of the school. Social skills were more important than academic skills, we were told, and that height was an equal consideration. She was

Our first home at 1550 Boxwood Way, Mississauga

not short, but only as tall as her class peers. Kids the next level up were a tad taller. And it was only through persistent requests that she was finally promoted to a higher grade, skipping a level.

Still living on Boxwood Way, our son Puta was to face difficulties at the High School level, Gordon Graydon, he being one of a handful of non-white children, most students being of white working class families. Getting a grade in the range of B in French, we had gone to talk to the teacher on the Parents' Night. We wondered about the Grade when his term, and class, grades had been higher. It was in disbelief we heard the teacher say, "Oh, he is smart enough to know not to do better". Huh, this from an educator?! But, er, she knew that to be known as a nerd was to be the target of bullying. Perhaps she was sheltering our son from abuse. Getting into the School band, he would, over time, play a variety of musical instruments.

Swarna and Mom Marynona, in Toronto

Father Sauris Silva at Boxwood Way rehearsing for TV appearance, with me at the drum

It was at this time that Swarna's mother came to live with us. It was shortly after when my father would visit us (1978) accompanied by Swarna's *loku ayya*, older brother, and his wife, *Bernie akka*. Accompanying them was the father in-law of Swarna's younger brother, by now living in Canada with us.

As a gift, loku ayya also had brought a batik painting of the annual *Esala Perahera*, the parade that brought out the elephants and dancers associated with the Palace of the Tooth Relic (of the Buddha) (*Dalada Maendura*). The batik has continued to adorn our living room since then.

It was difficulty of access to transportation primarily that made us move to

3315 Havenwood, where we lived in the early eighties. Attending OISE, and later working downtown, I would take public transportation, while Swarna would take the car to work, taking 30 to 45 minutes each way, even at that time. Walking 15 to 20 minutes from Havenwood, I would catch the bus to the subway, avoiding a second ticket fare.

It was also at Havenwood that Swarna's mother passed away. It was around the same time that my father passed away, too, in Sri Lanka, me returning to the country ten or so years after heading back to Canada. A State-honoured artiste and educator, he was honoured at the funeral parlour with a visit from Mrs. Sirimavo Bandaranaike, the first woman Prime Minister in the world.

Puta continued to be at Gordon Graydon, while Chutti had graduated to Allan A Martin. Both active in sports, the mantelpiece of the fireplace today displays their trophies, in baseball and karate.

Our Havenwood home saw an important event in Chutti's personal life. It was her coming of age (*malvara* 'noble flowering'), an event celebrated as a 'Treasure House Celebration' (*kotahalu mangula*) in the Sinhala Buddhist culture, and described by Swarna in a published paper. Welcomed by family and friends into a new stage in life – womanhood, she would receive gifts – clothing, jewellery, and money, when she goes around to all that had gathered, paying her respects, and welcoming them.

Not satisfied with public education, especially for an academically smart girl who had just come of age, a decision had been made to send Chutti to a private school. Our choice was Branksome Hall on Mt. Pleasant, north of Bloor. Though again she was just about the only non-white student in this stiff upper lip British-oriented school, she would come to be elected Deputy Head Girl of her House, every student belonging to one, as was also my experience back in Sri Lanka as a student at Nalanda Vidyalaya in Colombo. Involved in extra-curricular activities – tennis, music and House activities, many were the days that she would have to stay behind. And so there was now a need for a second car, primarily to pick her up, Swarna's school being in another direction.

But still considering two cars going in different directions, taking so much time, consuming much fuel, we looked to move to the city, without having in mind any particular location. Our primary consideration was proximity to Branksome. Having sought the services of the Real Estate Agent through whom we had bought our home on Havenwood, we were directed to a colleague of his who, he said, knew the city better.

The first house the new agent took us to was just beside Branksome, but it was right by the fast moving Mt. Pleasant, and had no visual appeal. A second house didn't catch our eye either. But taken to 3 Ardmore Rd, off Spadina Road, north of St Clair, we entered through the main entrance, to the left of which was the spiral stairwell in a polished velvety sheen. Looking up, it was not difficult to see why it appeared so bright and inviting. A tall window, with arching pieces of glass, let in a lot of sun, shining from the east. Swarna didn't have to look further. "This is what I want." And so was signed the deal. We had been given

Our home of over three decades at 3 Ardmore Road in Forest Hill

an overview of the features of the home – four bedrooms, three washrooms, oil-heated, etc. But, not knowing the city, we had no idea that it was in Forest Hill, a highly coveted *nouveau riche* neighbourhood. And we had made this our home for three decades.

Knocking down the garage, we would build an addition ten years later, giving us not only our favourite sun-room, but also southern exposure. With the addition of a gazebo, this is where Swarna and I, in our retirement years, were to spend a lot of time, surrounded by tall-enough trees, enjoying the fountain in the little pond that we had put in. Above the sunroom was my study, with its own washroom.

4.2 Swarna, the Professional

Always the Golden One at home, it was in Canada, however, that the real lustre of Swarna came to shine in the public domain. An early occasion was when she was evaluated to be 'thinking on her feet', in the estimation of her supervisory Professor at the Faculty of Education, University of Toronto, during her training period, in the late sixties.

Upon graduation, she had been turned down by the pre-multicultural hiring mandarins of the Boards of Education that they had 'better' applicants, the reference being to her younger class colleagues, with no teaching experience, but white. But, it didn't take long for Swarna to find permanent employment just a year after we had returned.

With a solid teaching record at Humber, she came to be a High School Teacher at Vaughan Road Collegiate Institute in 1974. Proving her mettle, not long after, she came to be hired by Prinicipal Larry Rogers of Weston Collegiate Institute in 1989, as Head of English as a Second Language, becoming the only visible minority Department Head at the York Board. She would also become part of the School Counselling team, particularly when it came to immigrant students, among whom she came to earn a name as a tough cookie, though compassionate.

Plaque given to Swarna by Vaughan Road Collegiate Institute

By way of a specific academic contribution she would make while teaching at Vaughan Road Collegiate Institute in the Borough of York, was an article published in *TESL TALK* (vol. 7 No 4, Sept 1976), "Structuring Structure: A Rationale". It is introduced by Editor Lillian Butovsky in the following words:

> *One of the central issues of language teaching is the selection and ordering of language items. The questions "What shall I teach?" and "In what order shall I teach it?" cause more unease among language teachers than the question "How shall I teach it?"*
>
> *Language is so complex, so vast, and the learners' needs so varied that we can never be certain that what we serve up will be appropriate. In the following paper, Swarna Sugunasiri tackles the two thorny issues in an essay which not only provides a workable rationale, but also touches upon some of the most important trends in language teaching.*

Drawing upon her theoretical as well as the practical experience, she had, as Head, developed a comprehensive Program of Studies, covering Grades 9 to 11 also writing the curriculum for the several courses, such as ESL for Math, ... for Science, ... Business, etc.

Faculty at Weston Collegiate Institute (Swarna, front row, 7th from R.)

Her task had come to be a formidable one. Working under this Visible Minority was a staff of 15, mostly white men, coming from disciplines such as Math, Science, Business, History and Art. Conducting monthly meetings would have been challenging, to say the least. The teachers, of course, would have had their own agenda, but happily, Swarna knew she could always count on the Principal.

But it was upon her retirement that I came to know who really she had been as a professional. At home, she had always presented the "Oh pity pretty please, look after this frail creature" act. But as Head of ESL at Weston Collegiate Institute, many a male Head of Department, not to mention members of her own department, knew her as a no-nonsense Head, who would tolerate no mediocrity, or laziness, from her departmental colleagues. While her demand for maintaining standards might have earned the wrath of some and more than a few enemies, her Principal, who had the most confidence in her, was her best ally. And if only the other Heads knew that her Department had been allocated the highest level of funding for books, in both lean and fat years! Comments made at her retirement blew my mind away. And so I was to read the poem, 'My New Love', at her Retirement Party held at the home of a colleague in 1998.

(*Celestial Conversations,* 2006, p. 4)

Becoming a bionic woman in the hey days of her career was another of her achievements, thanks to an Open Heart double valve replacement in the early nineties. But it is in the recovery process that her real discipline came to shine through, when she studiously kept to an exercise regimen. Though netball had given her the physical workout at school, and recreational ping pong at the university, physical activity had taken a toll in her life after university, marriage and raising two children not being helpful. If the treadmill thus came to earn a permanent place at home, paving a welcoming, and gliding, mat for her tender feet day in day out, the school running track in front of our house was the real bonus. And how glad I was when it was to become a double bonus, when I, too, returned to a regular physical activity, nearly forty years after school cricket and cadetting. It all began with me taking to the track only to give Swarna company.

The arrival of grandchildren brings out another skill in her: crochet and knitting, when she makes blankets for the little ones, loved by the little ones as much as the parents. Just as she had taught herself to cook, and then to sew, she had now taught herself to crochet and knit.

4.3 Swarna, the Food Connoisseur

Retirement would bring out another dimension of her lustre. Over time, Swarna had come to be known for her fabulous cooking. It was not just the family who looked forward to be at a dinner table gotten ready by her, but her Book Club colleagues, too, each member taking turns to provide a meal for a meeting. Puta and daughter Chutti, literally 'little one', as we always called them relationally, had encouraged mom to keep a record of her recipes, just as a family memorabilia. And so, would it be a surprise to them to be invited for a home book launch of *Cooking from My Heart: Loving Spoonfuls from a Sri Lankan Family Kitchen* (Jan. 11, 2009)? The words in the back cover, "Pleasing to the palate, exciting to the eye, soothing and healing for

Swarna launching her book, Cooking From My Heart: Loving Spoonfuls from a Sri Lankan Kitchen

the body and mind......", capture the essence of the collection.

Within days of publication, the title would come to have over 8 pages of interested sellers on the Internet!

The irony, nay, the intelligence, of course, is that she didn't know how to cook even as a young woman, having avoided the kitchen like the plague! I would only quip that I was happy to have been the guinea pig. And, on the day of the launch, I would write a poem: *Obama-Ji*, 2006, p. 2.

As if to prove her ongoing growth, among the latest of her interests was to always beat me at scrabble! Of course, she would console my strained ego by saying that I was multitasking on my laptop.

Her knees going wobbly a bit, Tai Chi comes to be her latest endeavour. In a return to an interest in her university days, she would translate my book on the Sinhala Short Story, under the title *The Origin and Development of the Sinhala Short Story,* still waiting to see the light of day. But happily, the latest to occupy her interest is writing fiction, once again becoming an avid reader of works of literature. This is in addition to her knitting on occasion.

4.4 Swarna, the Autobiographer

Though educated in the Sinhala medium in her early schooling, it was also in English that she was able to show her writing skills. Her *Girl Among Boys: Growing Up in Ceylon: Childhood Memories of Growing up in Ceylon* would amply speak to it. Here then is the write-up on the back page:

> *Girl Among Boys is the life story of a girl among seven boys growing up in an urban Sinhala Buddhist family in then Ceylon in the 1940's to the 1950's. A fun-loving nature-loving kid with a taste for good food, she learns to ride a bike in the dark of the night, away from the eyes of the family.*
>
> *She is the tomboy who manages to be top in her class, switch to the English medium in her teenage years and enter university as the only student from her school, making history. A book full of relationships, she recalls her life with great candor, the occasional punch and a not so rare self-mocking. Writing with obvious enjoyment, and aplomb, in narrative after narrative, Swarna, in this promising debut, shows her versatility as a writer with great control in the use of language.*

4.5 Swarna, the Golden One
'Swarna' means 'gold'. Hence the title.

An Ode to a Golden One
(Read at the 65th Birthday bash on Aug. 16, 2002, at home.)

I GROWING
There once was a beautiful and fair maiden,
    Maiden she was in Resplendent Island, a plush garden.
Garden-keepers, one and all in family, saw in a girl no burden.
    Burden how could she be, maiden that she was singularly Golden?........

II ENCOUNTER
... "A garland of poverty, a ride on risky wheels, all I offer", says me.
"What tradition, what wealth, when all I want is you", says she.
So begins the long march, ...

III LIFE
Heeding the call, taking to the masses' lane, I pull
    the golden rug from under my employment castle
In one big crash, money tree felled,
    tying life's pieces in a very small parcel,........
The juggling she doeth, ***wife fortitude***, unbattered,
    like in roaring winds a resolute post or pillar!

Making life a park, where feet kiss, the meandering and rolling
    ground of hill and dale,
Where we watch leaves dance in the wind, etching life's colours
    on butterfly wings in right royal regale.
Talking shop, the humdrum of life, humanity's follies and wisdoms,
    laughing hearty and hale
Taking to wings, crisscrossing the world, cruising in the Caribbean,
    having a time of a whale.
Breaking bread, a ***wife-wife*** arm around to leaven,
    with her, need I tell ya, who needs heaven!

....Wounded in social combat, mindbody benumbed
    by a mindless world, I lie bleeding,
Enters ***mother-wife***, poultice of sane words, a warm
    shoulder, voila, it's the magic healing...

Listening to songs of a yester year,
    in the evenings of Summer Winter,
Sister-wife always by my side,
    adding a sprite, as from a soda canister.
Telling old tales, a joke or two,
    bringing down the roof on occasion
It's when she gets me on my dancing feet,
    it becomes too much provocation.

Winning profs accolades, "You teach on your feet",
    earning another Bachelor's, this time in Teaching, ...
Here, then, is that *wife professional*, a gem in Canada's
    Educational Crown
No small feat, thru teenage hormones 'twas,
    she first encountered the English verb and noun.

Giving up jobs, diving into depths of knowledge,
    me in universities here there and everywhere,
Who but *bread-winner wife* put food on the table,
    you think she had any time to spare?...

Now you show me the *retired-wife*, where? Those
    busy nimble fingers doing the crochet loop?
Or is it the busy eyes, surfing the net, in a late late
    lovefest, for an e-mail snoop?
But what, pray tell me, are these words on a screen-
    words translated from a husband's book?
Or are they fond memories, leaping off a past,
    finding new life, in her own new book?

Swarna Sugunasiri playing billiards at the hotel in Varadero, Cuba, 2009

Sure she's cooked, all forty years, but you're on to a
    great big surprise
The *chef-wife*, untired of learning, knows now a hundred
    ways of cooking rice.....
"Table it must be, like a princely damsel,
    luring the food-lover, to be healthy and wise!"

Approaching that age, which ends you know where,
    how wonderful it is, to have a *spiritual-wife,*
To dig deep into the depths of existence, knitting together
    a dhammaic life.
Insights gained, analysis garnered, leafing through books,
    Western, more Buddhist,
Feet well grounded, in cultural tradition,
    the pragmatist the Golden One, she no idealist.

Stop me, or else, I'll go on, till cows come home,
    and the sun tomorrow rises from the east
gardening wife, athletic wife, house-wife only three,
    all part of a bountiful bubbling yeast
Martha Stewart Winnie Oprah Master Chefs and all,
    under her guiding hand and well-orchestrated care
Sampras and Serena on Centre Court vie
    to have of the Golden touch their own little share.

..... What better sentient being can be imaginable
    under the incredulous Karma's bidding?

..... Oh, Golden One, this the man in awe,
    here's a beauteous bouquet of flowers
For the castle you built, of health, wealth and good cheer,
    strong roof letting in no lightning showers.

IV THE TOAST
Now here's from everyone, a toast for you Swarna the Golden One,
    for health and long life of a century plus one!...
..... Rah rah rah! Mmmm! Mmmm Mmmm!

5. IN SEARCH OF LEARNING

5.1 Humanistic Nationism: a PhD from OISE

> *"A New theory of Development"*
>   - Prof. Joseph Farrell, Thesis supervisor
> *"The energy, range of scholarship, depth of scholarship..."*
>   - Prof. Douglas Ray, External Examiner
> *"..an extraordinary thesis"*
>   - Prof. Roby Kidd, Internal Examiner.

Now to return to my own studies back in Canada, with a Master's Degree from the same institute already under my belt, I was required to do a lesser course load of a doctoral program. And then there were the encouraging words of Prof. Gerald Caplan whom I had encountered during my Master's Studies. "If I can do it, Suwanda, anyone can do it."

I have never failed to be surprised when a doctoral student says, "Oh, I'm still fishing for a thesis topic." In my understanding, a topic, or at least an area of interest, should have been formed if not fixed in your mind when applying to do doctoral studies. But that may be more my naïve understanding, for many a student I have met did not seem to have a clue.

In my case, there was no doubt about my area of study, nor the reason for exploring it. Sure enough we were leaving Sri Lanka for good, but my experience at Sarvodaya had endeared me to rural development. I seem to have always had the vague notion that what plagued the country in terms of development was a lack of concern of the rurality, all policy and decision making being city-centric and English-centric. So it was that I wanted to explore the issue at some theoretical level.

So I was delighted, upon registering at OISE with such thoughts, that there were indeed several areas of study that touched on national development. Language Planning was one of them, and the perspective was not one I was unfamiliar with, having done a course on Educational Planning for my Master's. My doctoral thesis topic – or at least what I thought it was going to be, emerged, automatically and effortlessly – "A Language Plan for Sri Lanka". The language issue had been very much a thorn in the flesh of the body politic since at least S W R D Bandaranaike's socialist victory of 1956 when Sinhala was, after 500 years, enshrined, dethroning English, and later the 'reasonable use of Tamil'.

The Discipline of Language Planning had emerged in the context of the Developing World. My case study thus immediately suggested a political dimension. This, in turn, suggested an economic one, for after all, as far as the average person was concerned, it was putting food on the table that was the concern. At OISE, I was to find Professors such as Gerry Caplan and David Livingstone, making precisely such a connection between politics and economics, from the point of view of a Marxist critique.

The picture emerging from the literature was not pretty. After a quarter century of western development theories (directly economic, but tangentially political), and millions of dollars pumped into the non-western economies, researchers were digging out alarming data that suggested that the receiving countries may be worse off than earlier. A telling indicator was that the Economic Gap, measured in terms of GDP, between the poorer and the rich nations, was getting to be wider. The same seemed to hold as between the city and the village.

But as I continued reading up on the literature, something else emerged as being critical in development - *ethics* and *values*. Thus, specially given my background, namely, Master's Degree in Moral Philosophy academically, and Buddhism culturally, I began to entertain the distinct possibility of what I would call a Values Gap.

So now I had come to identify four areas that came to impinge on development - language, politics, economics and ethics. But, while there was much research in each of the areas in themselves, there didn't seem to be any research, either on the *interphase* among them, or within a *broader framework*. Here, then, emerged the next framework of my research. The issues were far too complex to be dealt with in relation to a single country. It was not only that Sri Lanka was too narrow a case study, but that the ramifications of the interplay of these multifarious issues were global. It was thus clear to me that my focus had to be what I would come to label the *Post-Colonial Nations* (PCN's), replacing the euphemism, 'Developing Countries', a self-delusion of the west that every nation would eventually catch up to it.

Little would I realize how my magic box of creativity and academic insight had given birth to a genie. It was an Octopian task I had set myself up to!

Luckily, my academic advisor, Prof. Joe Farrell, himself a specialist on Latin America, seemed to have no qualms about may ability to handle it. I was also able to convince Professors Fred Rainsbury, a specialistist in communication, and James Draper, a South Asian specialist to come on Board to help make my thesis committee. Dr Raymond Mougeon, with whom I had had the pleasure of working on some Field Research and Linguistic issues in relation to a Francophone community in Welland, Ontario, agreed to provide the Linguistics supervision.

By the end of the process of research, and disciplining myself to write a certain number of pages per day, I had managed to produce a 500 page doctoral thesis under the title, *A Language- and Ideology-based Language Plan for Post-*

Colonial Nations. It had primarily drawn upon several disciplines: Development, Language Planning, Sociology Political Theory, Adult Education and Buddhism.

At the end of this gargantuan cut and paste job – the original of my thesis still bears evidence to it, Prof. Farrell had a word of consolation: "Suwanda, don't worry. Now there's a machine that'll do all that cut & paste for you. It's called a computer".

"Thanks a lot, Professor. It couldn't have come sooner!"

But I couldn't resist taking a look at this wonderful machine. The year was 1978. It was a jungle of cables and wires, hooked on to a sea of metal, that I saw occupying a whole room, 30 by 20 perhaps! Now to that 8" laptop Swarna dished out $ 700 plus recently at Staples!!

One member of my Thesis Committee had an objection – that it was written in the first person, a no-no in academic study. Happily it came to be overruled by other members.

By the time the final draft came to be ready, my Chair had gone on a research leave. But it would be only under his recommendation that a final oral examination could be set up. How delighted I was then when Prof. David Wilson, under whom I had taken my Ed Planning course earlier, very kindly offered to take my 500 page epistle to be hand-delivered to Prof. Farrell in Latin America. How I would show my gratitude, he would never know. For it came by way of a poem, 'The Unbeatable Beat', to be written on his passing away, three decades later. Doing a private reading to his family at his home in North York, it was to my surprised delight that Prof. Vandra Masemann, also of OISE present at the reading, would decide to include my poem in a posthumous publication in his honour, *A Tribute to David Wilson*, picking the line, 'Clamouring for a better world' as the sub-title of the publication. Of Jewish background, one of his daughters would tell me that somehow she had an attraction to Buddhism, although she didn't know why, or knew much about it.

In later years, he would also personally deliver my final draft of the doctoral thesis to my supervisor, still on his research sabbatical year. If this appears to be no big deal, let us only be reminded that it was not the electronic era of today when files can simply be transported electronically. So, mailing a big parcel, specially to a Latin American country, was at best a risk. Loss of it would have pushed back my graduation by months or perhaps years. So, upon Prof. Wilson's passing away in 2007, I would read the poem, "Unbeatable Beat":

It was only as I write this Memoir that I discover that the *Language Planning Newsletter* of the East-West Centre in Hawai'i had, in a 1978 issue, noted my thesis, providing an overview. Here it is, as excerpted:

Humanistic Nationism: A Language- And Ideology-Based Model Of National Development, With Particular Reference To Post-Colonial Nations -Suwanda H, J. Sugunasiri, *Department of Curriculum, Modern Language Centre, OISE, 252 Bloor Street W., Toronto M5S 1V6, Canada.*

This dissertation attempts to develop a model of national development which has man as the focus. Analyzing man from the Buddhist point of view, the study examines the role of language in the maximization of the humanness of the individual as well as of the collectivity.

Approaching the issue from the Language Planning perspective, three specific issues are addressed to: the choice of a 'language of development' as between the exogenous language and the endogenous languages of a post-colonial nation, the choice of a language of development from among the endogenous languages, and the choice of a variety of a language as between the basilect(s) and the acrolect(s). Given the colonial past and the neocolonial present, the issues are examined in relation to social class, and an ideology which recognizes these realities.

In order to transfer this theoretical framework into the praxic, or plan implementation domain, the thesis proposes criteria for language determination and norm determination, and ways and means of language 'cultivation' in a manner that would likely minimize the linguistic and ideological dissensions that characterize the countries of Africa, Asia, Latin America and the Caribbean, the Middle East and Oceania.

THE UNBEATABLE BEAT
<for Prof. David Wilson>

For 22 minutes
under the piercing glare
of the Emergency Room lights
you mocked
the Dragon
waiting
claws on the ready,
stopping your beat
giving your heart
a well-earned reprieve,
sucking in
the surround-energy
of a loving family.

A-plus
for valiant effort
though soon

in claw's grip
of the inevitable,
bloodying
your heart's resolve,
your beat zings
unallayed,
to varying rhythms
in distant Mozambique Botswana
tropical Sri Lanka
in neighbourly Latin America
in frigid Canada on the home-run,
your unbeatable beat
clamouring
through and through
for a better world.

(*Obama-Ji*, 2009, p. 81-83)

I thank my friend from my Philadelphia days, Dr Lionel Steiman of the University of Manitoba, "to have taken time out of his Christmas vacation to go through my thesis for editorial comment", thanking his wife "for letting it happen".

Prof. Joe Farrell cleared the way to go for the orals with the following words, sent by letter to the Examination Committee, from Santiago, Chile:

> *Mr. Sugunasiri has undertaken a truly massive job... He has summarized and organized in a lucid and novel fashion a vast array of "development" literature from the West.. and which I find both fresh and intellectually challenging – has blended these with a Buddhist world view... He then combines this mixture with a series of concepts from modern linguistics to produce a new theory and model of development....*

Beginning the next paragraph with the words, "The breadth of knowledge shown in this long work is quite extraordinary", he ends by saying, "I wish I encountered more dissertations that challenge me intellectually as much as this one has".

Inviting me to his office, "Read the last page," said Prof. Roby Kidd, the Canadian father of Adult Education, much sought after in Africa in particular, as he handed over my thesis with his comments. He was the internal appraiser, at OISE. It read, "recommended to be accepted". In a letter he wrote his comments separately, which said in part,

> *Judged by many different criteria, this is an extraordinary thesis... it reveals both wide reading and much reflection...*
> *It is infused with humanism....*

Happy as I was, there was one more hurdle to be cleared: the Orals.

"Congratulations, Dr Sugunasiri," said the Chair of the Examining Committee, as he came with an outstretched hand to the waiting area outside the Oral Examination room at the Graduate Studies on St George Street "You did a wonderful defence", he continued, also making eye contact with Swarna who had accompanied me. Invited inside, members of the Examining Committee all extended their congratulations. As it turned out, my Orals had been, in the words of Prof. Douglas Ray, the External Examiner, from the University of Western Ontario, "one of the best [defences] in the memory of any of the Members of the Examining Committee". He also wrote,

> *The energy, range of scholarship, depth of scholarship, organizational competence, facility of expression, and painstaking attention to details of the author is amply demonstrated. The length of the thesis (477 pages plus Bibliography) makes the list of substantial concerns surprisingly short.*

While all this was exhilarating, it was anti-climactic in a sense, since, as far as I was concerned, the climax was the completion of the thesis, which had been more than a year earlier. The rest of the time was for the Professors to go through it.

Prof. Fredrick Case, the internal appraiser from within the University, advised that I not publish parts of it in the format of academic papers in journals. That would take the thunder away from the book version, he argued. While it was indeed sound advice, it had the unintended outcome of my research never leaving the pages of the thesis, or the thesis shelf at OISE and the Microfiche Collection at the Robarts Library. Submitted to the University of Toronto Press for consideration for publication, I got the unusual, but not entirely unreasonable, response that they were unable to find a suitable reader with the needed vast interdisciplinary knowledge.

Yes, drawing upon several disciplines was what had allowed a 'new model' to emerge. But that itself turned out to put me in territorial hot waters. The Curriculum Department wasn't too excited about it; the thesis was on Sociology! My Chair, though not from the department, was indeed a Sociologist. But Sociology wasn't excited either, since I was a student of Curriculum, where most of my courses were, too. It was with reluctance that the Modern Language Centre, my real home, even purchased a copy of the thesis, which was the tradition. The Chair, Dr Stern, in fact, had not been happy that he was not sought out by me to be on my Thesis committee.

But stepping off the elevator on the tenth floor two decades later, and walking to the home of my student days, what catches my eye in bold letters? "Department of Interdisciplinary Studies." Thanks a lot, Professors. Who said that being ahead of your times makes you popular! But I was happy I was not Galileo, and condemned to death for seeing the world in a different light, and could live to see the dawn of light in the academic skies.

Lengthy, and challenging as the PhD process had been, Swarna was also to

earn her own degree. At the end of the five years, basically financed by her after the first two years of partial funding, and for time, energy and encouragement, I had the distinct pleasure of conferring upon her the *PHT degree* – Putting Hubby Through. The Certificate, duly signed by me, still hangs on the same wall as my PhD Certificate.

5.2 Life at OISE

The fact that my thesis was on Development somehow or other landed me on the President's Advisory Committee on International Development, as one of two international students. Under the leadership of the Director, Prof. Ken Preuter, another academic member was Prof. Donald Brundage. But the membership also ended up in a personal surgery! I mean on my name. While I had thus far been called by my personal name (Sugunasiri), which in the Sinhala (and generally in many an Asian tradition) tradition follows the surname, now I came to be called Suwanda, the first part of my two-part surname. Suwanda, with 3 syllables, would be certainly easier than the 5 syllable Sugunasiri to the western tongue. But interestingly, the surgery seems to do justice to Swarna's decision to take on my personal name as her married, and the family's, surname. I guess she wanted us to have an identity for ourselves. To shed some cultural light here, a wife taking husband's family name is a recent practice of the westernized class, both my mother and Swarna's mother retaining their maiden names after marriage. In any case, the change of name was not the only time my name had undergone metamorphosis. Indeed inspired by all the name changes, I would write a poem, "The Many Names of the One" (see later).

OISE had always attracted international students, many a graduate eventually ending up adorning positions of responsibility and leadership around the Two Thirds World. In my own time were C K Seshadri of India, Grace Wright of Jamaica, Sam Ituen of Nigeria and Prapart Buddhiprabha of Thailand among others. Both by way of developing friendships and keeping ourselves informed of research trends and development, we had developed a practice of getting together for a Lunch-hour Colloquium when we would present our research to an Open House. Gerry Richards of Canada and Craig Chaudron of the US were regular participants as well.

Over time, this led to forming an International Student Association, the leadership coming from me, with lots of enthusiasm on the part of a Researcher Joya Sen. But once established, I would decline the honour of being its President, giving preference to finishing my thesis, and Joya taking over.

Another privilege I had at OISE is being Editor of *GRADOISIE*, the student newspaper. My only other experience working on a journal had been in Sri Lanka when, at a time of a strike, I had been holed up at the Government Printing Press, trying to put out the publication, Sri Lanka (in Sinhala). But at OISE, I was not playing second-fiddle. And it was on the job that I learned how to do cut and paste, add headlines, and write editorials. It was a lot of fun, as I also enjoyed the office space of a Professor, sometimes to the envy of fellow students.

In my final years, I also had the pleasure of working on a Francophone study, with Dr Raymond Mougeon (see above), becoming also a co-author of the only French language article associated with my name. In the publication that resulted, he thanks me for improving on the model, adding *"Sa competence, tant en linguistique qu'en anglais, et son esprit critique nous furent precieux pour l'analyse des données"* (p.iii).

Another research position I held was as Project Coordinator of a Gerontology Project, under the direction of Dr. Suzanne Cook, now a renowned Gerontologist. One of the questions asked of me at the interview still remains in my mind. "What do you think of working under a woman?" If I was taken aback, it might not have shown, my getting the job being the evidence. What she didn't perhaps know was that I came from a country which had produced the first woman Prime Minister in the world, Mrs. Sirimavo Bandaranaike. Or that Sri Lankan women got their franchise in the 1930's. Nor might she have known the respectful position held by woman in Sinhala Buddhist society, the Buddha always referring to 'mother and father' and not the other way around.

It must have been to test my patience, and compassion, that three people who had something to do with my leaving Sri Lanka for Canada came to be at OISE during my doctoral student days. The first was A T Ariyaratna, of Sarvodaya. It was a pleasure to help him around during his research at OISE.

But I can't say I had the same forgiving, and mature, mind when I was invited by my department to serve as hosting partner to the Senior Ministry Official. He was coming as a student at Ontario Institute for Studies in Education at University of Toronto. The hurt was still raw perhaps, in my heart, and my Buddhist compassion not mature enough. But it must have been particularly ironic that he was now at the very same institute that helped me write the Educational Plan he had held in scant regard when given to him in his official capacity in the Ministry. Of course, my unwillingness to be host to him, I knew, would have no bearing on his success during his stay in the city.

The third was Prof. L. Hewage who had advised me that it would be a mistake trying to work on a PhD in Buddhist Studies in Sri Lanka. While I tried to locate some funds to facilitate his visit, I was sorry that it didn't materialize.

5.3 MA in the Scientific Study of Buddhism

While, as noted above, my doctorate had benefited from insights from Buddhism, and I had read widely on the subject, I had never done any formal study of Buddhism. Now here in Canada, I was being looked upon as an authority on Buddhism, and looked up to for Buddhist leadership and guidance. There were few if any who could talk on Buddhism authoritatively in the medium of English, and for that reason alone, I was also being sought after to teach courses and give seminars on Buddhism, as e.g., University of Toronto extension division, the Learning Annex, TV, etc. (see later, under Buddhist Leadership). And it was all this that suggested to me that it was about time I got some academic

Prof. Don Wiebe, Associate Director, Centre for the Study of Religion, U of Toronto

credibility, too, in the field of Buddhist studies. It was also an opportunity for me to return to the expectation I had had in Sri Lanka to do academic study on the subject.

But given that I already had one Ph D from University of Toronto, I was made to understand that it was not technically feasible to be allowed to do a second Ph D. Thus I had to settle for a Master's degree, in which I would seek a specialization in Buddhism and the Scientific Study of Religion. Happily, the French I had passed at the Master's level at the University of Pennsylvania, came to be accepted as my 'second language' requirement, thanks very much to the understanding of Prof. Don Wiebe, then Associate Director of Centre for the Study of Religion. It was a privilege indeed to have been able to resolve some of the more complex concepts of Buddhism under the tutorship of Prof. A K Warder, as the only student, in fact, studying Buddhist Metaphysics (*Abhidhamma*), reminding me of my High School days at Ananda College when I was the only student taking Sanskrit under Mr. Sumana Lal Kekulawala, later Vice Chancellor following his doctoral studies. Studying Nagarjuna and the Madhyamaka

With Prof. A K Warder, U of Toronto

philosophy, as one of only two or three students, under Prof. Leonard Priestley, was another unique opportunity. Prof. Wiebe himself was, of course, the authority on the Methodology in the Study of Religion. While it was a full class of 20 or more, the Professor was more than accessible, and ready to guide this rookie.

And so it was that I got my third Master's Degree in 1992.

Prof. Leonard Priestley

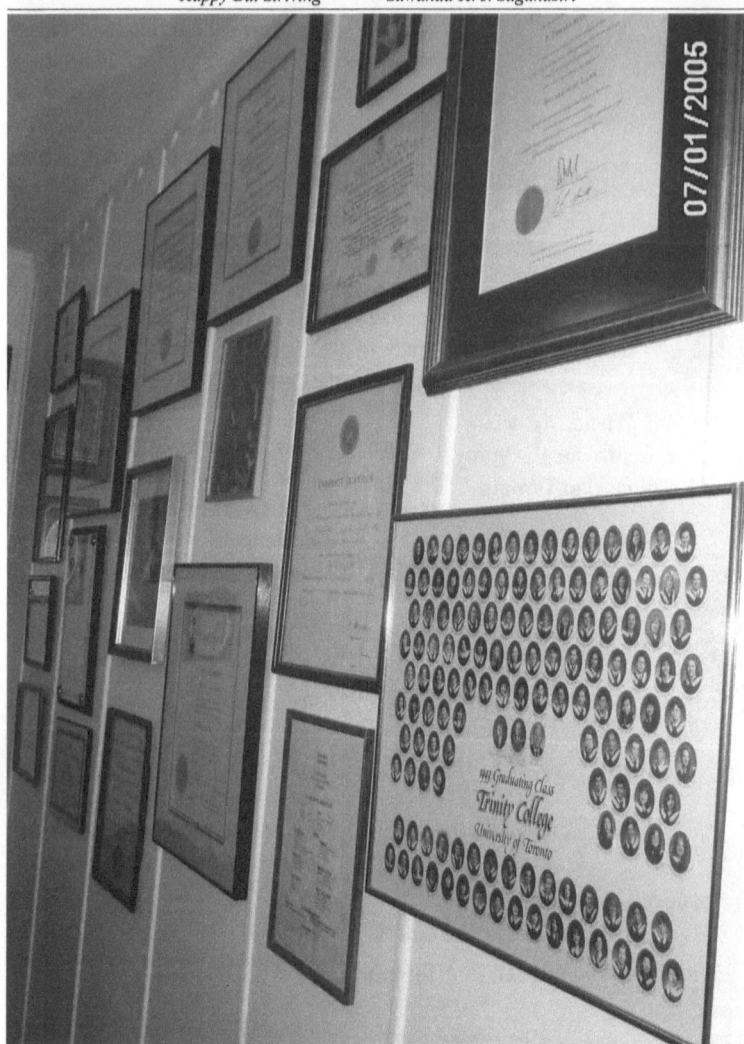

A Wall full of Degrees!

5.4 A Degree-loving Family

When I had the opportunity to garland Chutti at the University of Toronto convocation on June 15, 1993, it was to recognize her successful completion of BA at Trinity College, where I was by now a Research Associate. Now the family had another reason to be happy, and proud of. It was the 10th academic degree to be earned within the family! Except Swarna's BA from the University of Sri Lanka (at Peradeniya), and my own BA from the UK, and my Master's in Linguistics from the U of Pennsylvania, all the others had been earned in Canada. My two

Master's Degrees (Moral Philosophy in Education; Buddhism & the Scientific Study of Religion) and the Doctorate led the way, with another uncompleted Masters from Sri Lanka (in Sinhala Buddhist culture and civilization) in the wings. Swarna had earned her second degree in Toronto – Bachelor of Education. Puta would make his own contribution with a BA and MA from the University of Western Ontario, an LLB from Osgoode Hall, York University and an LLM from Dalhousie University in Halifax, Nova Scotia.

Not stopping at a Bachelor's, Chutti would go on to do her own Law Degree, as well as a Master's at the University of Windsor.

With that, the family will also have under its belt 1 PhD, 6 MA's and 7 Bachelor's degrees, accounting for a total of 40 years plus of life in the academy and research, allowing 5 years on the doctoral degree, two per each Master's and four years for each of the Bachelor's Degrees.

It is this crop of degrees, counting as well my Certificate in Teaching English as a Foreign Language from the University of Michigan, and the Teaching Certificates that each of Swarna and I had earned from University of Toronto, Canada that caught the imagination of Charles J Humber, Editor-in-Chief of the Heirloom publication, *Canada at the Millennium: a Transcultural Society* (2000). It was the latest in the Canada Heirloom Series, the earlier volumes being Vol I: *Canada: Sea to Sea*, Vol II: *Canada's Native Peoples*, Vol. III: *Allegiance: the Ontario Story*, the last with Introductory Messages from HRH Prince Andrew, Lieutenant-Governor Lincoln Alexander, Premier Bob Rae, and Social Activist Daniel Hill. I had also offered a photo of me shaking hands with the Hon. Joe Clark, the Minster of Constitutional Affairs under the Mulroney government, though not included.

As if not forgetting that one of the reasons for coming to Canada was for Puta to study French, he has come to study Canada's second language, enough to use it in professional settings, just as Chutti, too. It is true that I haven't gone far in the Old Persian, Gujerati and Swahili I had been exposed to in my studies in Linguistics at Penn, but I still had control of French learned to meet the second language requirement. But I am happy that my studies in Sanskrit, as the only student in the subject at Ananda College in Colombo, and Pali, both later to be subjects at the first degree level, have come to be of the most primary value in my Buddhist studies.

My parents, father in particular, would undoubtedly have been ecstatic, for the value placed by the four of us in learning and education. It was his foresight that had put me and my sisters in the only local English (Catholic) school, Christ Church College, and then sent us to Colombo, me at Ananda College and sisters Sunanda and Chitra at Ananda Balika Girls School, which was the best education at the time (and presumably continuing up to now). And if not for his primary grooming, I would not be even writing this.

With my parents Missinona Warnakulasuriya & S H Sauris Silva, and sisters Sunanda (older, at Right) and the next older Chitra, around 1956.

5.5 No Academic Love-in

Gerry, a colleague at OISE in the same Department I was in, looked forward to finishing his doctoral studies, to begin his academic career. So it was with surprise, and in dismay, that all he could find, earning the doctorate, was a job teaching in a High School! It is, of course, not that teaching was, by itself, a bad job, but that it did not call for five years of doctoral training and study.

Now my colleague was a 'true blue' Canadian – white, of European ancestry, and a native son of Alberta, with a PhD hot off the oven! He had all the credentials that Canada of the late seventies looked for. Yet an academic appointment didn't come his way. Was it perhaps the timing?

Exhilarated as I may have been by the laudatory comments of my examiners on my Doctoral thesis (as above), I had come to see the writing on the wall. Gerry's experience was not a good foreboding.

For one thing, the late nineteen seventies was a time of decline when it came to university hiring, with a greying Professoriate across Canada not retiring any time soon. At least not for another ten or more years. All that was offered to many a new PhD were sessional appointments. And I can't say I didn't benefit from it, teaching several courses in Sociology at OISE, invited by Professors David Livingstone and Margaret Eichler. I had also been invited to do things such as moderating Seminars, as e.g., , on "Heritage Language Education: Theoretical and Sociopolitical Perspectives", interestingly presented by the Departments of Socoiology of Education and Curriculum.

At the Faculty of Education, University of Toronto, I taught, for several years beginning in 1979, courses related to Multiculturalism, a brand new topic at the time. But when Prof Keith McLeod had initiated a full Certificate in Multiculturalism, I remember how on the day of the Open House and Registration, Dr. Inez Elliston and I who had been hired to teach along with Keith, waited in vain at the Faculty to welcome any applicants. The Multiculturalism Act had just been introduced in Parliament, but it had obviously not yet caught the imagination of professional educators.

But nothing seemed to materialize beyond these sessional appointments. I can think of many reasons that may have served as conditions for the resulting empty quest.

One may have been the very multidisciplinary nature of my thesis. While it, and my multidisciplinary academic background, did qualify me to teach in a variety of subject areas - Sociology, Linguistics, English as a Second Language Theory, Education, etc., this very breadth may have been seen to be an ill-fit. The well-respected criterion of scholarship in the West is specialization, which means depth – i.e., in my definition, knowing more and more of less and less, in a single area – discipline or sub-discipline. Even though the breadth achieved in my studies was not at the cost of depth, the hiring committees seemed to have not seen, or not wanted to look, at the potential in the budding scholar. What they were looking for may have been candidates who could teach an Introductory course in the Discipline, and related others in the Calendar, and this the day after – alright the semester after, hiring. Thus I could see that I, e.g., with no formal courses in Sociology, could hardly compete with an applicant who has had many Sociology courses under her belt. I had enough courses in Curriculum under my own belt, but my thesis wasn't in Curriculum! Can't win, can you now?!

But, of course, what the selection committees failed to, or did not apparently want to, see is the higher node connection. Both Curriculum and Sociology were departments of the same Graduate Faculty of Education, under the same Director and the same Board.

It also appears that I was being 'penalized' for being 10 or 15 years ahead of the Academy. Walking into OISE some years later, it was with some silent hilarity then that I would read the sign, *Interdisciplinary Studies,* housed under the same roof!

I was to read with interest a research article as well that talked about the difference between the US 'rebels', and the 'loyalist' Canadians (adjectives are from Yours Truly) when it came to academic hiring. American selection committees hired the best brain available and then developed courses around him /her, the scholarship itself being the magnet for increased enrolment. In Canada, by contrast, looking for the 'best fit' to existing courses was the preferred route.

I said that the selection committees hadn't 'noted'. But to 'note', one must look. So perhaps the problem was that nobody in the selection committee had taken the trouble to look in the first place.

To understand this, we may need to delve into a little multicultural history. The earliest immigrants to Canada were Europeans, responding to slogans like

'Only farmers need apply'. Italians came as labourers, the Chinese had come earlier to lay the train tracks and the Sikhs to work in the lumber industry in the West Coast. A common feature cut across them all. They spoke no English. They also had little or no formal education. By definition, not speaking English was to be dumb, and to have no brains! The resistance to official French until the eighties must serve as a hint.

But when the immigration door was set ajar a *yay* bit in the mid-nineteen fifties, allowing 250 'Indians' to immigrate, this including 50 from then Ceylon, Canada was to find that those who made it through the door could not be easily put under the dumb category. Lo and behold, practically all of them spoke English! And with a formal education, they could not be kept on the land either. Their professional choice was the white collar arena.

South Asians also came from the Commonwealth of which Canada was a member. And they were indeed 'Constitutional Equals' as well. In pragmatic terms, this meant that they could quote chapter and verse, from the very books – legal, political, economic or scientific, that the English-speaking Canadian had had exclusive privilege up to then. So it would then hardly be surprising that this new immigrant class – though not all or majority necessarily university educated, would not take things hands down. Thus emerged the 'Arrogant Brown' in the eyes of the establishment as well as the body politic.

But, for all their arrogance, these 'Hindoos' were a 'backward' people. So how could they be possibly tolerated among the civilized us?

If you thought that this was giving vent to some personal bias, you might want to read up on my study of Circular 14 Textbooks used in Ontario's High Schools (see 7.1 later). But continuing until then, it may be fair that you would say, 'oh, just an exception', 'an individual idiosyncrasy'. But what do we do with the research finding that Exec Search companies had strict instructions not to send any 'coloureds'? This was as late as the late eighties, a full ten or more years after my time. Blacks and South Asians made up the new Canadian group 'Visible Minority', a respectable replacement for 'Coloured' making its grand entry.

To add a slight variation on a theme, it didn't seem to matter, as it doesn't even today, that I was not Indian, or 'Hindoo' as the textbook authors had caricatured, but a Buddhist. Or indeed that all my degrees were earned in the West – UK, USA and Canada, and that the highest qualification, on the basis of which I was applying for university positions, itself was earned on Canadian soil. Apparently, it was enough that I was 'South Asian', 'Visible Minority', whatever, to be kept out, out, and out!

It was, then a case of, 'Apply apply no reply', to use that beautiful phrase of a Sri Lanka Canadian colleague, Edward de Silva! But no, there was indeed THE reply. Over time, I began to tire of the monotony of the response: "Your credentials are outstanding, but we do not have an opening that matches your qualifications." Translation: tunnel vision. It appeared as if the wordings concocted by some academic spin doctor had caught the imagination of the Canadian academy.

Regardless of the *"energy, range of scholarship, depth of scholarship..."*

in what was evaluated to be *"..an extraordinary thesis"* (as above), only two University selection committees seems to have been impressed enough to call me for an interview. Neither of them was in the area of my thesis specialization – National Development. Oh no, was that surely not the purview of White Canada! They had written the books, provided the models, coughed up the money. So no ignoramus coloured was going to get anywhere near that treasure! What indeed if I were to bring dangerous ideas like development from bottom up? The true and tried western method sold in the Two-Thirds World was development top down. Or bring the village – over 80% in any given country, into the decision-making process, seeking to bridge the Urban-Rural Gap, as well identified in research? Or incorporating a values system, in order to bridge the 'Values Gap' I had identified in my thesis? It would be several years before the Development Mafia – the World Bank, the IMF, and oh, in Canada, CIDA and IDRC, would begin to see the fault-lines of their approach, and actually go to consult people like Founder A T Ariyaratna of the Sarvodaya Shramadana Movement which had been in the development business since the 1950's.

What indeed if the *Buddhist world view* were to contaminate the dominant world view of the Development Mafia? After all, had I not adopted the Buddha's Four Noble Truths as my Research, and organizational, paradigm of the thesis? Underdevelopment was the *dukkha* (suffering), imposing the western model the *reason* for the suffering (2nd Truth), taking into consideration the local context the *solution* (3rd Truth) and a Language Planning in relation to a humanistic ideology the *Path* (4h Truth) to development. As already noted, my Internal Examiner Roby Kidd saw it as being "infused with humanism", another Buddhist thrust.

Approaching CIDA, a friend cautioned. If you don't have qualifications in Economics, you'll have a fat chance getting your toe in the door. It turned out to be prophetic.

So it was as if 'not looking' was what resulted in 'not seeing' the potential, the qualifications or the higher node.

Indeed the academy was to find another scaffold to stand on as well. By way of encouraging universities to hire younger scholars, the Government of Ontario had made available an 'Academic Renewal Fund'. In those early days of feminism, still primarily White, as Black women would point out, men could hardly compete. Especially when the decision was, as at OISE, e.g., determined by students, on the strength of a colloquium presented by the candidates. Would it be anomalous to allow the possibility that women students were no more enlightened, or less racist, than other segments of society? Feminism was on the rise. A presentation by me receiving no votes from the student body, I wrote to the Chair. Good luck!

Multiculturalism was yet to set in. In fact, the tunnel-visioned academy, with its head stuck in the muddy clouds of Eurocentricity, and oblivious to the winds of change around the corner, was among the last to listen to the call of Multiculturalism. "Forget that. We hire the best" was the mantra thrown at the Canadian legislation that prohibited hiring from overseas unless it can be shown that a suitable Canadian could not be found. But nobody pointed out that the academy didn't look to find.

It must have been the Year of the Pig, graduating in 1978! The Chinese Calendar read, "This is not your year if you are Male (with a capital M) and Brown, especially if too many of your neurons are firing together. You'll be pork before the phase is out when you'll still be casting pearls before swine." On the side-bar was indubitable Chinese wisdom: "Predicting, particularly the future, is dubious business!" But dubious it wasn't. The prediction held. In the Canadian pecking order of the time, the Brown Male was at the bottom. Being brainy, worse brilliant, i.e., 'too many of your neurons are firing together', could only make matters worse.

But luckily for Canada, and happily for me, the Calendar proved to be wrong, though over time. I am still not pork, and have lived to see the day not only pearls, but rubies and emeralds have come to adorn the necks of the Canadian academic necklace! Which goes to prove that timing is everything.

But, wait a minute. Was it my Karma perhaps – being born to a culture, specifically Buddhist, where knowledge was respected for its own sake? Or was it bad judgment on my part, or perhaps even a failure to be pragmatic.

In working towards my several degrees, I hadn't once asked myself, as I wouldn't today either, the pragmatic question as to what I would do with any them. I seem to have been smitten by the eastern bug of, can you imagine, learning for learning's sake! This is what indeed goes, in the Sinhala Buddhist, or in the entire Asian, tradition, into the making of the

Mr. D B Kuruppu, my Sinhala teacher at Ananda College, Colombo, Sri Lanka,

'Learned Man' – the Pundit: Learned in several disciplines, the Man of Wisdom emerging out of the interdisciplinary play. Indeed this – Pundit, is what my Sinhala teacher at Ananda College, Mr. D B Kuruppu, comes to call me later. So I must admit that I may have contributed to my own academic demise, by making the mistake of 'seeking wisdom' instead of mere knowledge and skills, and a piece of paper!

Now to that reason for not publishing my thesis – "Can't find a reader". Was there anything else behind it?

I don't know when in fact I began to sing the lines,

You can, from a hundred jobs, keep me away.
But from my interdisciplinary happiness? No darned way!

Professors undoubtedly deserve our respect as knowledge leaders. But I also understand them as human beings, sentient beings, with all the human foibles - *attachment, resentment* and *ignorance*, as the Buddha points out. To look for a specific tight fit in candidate selection may be seen as a discipline attachment, certainly needed for a successful career, but blinding when sitting in selection committees. Indeed had any of these selection committees been on my Fulbright Selection committee over four decades ago, I may never have hit the shores of North America. But, wait a minute…. there would have been a benefit to you. You may not have had to read this lengthy tome! Ha ha ha!

Resentment and anger, if also jealousy and a sense of threat, can be said to rise when faced with having to deal with intelligence of the outsider, the Brainy Brownie being the case study here. We only have to think of how Gandhi came to be only a 'naked fakir' to the colonial British. Canada was not Britain, or was it? And as for me, feeding the selection committee resentment could have been the misfortune of having five degrees which none on the Selection committee may have had. That this is a human phenomenon I know, because I had faced the same situation back in Sri Lanka when my two Master's degrees were said to be, as speculated by others, a bit too hot for those in charge who had less.

As for ignorance – and a touch of arrogance perhaps as well, here is one specific experience I had. Looking for a position, I had gone to seek advice from a newly appointed Department Head at OISE. I had had some acquaintance with him during my studies and work in the Director's Committee on International Studies. But he didn't know about my academic side. As if to impress him, I began talking about my thesis, and how highly it had been praised. But his offhanded comment was, "Oh, the theses of all our students are excellent!" He didn't want to hear that it was, in fact, the father of Adult Education, Roby Kidd, who had called it an "extraordinary thesis".

So it may be said that my Buddhist understanding may have best helped me to deal with any resentment that may have begun to swell up in me, remembering the *Dhammapada* lines (verses 3-4) as well:

He scolded me, beat me up, defeated me, robbed me.
In those who harbour such thoughts, hatred is not appeased.

In concluding this section, it must be emphasized that nothing of what has been said above should be taken to mean facing personal racism. I have only had but the best of relationships with all my Professors and the institutions. All the discussion points to is the presence of *systemic racism*, where the players may even be quite unconscious that they were harbouring racist attitudes. It is the environment, and the system, that makes them marionettes, dancing to the tune. As can be seen from the chart below, Browns were still the outgroup at the time in question:

And I was merely a possibly unintended victim. My only regret is that Canada was continuing to be underutilizing its human resources, as Sri Lanka, too, had done upon our return.

1 YEAR	2 PROTES-TANT ENGLISH	3 IRISH CATHOLIC	4 FRANCO-PHONE	5 E/W EURO-PEAN	6 JEWISH	7 VISIBLE MINORITY
1864	*in*	*out*	*out*	*out*	*out*	*out*
1899	*in*	*out/in*	*out/in*	*out*	*out*	*out*
1945	*in*	*in*	*in*	*out/in*	*out*	*out*
1967	*in*	*in*	*in*	*in*	*out/ in*	*out*
1999	*in*	*in*	*in*	*in*	*in*	*out / in*

Who is 'in' and who is 'out' in Canada, 1864 to 1999
(Suwanda Sugunasiri, *Towards Multicultural Growth, A look at Canada from Classical Racism to Neomulticulturalism*, 2001, p. 6)

5.6 Enjoying a Lemonade!

A Colombian friend in Canada shared with me his philosophy of life: "If all you have been handed is a lemon, make lemonade"! It was clear that Canada had handed me a lemon. An opportunity stolen. So making lemonade is exactly what I found myself doing soon.

Swarna had already made a success as a High School teacher. Conditions were not that bad. Good salary, good benefits, two months vacation. It was thanks to her encouragement, and practical wisdom, then, that I had enrolled in a Teacher Certification Program at the University of Toronto, not allowing even the smell of lemon to overwhelm me. As noted, a native son colleague at OISE had taken to teaching High School for the same reason. So having seen the writing on the wall, I took the plunge.

Having an MA in Linguistics from Philadelphia, and a Certificate in TESOL from the University of Michigan, the subject area had been cut out for me: English as a Second Language. The second subject area was 'Man in Society' – sorry, ladies, that's what it was called. Only skill in classroom teaching had to be established. As part of the Practicum, I was to teach a High School class. Evaluating my performance, the Professor was surprised that I had never taught at that level. It was possibly the genes of my father, I thought, a Teacher ending up as Principal.

My first appointment was to Danforth Technical School, interview conducted by the Head of English, Mr. John Terpstra, who I would come to to know later to be a poet, too. In addition to teaching English as a Second Language, I was deemed qualified enough to teach English as well. While teaching English in particular to a less than enthusiastic working-class student body, trade workshops being their pet subject, wasn't the easiest, the years went by comfortably enough.

But there was to be more joy teaching English as a Second Language to newcomers – from countries as varied as Burma, China, Guyana, Greece, Hong Kong, India, Vietnam and Yugoslavia. While they had all come with no English at all, it is a credit to their eagerness and language learning skill that some of them managed to come to a level of competence sufficient to participate in a school-wide Language Across the Curriculum essay competition. It all started as an exercise in essay writing. "The suggestion to seriously consider entering the competition was received by cynical laughter and disbelief... that they stood even an outside chance of winning", I write in the Preface to the subsequent publication, *Life in Canada*. But, "to everyone's surprise, one of the five entries submitted .. was selected a co-winner"! And this was an essay by William Aw of Burma, a Gr. 11 student.

One of the highlights of my years at Danforth was organizing the multicultural Open House. VP Aldo Morson thanked me for doing a fine job.

My time at Jones Avenue Adult Education Centre was equally enjoyable. For me personally, that is. Though an adult Learning Centre, it was bustling with activity with the participation of both teachers and students. At Christmas time, I helped another teacher to get the multicultural adult students, of mixed religious backgrounds, sing Christmas Carols, and occasionally participate in the annual Christmas concert. In charge of Badminton for the students, it was always a pleasure to get beaten at a friendly, after school game with the Principal, Randy Saylor. I was also happy to provide informal academic guidance to a fellow teacher working towards a PhD at OISE. At one of the Teacher Development days, I was honoured to be invited to give a keynote on Multiculturalism for the benefit of our own staff. When everybody became cross with me, however, was when I refused to join the picket lines, teachers going on strike for better wages. By way of showing my personal friendship, I had offered $ 50.00 so the picketers walking in the cold winter weather could get some donut and coffee. But it was returned with a thanks, but no thanks.

Lemonade, I was making alright, teaching in High school, and it was tasting good, the several degrees placing me at the top of the wage category, probably earning more than what I would have earned as a beginning Assistant Professor. Teaching 9 to 3, I had more free time as well, not to mention the two months of vacation. It was this opportunity, then, that allowed me to get involved in several other areas of interest – literature, Buddhism, Multiculturalism, journalism, etc.

BOOK II, PART 2

WATCH OUT!
SOCIAL ANIMAL ON THE PROWL

6. WITH THE CANADIAN SRI LANKAN COMMUNITY

6.1 On Stage

6.1.1 Celebrating Sinhala and Tamil New Year

During my entire time in North America, since coming overseas on the Fulbright scholarship in 1964, my engagement with learning, and earning degrees, compounded by the responsibilities of raising a family, had not allowed a place for society in my mind. But now, with more free time on hand, the call was loud and clear. And so in the next three decades, I would find myself in the comfortable role of a social animal on the prowl! And it begins with an involvement with the Canadian Sri Lankan Community. After five years in the academy, right into society I seem to have jumped!

The occasion was the New Year celebration, held at the Yorkwood Gate Community Centre in North York. The event falling on April 13th and 14th every year, and celebrated by both the Sinhala (75%) and the Tamil (then 12%, counting only the nativized population) communities, I make a pitch for unity inviting the event be called *not* 'Sinhala and Tamil New Year' ((secular) *alut auwrudda* in Sinhala and (religious) *pudu varadam* in Tamil), but a *National New Year*, with a plea for Muslims and Eurasians – the other two minority communities in Sri Lanka, too, to join in, all four communities making up the Canada Sri Lanka Association.

For the next few years, I would take joint leadership for the New Year celebration, along with Aloy Perera, a former journalist. The event provided the occasion to initiate the younger generation into the home culture as they came to perform on stage, mostly under the direction of, Hema Perera, a trained dancer and drummer.

A showcasing of the Sri Lanka Tamil community of the time was the a*rangetram,* the initiation to the dance world, of two young Tamil girls, the Lawrence sisters (both unfortunately victims of the Air India crash), following much training in Bharata Natyam in South India. I remember how, flying back to Toronto from out of town one day, I went to the theatre directly as I had promised the parents, and the talented sweet girls.

6.1.2 Directing the Sinhala Play Nari Bena

A more artistically demanding activity earlier was as Director of the popular Sinhala operatic play, *Nari Baena* 'Jackal son in law' produced in 1981, a creation of my colleague Dayananda Gunawardhana. In his letter authorizing the staging of it, he wrote that the play was "in good hands". He should know. Yours Truly was among the Founding group of *Aadhunika Natya sangamaya* 'Amateur Theatre Association', initiated by him at his high school.

The play produced in the eighties, the Canadian cast could be seen as a microcosm of the Sri Lanka community of the time. Deepthi Rajapaksa, a medical practitioner, and a Sinhala Christian, in the role of mother; Indrani Bellana, a recently arrived housewife, and Sinhala Buddhist, as the charming daughter; Nihal Silva, a Sinhala Christian, and leader of a rock group in Sri Lanka, in the main role of jackal; Hindu Tamil Karunesh, obviously fluent in Sinhala, as father, and Yours Truly as matchmaker. The narrator was Sunil Gunatunga, a Sinhala Buddhist, and helping on the stage were Nimal Perera, a Sinhala Christian, and Steven Selvadurai, a Tamil Christian, and uncle of Shyam Selvadurai who was yet to make Canada home. Shown to full houses both in Toronto and Ottawa, it also came to be adjudged one of the ten best non-English plays of the Province for 1980.

6.1.3 Dancing at the Toronto Harbourfront

Dancing at the Harbourfront, 1990's

At a cultural event at the Harbourfront under the leadership of Nimal Perera, in the early 1990's, I would partner the danseuse Hema Perera in presenting a variety of dance forms, both Low Country and Up Country. Included in the program were dancers by a group of young girls, among them our daughter Chutti, doing the winnowing dance (*kulu naetuma*).

6.2 Founding the Cultural Circle *Samskruti*

To keep the community in the cultural track off stage, I had also taken the initiative to form *Samskruti* 'Culture', under the sponsorship of which interested individuals would meet with some irregularly, to enjoy an evening of culture when we also shared food on a potluck basis. Indeed, the play was presented through its auspices, but over time, the light flickered out as interest waned.

But, a 'Proposed Program of Activities, 1980-1', written in my own handwriting, shows the following:

February	Sinhala theatre songs (Nadagam, Teetar, Contemporary) Folk songs (Tovil, Vannam, Carter songs, Boat songs).
March	Discussion on 'Cultural Unity' (a topic I had written up on in the New Year Program Publication).
April	Nari Baenaa (popular Sinhala play by my friend Dayananda Gunawardhena, and directed by me in Toronto).
May	Buddhist Devotional songs (the triple event of the Buddha's Birth, Enlightenment and Parinibbana, associated with May).
June	"Our children present..."
September	Muslim Devotional songs.
October	Informal discussion: 'Interfaith Dialogue'.
November	Tamil Devotional songs.
December	Sinhala film.

'Proposed Program of Activities, 1980-1', for *Samskruti*

6.3 Sri Lankans on TV

During the visit to Canada of my father the classical dancer, I would negotiate with Shan Chandrasekharan of the newly formed Multilingual TV, under the leadership of Dan Ianuzzi, to appear on the Program, *Sounds of the East*. Presenting the item on Sept 24, 1978, it was my privilege to provide the drum accompaniment for my father. Now this was an experience in itself! I had never learned to play the drum! But my father might have noted a certain knack in me, playing it at our Mississauga Boxwood Way home in preparation for the event. With 'eyes' of the drum, called the "low Country Drum' or 'Tovil Drum', facing away from each other, it was played with both hands, the camera focused on one of them. This is when the memorable moment came - during the performance, under the glare of light, the skin of the drum I was beating on, facing the camera, was to go bust! The director must have quickly directed the camera eye on to a different focus.

But my first serious foray into TV in Canada was when I successfully proposed (date in my notes: 80/1/23) to have a monthly program – in Sinhala, Tamil and English, on Rogers Cable 10. It was to be called "Sri Lanka: Resplendent, Multicultural & Different". My notes show that at that time there were about 3000 Sri Lankans, majority being the Sinhalas, reflective of the reality in Sri Lanka – over 75 %. It was to be a half-hour show.

The first program going on air on March 3, 1980, I begin with the welcoming word *Ayubowan* 'May you have long life', in typical Sinhala fashion. The first item on the show were a couple of women, led by Indrani Bellana, drumming on a wide circular drum called *rabaana*, sitting on 3 legs. This was followed by a Veena recital, an Indian instrument played by a Tamil woman, Rathi Surendra. Coming in next as host, I introduce the artistes and the discussants to follow. I then give an overview of Sri Lanka, the little known country at the tip of India but with a written record of two and half millennia. I explain how the Sinhalas and Tamils, Buddhists, Hindus, Christians and Muslims have lived in peace over millennia. The viewer is next introduced to "our multicultural community" - Hindu Tamil Rathi, Sinhala Christian Aloy Perera, and Swarna representing Sinhala Buddhists. I ask her to explain the special variation of the sari she is wearing – as my mother did, too, called the *osariya*.

Following a break, we open with a Sinhala song, from a traditional play, sung by Indrani – lament of a woman given in marriage to an ugly man! Then it is on to Tamil Karnata music, by Rathi, followed by Christian songs, sung by the male duo Aloy and Nimal Perera. Each item would also serve to introduce the different religiocultural backgrounds of the people of the land. Closing the program was a fast beat *baila* song, *purtugeesi kaarayaa*, inherited from the Portuguese. Highly popular, everyone – Sinhala, Tamil, Buddhist, Hindu, Christian all join in.

While another program, on April 29, 1980, follows the same multicultural format, it introduces an addition – a discussion, with three participants, and Yours Truly as host. Topic: 'Our Sri Lanka multicultural community in Canada', with Aloy Perera, Secretary of the Canada Sri Lanka Association, taking a stab at it first. He explains that most are English-educated, both professionals and blue collar workers. I also ask him to explain the National Dress he was attired in – a long sleeve top with an opening with only three buttons at the top over a wrap around lower garment *waittiya*.

Among others featured would be Muslims such as Hassan Sheriff and Christian Minister, Fr. Joseph. And the Tamil Lawrence Girls, the Bharata Natyam virtuosos. Then there were the lawyers such as Gamini Wanigasekara and Alavi Mohideen. My notes show our son, then a student of violin in the Japanese Suzuki method, presenting a violin solo, and Chutti, studying the piano at the Royal Conservatory, presenting a harmonium solo. But there were to be other children as well.

The program also would include visual images of the country's history, including stone inscriptions dating back 2000 years, and the Buddhist culture and civilization that rendered the island 'resplendent'. Another item introduced would be poetry reading, from the classics, particularly from the Medieval Golden Era, 12 to 15th c., following the Hindu invasion and before the first European – Portuguese, invasion.

In another one or more program, we would also feature Buddhist monks, one of them being Bhante Punnaji, then of the Toronto Mahavihara, but now in Malaysia. The well-known Ajhan Viradhammo, a white Canadian from Ottawa, was new in the robes, and was happy to participate.

How many more times we went on air I have no record of, but what is interesting is that while none of us had had TV experience, the programs were done live! Oops! Wish us luck!!!

Contacting the newly established TV Station, *Rupavahini*, in Sri Lanka, I had talked about a possible Canadian telecast. The goal of the program, as outlined in my letter, was "to introduce [a] Sri Lanka Canadians, and [b] Canada", sharing equal time. It was to be "educational and informative…". Further, "the Program aims to cover the whole of Canada", and was "to be aimed at the whole family". Most dimensions of the Program were to be telecast "in all three [official] languages" – Sinhala, Tamil and English. Intended to be entertaining, the first topic would include interviews, skits, cultural items by children, Sri Lanka events (like Wesak) in Canada, Sri Lankan visitors to Canada, etc.

As for introducing Canada, the following is what I show: Education in Canada, Geography, History, Make-up of Canadian society, Religion, Legal system, Media, Culture Canada: literature, theatre, music, film, recreation, folk culture, and Canadian visitors to Sri Lanka.

Receiving no acknowledgement, or response, I write a reminder. But it appears that the Proposal had not come to be pursued.

6.4 No Sinhala at the Sinhala Buddhist Wesak

It was not long after my PhD when a group of Sinhala Buddhist leaders came to see me at our home at 1550 Boxwood Way in Mississauga. Among them was, interestingly, a Muslim, Hassan Sheriff. There had been a crisis in leadership at the Toronto Mahavihara, and so, could I please help? Agreeing reluctantly, I would end up as a co-VP, the President being the incumbent chief monk, *ex officio*.

Still at OISE following graduation, working as Gerontology Project Director, I arrange to have the annual Wesak, the triple celebration of the Buddha's Birth, Enlightenment and the Final Demise (*parinibbana*), at OISE, in 1979. Historically

Bhante Gunaratana giving a Dhamma talk to participants at Wesak at OISE

held at the Temple premises, this was the first time the event was celebrated outside of the Mahavihara. The Chief Guest was Bhante Gunaratana, then of the Washington Buddhist Vihara, and later Founder of the Vipassana Bhavana Centre in West Virginia, and author of several popular books on Meditation, including *Mindfulness in Plain English*. Invited also was Prof. Bruce Mathews, a Christian

Addressing the participants at Wesak held at OISE

who had studied Buddhism in Sri Lanka.

While having these guests was well received by the community, a surprise awaited me. Identifying the different areas of the room, where Wesak was going to be celebrated, I had arranged to put up labels, all in Sinhala: *paavahan* (shoes), *mulutaen geya* (kitchen), *damsaba mandapaya* 'Dharma Hall', etc. But apparently this had run afoul of a segment of the leadership. "Why in Sinhala, 10,000 miles away?" They must have assuredly added, "This man must be nuts!" In pre-multicultural Canada, my attempt to contextualize the event to its home setting, and by way of retaining the language, for the benefit of the young in particular, was seen to be only a bit short of being total lunacy. Today, in multicultural Canada, I am glad that Sinhala classes are conducted.

6.5 Research and Writing

My earliest recorded involvement with the community is when I wrote a piece in a publication called '*Cultural Cameo*', presented by the Canada Sri Lanka Association in 1978, the year I was to earn my doctorate. It called for national unity under the rubric of the New Year Celebration (as above).

One of the major interests of the Multicultural History Society of Ontario, under the early leadership of Prof. Robert Harney, was to establish a data base of oral history of the peoples that made up the Canadian mosaic. It is in this context that I had successfully proposed a funded Project on Sri Lankan Canadians and Sinhala Buddhist Canadians.

This was the project that allowed me to get a more intimate knowledge of the community, and meet people face to face, conducting interviews of the Sri

Lankan community, interviews still available at the Multicultural History Society of Ontario Archives. This was when I had the privilege of meeting Tom Orchard, the first ever Ceylonese, as he would tell me, to be admitted to Canada, in 1955 the same year the (now) well-known Sir Christopher Ondaatje had been. I would interview members of the other three communities – Sinhala, Tamil and Muslim, as well. This included an early LTTE supporter, by his own claim, as well,

My piece in *Polyphony*, in 1984 on the basis of this research, provides an overview of the community. It points to three distinct time periods of arrival, beginning with the mid 1950's when Canada opened the doors to 250 South Asians, the allocation allowing for 50 from (then) Ceylon. The first to make use of the opportunity were the Eurasians, of mixed European and Sinhala / Tamil blood. The timing couldn't have been better. There had been a socialist political / cultural revolution in the country, which saw the dethroning of English, and among the most affected were the Burghers who, holding positions in the top echelons of society, had maintained their distance from the Sinhalas and the Tamils.

With Rienzie Crusz at his residence in Waterloo, Ontario

The next strand, continuing up until the 1980's, to arrive in Canada were the Sinhalas making use of the Canadian immigration policy of encouraging blue collar workers to man our factories. But benefiting from the opening were also professionals who spoke English. Reflecting the population make-up in the country, the majority here were the Sinhalas, while there were also the Tamils. Under the family re-unification plan, soon there would be many an immigrant who spoke only Sinhala or Tamil, even though English continued to be the language of communication among the educated class. The third strand began when the terrorist campaign began in the 1980's, when Tamils began to arrive through the 'refugee' door.-

6.6 Sinhala, Tamil & English Literature Under One Cover

In 1984, I bring out, with Prof. A V Suraweera of Sri Lanka, who would himself become a distinguished novelist, and later Junior Minister of Culture, a Special Issue of the *Toronto South Asian Review* (vol 3 no 2) on Sri Lankan Literature where for the first time, the literature written in all three languages – Sinhala, Tamil and English come to be brought together into a single anthology. It features Michael Ondaatje, and the other four Sri Lankan Canadian poets of the time – Rienzie Crusz, Tyrell Mendis, Krishanta Sri Bhaggiyadatta and Asoka Weerasinghe, and the very first English translation, by Lakshmi de Silva, of the runaway hit, *Maname*, by Prof Saracchandra, as well as the young fiction writer Gunadasa Amarasekara who had won an international prize. Included are also critical studies by Arun Prabha Mukherjee, "The Sri Lankan poets in Canada ...", A V Suraweera on "The Sinhala Novel and Short Story...", C. Kanaganayakam on "Tamil Writing in Sri Lanka" and D C R A Goonetilleke on "... the Efflorescence of Sri Lankan Literature in English". My own contribution, in addition to the "Introduction: Forces that Shaped Sri Lankan Literature", is a poem, Bridges'.

In Number 7.2, I seek to fill an important gap in the *Special Issue on Sri Lankan Literature*. Siri Gunasinghe though the pioneer of blankverse in poetry, the stream of consciousness in the novel, and a film director in a Sri Lankan context, had not produced anything creative in the context of Canada, limiting himself to his professional life as a Professor at University of Victoria, British Columbia. But, perhaps because the intent of the issue was to introduce writers in Sri Lanka, little known if any to the west, only those living in Sri Lanka at the moment came to be the focus. But when a decision was taken to include Sri Lankan Canadian writers – Ondaatje, Crusz, Weerasinghe, Mendis, etc., Gunasinghe did not seem to fit because he hadn't produced anything in Canada. So in a foolish rigidity, and much to my later regret, one of the leading literary figures of Ceylon came to be not featured. This was the gap I was seeking to fill when I interviewed him, TSAR 7.2 publishing a 'Conversation', under the names of Sugunasiri and Gunasinghe. In this piece Siri talks of how he came to introduce the term *nisandas* 'free of chandas (metre = poetic dicta)', meaning blankverse, in his first collection of poetry, translated 'Dry Bones' (*mas lay naeti aeta*), and to use the stream of consciousness technique associated with Jean Paul Sartre and James Joyce in his novel *Hevanaella* 'Shadow'. On the silver screen, he "tried to make the movie more cinematic", making "the visuals the main medium" in his film, *sat samudura* 'seven seas'. He used very little dialogue.

The issue also published a few of his poems – 'The Invisible Light', 'The Visible Darkness', 'Yesterday, the Day Before and the Day Before That' and 'Henry', all translated by his wife, Hemamali, herself a linguist and actress.

I would later, again a few decades later (1994), write a critique of Maname, a play in which I myself had acted in, "Sexism in Ediriweera Saracchandra's Sinhalese Operatic Play, *Maname*". Pointing to what I saw was the sexism in it, I however absolve the Director, placing the blame on patriarchal society. I offer, for fun, an alternative ending that would erase the perceived sexism.

Enjoying reading an appreciative work on Prof. Saracchandra by Sucarita Gamalath, I write a piece, published in 6 parts in the *Sunday Observer*, beginning with 23 March, 2003, under the title, "Musings of a Ghost from the Past". To show my appreciation of another national icon, music maestro Amaradeva, I write two pieces. The first to be published is 'Amaradeva: Art & Humanity Unite in Deathlessness', in the *Sunday Observer*, Aug. 20, 2000. A more recent piece appears in the online publication, *The LankaWeb*, under the title, "Visharada Pundit Amaradeva: Heaven-St(r)uck or In-stream?" (11/01/09).

7. HELPING SHAPE EDUCATION IN ONTARIO

7.1 "Smarten Up, Indians, & Go Western"

Surprised? Insulted? But this indeed was the reaction to the view of India and Indians contained in the Textbooks approved by the Ontario Ministry of Education under Circular 14 for use in High Schools. I had been commissioned by Alok Mukherjee, then President of the Graduate Students' Association of the University of Toronto (and the later Chair of the Toronto Police Commission) to do a Content Analysis of these books – written by Professors, mostly from University of Toronto. The title of my Report, *"Smarten up, Indians, and Go Western"*, captured the essence of my findings. In a word, Indians were backward, and Europeans were modern and forward looking. There is little reason to believe that this view, pumped into growing minds in the classroom, was not also shared by the body politic.

And so how indeed could such arrogance be allowed into the offices – government, journalistic or university? I can think of no better example than the case of my good friend, the late Hubert de Santana, to make the point. Born and bread in Ireland, he spoke impeccable English with an Irish accent. Back in Ireland, a creative writer, and journalist, and now in Canada, he had applied to work at a respectable Monthly publication published in Toronto. He was beyond himself when he was called for an interview. But he soon found himself digging the dirt on the floor when he saw the jaws of the men in the paneled office drop as he entered!

Organized by the South Asian Origins Liaison Committee of the Toronto Board of Education, when the Press Conference was going to be held for the release of my Content Analysis of Textbooks under Circular 14, the affable John Piper, of the Toronto Board of Education, had made contact with the *Toronto Star* for an exclusive, with the understanding that it would be given front page coverage. Preceding the Press Conference, I had been interviewed by a Reporter extensively, along with one or two others who had been involved. But then on the day of the Press Conference, the Reporter gets the diplomatic flu! And the Press conference comes to be reported in half a column or so on the inside pages, sans photos.

It is not for me to fathom the workings of a national press, but during the interviews, Piper had, possibly sensing some jostling, commented that not everyone can expect to be featured in the story. Even though the research was on India and Indians, I was myself not Indian. So did this sentiment have anything to do with the story getting short shrift? As I said, I can only speculate.

With our residence at 1550 Boxwood Way, a *cul de sac*, at the time, *The Mississauga Times* (June 7, 1978) would give coverage to my Content Analysis (see above). It reports:

> *According to the content analysis, Sugunasiri says that the student is likely to get a picture of India as backward and archaic, with the spectre of Hinduism everywhere and where there are sacred cows that roam all over at will, consuming or destroying the food [available for humans]. He found words like archaic, backward, inefficient, poor, primitive and ungraceful to describe India and Indians, while the West was described as advanced, brilliant, civilized, humane and progressive.*

Continuing, it quotes me as saying, "We don't want a flattering picture of India, but we want a realistic picture." The article identifies me as Chairman of UNICEF, Mississauga.

7.2 Multiculturalizing Canadian Literature

Teaching at Danforth Tech, I also had the pleasure of working with the new Head of English, John Borovilos. Drawing upon my expertise, it was thanks to his encouragement, and facilitation, that I happened to be able to introduce the notion of a 'Multicultural Literature' to the Heads of English at the Toronto Board of Education, backed up by my articles as well as several workshops at Professional Development Days and other conferences. I would also write two pieces in *Indirections* [10.1.4] published by the Ontario Council of Teachers of English, on both S Asian Canadian literature, and Multiculturalizing Canadian literature.

One of them was titled 'Step Down Shakespeare, The Stone Angel is Here', the reference being to Margaret Laurence's novel. I propose here a Canadian Literary Matrix (see next page).

To take you through it very quickly, the inner circle (along the 6 dimensions, going clockwise), from 'Canada (& US)' (under 'intended audience') to 'Anglo-Saxon' (under 'ethnocultural origin') to .. 'Judeo-Christian only' (under 'sensibility') represents the reality, in its ideal and purest form, that existed during the period of classical racism. Under this perception, 'Can lit' was considered to be the works of writers of Anglo-Saxon origin only, born and living Canada, written in the medium of English only on life in Canada based in a JudoChristian sensibility. The outer circle, by contrast, from 'elsewhere only' (under 'intended audience') to 'other/nonwestern Christian' (under 'sensibility'), represents more than the integrative multicultural antidote; it is the other extreme.

Capturing this emerging rich multicultural literature was the article that appeared in *Indirections* (Vol 9, No 2, June 1984), a journal of Canadian Teachers of English, titled "Multicultural Literature within the English Curriculum", for the benefit of the Secondary School student and teacher.

John, with his clout as a Head, would take me along to make presentations, he himself, of Greek background, being a willing learner of the emerging new literary landscape.

We would also co-author a 'Pro-File' for the Ontario Ministry of Education,

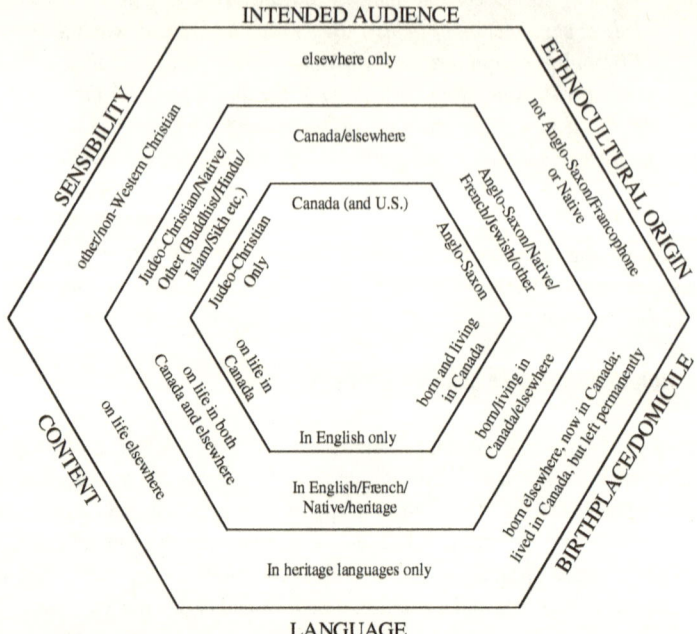

Figure 8. A Canadian Literary Matrix, showing the Continuum in Perspective from Pre-multiculturalism to Integrative Multiculturalism (from Sugunasiri, *Multicultural Education Journal*, 5.2, 1987)

under its Professional Development Series, "Multicultural Literature Within the English Curriculum" (1987).

Attending one of the workshops given by me, I was approached by a representative of a Textbook publishing company to do a multicultural literature textbook. But it was John, also in contact with a publisher, who eventually came out with the first Multicultural Literature textbook. While I was happy to see such a volume, I was surprised to see that I was nowhere in the picture – neither as co-author nor as poet, nor even of my leadership. While in our joint multicultural literature presentations, John had insisted that I do a reading of my own poetry, as model and example, none of my works got included either.

7.3 Toronto Board of Education Curriculum Consultant

While the Ontario Ministry of education was always ahead of other provinces in adopting multicultural policies, the Toronto Board of Education came to be ahead of the Ministry itself, sometimes even crossing its path. Thus they would set up 'Liaison Committees' in relation to the different ethnocultural communities they serve. The one I took a small role in participating was the S Asian Origins Liaison Committee, primarily made up of, reflecting the reality of the time,

Punjabi Canadians.

The Board would also establish a Sub-committee on Race Relations. Following the recommendations of the Final Report of this Sub-committee, interestingly enough, it is the Business Education Department that takes the initiative to undertake, as early as 1980, a review of texts relating to several areas that came under its umbrella – Accounting, Communications and Business Procedures, Consumer Education and Law. Committed to the principle of community presence, I would serve as the Representative, and Consultant, in the review of Texts in the last mentioned. The role of the Community Rep was "to review the materials prepared by the writing teams" who had been mandated to "... make recommendations concerning ... specific actions which can be taken by Toronto Board of Education and its teaching staff to combat the spread of racism in Toronto" (p. 1, General Remarks). What that entailed had been to go through texts and instructional material used in schools, as submitted by the Heads of Departments. The goal was to identify bias, pretty much as I had done in relation to Circular 14 Texts – identified specifically as 'Social bias', 'Ethnic bias' and 'Sexual bias'. My responsibility was to go through the Report developed by the two Reviewers of material in Consumer Education, Nancy Beaman of Eastdale Collegiate Institute and Mrs. Jean Probyn of Northern Secondary. Listed among the 'Print Materials Read' by the team in preparation for the review is *East Indians: Myth and Reality, a resource book*, A K Mukherjee (Ed.), which included my Content Analysis (see above).

Continuing the review in other areas of Business Education the following summer, there come to be reviewed texts in 1. Business Finance, 2. Typewriting and Secretarial Practice, and 3. Business Machines and Applications. In evaluating, the material comes to be examined for 'Classism', 'Ageism' and 'Handicapism' as well. Invited to serve as the Community Consultant for all three, I am thanked by the Reviewers, Corinne Hyatt of the Central High School of Commerce and Nancy Beaman of Eastdale Collegiate, "for.. helpful suggestions". Ronald Kendall of Humberside Collegiate Institute and Richard Lander of Oakwood Collegiate institute undertake the Review of area 1 while William McKay of Bickford Park High School works on 3.

I would also be invited to give a Keynote Address to the Business Teachers of the Board, when I talk on the topic, "What's Wrong with Name-calling?". This was the era when new immigrants were labeled FOB's – Fresh off the Boat – luckily, not SOB's! The labels reserved for the resident Canadians were less neutral: the Anglos earned the name 'WASP' – White Anglo-Saxon Protestant, the French 'FROG', the Italians 'WOP', the Blacks 'NIGGER', the Chinese CHINKS, and the Browns 'PAKI'. Marrying a white woman, a Sri Lankan colleague would make light of it on with a Lord's Prayer, reflecting his wedding day, talking about, to roaring laughter, the day when 'Jackie met the Paki'! The humour of the occasion, of course, was not to blind us to the serious matter of taking the individuality out of a person through stereotyping, as well as creating friction in society.

7.4 School Opening Exercises

Historically, Schools in Ontario had opened with the Christian origins of the land. But the practice had been struck down by the Ontario Court of Appeal on Sept. 23, 1988, also noting that "the content of opening or closing exercises must recognize and reflect the multicultural realities and traditions of Ontario Society...". In response to the passing of the Federal Multicultural Act in 1979, The Ontario Human Rights Code had been set up as well, by Attorney General Roy McMurtry in the William Davis government. And then there was the entrenchment of the Charter of Rights and Freedoms under the Constitution Act of 1982. It was in that context, then that the Lord's Prayer had been challenged successfully. Deciding not to appeal the decision, the Government of Ontario set to work to abide by it. One of the outcomes was developing a Working document, eventually published by the title, *Opening or Closing Exercises for Public Schools in Ontario,* 1993 (Document hereafter).

I was pleased, both as a committed multiculturalist, but also as the Author of the critique of the Social Studies Textbooks under Circulr 14, fifteen years earlier, that the Ministry had come a long way in responding to the changing society. I was also pleased that I was nominated by the Ontario Provincial Interfaith Committee on Chaplaincy, the Buddhist Rep on the body, to represent its interests, thus becoming a participant in the process of developing the Document and the material (as acknowledged under 'Advisory Committee' (p. 86)). The expressed vision of the Ministry of Education & Training Committee was as set out by the respected Ontario educator, Egerton Ryerson, whose statue still adorns the Ryerson University compound. He envisioned a school system, "open to all upon equal terms, and upon principles common to all" (p. 7). This had resonance with me, the Buddha's wish being, "May all beings be well".

Not excluding the Lord's Prayer by any means (see p. 35), the Document gives four general Criteria for selection of suitable items, one of them being that they "...fulfil the stated patriotic and educational purposes, imparting social, moral or spiritual values..." (p. 22). Then it goes on to include 38 pages of 'Sample Readings' (ch. 6, p. 29-66) that the Boards and Schools could draw upon for their Opening / Closing Exercises, organized under ten headings: 1. Respect & care for others; 2. Respect and care for self; 3. Commitment to Honesty, Equity & Justice; 4. Commitment to Non-violent Problem Solving; 5. Respect and Care for the Environment; 6. Pride in Canada – Its Heritage, Diversity, and Ideals; 7.Sense of Community; 8. Appreciation of the Human Spirit in its Capacity to Wonder, Joy, and Love; 9. Appreciation of Learning as a Lifelong Process; and 10. Sense of Transcendence.

Under the 3, 4 and 7 come to be included excerpts from the Buddhist work, *Dhammapada* (pp. 36, 41, 56), brought to the attention of the committee though not by me. The Document describes it as "a collection of aphorisms and parables that are ascribed to Buddha and that underline humanity's moral struggles and the ongoing need to conquer the self." I would have worded it differently, especially replacing the last word 'self' with 'oneself'. Among other selections included are excerpts from the Corinthians (Bible), and Ralph Waldo Emerson, 'American essayist, ... Unitarian minister....''

But I was also humbled to find myself, in the Selections, in the lofty company of John Diefenbaker, Prime Minister of Canada, Adrienne Clarkson, later Governor-General of Canada, Joy Kogawa, Obasan (novelist) and Martin Luther King Jr., among others. My specific contribution, under "Pride in Canada" (p. 46), was a *Saturday Star* column I had written on Feb. 4, 1989 under the title, "Who, Then, is a Canadian?":

7.5 Buddhism, in *Religions of India*

Participating in the South Asians Origins Liaison Committee of the Toronto Board of Education, I was to be invited to be a member of 'a work group', to work with the Language Study Centre headed by Jim Henderson. The task was to develop what eventually came to be a publication titled *Religions of the Indian Sub-continent*, "destined to provide Toronto teachers with a greater understanding of the major religions of the Indian sub-continent". Included were pieces on Buddhism, Christianity, Hinduism, Islam, Jainism, Sikhism and Zoroastrianism, representing a whole spiritual range – from atheistic Buddhism, to monotheistic Zoroastrianism (the precursor to Judaism), to polytheistic Hinduism. The most contentious was the one on Sikhism, which had to receive approval from the Head Office in India itself.

Writing an 18 page long piece on Buddhism, I would again adopt the dialogue format, often used by the Buddha himself, setting the scene in a Sri Lankan temple. Resident Bhikkhu Ananda is responding to Questions by an inquisitive Kay, "a Canadian teacher on tour". Making no claim to comprehensiveness, I point out that the attempt is rather "to draw the readers' attention to the social dimension". Among the topics covered are Buddha's attitude towards sex ("neither a sin nor ... held on a pedestal for worship"), towards women ("no different from his attitude to men.."), pointing to the principle of reciprocity between husband and wife, and as a Religion for the layperson. Pointed out in relation to the last is also the 'four states of mind' one needs to cultivate towards harmonious social living: friendliness (*metta*), compassion (*karuna*), altruistic joy (*mudita*) and equanimity (*upekkha*). Added are also the four behaviours recommended by the Buddha: sharing, pleasant speech, social good and equalitarianism. Listed are also the five precepts, to be taken voluntarily –

To *abstain* from:
1. *taking life.*
2. *taking what is not given.*
3. *sexual misconduct.*
4. *false speech.*
5. *taking intoxicating drinks leading to non-diligence.*

Major Teachings such as *dukkha* 'suffering', *nibbana* 'blowing out', meaning liberation, impermanence (*anicca*), come to be explained as well, lisiting also the Noble Eightfold Path:

> *Excellent View.*
> *Excellent Intention.*
> *Excellent Speech.*
> *Excellent Action.*
> *Excellent Livelihood.*
> *Excellent Effort.*
> *Excellent Mindfulness.*
> *Excellent Concentration.*

Bhikkhu Ananda has been such a good communicator of the spirit of the Buddha's Teachings that by the end, Kay herself answers her own Question about Buddha's Teachings towards eating meat: "that the individual should be able to decide this for himself or herself".

Hot from completing my doctoral thesis at OISE titled *Humanistic Nationism*, I list a section in it under 'Sources and Recommended Reading': "What is Humanness? A Buddhist Interpretation".

7.6 ESL/D Teacher and Language Across the Curriculum

Another area in which I would seek to provide an alternative, serving to educate the profession as well, was in English as a Second Language. Writing a theoretical paper, "ESL/D Teacher and Language Across the Curriculum", in *TESL TALK*, (13:2), the *Journal of English as a Second Language* professionals, drawing upon my background in Linguistics studied at University of Pennsylvania, Second language Methodology learned at the University of Michigan and Pedagogical Principles discovered at Ontario Institute for Studies in Education at University of Toronto. Here I offer "an expanded paradigm, elaborating how the English as a Second Language /Dialect Teacher could draw upon every subject in teaching newcomers". A chart I would develop seeks to pull in all such dimensions: In the article, I talk about working within Ministry guidelines in teaching 'Language across the curriculum' (LAC), showing it visually with another diagram: I also point to the benefits of an LAC approach to the ESL teacher, teachers of other subjects and the learner.

7.7 Teacher Training in the People's Republic of China

I had gone to China, with Swarna and Puta, in 1972, on our return to Ceylon, when the country was still closed to the world, the West in particular. As an educator, I was naturally interested in Chinese education. So we had been provided the opportunity to visit a school at my request, as well as meet with two

Chinese Professors. And, I was to share my experience with Ontario and Canadian educators in a paper titled 'Teacher Training in the People's Republic of China', in OISE publication, *Orbit*. Taking a descriptive approach, but making comparisons with our own western system where relevant, I point out among others, the following:

Physical exercises in a school in China 1972

- Streaming begins at the high school level itself, the four areas being Medical, Agricultural, Industrial and Standard. The thrust towards preparation for the work world here should be obvious.
- While the day to day operations are done by the Chair of a Team, itself is made up of Reps from a Teaching committee, Production committee, Political Committee and Logistics committee.
- Physical Education is mandatory for all, as in Chairman Mao's thought.

As for Teacher Training,

- A candidate applying for teacher training must have had at least two years of work experience, though not necessarily as a teacher.
- Educational Psychology is not taught [this was in 1972] since no textbooks were available, the earlier ones being of Russian origin, no longer in use after the Cultural Revolution.
- Teacher Training lasts three years, because it also includes training in a field such as military training, apparently preparing every teacher to be ready to defend the Revolution, even with arms if needed.
- Interestingly, no Certificate is issued at the end of the Course, since "Everybody serves the people".

As for Professors themselves,

- Teaching at the Training College is only a part time job for the Professors. They also move to the country 'to take education to the middle schools'.
- Professional development is mandatory for Professors, and is handled by a Special Teaching and Research Group.

8 LIFE IN THE LITERARY LANE

8.1 "*The Search for Meaning*:
Literature of the Canadians of South Asian Origins"

"Research Proposals Invited" in the May 17, 1979 issue of the *The Canada India Times,* caught my eye. It was in the name of Judy Young of the Multiculturalism Directorate of the Secretary of State Department, Ottawa. My antenna went up. While it was far, far away from the topic of my doctoral research just completed, namely, National Development, literature had apparently never left my heart.

I had published three collections of short fiction in Sinhala before leaving Ceylon on the Scholarship, and completed a Master's thesis on the 'Origins and the Development of the Sinhala Short Story'. But, I had had very little association with literature since leaving in 1964, except perhaps to read one or another creative work. For some odd reason, however, I had done a course on Children's Literature as part of my Diploma in Teaching English to Speakers of Other Languages (TESOL) at the University of Michigan, perhaps my literary fires seeking a little re-kindling. Just about that time, a translation of one of my stories, titled 'The Ingrate' had come to be published while still in the US, in a journal called *Mahfil*, a *Quarterly of South Asian Literature*.

But there was little attention to creativity upon arriving in Canada, with my nose in academic study, in Moral Philosophy, Linguistics, Pedagogical Linguistics and National Development. However, having completed the doctorate in 1978, I was looking for employment beyond the one year Project Coordinator contract in Gerontology. It was then that the advertisement appeared.

Looking for paid work, I put in a Proposal.

Although the original invitation called for proposals "to undertake a study of the writers and writing of any one of the groups (Chinese, Japanese, Vietnamese, Indian, Pakistani, etc." in submitting the proposal, "the present editor argued that the whole of South Asia should be treated as a single unit..." In this wide net was to be included not only those from India, Sri Lanka, Pakistan and Bangla Desh, but also from the West Indies and Africa. It was to capture this reality that I had come to use the rather cumbersome but more accurately descriptive phrase, 'Canadians of South Asian Origins'.

If my freshly minted PhD and the just completed Content Analysis had provided my Canadian credibility, my literary background in Sri Lanka gave the literary credibility. To my great excitement, finding my argument to be cogent, I was invited to take on the project. Little did I know it was a project that nobody had wanted to touch! Indeed I had rushed to where angels had feared to tread. Prof. Uma Parameswaran had turned it down, as she would tell me, meeting her at the University of Winnipeg on my research tour across Canada.

Whatever else the Project was, for me, it also had a bonus. It gave me the rare opportunity to see Canada by train! Getting on the CN-CP train on the evening, I spent the first night sleeping sitting up, as I would for three more nights, before getting off the train in Vancouver the morning of the fourth day. The travel money in the budget did not allow the luxury of a sleeping berth! At Sudbury I believe it was, passengers had to change trains. The first stop was Winnipeg, when my friend from Philadelphia, Prof. Lionel Steiman came to meet me at the Station, during the short stop. The next two days were nothing but the plain-lands – of wheat and more wheat, or whatever other crop was growing on the flat land extending to the horizon on both sides of the train and for miles and miles. The monotony was to be broken only by the very frequent stops on that stretch when a few passengers would get off and on. On occasion when the train went around a corner, it was like a snake snailing its way through the undergrowth under a clear blue sky.

I could now understand how the Sikhs might have come to be impressed by Canada. Members of a (British) Hong Kong Battalion and hence traveling from Hong Kong, they had traveled through Canada to and from attending the coronation of Edward VII in 1902. Following the pattern set by the celebration of Queen Victoria's Diamond Jubilee of five years before, representatives came to London from across the Empire. Travelling through Canada by train would have been enough to attract the farming eyes of the Punjabis, from the 'Land of the Five Rivers', Punjab literally from Sanskrit *panc* 'five' + *aap* 'waters'.

The scene as the train approached the Rockies, a huge boulder, was breathtaking. It was a scene which Swarna and I would take in later in life as well, enjoying the hot springs up in the mountain, and watching coyotes from the hotel room over breakfast. It was the lumber moving down the Fraser Valley that caught my fascination the fourth day before we landed. I could well imagine how in pioneering days, this was the only mode of transporting wood, to and from the sawmills. Of course, I did have my reading and writing material to keep me busy through the trip. Following my extensive research on Punjabi literature in Vancouver and the suburbs, still vibrant after 80 years, I returned by air, touching down on Calgary, Edmonton and Montreal, to complete the work in Toronto. The research had discovered a total of 159 writers, 75 in English, 65 in Punjabi and 19 in Gujarati, among them 20% women in each of English and Gujarati, and 6% in Punjabi. The research also reported that "Out of a South Asian population of 326,000 [1981], writers constitute .049%".

If the Project allowed me to dip my feet back in familiar literary waters I had left behind, I was also dipping into the unfamiliar, but, as I would find out, richly rewarding, Canadian waters as well. Coming from Sri Lanka, I spoke, in addition to English, nothing but Sinhala, and no Indian language. Luckily it was no barrier, thanks to the many English-speaking South Asians who were kind to help, among them Professors Inder Nath Kher and Mathew Zachariah of Calgary, Uma Parameswaran of Winnipeg and Ashok Aklujkar of Alberta. I was kindly hosted by Prof Zachariah during my stay at Calgary. A pleasant surprise was meeting Science Professor, Chandana Wirasinghe, of Sri Lanka, later Dean of Science. Of help was also Prof. Brenda Beck, a Tamil scholar, at the University of British Columbia.

My research originally sought to examine the literature in several languages - in alpha order, *"Arabic, Bengali, Gujarati, Hindi, Kannada, Konkani,*

Search For Meaning

The Literature of Canadians of South Asian Origins

Suwanda H. J. Sugunasiri, Ph.D.(Ed.)

Report submitted to:
The Secretary of State, Ottawa
September 1983

Malayalm, Marathi, Punjabi, Sinhala, Swahili, Tamil, Telugu, Urdu, and of course, English and French.". Even though a preliminary survey showed that there was literary activity in Canada only in English, Punjabi and Gujarati, to just make doubly sure, "... three other researchers were hired, one for Hindi in Toronto, and two for the Dravidian languages, both Tamil, in Toronto and Vancouver. The finding of these researchers were that "there exists no literary activity [in Canada] in these languages". During my research in Vancouver, I had also met a young PhD student from Sri Lanka. This was Chelva Kanaganayakam, later Professor at Trinity college, University of Toronto. On the faculty of Jaffna University, he was doing research on English Literature at UBC. Given the finding of the Tamil researchers, I remember encouraging him to encourage Tamil Canadians to take to literary creativity.

My Report, titled *The Search for Meaning: the Literature of Canadians of South Asian Origin*, was submitted to the Secretary of State by date of September 1983. In submitting I said,

> *I sincerely hope that this basic research [the results of three years of work] [1] will generate discussion and further research among scholars, both South Asian and other. Perhaps more importantly, this study will, I hope, [2] serve to bring together the South Asian Canadian writers of varying ethnic, linguistic, geographic, national and religious backgrounds. It would be encouraging as well if this effort were to [3] serve the cause of bringing South Asian Canadian literature and the writers themselves to the attention of Canadians, in order that they may gain their rightful place in Canadian society. Such a consciousness-raising exercise would, one hopes, [4] serve the larger goal of developing an increasing respect for the South Asian Canadian community in general. It is, of course, [5] up to the community itself, and to the writers, to continue to earn this respect through their continuing contributions.* (p. 3).

One only has to think of Michael Ondaatje, Neil Bissoondath, Rohinton Mistry, Moyez Vassanji, Shyam Selvadurai and Randy Boyagoda, the list reflecting the order in which each came into prominence, to see how my final expectation (# 5) of a blossoming of S. Asian Canadian literature have come to be actualized. Anyone present at the recent Conference organized by the TSAR and the Centre for South Asian Studies at the University of Toronto to commemorate 25 years of the Conference releasing my report, would have had no difficulty assessing to what extent my expectation # 2 has come to fruition. As for #1, hardly any scholar of literature can now discuss Canadian literature without reference to South Asian Canadian writers. Equally significantly, among the Professors of Literature in Canadian university are many that are of South Asian Canadian origins. With the Visible *Minority* community in a city like Toronto projected to become the Visible *Majority* not in the distant future, one need hardly argue for #3 and # 4. I know now I can rest in peace in the thought that my minor effort has borne fruit for the building of a multicultural Canadian society.

Dr. Arun Prabha Mukherjee seems to have earned her Doctorate in Literature at York just at the right time. At least as far as I was concerned! Not yet secured a faculty position, I was lucky to have been able to recruit her to report on the poetry written in English. Her paper, presented at the Conference organized "to mark the release" of my Report, looked at Michael Ondaatje's poetry against the poetry of a little known Ottawa writer Cyril Dabydeen of West Indian origin. The pungent critique of Ondaatje was a hit! It established her as a new minority and feminist critical voice that would make waves in the Canadian literary establishment. Indeed launched was, it can be said, an academic career!

Dr Prajna Enros was hired for Gujarati and Surjeet Kalsey, a poetess from Vancouver, who had also helped me immensely with the research itself, for Punjabi. It was a labour of love from Prof. Frank Birbalsingh of York University, Toronto, analyzing the 10 novels in English written by that time.

Taking three years, "traveling and meeting people personally" (p. 7), the research "was completed in 1983" (p. 9). I would send everyone who helped a letter of thanks dated May 12,1983. It would be five or so years later when *The Search for Meaning* comes to be published by the Secretary of State, with a French translation, along with the Reports on the Literature in other languages – Hispanic, Hungarian, Italian, Polish and Urdu, in addition to the one on *Literary Writing by Blacks in Canada*, commissioned, and completed "between 1979 and 1986".

8.2 Joining Moyez Vassanji, Co-Founding *Toronto South Asian Review*

One of the most persistent concerns expressed by South Asian Canadian writers throughout my research was the unavailability of an outlet that would be responsive to their writing. They were basically asking for a Journal expressly for South Asian works. During the period of my research, I had had the pleasure of meeting Dr. M G Vassanji, a physicist, with a doctorate from the MIT in the US, hailing from Kenya, doing physics research at University of Toronto. It had been his long-time dream, as he would tell me later, to publish a literary journal. And that would jive well with my interest, if for nothing more than to honour a commitment I had given to writers to do my best to see if such a journal was feasible. So I thank him in my Report "for inviting me to participate in the *Toronto South Asian Review*" (TSAR). Helping in our planning, and present at our initial meetings - held possibly in an office I had at OISE or in his own office on campus, was M H K Qureshi at Vassanji's invitation.

Having taken the decision to dare, given that it was, in the eighties, still WASP country, Moyez would come to the next meeting with a selection of material he had put together for a first issue. Qureshi and I both agreeing that it would be too cumbersome for three people to be involved in editorial decision making, it was left in the hands of Moyez. The maiden issue (1982) thus shows Vassanji as Editor, Suwanda Sugunasiri as Consulting Editor and Qureshi, along with Cathy Hassam and Surjeet Kalsey as Associate Editors. It also includes a translation of a story of mine, 'Fellow Travellers', and two poems by Qureshi.

Two of my poems, 'Which is Fun?', 'Expectations', come to be featured in Vol. 2, No. 2 and 'Women on Tape' made up of four poems in 4.1.

Vol. 2 Number 2 carries an article by me, Bibliography: 'South Asian Canadian Fiction in English' (-1982), drawn upon my larger study.

The TSAR, printed and bound at the University of Toronto Press, comes to be respectably received by the academy and the literary circles, right from its very first issues, though the numbers would still be countable on fingers. If it was thanks to Moyez's high standards in selecting the material, which as my Report showed, was in no short supply, and his discerning eye in copy editing, it was also thanks to "the amount of work that went in ... the full nights of paste ups, proofreading, putting in errors using rulers, T-squares, etc.... putting the magazines in envelopes and taking them to the post office", as he would tell me in later correspondence. I was reminded of my time a few years earlier as Editor of *Gradiosie* at OISE. Not only was it "like having two full-time jobs", his own writing comes to suffer as well, because "I have not been able to give it sufficient time." Happily all the hard work paying dividends, soon the journal would come to be recognized by the academy as equal to any literary magazine in Canada, not only adding a South Asian voice, but making Vassanji earn respectability among editors and the literary establishment.

Undoubtedly, however, its success was in no small measure due to a high profile Conference organized in 1983, with funding from the Secretary of State. My Report submitted to the Multiculturalism Directorate earlier in the year, the Conference was organized "to mark the completion of the initial report" (*The Search for Meaning)*. The initial get together that resulted in the Conference was a dinner held at our residence at 3315 Havenwood. The invited guests were Moyez Vassanji and his wife Nurjehan Aziz, Alok and Arun Mukherjee and Austin Clarke, who by now was himself beginning to establish a name as a writer. Austin would have only but the highest appreciative comments on the food Swarna had prepared.

Life in the literary lane

THE TORONTO SOUTH ASIAN REVIEW
Volume 3, Number 2   Fall 1984

Editor	M G Vassanji
Associate Editors	Cathie Hassam
	M H K Qureshi
	Surjeet Kalsey (Vancouver)
Consulting Editor	Suwanda Sugunasiri
Business Manager	Iqbal Dewji
Administrative Assistant	Nurjehan Aziz

SPECIAL ISSUE ON SRI LANKAN LITERATURE
guest edited by
SUWANDA SUGUNASIRI AND A.V. SURAWEERA

All of us Browns being unknown entities, we needed a way of highlighting both the Journal and my research. And so in my Report, I thank Dr Vassanji for inviting me to "help organize a Conference to mark the release of the ... report." (p. 3). Vassanji assumed the position of Chair of the Conference, with me as Co-Chair. In his Remarks, he thanked "Suwanda for his aggressive publicity efforts". These efforts are partly reflected in my letter of thanks, of May 12, 1983, written on the *Toronto South Asian Review* letterhead, sent to all those who helped in the Research Project. In it I state,

> As will be noted from the letterhead, we now have a journal, thanks to the efforts of its energetic editor, Dr M G Vassanji, devoted entirely to the Literature of the Canadians of South Asian Origin. .. Part of the reason for the birth of the [Journal] was the concern expressed by many of you regarding the absence of a serious forum for your literary works. .. We have featured over 40 Canadian South Asian writers in our first three issues, and have subscribers from across Canada, the US, Europe and Asia. It is our hope that you'll help in its continued success, and there are three ways you can do it: (a) by sending your works ... for publication, review, etc.; (b) by subscribing to it; (c) by getting subscriptions from your associates." I give my home phone number, 416-625-8746, inviting them "to help me keep the ... research updated".

I also thank Nurjehan in my Report, not just for being the wife behind every successful man but also the person behind the success of the *Toronto South Asian Review* itself. She was obviously part of the 'full nights' that went into producing it. It continued to grow over the next many years, until it came to be the (now defunct) *Toronto Review*, expanding the mandate to include any, primarily though not exclusively, writers of any minority, though writers of the majority community also found themselves featured.

The papers read at the launch would appear in the same year (1983), however, under the title, *A Meeting of Streams,* showing Vassanji as Editor. While I was not too happy that my name didn't appear, since the papers, except one or two, were basically by the researchers hired by me, there was no question that all the hard work that went into editing was solely a labour of love on his part. However, unfortunately, as I was to discover more recently, the publication has resulted in perverting history. In an article written three decades later (2015), the publication is seen as marking "The arrival... of South Asian Canadian literature" (*Studies in Canadian Literature*, 40, 1, p.10), "followed by ...*The Search for Meaning*", my pioneering role buried under chronological accuracy.

Continuing our friendship, it was with a lot of confidence that I would invite Moyez to join me for some of the TV programs I had been invited to, on Rogers Cable among them. I was also happy, in his early years as a writer, to write a letter of recommendation on his behalf in support of his application to attend a Writer's Workshop at the Banff Centre, School of Fine Arts. He was seeking to work on the collection of stories that would eventually appear under the title, *Uhuru Street* (1992). Some of the stories shared with me, I would write in my letter of recommendation of March 3, 1986, as follows:

> *Among the strengths I see in his works are an artistic delineation of his characters and setting, with an economy of language, the effective use of symbolism, both traditional and not-so-traditional, a marriage between an African context and a classical Indian idiom, and a flow in story development.*

Thus I urged that an opportunity be given, "to allow Vassanji to reach his goal of perfectionism which I know he constantly aspires to in all his work."

While mine was no big name in establishment circles, at least I had justly earned the apt image of the Arrogant Brown with my critique of the Circular 14 Textbooks (see 3.2 above). But I might have had earned a more positive image through my Research Report to the Secretary of State. I was also additionally a 'home-grown' PhD.

Unfortunately though, it turns out that I still didn't have enough clout. Moyez was not selected for the Program! This was a time when S Asian Canadian writers were struggling to find acceptance by the Canadian literary establishment. Reshard Gool, from South Africa, is a case in point. Professor of English at the University of Prince Edward Island, he had published two novels, one of them,

Nemesis Casket, around two upper middle class British families in a Toronto context. Hailed as "the most brilliant example so far" of what critic Prof Roland Sutherland (writing in 1983) calls "Twentieth century Canadian Baroque", his works were never to make it into the literary establishment in his lifetime.

It was much the same story with Vassanji. Unable to find a Canadian publisher, his first collection, *Gunny Sack* (1989), came to be published in the UK by Heinemann under the 'African Writers Series'.

The first to breakthrough this literary race barrier was Neil Bissoondath, with his publication, *Digging Up the Mountains* (1985), published by Macmillan, the same publisher as his Uncle V S Naipaul's. The back cover blurb indeed publishes Naipaul's recommendation: "I welcome this book by my nephew. I'm staggered by the talent which is already so developed..". Margaret Laurence, in another blurb, refers to "A strong new voice with an impressive range". Ken Adachi, reviewing the work for the *Toronto Star,* calls it a "major work and a welcome addition to a slowly increasing body of first-rate work produced by immigrants to Canada".

So it was with great deal of happiness that I welcomed the news that Moyez's *The Book of Secrets* (1994) had won the very first Giller Prize. And then again in 2003 for his, *The In-Between World of Vikram Lall*. No more evidence was needed as to how wrong the Banff Centre School of Fine Arts had been. It must have been with difficulty I resisted the temptation to call it racist.

A more recent contact with the Vassanjis was when they came for a book launch of Swarna's cookbook, *Cooking from my Heart: Loving Spoonfuls from a Sri Lanka Kitchen.*

Most recently, I had the pleasure of working with Moyez and Nurjehan at the Festival *of South Asian literature,* held on Sept. 25-26, 2009, to commemorate 25 years since releasing my Report, and the publication of *A Meeting of Streams*. It was jointly sponsored by TSAR Publishing and the Centre for South Asian Studies at the Munk Centre. In her opening remarks, Nurjehan was kind enough to say something to the effect, *"We are here today celebrating twenty five years of South Asian Canadian Literature. And the person who started it all is Suwanda Sugunasiri, who is with us today."* Though not called upon to identify myself, I was happy that my place in history had been publicly acknowledged, specially in the presence of younger scholars and writers who had not been around during the pioneering years.

I would call to congratulate Moyez upon winning the Governor-General's

With Moyez Vassanji and Swarna at our home

Award for non-fiction writing, *A Place Within*, based on his explorations of India, having been born in Africa. I had earlier called to congratulate him upon being named to the Order of Canada.

The success of Moyez, and others such as Rohinton Mistry, Neil Bissoondath, Shyam Selvadurai, and most recently, Randy Boyagoda during the last quarter century was for me humbling cause enough for a silent glee of satisfaction that I had had a pioneering if minor role in unravelling such quality, and planting a seed towards the efflorescence of South Asian Canadian Literature and the public recognition of it.

8.3 A Few Pieces of Critical Writing

My research found expression, in addition to my own Report and a *Meeting of Streams*, in several other formats. One was in *Canadian Ethnic Studies*, and another, in the Multicultural History Society of Ontario. A third was at a conference in Ottawa on 'Language, Culture and Literary Identity in Canada'. I would also write a piece on 'Reality and Symbolism in South Asian Canadian Short Story' in *World Literature Written in English* (1986).

Over the next few years, I also wrote a few more pieces on *Canadian literature*, among them one under the provocative title, "Sri Lankan Canadian poets: the Bourgeoisie that fled the Revolution". In this study, I review the poetry of Michael Ondaatje, Rienzie Crusz, Asoka Weerasingha and Krishanta Sri Bhaggiyyadatta. The Revolution referred to is the Socialist Revolution under the leadership of S W R D Bandaranaike when English came to be dethroned. The point I made was that these were all writers who fled, unable to take the heat entailed by the radical linguistic, cultural and social change. This may be seen, in hindsight, as a continuation with my social consciousness displayed in my pieces written to the Sinhala media before leaving Sri Lanka. I had also made a critical note of the fact that Arun Mukherjee, who had taken Ondaatje to task for not being 'South Asian' enough, had herself not been any more 'South Asian'. There was no evidence in her critique, of Ondaatje or in her study for me, of drawing upon the rich Indian literary critical tradition, relying solely on the Western.

I was also inspired when Howard Aster of Mosaic Press, Oakville, Professor at McMaster University, invited me to do an Anthology of South Asian Fiction. *Whistling Thorn*. This was the first collection that brought to the attention of the wider Canadian public the rich literary creativity of South Asian Canadian writers of fiction, and I make use of the opportunity to take a little jab at the establishment, that the collection may well "serve as a thorn in the flesh of the Canadian literati". I was happy to have been able to feature writers such as Neil Bissoondath, Cyril Dabydeen, Rohinton Mistry and Moyez Vassanji (listed in alpha order), household names today, but still early in their career. Among others to be featured were Iqbal Ahmad, his story "Kumbh Fair" being "the earliest [known] [short story] to be written in Canada in English" ('Selections Introduced'), and Hubert de Santana, his story "Dublin Divertimento" being [at that time] the latest. It also featured three women writers - Uma Parameswaran, a University Professor in Winnipeg, Surjeet Kalsey, better known for her Punjabi writing and a newscaster on All-India Radio prior to arriving in Canada, and Laksmi Gill, winner of the Poetry Prize at Western Washington University, USA. Reshard Gool, Professor of English at the University of Prince Edward Islands, Arnold Itwaru, later of New College, University of Toronto and Sasenerine Persaud, were others, very new on the scene. My own story, *Fellow Travellers*, was the only translation, included at the specific request of the publisher.

The Whistling Thorn gave the Canadian reader a peek into the rich diversity of what I would come to label Canadians of South Asian Origins. Cumbersome as it sounds, I was seeking to capture the wide variety that falls under its rubric, not captured in the later, and the more popular label 'South Asian Canadians'. If most were from India and Sri Lanka, there were those from South Africa, West Africa, Guyana and Ireland as well, also reflecting the diverse religious sensibilities: Buddhist, Hindu, Sikh and Christian. A wider representation would be hard to find. A Review of the work would appear in *blood + aphorisms*, a journal of literary fiction, No 23, Summer 1996. Saying that the collection "merely begs for a second volume to follow up the quality here", reviewer Philip D'Sousa ends with the words, "let us appreciate some more".

Writing a piece titled, "Hung Between Two Thoughts" in *Books In Canada*, Andrew Faiz writes:

> ... *The Whistling Thorn* is an example of how to do things right. He lets stories reign, pulling in the politics. .....
>
> The exciting thing about Sugunasiri's collection is that the characters are allowed their own lives. They are not judged in relation to their chosen countries, nor do they judge that country. What is explored is the static between countries and characters. This sounds simple and obvious, yet it is rare to find, especially in ideological anthologies. Most of these stories are about making a heaven for yourself while suspended between two worlds.

I would also be invited to write a piece on South Asian Literature – remember, now I was the specialist, for *The Asianadian*. Identified on the cover page itself, I would write a three-page article under the title "Emerging themes in South Asian Canadian Literature", based on a talk given at the Sixth Triennial Conference of the Association of Commonwealth Literature and Language Studies, held at the University of Guelph. I identify some of the themes as follows: the Immigrant Experience, Life in the Homeland, Love, Woman's Place in Society, and the Canadian mainstream. I excerpt from three poets as well: Sinhala Burgher Rienzie Crusz, and Punjabi Surjeet Kalsey and Dhanjal.

In 1995, the journal now becoming publisher, TSAR Publishing would bring out my first collection of poetry, *The Faces of Galle Face Green*, title reflecting Vassanji's artistic acumen. It included the very first poem I would pen, *Disarming Death* (see later). But he, now in his role as publisher, comes to be understandably frustrated to discover that the Sinhala Canadian community was not ethnocentric enough to line up to buy it up! Over time, of course, the stock comes to be exhausted, through my own efforts, with a second edition coming to be published in Sri Lanka 6 years later, by Sarasawi Publishers.

It was with a sense of humble delight, then, that I was to discover in 2010 that I had been featured in the *Encyclopedia of Literature in Canada* put out by Prof. William H. New of University of British Columbia, since 2002. I also come to be featured in *Asian-American poets: a bio-bibliographical critical sourcebook*. As an overview of Asian American poetry, making a reference to me in the words "in her article", this volume synthesizes current research and points to the urgent need for additional scholarship.

8.4 A Brown among Browns: a Marginalization

If, through my 67-page Content Analysis and Critique of Circular 14 Textbooks in 1978 I had pierced the consciousness of the establishment, through my research on the rich Literature of the Canadians of South Asian Origins in 1980, I can be said to have put up a dais at which the S. Asian Canadian community could stand tall, with head up, to be counted for a Gold. In that sense, I may have played a small, and humble, role for the paradigmatic shift that was to ensue regarding white Canadian attitudes vis-à-vis the 'Arrogant Brown'.

I may have made a small contribution towards multiculturalizing Canada as well by bringing white Canada to the second stage of change. As theorized by Rapaport, this next stage was to take a good, hard look at these strangers within the borders. Writers like Margaret Atwood and Margaret Laurence, poets like Al Purdy and Professors like Roland Sutherland and Michael Thorpe were among the trailblazers in beginning to take this serious look at the newcomers.

If my role should make me a respected *insider* among the Browns, the irony is that that I have always sensed to be left at the margins of the Brown Canadian consciousness. A fragile ego perhaps? But take a look.

Scene: **Toronto Board of Education, 1980's: A meeting of South Asian Origins Liaison Committee of the Toronto Board of Education.**

During the break, we break up alright, but soon, I begin to notice how people are clustered in their exclusive groups - speaking Punjabi, Hindi, Bengali, Gujerati, ...whatever. When the odd one does me the favour of talking to me, the smile is accompanied by a torrent of sounds of their language. As I draw a blank, they seem genuinely puzzled:

"You don't speak Punjabi [Hindi / Bengali / Gujarati]?"
"No, I'm from Sri Lanka."
"And you don't speak Punjabi [Hindi / Bengali / Gujerati]!"
"No...."
"Oh, soon you will"

Or, for a variation,

"*You don't speak Punjabi [Hindi / Bengali / Gujarati]?*"
"*No, I'm from Sri Lanka.*"
"*So whaddaya speak?*"
"*Sinhala.*"

With a condescending look that suggests, 'Never heard of it', a question follows:

"*But it's like Punjabi (Hindi / Gujarati, etc.), right?*"
"*Well, not quite.*"
"*But you were part of India, right?*"
"*Never in the history!*"

I smile, as s/he walks away to their in-group, little realizing that I was the pioneer who pointed out to the authorities how Indians were portrayed in condescending terms in school textbooks, which were to be eventually replaced.

How could I blame the innocent Punjabi, or the other Indians, who naively think that Lanka the island was or has been part of their country? That, of course, would have been too much to believe. After all, Pakistan and Bangla Desh at one time WERE, part of India! *So how could puny Sri Lanka not have been? Just who are you trying to kid, eh!*

But how could it be only a matter of time before I would come to my senses and speak an Indian language? For after all, does not one of Sri Lanka's minorities speak an Indian language – Tamil?

I can only view the above scene as symptomatic of a psychological expulsion of the Sri Lanka Brown from the Indian Brown psyche. Biased statement?

Here is some more fodder for the gristmill.

The *Toronto Star* does a supplement on South Asian religions. It includes even Christianity, but on Buddhism, there is a small write up, under no name, which says that Buddhism is present in Nepal, and that there are about a 1000 Nepalese Buddhists! Somebody forgot to tell that Nepal was (at that time), the only officially Hindu country. And, of course, nobody remembered Sri Lanka – that there were by now nearly 10,000 or so Sinhala Buddhists in Canada. I am told that the supplement was overseen by a Committee, drawn from the Canadian South Asian Community. Any more evidence needed for the mantra that India is Sri Lanka, and Hinduism is Buddhism? This Committee, and the *Toronto Star* itself, apparently didn't want to know that there indeed was a specialist on Buddhism in the city – a fellow called Sugunasiri who had only been a columnist for the Star on Buddhism!

The thinking that Sri Lanka is nothing other than India seems to be so pervasive that it appears to have pervaded the Canadian academy, too.

Scene: **Conference on South Asia. Year, late 1980's.** *Speaker: History Professor, and specialist on S Asia.*

> *In his presentation, he shows, using UN data, how India is low on the critical indices such as literacy, infant mortality, longevity, poverty, etc. "And that's generally true of the region." Of course, the Professor was on good grounds, since the Indian figures are indeed generalizable to Pakistan and Bangla Desh; they were once, not very long ago, part of India. The Professors who wrote the Circular 14 Books (I had analyzed in my study (see above) would have been more than thrilled to pieces that they had finally been vindicated.*
>
> *But the Professor was apparently busy being the specialist – fitting my pet definition of a specialist as being 'someone who knows more and more of less and less'. So when he was so well informed of India – the country that really matters, why would he pay attention to the erratic, and troublesome, little mouse, the small player who would ruin his picture of misery with an unwarranted intrusion of sunshine?*
>
> *And so it was not comfortably that I got up to point out that the UN data on Sri Lanka, printed on the back side of the very literature distributed at the conference itself, told a markedly different story - how Sri Lanka was different in all these indices: high literacy, low infant mortality, longer life-span and lesser poverty. Of course, Sri Lanka was never part of India, a fact that few seem to want to know, or to hear.*

Many years later, nothing seems to have changed regarding the place of the Sinhala Canadian in the pecking order.

At the FSALA Conference at the University of Toronto (above), I had been invited to Moderate a Reading Session. Using the Chair's prerogative at the end of the session, I present two Sinhala poems from the 13th Sinhala Long poem *Kawsilumina* 'Crest Gem of Poetry', by King Parakramabahu II. One was a description of dainty damsels dancing, and the other the scene of a group of drunken men. Taking off my jacket, but still in tie, I broke into dance, flailing my arms "like hands drawing a thousand pictures, as if they were rays of lightning", to quote the first line. The total poem I sang as I danced – you can imagine how ridiculous it must have been... oh never mind, went something like this:

> *Hands flailing, as if etchings many a figure, in streaks of lightning,*
> *Keeping their feet to the tune of the Veena strumming out golden chimes,*
> *Casting glances with corners of eyes like darts sent by the God of Love*
> *Just how could I say these noble heavenly nymphs perform their dances?*

The drunken scene, as can be seen from the shortness itself as seen below, was quite in contrast in pace and language, with consonantal endings and short syllables:

> *Jug in hand, liquor-brimmed,*
> *Eyes dark red, as in lotus petals.*
> *Not knowing a thing, in their unsteady gait*
> *Some dance in their very own stupor.*

I must have looked quite the clumsy, flailing my arms and swirling around, all in full suit! But...

If this was in part to add colour, in my naive way, to the Conference which only had an instrumental recital at the Opening, it was also to take the opportunity to highlight Sinhala literature. Told that the conference would feature presentations in English, Punjabi, Urdu and Tamil, I had attempted to have Sinhala included. My argument was simply that to exclude Sinhala would be to exclude a whole country, and the whole Buddhist culture, given that all the other three religions of the sub-continent - Hinduism, Islam and Sikhism, were represented. I was happy that Sri Lankan Tamil literature was well represented. As noted above, during my research on South Asian Canadian Literature, the two Tamil researchers I had hired found no evidence of Tamil literature in Canada (in the early 1980's). And I had encouraged them to encourage the community to produce literary works. And so I was delighted to see not just one but three Tamil presentations as part of the conference. But I was saddened there wasn't even one representing Sinhala Canadians. To have Tamil alone as representing Sri Lanka would be like including French programs as representing Canada, but nothing on English. Obviously I had not been persuasive enough.

What, then, explains the marginalization of the Sinhala Buddhists in the Canadian psyche, by both the Indian and the non-Indian, making them occupy the bottom of the Canadian multicultural barrel? I shall leave that with you for future research.

9 HELPING SHAPE MULTICULTURALISM

9.1 Opening Salvos in Multiculturalism

Looking back on my involvement in the multicultural scene, I seem to have gotten into the multicultural act not long after the Multicultural Act of 1979. My opening salvos have been with my pen, if also oratorically, when I am invited by the Peel Board of Education to give an Address to the Summer ESL Staff (June 18, 1981) at the J A Turner Secondary School in Mississauga. Putting the responsibility right on the individual, I capture the sense in my title, "Multiculturalism is Humanizing Action – Personally and Socially".

At the initiative of lawyer and social activist, it comes to be published, in an edited version, in a special issue of *Rikka* (Winter 1981), and Guest Editor, Charles Roach, a quarterly produced by 'an editorial collective'. This particular issue (vol 8, no 4), as characterized in the Editorial, "contains articles that critically analyse the Canadian experience of Multiculturalism from 1971 to 1981", the first date being the year when Prime Minister Trudeau announced the Multicultural Policy in the House of Commons, with the support of both Opposition Leaders, Robert Stanfield of the Liberals and David Lewis of the NDP.

Re-titled "Cross-fertilization and Cultural Pluralism",

With Charles Roach, Guest Editor, *Rikka*

I begin by pointing out that while we have been bombarded with the term 'Multiculturalism' since the adoption of the policy in 1971, there has been no clarity. "Perhaps there has been more sound than light; for it is rare that this concept ... comes to be explained with any clarity". Never not the fool to rush where angels fear to tread, I offer to share "my own attempt at understanding this somewhat elusive concept."

Having gone through several scenarios which to me didn't seem to capture the concept of Multiculturalism well, I suggest that the "first sign of Multiculturalism in practice [is] a questioning attitude toward hallowed Canadian patterns of behaviour, thought and speech", the threesome clearly drawn from the Buddha's teaching of mind, body and speech as the 'three doors'. And the suggestion is not one churned out philosophically, but based in some real examples from Canadian society itself. Maureen McAteer, wife of Prime Minister Joe Clark, prefers to retain her maiden name, going against the Canadian practice of taking the husband's name, as has always been the practice in Buddhist Sri Lanka up to later times. The Chairman of the Chamber of Commerce declares that pinball machines tend to corrupt the young. Toronto Board of Education prepares a booklet providing alternative readings to the Lord's Prayer. And I suggest that we become multicultural by "promoting this questioning attitude", and "seeking to learn from others, aspects of culture that are conducive to our mental health and physical well-being", this regardless of the source of origin of the alternative. I seek to capture my understanding with a diagram, which shows, in true Buddhist fashion, a cyclical process:

I urge that newcomers, too, maintain this questioning attitude, presumably of their own culture.

Saying that questioning is not enough, I suggest that we should consider it our responsibility "to ensure that our student, and their families, have equal opportunities in Canadian society". This again is no philosophical stance, but stems from the reality as it existed then. I give a few research findings:

- *The Toronto Sun sends a white and a South Asian to find rental accommodation to discover that not all the places offered to the white person were available to the South Asian, and where available, the rent quoted was higher.*
- *Consistently, in all provinces, French Canadians earn less than the Provincial income averages (research drawn upon Stats Can 1969).*
- *The more educated an immigrant is, the more difficult it is to find work at their own level (research based in research in Montreal and Toronto).*

When you consider that immigrant doctors are still said to drive taxis, it appears as if not much has changed in nearly four decades!

I end by proclaiming that "Multiculturalism is humanizing action, personally and socially". And I end with a quote, perhaps to the chagrin of some even today, Chairman Mao Tes-Tung: "Let a hundred flowers bloom". I remember the kindly Charles Roach being concerned about my own future in Canada! I was still looking for work.

The same year, I am published in the Ontario Human Rights publication, *Affirmation*, edited by Rabbi Gunther Plaut, V. chair of the Commission. Titled "Human Rights entail obligation – a Buddhist View". In this very short two-column piece, making reference to the Buddha's Teachings, I argue that "In order to make the concept of Human Rights more balanced, comprehensive and humane, it is imperative that we enshrine *human obligations* as part and parcel of Human Rights" (italics added). I end with the following lines, again in typical Buddhist fashion:

> "While we should fight for our own rights, we should fight, with equal commitment, for the rights of others. Further, each act of asserting our rights must be matched by an act of meeting our obligations. *As we give, so others get; we also get as others give* (italics in original)."

The theme would come to be given a lengthier treatment in a paper, 'Human Rights: A Buddhist Critique', Second Interdisciplinary Conference on the Evolution of the World Order under the theme "Global and Local Responsibilities for a Just and Sustainable Civilization", Ryerson University, Toronto, "Media and Multiculturalism: a sociopolitical view", would appear in *Multiculturalism* (October, 1983).

A similar lengthier treatment, in a related field, Drawing upon John Porter's *Vertical Mosaic*, I seek to explore "the problem of media non-Multiculturalism" – meaning that it "has failed or refused to see that Canada is no longer ... White alone.". In this process, I point out (a) that the media is owned and operated by the same class and ethnicity – white, and basically, Anglo-Saxon; (b) that there is no such thing called 'objectivity' when it comes to the media; (c) that there needs to be a sense of obligation to the public going beyond the bottom line; and (d) that the media functions at the level of "a good boy orientation" when it comes to morals. I therefore argue that "Each of us must be held accountable for our media multicultural ills, because, in a very real sense, we are the media!" I then go on to list a questionnaire along which an individual may make his / her own judgments when it came to the media, and then urge that we as individuals take the responsibility to "give the media its direction". And this we can do it not with a "song and dance Multiculturalism" when we applaud and return to our own cultural ghettoes, but only with ourselves being multicultural in our personal lives. Then when the media begins to report the happenings of society, reporting Multiculturalism in action in individual and collective lives, the media will be found to be automatically multicultural!

I leave it to the judgment of the reader if indeed my theoretical model has accurately projected future reality, as judged from today's media. Perhaps I myself provide a case study. At the time of writing, I had pointed out that only 'Judeo-Christian' was in their psyche, but not Buddhism, Hinduism, Islam, Sikhism, etc. But, first, I become a columnist at the *Toronto Star*. And then I was happy the Editors responded to my suggestion that the Religion page reflect these other religions, too. And invited to write my first piece in 1983, I would come to write a Buddhist column, sharing the space with other religionists. (See later under 'A Buddhist Columnist'.)

So it is that I see myself as playing another tandem midwifery role in both making the Canadians to understand the mouthful m.u.l.t.i.c.u.l.t.u.r.a.l.i.s.m, but also helped widen their horizons. There may be many a specialist scholar today in the field, but I was just planting some early seeds.

9.2 An Order-in-Council Appointment:
Ontario Advisory Council on Multiculturalism & Citizenship

It was a normal Sunday at home with the family when my phone rang. It was John Nicholls at the other end of the line, calling from the Premier's office. I had met John when I had invited the Provincial Minister of Multiculturalism and Citizenship, Mr. Bruce McCaffrey, to be guest of honour at a Wesak celebration organized by the Buddhist Federation of Toronto. I had convinced my colleagues in the Buddhist community of the need to make political links as a way of raising our profile. John, an aide to Premier William Davis, had attended as the Minister's assistant, not unlikely, fishing for party members as well.

John was calling to invite me to accept an appointment as member of the *Ontario Advisory Council on Multiculturalism and Citizenship* (OACMC hereafter) of which I had known nothing. As I would learn later, this was the Ontario Provincial counterpart of a similar body at the federal level, with a mandate to advise the government on matters multicultural. Premier William Davis, who would be a key player in the battle for Canadian unity, was a keen supporter of Multiculturalism, and ably assisted by his Minister of Justice, Roy McMurtry who would eventually set up the Ontario Human Rights Commission.

Asking for time to consider, and after consulting with Swarna, I call back to tell him that I would accept the invitation. I made it clear, however, that I was representing nobody, and that I was on the Council in my own right. Appointed by Order-in-Council, I would become one of a large body of 60 members, representing the various ethnocultural and religious groups. Meetings held at one of the big rooms at the Mowat Block, there was a per diem of $ 60.00 for attendance at meetings, lowest, as I came to understand, for similar advisory work. But it was understandable, too. There were 60 of us, not the one or two as when it came to other advisory bodies. My appointment comes to be reported in the Sri Lankan leading Sunday paper, *Sunday Observer* of April 17, 1983.

John would also call me later to do a little background check on someone who had made a request for a Message from the Premier for a paper called *Sri Lanka Times*. I called back to say that my research showed that the request was authentic.

Sitting around a table that sat 60 people in a room at the Mowat Block was overwhelming to say the least. I had not had such an experience. But over time, we also seemed to get used to it. We each had a microphone sitting right in front of us built into the desk, and when we wanted to talk, we would push the red button for 120 ears to listen.

At the invitation of Dr. Mavis Burke, Chair of OACMC, I would later become the Regional Coordinator for the Toronto Region – with the largest number of members, and ex officio, Executive committee member. In these early days of Multiculturalism, we were looking to see how sensitive the two major newspapers were to the issue. Our methodology was rather unsophisticated – merely to look at the occurrence of the word 'Multiculturalism' in the body of the stories. The fact that the newspapers were beginning to develop an electronic archives was helpful. While we had hypothesized that the left-leaning *Toronto Star* would be the hands down 'winner', it was to our surprise when we found out it was the other way around. The *Globe & Mail* was found to have the most number of occurrences of the term. This was perhaps because, being the 'national newspaper' by its own claim, it reported on national matters more than the localized *Toronto Star*.

It was our

With Lily Munroe, Minister of Citizenship and Culture of the David Peterson, Government of Ontario (1987)

expectation to present the findings to the Editor-in-Chief of each of the newspapers, but, not being a rigorous study, the sub-committee's recommendation, headed by me, was to be shot down by the Exec: "Your research methodology is full of holes". The findings thus never came to be shared with the Publishers.

Appointment renewed once more, my tenure comes to end in 1987, when I get a certificate dated March 14, 1987, signed by the Hon. Lily Munroe, Minister of Citizenship and Culture, and the Hon. David Peterson, Premier of Ontario. It thanks me for the "distinguished service .. rendered to the citizens of Ontario".

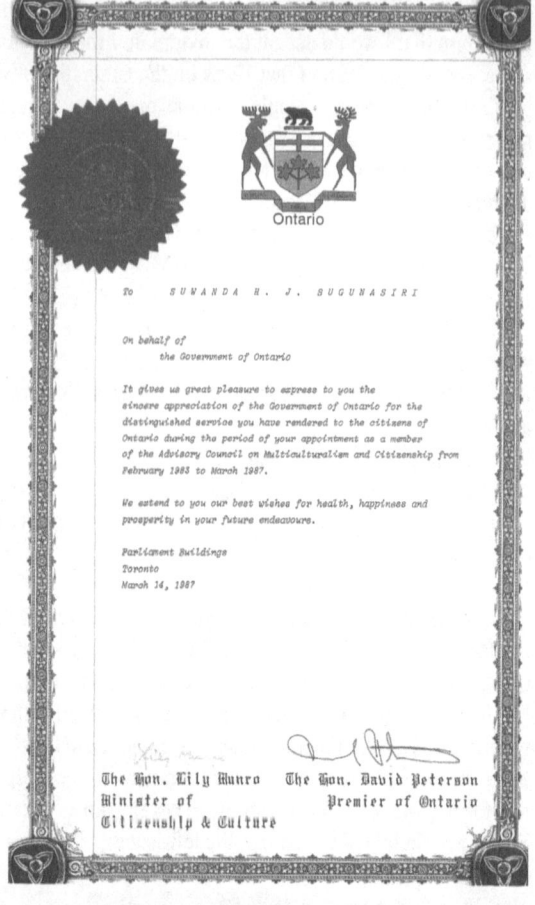

9.3 Public Speaking

Organizing a Conference, Tracey Brieger, of the International Program of the University of Trent, Peterborough would invite me to be one of three speakers at the Asia Dialogue 1994, to be held on Nov. 19, 1994. I was also to have a Q & A period to respond to specific questions students would have and given to me ahead of time. In the letter of invitation, I seemed to be asked to cover the universe! The suggested topics were:

    a) survey of Multiculturalism in Canada;
    b) its implications for Asian immigrants;
    c) instances of racism / hypocrisy towards Asians in Canadian immigration policy;

d) evaluation of the 'mosaic' theory of Canada as it pertained to Asians;
e) Neil Bissoondath's book *Selling Illusions* critical of Multiculturalism, creating a furore in the multicultural establishment;
f) generational difference in the South Asian Canadian literature.

The other two suggested topics combined Sociology and Buddhism:

g) problems of adaptation for people entering western liberal individualist society from cultural backgrounds that place more emphasis on the interdependence of the cosmos, and
h) if Buddhism has served to significantly bind immigrant communities.

Happily I wasn't asked to cover Einstein's Theory of Relativity! But it was an enjoyable experience since it allowed me to bring my strengths in Multiculturalism, South Asian Canadian Literature and Buddhism. Clearly somebody had been keeping track of my multiple tracks.

By 1994, Markham had come to be heavily developed, with many a new immigrant group settling down in the new sub-divisions, adding their own colour (both metaphorically and literally) and cultural prejudices and biases. The traditionally white neighbourhood couldn't help noticing the 'encroachment' either. Some issues apparently thus emerging, there comes to be formed a Committee on Race and Ethnocultural Equity of Markham (CREEM). By letter of Aug 22, 1994, and in the names of Harvey Goodman, CREEM Chair and Paul Marcus, Conference Chair, I would get an invitation to make a presentation at a Community Forum on "Community Response to Hate Crimes" to be held on October 2, 1994, co-sponsored by the Ministry of Citizenship. On the Panel with me, "Developing a Community Model to Respond to Hate Group Activities" was Madge Logan, Superintendent, North York Board of Education, David Tsubouchi, Town of Markham Councillor, Mark Sandler, Senior Legal Counsel, League for Human Rights of B'nai Brith of Canada, and Sun columnist Bill Dunphy. Educator Dr Helene Ijaz served as Moderator.

I talk on "Responding to Hate with Understanding", not taking an oppositional stance but making the point that "Entangled in one infinite net, we are all haters and the hated". I base this on the story of the Jewel Net of Indra (Lord of gods in popular Buddhism): "... there is a wonderful net that stretches out from the abode of Indra, infinitely, and in all directions. In each eye of the net is a glittering jewel, and since the net is infinite, the jewels are infinite, too. Now if we looked at any one of them closely, we'll find that *all* the jewels are reflected in the polished surface of this one jewel. And each of the jewels reflected in this one jewel also reflects all the other jewels". Thus every human being is connected to one and all, and by extension, hate groups come to be conditioned by those hated. This reciprocity is also based in the Buddha's Teaching of Conditioned Co-origination, where nothing comes out of nothing and that and every phenomenon results from other phenomena.

I would later use my column in the *Toronto Star* Nov 26, 1994 to write a piece under the title, "There's a Little Piece of Hatred in Every One of Us". Here I was making the point about Buddha's Teaching how constituting every sentient being (i.e., each of us, having six senses) are passion, anger and ignorance.

While there would be many an other presentation – to church groups, synagogues and secular groups, one that seemed to have thrown a stone to a hornet's nest was when invited to speak to the Ontario Advisory Council on Multiculturalism and Citizenship of which I had been a member for 5 years. Such Councils had been set up both at the Federal and the Provincial levels, and had served a very useful function at a time when nobody had a handle on Multiculturalism. The members appointed to them coming from the different communities, the Councils provided the raw data of a field study upon which to develop policy. Indeed, while many a proposal that would come from us to the government would make the officials hem and haw, we find them seeping into government policy and practice over time.

But by the late eighties, Multiculturalism had established itself firmly as Canadian policy and practice, and there was enough information and policies already in place at all levels – from governments to Boards of Education to Chambers of Commerce. Thus, invited back by the OACMC to make a presentation, I would argue, to the horror of the membership, among which were some of the colleagues I had worked with, that the next best recommendation to the government would be *to disband the Council itself*! It must have come as a real bombshell, particularly to some for whom membership helped establish leadership in the community, and political clout. Multiculturalism was also by now a sacred cow, explaining why Neil Bissoondath's *Selling Illusions* clearly touched a raw nerve. It also explains why no publisher also wanted to touch my own publication, *How to Kick Multiculturalism in its Teeth* (see next), not even its sub-title 'with critical compassion' helping to soothe the nerves. I claim no credit, but the Council was indeed disbanded not much later, the government itself coming to realize that it was no longer functional.

9.4 Kicking Multiculturalism in Its Teeth! History of a book

Having been a foot soldier in the trenches of Multiculturalism to help make Canada a better place for all of us to live in peace, prosperity and harmony, I was getting somewhat anxious and jittery of what I came to

With Vian Ewart, *Saturday Star* Editor,

be increasingly seeing as the abuse of Multiculturalism by minorities, and the poor way things were being managed by the authorities and the mainstream. Expressing this opinion to Vian Ewart, my *Saturday Star* Editor, over lunch, one of several we would have over the years, he opines, "Why don't you write a book?" By now, Neil Bissoondath had stirred the multicultural pot with his book, *Selling Illusions*. So, taking Vian's suggestion seriously, I mull over it, when I begin to work on it, partly to thank Canada for nurturing me for 25 years since returning from Sri Lanka.

The work was an insider critique, based in my experience as an Executive Member of the Ontario Advisory Council on Multiculturalism and Citizenship, advisor to governments, member of the Ontario Provincial Interfaith Committee on Chaplaincy, grassroots membership in a host of other governmental, institutional, secular, religious and interfaith activities at the grassroots level as well as teaching at both the post-secondary and secondary levels.

The book was in a sense perhaps a *mea culpa* as well. In my earliest articles on Multiculturalism, there was every reason for the majority community to be mad as hell with me, as the few readers who would respond to my columns made no bones about. I was advocating the dismantling of many a hallowed tradition upon which the nation of Canada had been built. Mind you, it was not that I should be credited with any original thinking in all of this. It was merely an attempt at furthering the intent of the Multiculturalism Act. Unlike now, there were no experts on the issue at the time, and I happened to have some personal experience. And I had just stepped into the waiting shoes.

But where I erred is perhaps that I had taken a completely oppositional stance. Doing my doctoral studies at OISE, I had been exposed to Marxist sociology, and having dug canals to divert water to thirsty fields in Sri Lanka as a Sarvodaya worker, my thesis itself had come to be a critique of western developmental models.

But beginning to note how the mainstream was now beginning to cave in under minority pressures, I had begun to be critical of the other side of the divide, beginning in 1990 (Oct 29) with my Star column, "Minority Ethnics' Build Walls of Seclusion'. Having been a Member of the Canada Day Committee, I had filed a commentary for broadcast, though not broadcast, over CBC Radio "In Praise of Canada" the same year (June 26, in commemoration of Canada Day). A piece written in 1993, "When a Majority People is Pushed against the Wall" though not published, brought the issue into the open limelight, at least in my mind. Later, "Let's Have Some Rules for Family" spoke to an issue that was close to the Christian community as it was to a Buddhist, not to mention other spiritual persuasions, including the Secular Humanist. A December 9, 1995 column, "Let's Help Christians Celebrate" was in response to what I saw was the unfair treatment that the Christian community had now come to be subjected to, manoevering Christmas into some politically correct 'Holiday season'. I would write a Letter to the Editor in the Star, titled "British population of Toronto suffers reverse racism" (Sept. 7, 1999), in defence of the British

Canadians, Linda Cuthbert responding, "As Sugunasiri says, the British culture and influence in Canada should be recognized and celebrated and not shoved aside in the pursuit of Multiculturalism" (Sept 15, 1999, A 21). Earlier she says that "Sugunasiri eloquently expresses what I have often thought but wouldn't dare express publicly in our politically correct environment".

So I had now in a small way begun to draw the attention of my readers and listeners to the other side of the divide, having earlier come through from the Multiculturalism *rah rah rah* perspective, and in the Globe & Mail piece of July 18, 1991, I had actually sought to give a balanced view, both castigating and encouraging the mainstream as well as the sidestream.

In its manuscript form, my book had the rather sober, and sophisticated-sounding title, but perhaps also rather symbolic title, *The Crosswalk and the Strap: Towards multicultural Healing through Critical Compassion*. The 'crosswalk' reference was to the many layers of legal protection available to new Canadians, that would encourage, as I would argue, the misuse and abuse of the Canadian largesse, with a spadeful of help from the ever-ready lawyer. And the 'strap' stood for a checks and balances component, as in responsible public or private undertaking, to our policy of Multiculturalism. The intent of healing reflected my view that society was bleeding from Multiculturalism, and the critical compassion again to underscore the importance of being both compassionate but also critical, a combination that stems from my Buddhist background. In an apparent self-maturation into my Buddhist Middle Path, and continuing my *kalyana mitta* 'bosom buddy life-long pal' mode, it came to have a sub-title, 'towards multicultural healing with critical compassion'.

With a view to bring about some healing, I would write a section, "In Defence of Canada":

In Defence of Canada

If in the last chapter, we used our brush of classical and systemic racism on Canada lavishly, we must now.. stand up before the International Court of Justice in the defence of Canada:

Mi-Lords & mi-ladies, we accept our responsibility for the mistreatment of toutes les autrephones (all othertongue speakers) who came upon our shores, but we simply couldn't have been any different, given the historical times and conditions. No other European power, nor indeed for that matter any other non-European nation we know of, acted differently either, we submit your Honours.

Ethnocentrism was the tacitly accepted international norm. We know of no ethno-cultural community, or nationality or nation in power, that did not mistreat one or another community within its political boundaries, be it at the national, community, tribe or clan level. We bow our heads in deep respect if indeed there were to be such examples of humanity from which we certainly were not fortunate enough to benefit.

But if our past was bad, we submit we have tried hard, darned hard, if I may be permitted a slang to emphasize the point, over the last two and a half decades to be exemplary. While we note that most other countries north south east or west, continue to be 'classically racist', to offer the same garland we have been honoured with, we alone pioneered steps to rectify our thinking-behaviour.

We accept that we sometimes stumbled, and fell by the wayside, but we quickly picked up and continued the journey. We are so far away from where we started that our forefathers might not recognize their land. But we are humbly proud, mi-lords and mi-ladies, that we have taken these giant steps to make all our peoples feel fully Canadian.

In order that you may get a first-hand taste of what we are today, we invite you into our supermarkets to see what kind of exotic foods are stacked up in the shelves and how garlic, once the very epitome of what was wrong with the non-European, has become not only 'haute cuisine' but 'cuisine bourgeoisie' as well, which the dictionary translates as 'homely fare'.

While we invite you to get the benefit of our westerntrained doctors for your run of the mill illnesses and surgical needs, allow us to introduce you to your alternative therapies: Chinese acupuncture and Indian Ayurveda, Tai Chi and yoga, energy-rejuvenating Chi-gong, Transcendental meditation and Buddhist meditation.

Watch our TV channels to enchant your eyes with our multi-colourful newscasters, commentators and ad appearances. Or open up the pages of our newspapers .. Go to any office, bank or school to see our multicolored and multitalented people. The list can go on and on.

To sum up, then, your Honours, judge us not from our past sins and misdemeanours, but from our present efforts and endeavours. We thank you for bringing us to your presence so we can make a statement the whole world can hear. And if anybody, from within the world community or from within our own national community, has any suggestions to help us do things better multicultural, we are only a phone call away.

We have, in our submission, leapfrogged 25 years of history merely to begin to show that painting Canada with the brush of classical racism and leaving it at that is only to tell half the story. For the other half tells of a Canada equally non-racist and large-minded

But before continuing, just a comparative comment on my comment that "ethnocentrism was the tacitly accepted international norm", etc. Taking the period of time in question relating to Canada, i.e., 1867 on, it would be equally true in the case of Sri Lanka during this British occupation when the Sinhala, the majority people, were not even allowed to practice their religion. While the colonizers undertook to respect the "Boodoo religion" at the Kandyan Treaty of 1818, as a condition of surrender, "the ink on the paper had not dried out when they went back on their word". As if almost taking a cue, later in the thirties, when the Buddhists went in a religious procession, it was stoned by the Sinhala Christians! It was after the petitioning the British government in person by the American Col. Olcott that they finally could celebrate Wesak (Rick Fields, 1981, 97ff). To give another example from personal knowledge, as School Principal, my father earned half the salary of one in the English medium. So the statement would be equally true in the case of colonial Ceylon.

In the closing chapter, I add the following:

And now if I were to pick a single Canadian ethnocultural community deserving praise, it would be... not the Western, or the Eastern European, but the British. How ironic! Wasn't this the very group that was culpable of keeping all other groups out? Yes, but it is also they who used their power to change things around.

If I were to now pick a specific religious community who earns the highest credit for promoting Multiculturalism it would not be, however, the Anglican Church of the British stock. Not the Catholic either. It would be the home-grown United Church of Canada. It alone had, during this formative Multiculturalism, an interfaith policy, and a paid employee specifically charged with the task of outreaching to other faith groups and working within its own congregations to make them accepting of Multiculturalism and multifaith......

So I invite the reader, of whatever colour, to look at the next White woman and man you meet, and offer a smile, for offering us an olive branch, and ushering in the multicultural spring we are enjoying today, and for continuing to water its plants and flowers to make this land of ours even more beautiful, more fragrant, more luscious and more precious.

Though I was not unknown in multicultural circles, in order to gain additional legitimacy, I had also requested endorsements by some well known figures.

In his Preface, Prof. George Bancroft, one time multicultural Director of the Ontario Ministry of Citizenship calls the work " ... informative, insightful and passionately written ... I think you have written a rather controversial document." Prof. Uma Parameswaran of the University of Winnipeg, herself an author, sees me "courageously" taking up "the risk of losing the sympathy of his readers, both white and non-white, to say what he consider needs to be said in unequivocal terms. He throws satirical punches at both." York University Professor Frank Birbalsingh, on the back cover, notes: "Through perceptive, balanced insights, and a style that is both informed and witty, the book provides an informed and lucid position of Canadian Multiculturalism... supported by wide-ranging research, authoritative personal anecdotes and a passionate commitment to Canada." June Callwood, characterizes it in the words, "This is an astonishing book – sometimes profound and wise, sometimes maddening, but always lively and full of élan." Sheena Sharp, an architect, and a senior member of the Humanist Association, says that the book "pulls issues and ideas about our multicultural experiment out of the hidden recesses of society into the sunlight. Patricia Weldon, a Senior Educator and Administrator notes how "there is enough ammunition for all sides in the debate on Multiculturalism."

Though the manuscript comes to be over 200 printed pages, writing was, as I would soon find out, the easy part. Getting it published by the establishment, however, was something else. Multiculturalism was the sacred cow nobody would touch. No publisher, from McLelland & Stewart (1995), Macmillan (1996), Key Porter, Penguin Canada, McGill/Queen's University Press (1997) and Anglican Church Publishing went for it. While another said "your book has merit", it didn't "fit right now with our current editorial plans." Another noting similarly that "it isn't right for us", encourages me to submit it to other publishers. Submitted to another, it is suggested that I approach "a trade publisher with a list that includes ethnic and multicultural issues". Was I getting the run around or was I getting the run around!

York University Professor Frank Birbalsingh

The United Church alone shared with me its views of the manuscript. In answer to their first criterion, "Does the book meet a perceived need?" the answer given is "yes". Does the book ring true? Yes "in many ways...." Will the work be useful for the intended audience? "Definitely - would be useful for students, inspirational to leaders, politicians, educators, immigrants and general readers." I couldn't think of a wider audience. Answering a question as to what other works compete with it, "Bissoondath's 'Selling Illusions" is the only one... It's written from a different perspective." Would you recommend publication? "Yes, I think it has a good spiritual content.. and is an honest attempt to look at Multiculturalism from different angles. This is a subject that many people have strong views about. This book might help others to understand their own feelings better."

Asked by an Author's Agent how my manuscript differs from other books, I had spoken to the same issue:

> "Indeed what specifically prompted me to write this book is a comment made by a reviewer of Bissoondath's *Selling Illusions* that when it comes to Multiculturalism, there are only two sides – for or against. But my immediate reaction was, "No, there is middle position, too" And it is that

middle position that the ms seeks to capture. That is to say that I am both sympathetic to and critical of both sides of the multicultural divide.." (Letter of May 20, 1996).

The reply I got from the Agent was basically the same as what I got from the publishers. "I'm sorry to say that I will not be able to offer you representation. The personal autobiographical approach didn't quite work for me ..." Another publisher saw it differently: "it may be a bit too academic"!

Finally, asked by an agent what I would suggest for the back cover for promotional purposes, I suggest the following: "the book may provoke some and appease others ... [But it is] written out of a felt need, and out of an understanding of both the 'Minority' and the 'Majority'."

Everything needing a professional touch had been attended to: getting in touch with the Writers' Union of Canada, getting a list of Canadian Literary Agents, sending a few sample pages along with an outline, a letter of introduction giving my qualifications - Executive Member, Ontario Advisory Council on Multiculturalism and Citizenship; Member, Ontario Provincial Interfaith Committee on Chaplaincy; Member, Canada Day Committee (Ontario), *Toronto Star* Columnist, et cetera, et cetera et cetera... I had appended a few of my *Toronto Star* columns as well.

Yet a publisher's reply opines, ".. the book's potential in the marketplace is a matter of concern for us". So it was the bottom line that was the concern of every publisher. Hmmmm! Now I began to wonder. May be I was a cruel publisher myself in a past life, only looking for the bottom line! Thank you, kamma hand.

Frustrated though I was, I was in good company. Vassanji, as noted, had to go to the UK to get his first collection of short stories, *Uhuru Street*, published. The now well respected writer Nourbese Phillips, whose novel *Harriett's Daughter* I had reviewed for the *Toronto Star*, would once tell me of her experience of being told that her stories would never be touched by the Canadian reader because the characters were Black.

Energized by the frustration perhaps, and as advised by the Course Director of a self-publishing course I had taken, I set up the *Village Publishing House*, and self-published it, having the manuscript copy-edited. And Course Director Steve Manning thought that my title was too pansy. People like to know 'how' things are done. Hence the popularity of 'How to do' manual type books. Reflecting perhaps my unhappiness at the direction the country was going under Multiculturalism, now emerged the angry title *How to Kick Multiculturalism in Its Teeth,* with a subtitle intended to mitigate the blow *'an insider look with critical compassion'*. While the book indeed talked about the welfare cheaters, multicultural criminals, bogus refugee claimants, etc. the reader that responded to my Star piece had talked about, the educator in me would go on to provide an alternative model, a publishing Agent thinking it not fitting. Still a hundred or so left out of an original print of 1000, the title was again changed to a tamer one, *Towards multicultural Growth: a look at Canada from Classical Racism to Neo- Multiculturalism* In its latest rendition, a digital version of the book has come to be published online by Mr. Sheriyar Patel of COOPERJAL Limited U.K, under its IDEAINDIA.COM series.

If the publishing hurdle was cleared by throwing my own money at it, it didn't take me long to face the next hurdle – getting it reviewed. Sent to the major newspapers, I was to be told that self-published works were not reviewed by them. By now,

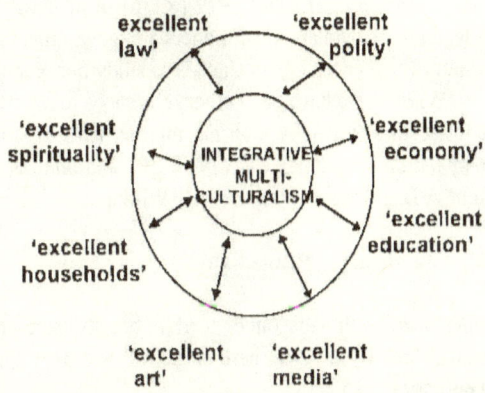

The 'Excellent Social Hadron' for building the Second Multicultural Cycle

my own contacts with the *Star* having faded, I was dealing with a new crop of Editors who barely knew me. Ahem, I must have said to myself. So my effort came to be scuttled by what I have come to call a joint Agent-Publisher-Reviewer Mafia!

But it did get reviewed by two academics. One of them practically dismissed it, having only read the first part, and not bothering with the more creative part where I had developed what I called the 'Excellent Social Hadron' for building the Second Multicultural Cycle.

Prof. Suzanne Majhanovich of the University of Western Ontario saw it in a different, and more positive, light:

> *In summary, this is a useful book written in an informal, conversational style – the better, no doubt, to engage Canadians in general in the discussion. ... the author states he makes no pretensions of having produced a scholarly tome aimed at academics. Still, he has included some very useful information on the development of Multiculturalism from his informed perspective, and his challenge to Canadians to enter the debate to rescue what is good in Multiculturalism is heartfelt and worthy. Even if some of his suggestions are outrageous and provocative, they do make the reader think. Perhaps they were offered in sly irony to entice the reader into thinking about the issues in new ways. Even the title of the book, "Kick Multiculturalism in its [rather than the] teeth" may suggest that Canadians should eliminate not Multiculturalism itself, but the teeth of Multiculturalism that have impeded the social benefits the policy could bring to the country.*

It was on the basis of the book that I came to be interviewed by Karlheinz Maiterth for a piece that would appear in a Canadian German publication,

Canada Journal, October 1999 (p. 36). And it was with interest that I met a delegation of scholars, practitioners and government personnel from a European country (Netherlands?), in Canada to study our practice of Multiculturalism.

While there have been other references to my work here and there, I found it interesting to discover on the internet (in 2010) that it finds a reference in *Brunner and Suddarth's Textbook of Canadian Medical-Surgical Nursing* by Rene A Day, Pauline Paul, Beverly Williams.

9.5 Who, then, is a 'Canadian'?

If the Opening Prayers, out of need for brevity, excerpted the definitive paragraph from it (below, in bold), here is the full text as it appeared in the *Toronto Star* (February 4, 1989):

> *Alien hordes. That's what the term 'ethnic' came to be associated with in prewar years. By 1930, an ethnic was, by dictionary definition, someone who was 'neither Christian nor Jewish,' the implication was "a heathen."*
>
> *Today sociologists define an ethnic community as "an involuntary group of people who share the same culture."*
>
> *So, none of us can help it. We are - Anglo-Saxons, Jews, Francophones, Native People, Blacks, Chinese, South Asians, Arabs, Latin Americans - all ethnics! Just as Margaret Atwood says, we're all immigrants, even if we were born here.*
>
> *No doubt some, like the Native People who were the exclusive inhabitants of Canada 10,000 years ago and the Anglo-Saxons and Francophones who laid claim to the land 200 years ago, are "old ethnics" compared to the "new ethnics."*
>
> *Who, then is a "Canadian?"*
>
> *A family friend, of English origins, highlighted the issue for me recently when he wondered out loud who in his family would be a Canadian and who not. He and his wife were born and raised in England, their 20-year-old son was only a year when he came here, and their daughter was born in Canada.*
>
> *By International law, of course, the daughter is "Canadian." But the brother, six years her elder, is hardly any different from her - in language, food, taste in fashion and music, etc. Naturally. They were both educated in Canadian schools. So is he not Canadian?*
>
> *When it comes to parents, they still prefer Beethoven to the Beatles, or to Gordon Lightfoot.*
>
> *Their Canadianness has never been questioned. But the issue cam to be raised because we have mutual friends, among both old ethnics and new ethnics, of white, black, brown, yellow skin colour, and in between, who have the same history but have had a different experience.*
>
> *Indeed some of these friends have their roots among the loyalist*

Black Canadians of Nova Scotia. The children, whatever the ethnic origin, watch Hockey Night in Canada as they eat popcorn, wear Roots sweatshirts and speak Canadian English fluently. Their parents drink Canadian lager, pay $50 for a dinner with a rotating view from atop the CN Tower and attend concerts at Roy Thomson Hall.

Some of them are Christians - Catholics, Protestants, Rastafarians, Geek Orthodox. Others are Jewish, Muslim, Hindu, Buddhist, Sikh, Zoroastrian, not to mention non-believers and Rational Humanists...and heathens.

The traditional model of the "nation-state," born of the European experience, where an entire people bound by a national border share the same ethnicity, birth status, language, culture, etc. and believe in the same god, clearly does not fit the Canadian experience.

We can, of course, come close to it by defining a Canadian as one with links to the Old Boys' Network and has access to jobs, privilege, wealth, power and social recognition. But the Canadian sensibility would no doubt loathe such a narrow definition.

[Governor-General] *Jeanne Sauve speaks French as her first language. The premier of P.E.I.* [Joe Ghiz] *is of Lebanese origin.* [Enviornmentalist-Scientist] *David Suzuki is a Japanese Canadian.* [Poet] *Irving Layton was born in Romania.* [Federal MP] *Charles Caccia speaks English with a non-British accent. And many a Professor in Canadian universities still retains his American citizenship.*

A Country of immigrants and ethnics, old or new, calls for a more flexible definition of Canadianness. Try this one on for psychological comfort:

A Canadian is someone living in Canada; considers Canada to be his or her permanent home, come hell or high water, is able to communicate with other Canadians, in English or French, in whatever accent and dialect, but without giving up any original language facility, respects, and is willing to share other people's values, customs, etc. in such a way as to contribute to a developing and changing Canadian culture, and proudly claims "Je suis canadien(ne)" or "I'm Canadian," not by the involuntary accident of birth but by conscious choice.

To be sure, such a definition is not neat and tidy, it may even be nebulous and slippery. But such is the nature of Canadian society. Perhaps with time we might be able to do some tightening up.

However, what we really need is not definitions. Simply our traditional Canadian large-heartedness. **The moment we stop asking the question, "Where are we from?" we will cease to see alien hordes. The moment we begin to recognize and accept, the claims to Canadian nationality, we will see 25 million Canadians old and new ethnics, walking through the frontier of our hearts.** [Bold added.]

A very popular piece, it had already found its way, in its full version, to an Anthology, just a year after its publication, by a Commercial Publisher, Nelson Canada. This was in *Viewpoints: Reflections in Non-fiction* (1990), edited by Christine McClaymont, under the heading , "Oh Canada". Among others featured in the anthology were Naturalist and Scientist David Suzuki, CBC journalist Erika Ritter, writer and academic Myrna Kostash, author Farley Mowat, Journalists Christie Blatchford and Ian Brown, and Margaret Visser, to pick up the public names I am familiar with.

The piece would find its way to another Anthology in 1996, *Dimensions II*, sub-titled, "Precise Thought and Language in the Essay", edited by Glen Kirkland & Richard Davies, for Gage Publishers in Toronto. Here again, I would find myself in high company, first finding berth with Nelson Mandela in the section under the heading 'Transitions'. Keeping me company in other sections would be June Callwood, David Suzuki, Roberta Bondar and Bertrand Russell.

The piece still apparently in circulation fourteen years after its first publication, it would find its way to yet another Government of Ontario publication, *Moving On*, in a 'Readings Selection for Canadian Students' (1993), edited by a foursome, Christine Strauss, Marie Clayden, Dianne Fenner and Christine McAdam. Here I am in the company of the CBC Anchor of a quarter century or more, Peter Gzowski, humourist Stephen Leacock, David Chilton of *The Wealthy Barber* fame, Carol Shields, Justin Trudeau, Maya Angelou, EJ Pratt and Joy Kogawa among others.

10 LIFE IN THE INTERFAITH LANE

10.1 Envisioning Vision TV: a Midwifery Role

My entry to Interfaith activities had, of course, taken place around 1979 when I joined the World Conference on Religion for Peace just following completion of my PhD, and which initiated me into all my Buddhist activities. But my next involvement came to be about 8 years later, when I became a member of the Interfaith Sub-Committee of the Ontario Advisory Council on Multiculturalism and Citizenship. The only Buddhist in the 60 member body, my membership was automatic. Chaired by the late Dr Vara Singh, we dealt with many an issue relating to Interfaith relations, beginning with the very definition of 'Interfaith'.

Religion had come to be part of Multiculturalism since the Consultation we had been invited to by the federal Assistant Deputy Minister, Dr. Noel Kinsella. Pursuant to that decision, the Canadian Radio and Telecommunication Commission (CRTC hereafter) had issued a challenge to the Religious communities to come together to establish an Interfaith TV station. At that time, the only religious community to have their own TV network was the Christian Evangelical, 100 Huntley Street, and it must have been with the intent of opening up the airwaves to other communities as well, by way of leveling the playing field, that the Commission must have hit upon the idea.

The call had come to the Chair of the OACMC, perhaps as the largest of the Provincial Multicultural bodies, and Dr Mavis Burke would pass it along to the sub-committee. Any kind of Interfaith activity in Canada had come to be primarily if not exclusively a mere Christian interdenominational exchange. The exception perhaps was the Canadian Council of Christians and Jews. A Papal document had by now come to encourage Catholics to work with Protestants, and by extension, with other religious communities. But there was not much action on the ground. So it was not surprising that there was some footdragging at the Sub-Committee about the chance of success at such an initiative. First of all, what authority did we, a self-appointed hodge-podge group of adherents of different religious communities, have over, e.g., the already well-established Christian communities? And other than the Jews, minority religious communities did not have any overall organizational structure either. And, even if we were able to bring together a group of people from the different communities, however unrepresentative they may be, will they agree to work together? There had never been a history of any such intrafaith – meaning within the religion, or interfaith, across religions, many a minority religious community new to Canada and barely trying to keep their heads above water. Who in each of these communities would we even talk to?

While all these legitimate questions were being raised, my fingers were itching. There was this challenge from the CRTC, and it would be a shame to let go of an opportunity to work together. I had written a piece in the *Toronto Star*, "Let's speed up the good work of Dialogue" (Jan 21, 1984). Besides, with every religion advocating kindness, tolerance and such other values, it would be a good test of these values, with Multiculturalism providing an additional impetus. So I would sketch a series of steps that could result in bringing the religious communities together under the auspices of the OACMC sub-committee.

It was with delight then that Dr Vara Singh welcomed the religious reps to a luncheon meeting. Conspicuous by their absence were the Catholics and the Jews. The CRTC call presented, we were happy to see the participants agreeing to explore the possibility of working towards a multifaith channel. One of the immediate outcomes of the meeting was that two sub-groups came to be formed. One was the Canadian Interfaith Network (CIN), to work as an umbrella group under which all Christian communities could come together, the United Church of Canada taking the leadership. The other was the Canadian Interfaith Coalition (CIC), an umbrella group under which all the *minority* religious communities could work together. This would include the Zoroastrians, Hindus, Buddhists, Muslims, Sikhs and Unitarians, to list them in their historical order. All basically from the sub-continent of South Asia, the group represented practically the whole gamut of spirituality, from the monotheistic Zoroastrianism and Islam, polytheistic Hinduism, to non-theistic Buddhism, to Sikhism that had emerged as an amalgam of Hinduism and Islam. The Unitarians happened to be the only surprise. Primarily a white community, it was, as I was made to understand, a mixed community serious about spirituality but with a variety of belief systems.

While there were believers in a Christian–like God, there were also Buddhists with no belief in God. The thread that united them was the interest in promoting unity. Native spirituality had no particular representation, although the Christian churches had come to be making contacts with the Native people, many of them now Christian.

With Deo Kernahan and Charles J Humber, Editor, *Canada at the Millennium*

While the CIN was generally constituted of official representatives, the CIC came to be made up of self-appointed Reps. Such as Yours Truly. Having stepped down from the position of Coordinator of the Buddhist Federation of Toronto, I played no formal or official part in any Buddhist organization. Thus, a 'free agent' so to speak, I came to volunteer since there was no one around who seems to be interested in mounting an interfaith channel. Among my colleagues would be Muin Muinuddin for the Muslim community, and Deo Kernahan from the Hindu community. The Unitarians were kind enough to provide space for our meetings at the recently renovated Unitarian Church on St Clair at Avenue Road.

While the CIN group could speak for over 80% of the population, that would still be Christian, and would not meet the CRTC mandate of being interfaith. In other words, without the active support of the CIC, no application to establish a TV station would have gone very far. Dr David Nostbakken, who had by now been hired to lead the charge in working towards meeting the CRTC challenge, had successfully garnered the support of the Christian communities across Canada, traveling together with other representative members, including the Buddhist, Prof Stanley Fefferman. But, the strategist that he was, David, a doctoral colleague of mine at OISE, also made it a point to meet with each of the members of the CIC.

A broad-based support enlisted, CIN successfully applied for a licence, in 1988, to operate an Interfaith Channel, indeed hiring some capable TV personalities, with Peter Flemington as Director of Programing. But those of us in the CIC were to be disappointed when we found out that although without our support, there would have been no approval, when it came to hiring, none of us had been consulted, or invited to serve. Not even at the Board level were we invited to serve. The outfit thus ended being basically white, this after years of Multiculturalism! However, the choice of Rita Deverell, of West Indian Black background, as co-host of the regular daily Vision TV telecast along with Ron Keast, and later, the respected veteran journalist, Tom Harpur, mitigated some of our concerns. The administration seems to have responded to some of the criticism by drawing upon, by 1994, the able on-air TV Presence of writer Neil Bissoondath as host of a film series, and Deo Kernahan as another member of the Skylight Team.

I also had been invited to appear on the newly minted Vision TV (1992, 1994) in relation to the Canadian Constitution, as a member of the Ad Hoc Interfaith Committee. But the more memorable appearance was when, in a commentary, I urged fellow Canadians to light bulbs on all roof tops across the nation to celebrate the birth of Jesus Christ! The Government of Ontario had put an official stop to putting up decorations at Queen's Park, obviously under pressure from minority religions. While I, as a Buddhist, was irritated enough to write a piece in the *Toronto Star*, I would also go on Vision TV. The well-known amiable host Rita Deverell, a Christian herself, would comment that, "Oh, it must surely be uniquely Buddhist!", for no Christian would presumably dare do so, put firmly under the minority foot. Reading my *Toronto Star* piece more recently at the Toronto School of Theology Christmas party, I would send copies to MPP's of the Ontario Legislature.

I came to be truly humbled when I was invited to appear on June Callwood's continuing Program, 'National Treasures'. Appearing on the program on December 22, 1994, I had been asked about how to deal with cultural pluralism. I had told her the basis I would use to determine which idiosyncrasy of my own culture and upbringing I should hold on to in a pluralistic context, and which I shouldn't, as I continued to live in Canada. I would ask two questions of myself:

1. Is this (trait, value, habit I cherish so dearly) good for me?
2. Is it good for society?

> *If the answer to both is yes, I would continue to root for it. But if the answer to the first is yes, and no to the second, then I'd ditch it.*

She was to say that she had never heard of such an approach..

I frankly did not know what is it that June Callwood saw in me to be invited to appear on her Program. Doing research for this Memoir, I was to come across some information on her program, which came to be be characterized as "a marvelous sampling of the outstanding Canadians" (Vision TV, *Great Viewer's Guide*, October 1994, v. 6, no 6, p. 32). In the proposal she had submitted to Vision TV, she had listed the criteria to be used in selecting the 'Canadian Treasure':

1. The person is known nationally.
2. The person is respected.
3. There is something special about the way the person lives his/her life (not what the person does).
4. The person has a thought out, as opposed to random and reactive, existence.
5. The person is able to define himself or herself.

(Vision TV, *Great Viewer's Guide*, October 1994, v. 6, no 7, p. 44).

Wow! So was I known nationally? I don't know! But, of course, I had travelled across the land, researching S Asian Canadian Literature, working in Interfaith relations, and as we shall see, setting up Chapters of the Buddhist Council of Canada and promoting Nalanda College of Buddhist Studies. But I was humbled to be among writers, artistes, actors and activists such as Margaret Atwood, Maureen Forrester, William Hutt, Farley Mowat, Buffy Sainte-Marie, Charles Pachter, Phil Fontaine and Rosemary Brown. And of course, I had come to be the Buddhist spokesperson for over a decade a (See Hori & McLellan, in *Wild Geese, Buddhism in Canada* (McGill U Press)).

Dr. Steven Aung, VP, Buddhist Council of Canada (awarded Order of Canada)

Vision would also open up air-time to groups to present their own programs. While I had on several occasions offered to provide leadership in presenting a regular series on Buddhism, there seemed to be no interest within the community to find the money, even for the lowest rate - shoulder time (past midnight).

Richard Landau, in charge of diversity programming, had found some money so there could be more local material on Vision TV. Finding an opportunity to present Buddhist material, I would get the nod to do two video productions. One was to do a film on Dr. Steven Aung of Edmonton, a past VP of Buddhist Council of Canada, and active in the Buddhist community in Edmonton. A General Practitioner who was also a Qui Gong Master, he had come to successfully incorporate Chinese medicine with western Medicine in his practice. The government of Canada was to honour him later with the Order of Canada. Flying into Edmonton, I hired a cameraman who helped me with extensive filming. Dr Aung's extensive collection of Buddha figures from all around the world was impressive. And it was a delight to see him practice Qi Gong every morning, an activity we would capture on film, bright and

with Sister Benedetta

early on a very cold day.

The other video was to be on Sister Benedetta, a Roman Catholic nun, who had had the privilege of being in encounter with the late Tibetan teacher Chogyam Trungpa in Boulder, Colorado. This time my cameraman was Helmfried Muller, a practicing Buddhist from the Dharmadhatu on Bloor West. Again, I did hours of filming on site at the seminary in Oakville.

But organizing my material into a story, and bringing them to the studio, it failed to pass muster at the hands of an Editor assigned to me. By way of preparing myself for my new role as Film Director in the field of Cinematography, I had studiously gone through a handbook, *Videography – the guide to making videos* (1992), co-written by Peter Hitchcock and Richard Landau. Apparently I had not mastered well enough the art of producing good videos. Retaining a copy which I still have with me, I returned the original tapes to Dr. Aung, with apologies, and with a request that a film be done by a more able hand. The original tapes done on Sr. Benedetta, for anyone interested, remains with me.

10.2 Buddhist-Christian Dialogue

One of the activities that Prof. Stanley Fefferman had started upon as President of the Buddhist Council of Canada was to engage in a dialogue with Christians. As the Buddhist rep on the CIN - Canadian Interfaith Network, he had been traveling with them across Canada towards soliciting support for what emerged as Vision TV. It was the United Church

John Berthrong, Interfaith Officer, United Church of Canada, speaking at a luncheon at a Chinese Buddhist temple honouring him. At the table are Paul Hardman, Joe Than and Darshan Chaudharay

that had come to spearhead this thrust, it also being the only Christian sect to take its multicultural mandate serious enough to have a paid position. It is thus that Prof. Fefferman had come to arrange a series of dialogues along with Dr. John Berthrong, the Interfaith Officer of the United Church, and Chinese scholar. Later he would join the Boston School of Theology as Associate Director.

Continuing the thrust after becoming the President, Buddhist Council of Canada, I sought a different direction in the B-C Dialogue. The focus of the Dialogue thus far had been on how similar Buddhism and Christianity were. But, if that were the case, I was to ask Dr Berthrong, why keep our labels – Buddhist and Christian? If clearly, then, the two are, surprise surprise, different from each other, I wondered why the Dialogue shouldn't be about our differences (as well)? Agreement from John was swift! Participating in the Dialogues were sister Benedetta herself, and Professors Will Oxtoby and David Waterhouse, among others. The tapes of the Dialogues remain in the repository of the Multicultural History Society of Ontario.

In a continuing attempt to maintain our relationship, John would invite me to their Annual Conventions when Rev Farquarson was elected the Moderator. It was indeed a pleasure to be able to meet a large number of dedicated Christians at such gatherings where we would make additional friendships. Not rarely would such connections end up in an invitation to talk at their church.

It was during this time that the World Council of Churches Annual Meeting came to be held in Seoul, Korea. Dr. Berthrong saw in this an opportunity to give real meaning to the concept of Interfaith Dialogue with Buddhists when he invited me to represent the Buddhists in Canada, taking his place. Accepting the gracious offer, I came to be one of the two Canadian delegates to the WCC meeting in Korea. This is how it was reported in *Buddhist-Christian Studies*, 1989, in a Report under News and Notes, by Prof. David Lockhead of the Vancouver School of Theology under the title, "Buddhists and Christians in the Search for Peace with Justice":

With United Church Moderator Rev. Walter Farquharson and Muin Muinidin

> *"Justice, Peace, and the Integrity of Creation" is the current theme for the work of the World Council of Churches. The Council's unit on Dialogue with People of Other Faiths has attempted to use that theme as the focus of Interfaith meetings which it has sponsored in recent years.*
>
> *The Christian concept of "creation" is one that presents some problems for Buddhists. As a result, when a meeting between Asian Buddhists and Christians was organized to meet in Seoul, Korea, in November 1988, the theme was announced as "Peace and Justice", Christians and Buddhist participants representing seven Asian countries: Sri Lanka, Tibet, Burma, Thailand, Hong Kong, Korea and Japan. Three North American observers were invited: Sandy Boucher, a Buddhist writer from Berkeley; David Lockhead, a Christian theologian from Vancouver; and Suwanda Sugunasiri, the president of the Buddhist Council of Canada.*

Stopping over in Japan en route to Korea, John would make arrangements for me to visit the Nanzan Institute in Kyoto, a Christian outfit working in the area of Japanese religions including Buddhism. It was headed by James W Heisig, and the two days I spent there also served as a reprieve from my jet lag.

Being only an observer, there was, luckily, not much I had to do at the Korean meeting, except add my two cents' worth in the various discussions. I would also meet Wesley Ariyarajah, a Tamil from Sri Lanka, who was the Secretary of the WCC.

The visiting delegates also came to be treated to a typical Korean wedding by way of an outing. While it may have been of cultural interest to the European delegates, there was nothing exciting about it for me who, coming from an eastern country, 'cultural weddings' were no surprise.

But I also had taken the opportunity to visit some Buddhist temples, one of them being the Headquarters of the Chogye Order, with an official temple in Toronto, the Bul Gwang Sa headed by Kwang Ok Sunim whom I would feature in a work edited by me, *Thus Spake the Sangha: Early History of Buddhism in Toronto* (2008). But the more memorable visit was to a temple up in the mountains, quite a bit of a climb even after going part of the way up by car. Meeting no resident monks, we had a look from the outside. I was impressed by the heating system, using hot water running along pipes running just under the floorboard.

But even more memorable would be what I saw coming down from the mountain and driving into the city centre - an Evangelical Christian Church that would hold 2000 people in a country that a generation ago was primarily Buddhist. The evangelicals had done a marvelous job of imprinting an image of a backward Buddhism in the backwoods, with nothing to offer for modern day living, and by contrast, a modern Christianity, serving as the wish-fulfilling tree for young Koreans in particular - to go western, make it to the west, learn English, and benefit from the largess of capitalism. Visiting an exclusive women's university, the message was writ large – on a T-shirt sold at a boutique: an emblem of the British Crown, with the words, 'God Save the Queen'! If the phenomenon of an increasingly Christianization made the Korean Buddhists uncomfortable, it was the Korean Christians, judging by the ones I met at least, who were concerned - that young Koreans were moving to Christianity for the wrong reasons. But the Evangelicals had all the reasons to be smiling from ear to ear. Working with Korean Buddhists in Canada later, it was with sadness that I would hear that Korean Christians and Korean Buddhists living in Canada did not get along well. Conflicts were within the family itself, where one or more members had seen the wisdom of retaining the tradition while others had come to embrace the western religion.

The traveling seemed to have prompted a poem related to flying:
CRY OF THE GREAT BIRD
Plane carrying the country's most powerful crash in Africa.
– news item.

I

Stretched wings aerating the arid land
Moscow to Washington, the Great Bird glides
On to the tarmac, pride in its passengers teeming,
Shrinking the world in half.

Huddled within paneled-oaks under the eagle eye
The very best concur, signing out wars
Setting on its way pigeons in a beeline.
That was forty five.

II

Decorated for its role, wearing the decal
In the music of its humming wings, the Great Bird
Spirits away the best, Ho Chi Ming City to Vatican City
Shrinking the world by a half and half again.

Glasses lifted, burning the midnight oil
The best compliment, stare, eat up a thousand pads.
But viewing in the table mirror their depleting heads
They dash to the bird in search of solace.

III

Offering the load to the heavens in uproar
In homage, vibrrrrating in...to.. a trance
In a grand finale of a suicidal act
The Great Bird sheds its wings, dousing
The engine with tears wrenched off the think tank,
Hiding in hot shame in a yellow, red blanket,
nosediving its anger in heated explosion
As it kisses the earth, renting
Miles apart heads and limbs
Of the very best that failed!
      (1988, Soeul, Korea)
      The Faces of Galle Face Green, 1995 (P. 40).

Before heading to take up his position at the Boston School of Theology, John was kind enough to invite Swarna and me to a lunch at a nearby restaurant. Not only was it that, in our estimation, he was one who could not be easily replaced, but I had worked with him so closely that I literally felt I was losing a brother! However, I was happy that he was moving on to better pastures, not in monetary or country terms, but in terms of the academic environment where he could better put to use his extensive Chinese scholarship.

With Paul Newman, Interfaith Officer, United Church of Canada

I was to be proven wrong when Rev. Paul Newman – oh, please don't line up, it's not the namesake on the silver screen!, came to replace John Berthrong. Author of *A Spirit Christology: Recovering the Biblical Paradigm of Christian Faith*, Paul and I would come to be, as with John, personal friends, enjoying many a chat at the United Church of Canada headquarters on St Clair between Yonge and Bay before it fell prey to the demolition crew in preparation of a new residence highrise. We would also jointly teach a course, Dynamics of Interfaith

He would also invite me to teach at a Summer Christian camp in beautiful Naramata. Going there with Swarna, we were to break journey at the Rocky Mountains, our first experience of the breathtaking splendour of the mountain range, reminding me of the Sigirya Rock of Sri Lanka, home to King Kassapa of the 7th-8th c.

Dipping into the pool, fed by a hot water spring, was an experience by itself. The next morning, it was in amazement we gazed at the rising sun over the peak, again reminding Swarna of the scene she had seen, climbing the Sripada mountain in Sri Lanka, holy to Buddhists, Christians and Muslims, where many a pilgrim would get to the top just to view the 'sun service' (*ira sevaya*), as the rising sun would dip as if in veneration of the peak. Breakfast, overlooking the wide green slopes was another great experience as we watched a wolf or two, and other animals, sauntering in search of food.

I was happy to be able to attend the World

On the way to Naramata, Swarna, and I were to break journey at the Rocky Mountains.

Parliament of Religions in 1993, reading with interest a news item, "World Religions Meet in Real Dialogue with the Devil". It was in the newspaper, *The New Federalist* (Aug. 30th), characterizing itself as the 'National Newspaper of the American System'. The Editorial had the title, "Save Christian Civilization". It was thanks to Paul and the

Sigirya Rock of Sri Lanka, home to King Kassapa of the 7th-8th c.

United Church of Canada that I was able to go to Chicago. While I was able to foot the travel bill, it was thanks to the generosity of UCC that I came to be one of four or five men sharing a hotel room. In the manner of the First Parliament in 1893, it was held in Chicago, with over 5000 religious people coming together for a few days of deliberation. Though not a speaker at a Plenary, but just sitting in the Assembly, I tried to imagine how Anagarika Dharmapala of Sri Lanka, as reported, must have electrified the august gathering a hundred years earlier with his renowned oratorical masterpiece, "The World's Debt to Buddha".

: While I was too small a player to be a Plenary speaker, I would make two presentations at smaller seminars, one of them titled, "The Science of Spirituality Across the Curriculum: Foundations to a School Spiritual Culture", a theme I would present at Queen's University in Kingston, Ontario, later.

Making a presentation at the World Parliament of Religions, 1993, Chicago

At the end of the World Parliament of Religions, I would write a piece in frustration, "Spiritual Tolerance Betrayed", but never getting published. *Toronto Star* Religion Editor, Michael McAteer, writing on the Parliament quotes that I was "disappointed by the triumphalism" of some faith groups "who aggressively promoted their particular brand of religion". Earlier (Aug 24, 1991), I come to be featured in a full page piece in the *Toronto Star* by Michael McAteer, with a half-page blow-up of a bust of Yours Truly alongside Archbishop Ted Scott, former Anglican Primate.

While in Chicago, I also took the opportunity to visit Samu Sunim's Temple, and meet Sujata, the resident teacher. It was a pleasure to meet her after quite some time, reflecting on how she had done the poster for the first WESAK in 1981. I was accompanied by Prof. Chatsumarn Kabilsingh, from Thailand, who would later go on to make history by being the first Thai woman to be ordained formally, thereby establishing the Thai Bhikkhuni (Nun's) Order.

10.3 'Tis no Reason to Steal Lord Jesus!

You will remember the reference above to the banning of Christmas lights from the Ontario Legislature. This was something that this Buddhist couldn't stomach! After all, Multiculturalism was ushered in by Christians. And minority communities had come to cry from their rooftops how wonderful their religions were and how multicultural Canada should not fail to allow, nay encourage, to practice them. But in the same breath, the majority community was being denied their right to practice their own. And that's when I went on air on *Vision TV* to urge all Canadians to light up all of their houses and government buildings to share the good news of the birth of Jesus. Here are, for your entertainment, the lines I wrote later in my *Toronto Star* column, of Dec 9, 1995. When I was featured at the Toronto's Harbourfront Reading Series (March 10, 1996) upon publication of my first collection of poetry, *The Faces of Galle Face Green*, 1995, I sang it it to the tune of 'Deck the Halls . .', inviting the audience to join in. So here go the lines:

Poetry reading at Toronto's Harbourfront International Reading Series (March 10, 1996)

> *Deck the buildings with boughs of holly*
> *fa la la la laa la laa laa laa.*
> *Stem this tide of multicultural folly*
> *fuddle duddle daa da daa daa daa.*
> *Born this nation of Christianity,*
> *fa la laa la la laa laa laa laa.*
> *Like you not this stubborn reality?*
> *Fa la la la laa, la laa laa laa...*

Light your candles for Deewaali Hanukkah
fa la la la laa la laa laa laa.
Night and day pray, pray to Allah,
fa la la la laa la laa laa laa.
Turn the Buddha's wheel that's timeless
fa la la laa la la laa laa laa la.
'tis no reason to steal Lord Jesus
fa la la la laa, la laa laa laa...

Come ye adults, lads and lasses
fa la la la laa la laa laa laa.
Clean up your blinding secular glasses
fa la la la laa la laa laa laa.
Don't you see our Christians bleeding?
Fa la laa la la laa laa laa laa.
Won't you lick wounds, do some healing?
Fa la la la laa, la laa laa laa....

'Tis the season to build community
fa la la la laa la laa laa laa.
Kiss goodbye to our own insecurity
fa la la la laa la laa laa laa.
Let's join hands in good spirituality
fa la la laa la la laa laa laa laa.
Climb the chariot of lofty humanity
fa la la la laa la
fa la la la laa la
fa la la la laa la laa laa
laa.

A few years later, I would invite everyone at a Christmas Party at the Toronto School of Theology to join me in singing it to everyone's delight.

Publishing the piece in the *Toronto Star*, it was published not as a poem, but as continuous prose. Mary Fraser, Editor of the *Theological Digest and Outlook*, on the other hand, published the total piece, along with the poem as poem, in its July 1996 issue,

Swarna on an Interfaith Panel with Fredelle Brief and Toni Mehran
(Photo credit: Hamilton Spectator)

saying that, although it is "slightly out of season, it is too good to be ignored." And she adds, "What a wonderful antidote for the apologist disease that's slowly debilitating the once vibrant Christian faith of our United Church".

It was perhaps on the basis of my work in the Interfaith field that Scarboro Missions Magazine, April 1991 lists me, along with my home address at 3 Ardmore Road, Toronto, and phone number, for more information on Buddhism in Canada. Listed is also Samu Sunim of the Zen Buddhist Temple at 86 Vaughan Road Toronto.

Participating as a member of an Interfaith Panel at the 25th anniversary celebration of United Church Women in July 1987, and making her own contribution to Interfaith dialogue, Swarna would share the story of Chutti's coming of age. She would also come to be featured in the *Hamilton Spectator* (July 25, 1987, c11), along with Fredelle Brief and Toni Mehran, in a Column on Religion by Jim Cairney. The article began as follows:

> *What is the experience of women in Canada with different faith communities?*
>
> *That Question prompted the organizers of a 25th anniversary event for United Church women to invite a Buddhist woman, a Jewish woman and a Muslim woman to share their experience with the 750 United Church Women gathered from across Canada at the University of Waterloo this week.*

Earlier Swarna would write a piece, "Women in Buddhism: a Personal Note in *Canadian Woman Studies*".

10.4 Buddhist-Jewish Dialogue

Walking along the streets of the Haight-Ashbury district in San Francisco, California, in 1967 while studying in the US, little would I know that among the hippies – who had 'opted out', were many a Jewish kid. Nor would I imagine that many of them would by the eighties and nineties become Buddhist practitioners if not Buddhist leaders of America. Though to a lesser degree, the phenomenon was to be played out in Canada as well.

In my activities in Buddhist – Christian Dialogue as well as at other interfaith activities, I would encounter Jewish leaders who were curious about Buddhism – a religion they had never encountered. One of them was Rabbi Marmur, of the Holy Blossom Temple, on Bathurst Street. Invited to the Temple, I would lead a group of Buddhists that included the Burmese Buddhist. Rosemary Than, VP of Buddhist Council of Canada. After the pleasantries, it was time to get to serious business. While I made a presentation on Buddhism, sitting around a table, one of the Rabbis present would come out and make no bones as to why he was there. He wanted to plug the hole of Jews becoming Buddhist! He was talking about the phenomenon of *Ju-Bu*'s – Jews who had turned Buddhist. To be

At the Holy Blossom Temple on Bathurst Street, Toronto.

'Jewish', as traditionally defined, was to be so in both religion and culture. But now here were Jews who would attend Bar- and Bat-mizvahs, culturally, and take Jewish holidays, but would keep away from the religious practices. This was a phenomenon that he could not fathom.

While our very open and frank discussion ended with an expectation to reciprocate on the part of the Buddhists, it is to my regret that it never did not happen before I stepped down. But I was pleased that Rabbi Marmur would continue to consider me to be "my Buddhist friend" and colleague, as he would not fail to mention at public gatherings where we would both be present.

While I know of no other formal Buddhist-Jewish dialogue that took place before or after, I was to have another opportunity to share some Buddhist insights when I was invited to the Beth Tzedek Synagogue, the Conservative Jewish Temple, just next to the Holy Blossom on Bathurst Street, and just around the corner from Ardmore Road where we lived. The invitation was to be part of a Rosh Hashanah Jewish midnight event in which only men would participate. I was asked to speak on the topic, "What Happens after I die?" (1997/09/27) from a Buddhist perspective. I started with a tease. "In inviting me, Rabbi Frydman-Kohl's said Buddhism would be interesting, "because there is no 'I' in Buddhism". Whaddya mean there's no I? I can assure you that despite what the learned Rabbi thinks, I'm here. See my body? Can you hear some sounds? Hi! That's me talking... The other day, I went to the Supermarket. I even have the receipt for proof." But, then, of course, I went on to explain what the Rabbi had read about – the concept of *anatta* 'asoulity', or the absence of anything called 'soul'. I also gave the simple answer to the question, "What Happens after I die?". I'm born again! I don't know about anybody else, but I know that I am still working on overcoming my own inner devils of attachment, which the Buddha tells is what keeps us in Samsara and suffering. In my presentation, I had of course, talked about the Buddhist view of consciousness.

I would be invited to the Holy Blossom Temple for a Seder on the issue of social justice. What I remember vividly was how, walking outside after the event, I, along with others, joined hands with Bob Rae to sing the *Internationale*, "We shall overcome …".

10.5 "Buddhist Protests 'God' in Constitution Preamble"

In 1991, an Ad Hoc Committee on the Canadian Constitution came to be formed to make recommendations, from an interfaith perspective, to the Special Joint Committee on a Renewed Canada. Formally called the 'National Interfaith Working Group', it was under the Chairpersonship of Archbishop E. W. Scott, Former Primate, Anglican Churches of Canada. Mr. Wilber Sutherland served as the Coordinator and Mr. Gerald Vandezande, National Public Affairs Director, Citizens for Public Justice, as the other leading hand.

Continuing to be involved in interfaith relations, I, as President of the Buddhist Council of Canada, was happy to be invited to serve on the committee. Other members were, in alpha order, Dr Muhammed Ashraf (Islam), Dr Stuart Brown (Canadian Council of Churches), Dr Bhudendra Doobay (Hindu), Mr.. Manohar Singh Bal (Sikh), Ms. Caroline DiGiovanni (Ontario Separate Schools' Trustees Assoc.), Rabbi D. Gotlieb (Jewish), Dr. William Jantzen (Mennonite Central Committee), Father Edward Sheridan (representing Father Taché), Ms. Eileen Van Ginkle (Social Action Committee, E. F. C.), Rabbi Guenther Plautt (Jewish), Rev. Brian Stiller (Evangelical Fellowship of Canada) and Father Alexander Taché (Canadian Council of Catholic Bishops). I was excited! What a broad representation of spiritual views! And there were others as well who would attend some sessions as guests or representing Committee members who couldn't make it to a meeting for one reason or another.

Former Prime Minister Joe Clark had been appointed Minister in charge of the Constitution by the new Prime Minister Brian Mulroney. And the Ad Hoc committee's interest was to provide input in relation to the Preamble of the Constitution.

Having had several meetings, we very enthusiastically participated in a Press Conference from the Press Gallery in Ottawa. We, religious leaders, provided a visible example of interfaith relations in action. Following the Press Conference, we met with the Honourable Joe Clark, Minister of Constitutional Affairs, at a meeting arranged at the Royal York Hotel in Toronto, to make two points: (a) that the Constitution needed a spiritual dimension, and (b) that the way spirituality was expressed must be inclusive, i.e.,. embrace everyone. In this spirit, following our meeting with the Minister, a proposal was made to the Beaudoin-Dobbie Committee, an all party House of Commons Committee appointed to formulate a Constitutional package.

But when the House Committee released its report in the Spring of 1991, the proposal to have a spiritual dimension to the Constitution had made its way into it alright. But, to our surprise, and dismay, the Preamble came nowhere near paying attention to our second recommendation: about being inclusive. The wording only made reference to "the supremacy of God". That there were more than four million Canadians – Buddhists, atheists, agnostics and those with no religion, who had no belief in God, making up 18% of the population (Stats Can 1991), had fallen on deaf ears.

As it turned out, invited by a "MP member of the [Parliamentary] Special Joint Committee for a Renewed Canada',

Author at the Ottawa Press Gallery with Religious Leaders.

a Christian member of the Ad Hoc Committee, of whom the MP was 'a personal friend', had contacted two other members of the Ad Hoc committee, both Christian, and written a version. ('Memorandum on Meeting [of the Ad Hoc Committee] held 7.30 PM, April 23, 1992'). I had suggested a series of changes, notes the Memorandum, "particularly with reference to the quotation …. referring to "the supremacy of God"', and that my suggestions "were faxed to the MP that night for his consideration … before his presentation to the Beaudoin Dobbie Committee". But my views had obviously not made an impact on anybody! I was one of the non-Christian voices at the Press Gallery in Ottawa that urged Canadians to support the new Canadian Constitution.

Just to satisfy your curiosity, so what is it that didn't make it to the report? It was an inclusive wording submitted by Yours Truly, and supported by, among others, NDP leader Audrey McLaughlin and former Tory Cabinet minister, Rev. Walter McLean. The two versions are listed side by side for comparison, the bold lettering highlighting the additions:

BEAUDOIN-DOBBIE	SUGUNASIRI
We affirm that our country is founded upon principles that acknowledge the supremacy of God	We affirm that our country is founded upon principles that acknowledge the supremacy of God **Now cradles others, too, seeking spirituality exclusively from within.**
The dignity of each person the importance of family the value of community.	**We treasure** the dignity of each person, the importance of family, and the value of community, **in relationship with each other in relationship with nature.**

Even though I see God as a fiction of the human imagination (as I had boomed into Christian homes on 100 Huntley Street some years earlier), I, as a Buddhist, certainly wanted to respect the God believing spirituality of the majority of Canadians. But I also wanted the non-theistic spirituality included.

As Reginald Bibby, University of Lethbridge chronicler of our Canadian religiospace, tells us on the basis of his 10 year study, *relationships* is the value we Canadians of all ages ("some 90% of the country's adults and young people") seem to cherish. Since it also lives well with the natural reality of interconnectedness of humanity, I wanted that included, not forgetting the smaller unit of family, and the individual.

But after two decades of Multiculturalism, Christian fundamentalists wanted to have nothing to do with any expressions of spirituality other than theistic, even when God was left right in the centre!

Michael McAteer, Religion Editor, would ensure that the story would get a full front page spread on the Saturday Star of May 23, 1992, under the banner Heading, "Buddhist Protests 'God' in Constitution Preamble".

I would write a Letter to the Editor on May 30th explaining that "Even though I don't believe in God, I want to go on record that I DO want God in the Constitution ... because it is foundational to the spirituality of my many Christian, Native, Jewish, Hindu, Muslim, Wiccan and other sisters and brothers, and, as a Buddhist, I want to respect that." Apparently troubled by the banner story, Dr. Brian Stiller, a member of our Ad Hoc Committee, and of Evangelical persuasion, would meet me at a luncheon at Royal York Hotel to discuss the matter. I had nothing more to add, and nothing changed either.

Buddhist protests 'God' in Constitution preamble

Author Featured in *Toronto Star*

But letting it sit there was perhaps a little too little to ask of myself. So here I was then making contact here, there and everywhere, just to make sure that my lone voice did not remain a lone voice and that the critical segments of diverse opinion makers and power brokers shared my vision.

The first was a letter to the Hon. Joe Clark himself, Minister of Constitutional Affairs, dated May 4, 1992. It began by saying that I was writing to him "with a deep sense of betrayal, but also with a great sense of expectation".

Seeking his support to ensure the inclusion of a spiritual thrust in the Constitution in a manner that includes all Canadians, I wrote, "It is my firm conviction that we are <u>all</u> spiritual beings. There is a basic goodness in each of us, by virtue of simply being human. Some may see here mysterious, 'transcendental' or 'divine' associations. Though we may not always be able to be at our best, we humans try to seek a balance, and peace, within ourselves. This, to me, is spirituality…". It was a simple definition of spirituality alright, but it certainly helps to include everyone.

I go on to argue that "While … historical consciousness [country being of Christian origins] and gratitude [to Christianity] are not to be taken lightly, a constitution seeking to rejuvenate a nation must consciously seek to reflect the present realty as well as allow for future growth…" I further point out that 'God' means now different things to different people, both within Christianity as well as other spiritualities of a theistic orientation – Native, Jewish, Muslim Hindu, Sikh, African and nameless spiritualities, for whom the historical Canadian god – white and blue-eyed, means at best nothing, and at worst, oppression". And so I propose that God be replaced by 'Ultimate Reality' [as proposed by a Christian scholar of eminence], intended to be both personal and impersonal, non-sexist and be inclusive ..". I seek a 'respect for moral and spiritual values' as well. In conclusion I put the ball on Mr. Clark's court: "you have the credibility and the skills of moral suasion to convince your political colleagues, federal and provincial, to incorporate an inclusive spirituality in our Constitution, one that may, incidentally, not face a court challenge under the Charter".

Looking for support for my perspective was a series of faxes, attaching my letter to Mr. Clark. Among the recipients were:

- Members of the Interfaith Ad Hoc committee;
- Governor-General Ray Hnatishin;
- Provincial Lieutenant-governors;
- Prime Minister Brian Mulroney;
- Cabinet Members;
- Leader of the Opposition, Jean Chretien;
- Federal and Provincial Party Leaders;
- Provincial and Territorial Premiers;
- Christian Leaders;
- Buddhist Leaders;
- Multicultural Leaders;
- Educational Leaders;
- Civil Rights Leaders;
- Professors of Religious Studies;
- Print and electronic Media;
- Religion Editors and Columnists.

Writing to Mr Dick Vinnels, Director of News, Canadian Broadcasting

Corporation Radio News, e.g., I say "I thought you might be interested in pursuing the matter, in the form of a commentary or other", also noting that Mr. Clark is "going to be in Toronto Tuesday through Friday".

This was to be followed by another letter, dated June 11, 1992, though to a smaller circle that included some others, urging support and endorsement of my thrust. Happily, I was to receive support from several quarters including a Cabinet Minister, and representatives from the Christian, Jewish and Buddhist Communities, among them academics.

I would also write to the Hon. Gerry Weiner, Minister of Multiculturalism, opening with the words, "I need your help! Millions of Canadians, in fact, do....". I also appeal to his spiritual and public conscience: "I know that your own spirituality based in the teaching of the Torah, your philosophical principles of justice and fairplay, your Parliamentary responsibility of preserving the intent and the spirit of the Charter and the pragmatic sense of not wanting to face a Charter challenge will dictate your conscience. My specific request, then, is that you take that deep conscience to the Cabinet table to vehemently argue for the spiritual inclusive version I have proposed, in the furtherance of multiculturalism for which I know you have fought so hard over the years." I attach my Proposed alternative version, the Preamble adopted in the Parliamentary Committee Report, my earlier correspondence with the Hon. Clark and the *Toronto Star* piece front-paging me.

Sadly, for all my unending efforts, but happily, as I could say from my Buddhist perspective, for the majority of Canadians who are Christian, the *Constitution Act of 1982* continues to be "founded upon principles that recognize the supremacy of God ...". I can only hope that, as in my letter to Minister Weiner, that "mother Canada will not have to grieve the loss of spirituality for another 125 years through the squabbling of her children, over the past and present, and theism and non-theism." I repeat my question: "As we go into the twentieth century, do we not want a Canada that will be a shining light to the world?"

10.6 Multifaith Participation

My involvement in Buddhist-Christian Dialogue and Buddhist-Jewish Dialogue would naturally lead me to multifaith participation. One of the earliest was a presentation under the title, "Be a Lamp Unto Yourself", at the Interfaith Service of the *Mississauga Rainbow Festival* held on July 10, 1983. In my brief talk, I go on to say, "Buddha himself claimed to be merely one who maximized that potential which is in each one of us, but with no divine intervention. He is superhuman only in that sense – more like Tarzan, the Wonder Woman, or Neil Armstrong, the first man on moon, each of whom can only be an embodiment of the maximization of one's potential. So the Buddha, in exhorting us to be a lamp unto ourselves, is telling us all: You are all equal; you have similar strengths; so work on them, without waiting for others to do it for you...".

Another body I came to be involved in was the *Ontario Provincial*

Interfaith Committee on Chaplaincy (OPIFCC). This was the body that had the responsibility of overseeing Chaplaincy services to primarily prison inmates. Originally an exclusive Christian outfit, it had come to be multifaith, following our Multicultural policy. One of my initiatives serving on the body was to propose an Interfaith Chaplaincy Training Program under which there had come to be selected trainees from several religions: Buddhist, Hindu, Islam, Jewish and Native Spirituality. For various reasons, only the Buddhist ended up completing the training. Her work was so solid that even the jail guards would come to her for spiritual guidance. Yet, when it came to hiring, the male-dominated establishment did not appear to be able to find any openings for her! When I stepped down from OPIFCC, I was happy to nominate Anila Kalsang, Founder of Tengye Lin, and formerly of the Buddhist Council of Canada, as my replacement.

Invited by Charles McAvity, a committed Christian, with a visit to our residence, I would come to belong to the World Interfaith Educational Association (WIFEA). The Association had been set with the excellent idea of bringing together students of different religious backgrounds towards interfaith understanding. While the goal was excellent, I thought the *modus operandi* of achieving it had a counterproductive dimension. The proposal was to bring the students to Canada to study towards the International Baccalaureate, offered by the UK. While students from different cultures and religions studying together would certainly be promotive of cultural understanding and religious sensitivity, there were, I argued, speaking from my background of national development, two problems. First, it would create a social class within a given society from which the students would be selected, given that they would be English-speaking. Second, it would ensure that those so trained and educated would not remain in the home country, but would quickly head for greener pastures, adding to the Brain Drain the non western countries were already suffering from. But I remember my views expressed at one of our annual meetings at the Pearson College in Vancouver not going too well with some of the membership.

I would, by contrast, turn down a request to be the Buddhist Rep on an Interfaith Coalition with a goal of getting government funding for sectarian religious schools at the secondary level. This was on the grounds that we did not want yet another basis to rip apart our Canadian society, already far too *rainbowed*, to create a term here, along far too many colours. The argument of the coalition was that since the Catholics were getting public funding, it was just a matter of parity to give the same benefit to other religions. But I had my own solution to the problem. In a *Toronto Star* Column, I wrote that it was "Time to end Cash Flow to RC schools". Did I hear from the Catholics!

During the Papal visit in the nineties, I had the honour of being with the Pope on the stage, behind him, at a Cathedral on Bloor Street. Unfortunately, non-Christians were not welcome at an event following, when His Holiness had the opportunity to meet with people. I had also been given a pass to attend the Open Air Mass as a 'Dignitary' at the Downsview Airport in North York. I put it to better use by giving it to a practicing Catholic friend, a Sri Lankan Canadian,

Ranjini Perera, who expresses her thanks to this day.

In May 1991, I also had the humbling honour to give a Buddhist blessing at the Convocation Hall of the University of Toronto, at the Opening Benediction at the Templeton Award on Interfaith understanding, to Sir Sigmund Sternberg, Chairman of the Exec Committee of the International Council of Christians and Jews located in London, UK. Sir Sigmund would send me a note of appreciative thanks (31 May 1991) following the event at which I was to meet members of the Templeton Foundation as well.

A multifaith involvement in 1993 was with the Institute for the Prevention of Child Abuse at 25 Spadina Avenue. This first related to a consultation on an Interfaith Video Presentation on Child Abuse, titled 'Help Me', for use by different professional groups, a similar one already in place for physicians and teachers. While I was invited as a Faith Leader, Swarna had come to be on the Advisory Committee. A second activity was being part of the Video itself, 'acting out' a minor scripted role. The video was also aired on TVO.

My participation at the Trinity Divinity Associates 1996 Conference (June 25-27, 1996) was as an Interfaith Panelist, under the topic "Strange Attractors: Wonder and Mystery in Faith and Science". My fellow panelists were Rabbi Dow Marmur of Holy Blossom, Robert Vander Vennen, Director of Educational Service at the Institute of Christian Studies in Toronto, and Lyle Young of Christian Science. Prof. Don Wiebe, Dean of Divinity at Trinity served as Moderator.

Invited by the The Campus Chaplains Association of the University of Toronto, "Celebrating Our Diversity", I would serve on an Interfaith Panel on Death and Dying (Nov 26, 1997), following a Keynote given by Dr Ralph Masi of the Faculty of Medicine, and Founding President of the Canadian Council of Multicultural Health.

Invited to a Conference, "Faith and the Public Life: Challenges, Choices ad Opportunities", at Queen's University, Kingston, Ontario, in 1999, I would speak on "Points of contact and Divergence: A Buddhist Contribution". I used my time to cover three of the five areas we had been asked to speak on: being involved innovatively, influencing public life more constructively, and challenges that need to be addressed. I end my presentation to the academics with a 'meditation', inviting them to join me as I read it:

> *May I be free from greed.*
> *May I be free from anger.*
> *May I be free from hatred.*
> *May I be free from vengeance.*
> *May I be free from stress.*
> *May I keep myself happy!*

Turned into a booklet, I would send it to the politicians, at both the Provincial and Federal levels, receiving notes of thanks and appreciation from several.

At a more personal as well as professional level, I was to be invited to become a Partner in a private outfit called Interfaith Associates, initiated by Dr. Keith Lowe, working with the Ontario Ministry of Higher Education. The two other members were Vandra Maseman, a Sociology Professor at OISE, and Karen Mock who would later take on a leading role at the Canadian Human Rights Commission.

I would also be invited to participate in an event organized by Prof. Edmund Sullivan of The Transformative Learning Centre (OISE/UT), under the title, *'Spirit Matters: Wisdom Traditions & The 'Great Work'* (March 2004). If it was to honour the Christian theologian Thomas Berry, not present due to illness but well captured on screen shown at the event. Represented was "a range of Spiritual Wisdoms, including First Nations Indigenous, Celtic, Women's, Indigenous African, Buddhist, Hindu, Islamic, Christian Creation-Centered, African American, Chinese, Pagan, Jewish Renewal, agnostic and others" Presenting the different perspectives were, among others, another Christian theologian Matthew Fox, Vandana Shiva, the Indian expert on development, Michael Lerner of the US whose thinking we had studied at my Master's in Moral Philosophy, the well-known Buddhist practitioner bell hooks (lower case her choice), Canadian educators Margrit Eichler and George Dei, lawyer Roxana Ng, and the Canadian scientist Ursula Franklin.

My most recent multifaith participation was in the Blair-Stronach initiative to work on development in Africa. Finding the activity to be in good hands – young eager beavers, I would step down after a few meetings, seeing no particular contribution I could make.

10.7 Dynamics of Interfaith

While interfaith relations were going well on the ground, it was felt by us that the next step should be to take it to the academic level. It was in this context that I was invited to design a course which upon completion came to have the title *Dynamics of Interfaith*. Originally offered through the Ecumenical Centre at 10 Madison Avenue, it came to be taught, by Paul Newman and me, through the Toronto School of Theology. It would eventually find its way to the Divinity Faculty at Trinity College where I would teach the course by myself, to Christian students preparing for the Ministry.

By way of not only making everyone comfortable to share ideas during class discussions on the sensitive topic of interfaith relations, but also as a pragmatic exercise in interfaith relations, it was my practice to begin the course by asking the students, all Christian, to form themselves into groups of three or four, making sure that they came from different denominations. And it was to my surprise that I came to understand that a Catholic student would meet an Anglican or a Lutheran, etc, for the first time in my class, even though they had lived all their lives in Canada, in fact, several in this very city of Toronto!

The experience was an eye opener to them in the realization that, despite their sectarian theological stances, there was so much in common among them when it came to spirituality. And though somewhat threatening at first encounter, they all seemed to appreciate the psychological breakthrough. It helped them to talk to each other as practicing Christians, and not card carrying members of a given denomination, without by any means giving up on their received heritage. I would like to think that the process was also facilitated by my opening remarks at the beginning of each class that they should keep their affiliations at the door before entering the classroom! This was by way of encouraging openness.

To my great academic satisfaction was a change that seems to have taken place in the students' perception. While at the beginning of the course, they would, to a voice, invariably take the terms 'spirituality' and 'religion' as being interchangeable, it was rarely the case that by the end of the course, anyone was not convinced that indeed they were distinct, although with certain overlap. I had defined *religion* as "a culture-specific expression of spirituality", while *spirituality* itself was defined as 'a genetic potential in a given sentient being for psychophysical homeostasis'.

The following is a Chart (modified) that was helpful in makng the point:

LEVEL	LINGUALITY	EXPRESSION	SPIRITUALITY	EXPRESSION
PROTOTYPE	Language	English (British)	Religion	Christianity
SOCIETAL	Sociolect	Canadian; American	Socio-Spirituality	Roman Catholic; Protestant
COMMUNITY	Dialect	Eastern Canadian	Dia-Spirituality	United Church of Canada
SUB-COMMUNITY	Dia-Dialect	Newfoundland English	Dia-Dia-Spirituality	Seventh Day Adventist
INDIVIDUAL	Idiolect	Personal	Idio-Spirituality	Personal

Spirituality Paralleling Linguality in Terms of Expression

As in Col. 3, English (British) is an example of a Language (Col 2) that is an expression of human 'linguality' (to coin a term, a back-formation of 'spirituality'). But over time, with geographic and cultural spread, it comes to change, as e.g., Canadian and American English, giving us sociolects. Canadian English in turn comes to have variation giving us dialects, and language still changing by community, we come to a context when Newfoundland English may not be understood in the mainland. And then, in practice, regardless of the community variety, language usage comes to be even more honed in at the hands of a given individual, giving us as many number of idiolects as there are speakers.

Spirituality (Col 4), though still waiting to earn its rightful place in human thought, is a quality, nameless as it may be, inherent to all sentient beings, including animals, the Buddha's term satta meaning both human and animal. The fight or flight thrust and protecting one's only child with one's own life, common to both humans and animals, need no elaboration.

But leaving the broader issue aside, the point is that Spirituality, too, comes to be formally expressed in terms of a given organized Religion (L 2), our example being Christianity (Col 5), which over time, and geographic spread as in relation to language, come to change. And again, in practice, it comes to be even more honed in at the hands of a given individual, giving us as many number of idiospiritualities (Last Row) as there are followers of a given Religion.

And so, Religion can be defined as 'a cultural expression of spirituality'. The point not readily taken by my Trinity students (primarily Christian) at the beginning of the course, finds acceptance in general by the end of the course. And within ten years, I come to see an acceptance of it from the very beginning.

Helping usher in such an understanding may have been the exposure they got to a spiritual diversity that ranged from belief in God to no belief at all. With Christianity under their belt as the example of a spiritual expression with belief in God, they would be introduced to Taoism as an example of an expression with a belief in some super power – the Tao, the Founder Lao Tzu itself with no historical authenticity. Reading a text like the Humanist Manifesto, in Corliss Lamont (1990), it would be difficult to say that Humanists, with only a belief in rationality and nothing outside the present human experience, didn't share the same values as advanced in other religions, such as truthfulness, kindness, etc. Buddhism, however, would be the bridge: like Christianity, a religion, but unlike Christianity, with no belief in God, or soul. On the other hand, it was like Humanism when it came to empiricism and rational analysis, but goes beyond a mere human materialist experience, with mind playing a critical role.

As if to indicate that the thinking of the Canadian body politic itself was changing, in my later classes there came to be more students that came to the class in the understanding that spirituality and religion were not one and the same. It is also as if with the advent of multireligism in the Canadian landscape, they had come to see the reality of many an expression of spirituality in the form of other religions. In other words, they had come to see that Christianity was no longer the only way to heaven!

Another change I would notice, accompanying this understanding, was in the concept of God itself. The bearded white and Euopean male God was gradually giving way to a God that could be this, or could be that – male or female, personal or impersonal, and white or non-white. It could even be more than one, or even none – just a spirit, a force, an unseen power, etc. The indelible sea change that Multiculturalism had ushered in could not be missed. And students in my course appeared to be a microcosm of this changing sea.

Following a theoretical discussion of criteria by which one's level of spirituality may be evaluated, each of the students was given an opportunity to judge for themselves where they would be personally, on a given date, or time period, in relation to other expressions of spirituality other than one's own. As a way of continuing to measure themselves once the course had ended, each would also get a *'Spirituometer'* (the concept and the term coined) to be put up on the fridge. It was, as a student would quip, like taking one's temperature everyday! While some thought it was a cool idea, there were others who were not sure they would be comfortable looking in the mirror everyday.

10.8 A few Publications

An idea that came to be rooted in my mind teaching the Dynamics of Interfaith was how the phrase 'Interfaith Dialogue' did not capture the full essence of what went on under it, nor was it accurate. Thus would I publish a paper in *Buddhist – Christian Studies* a paper, "Spiritual Interaction, not 'Interfaith Dialogue': a Buddhistic Contribution". Critiquing separately each of 'interfaith' and 'dialogue' that make up the compound, it provides the alternative 'Spiritual Interaction', arguing again, how each of the components is an improvement on the label in current usage.

Another short piece of mine would appear in *World Faiths Encounter*, a joint British and American Publication. Titled "Returning Spirituality to the People" (1993), it is an abridged version of a Keynote Address given in Buffalo, New York, at the First Conference of the North Atlantic Region Interfaith Forum, 1991. In the published abridged version, providing a classification, I argue that spirituality can be studied objectively, and empirically, but that the methodology needs to allow a place for the mind, and intuition, not only as per the Buddha, but as also pleaded by Haeraclitus and Pythogaras. But I shall let a paragraph in my concluding page disclose for you my punchline:

> *We have a choice here. We could be stubborn, and continue to keep our kith and kin in perpetual spiritual starvation, like the poor man, who when asked how he was doing, said, "'How 'm I doin'? With God's help, I starve three times a day"! Or we could return spirituality to where it belongs - to people, by letting go of our hallowed traditions, if found wanting under the critical scrutiny of the objective science of personal verification, and adopting new ones, discovered, rediscovered, created or even borrowed, if more conducive to spirituality.* (p. 34).

Always in the forefront in promoting interfaith understanding, it was no surprise that the United Church would come to realize that while there were any number of academic publications on the different religions that made up the Canadian **religioscape** (new term), there was nothing that would bring all the various religions within the same cover, readily available, and accessible, to the average reader. It is thus that they would take the initiative to produce a publication, *Faith in my Neighbour – World Religions in Canada: an Introduction*, that would include not just the World Religions – Buddhism, Christianity, Hinduism, Islam, Judaism, but also the lesser known ones such as

Baha'i, Native Spirituality Sikhism, Wicca and Zoroastrianism, and the rarely featured among religions, Humanism. My contribution was a 10-page piece on "Buddhism", in which once again I adopted the Dialogue format. A Toronto teacher Marie is visiting a Sinhala Buddhist temple in Toronto, and Suwanda is trying to help her understand what takes place at a Homage ritual. He begins by falling prostrate, next explaining that he was taking refuge in the three refuges – Buddha, Dhamma and Sangha. Asked about the flowers, incense and food on the altar, he explains the significance and the symbolism. Outlining in brief the difference between Theravada and Mahayana, he explains in brief the Four Noble Truths as well: suffering (as *a* reality of life, though not the only), why the suffering, that *Nibbana* is when the suffering is brought to an end and how it can be done (the Path). The piece ends with some statistics on Buddhists in Canada.

BOOK II, PART 3

PLANTING BUDDHIST SEEDS ON CANADIAN SOIL

11. WORLD BUDDHISTS UNDER ONE UMBRELLA
11.1 An Invitation to Participate

The red brick two-storied house with a basement at 10 Madison Ave. off Bloor Street, east of Spadina Avenue, and right in front of the Faculty of Education, University of Toronto, housed the Ecumenical Forum. Strongly supported by the United Church of Canada, the largest Protestant Denomination in Canada, it was home to many a meeting of the Canadian Council of Christians and Jews, as well as to many other ecumenical and interfaith activities: Christian-Native; Christian–Muslim, etc.

Another organization, of Japanese origin, that made it its home there was the World Conference on Religion for Peace. Soon after the completion of my doctoral studies, or thereabouts, I had come to be a member of this organization. How it happened or why I joined I just have no recollection of. It was perhaps an extension of my interest in International education. Only a block away from OISE, I would come to meet Christians of different denominations, active in promoting world peace. In the heels of the Canadian policy of Multiculturalism, first introduced in 1971 by Trudeau, the Christians were among those first off the gate, especially the United Church of Canada. I was also delighted to meet

Bloor United Church

Rev Fujikawa Sensei of the Toronto Buddhist Church, as another member of the Education sub-committee.

In 1980, the WCRP had decided to hold a Peace Service, and Fujikawa Sensei and I were asked to bring a Buddhist delegation. A Buddhist delegation? I had only known the existence of the Chinese Cham Shan Temple, the Sinhala Toronto Mahavihara and now the Japanese Buddhist Church. But it was our task to round up as many Buddhists as possible. And so it was to our pleasant surprise that no less than 75 Buddhists walked through the doors of the Bloor United Church, one street over from Madison. Perhaps for the first time, Christians came to see the living face of Buddhism in Toronto, and perhaps many relieved to see that these strangers within their borders also had only two eyes, with a nose in between, two ears, one head, two hands, two legs and a body like their own! It may also have been the first time they were to encounter believers in a religion that had no belief in a God or a soul.

Each faith community asked to make a presentation, the responsibility fell on me. And I clearly remember the wise-crack I made to roaring laughter. New in Canada, and looking for work, I had been asked what my SIN was. "Stunned", I scanned the audience, including those in the balcony, "I said that I was a Buddhist and that I had no sins to confess! Later only would I know that it was my Social Insurance Number they wanted, and not the number of sins I had committed since opening my eyes!" This was the first of many a presentation I would give on Buddhism at various church groups in the years to come.

11.2 Buddhists Come together

In response to the invitation by the WCRP to attend the Peace service, Rev Fujikawa and I were to take the initiative to organize the very first meeting of Buddhists anywhere in Canada, on Nov 9, 1980, at the Ontario Institute of Studies in Education where I had just earned my doctorate. As reported in *Spring Wind*, Buddhist Cultural Forum (Spring/Summer 1985, 192):

> *The Buddhist Council of Canada is a multi-denominational organization promoting cooperation between different Buddhist groups in Canada and elsewhere..... The Council, originally the Toronto Buddhist Federation, had its origin in a gathering of Buddhists at the Ontario Institute of Studies in Education on Nov 9, 1980. Their initial objective was to respond to an invitation issued to the Council's founders, Dr. Suwanda Sugunasiri and Rev. Fujikawa of the Toronto Buddhist Church to bring a delegation to a multireligious service organized by the Toronto Chapter of WCRP-Canada (World Conference on Religion for Peace) at Bloor Street United Church in Toronto.*
>
> *At its founding, the Council included representatives of all three major schools of Buddhism, from both ethnic and North American groups, and its membership continues to be broadly based....*

Having also agreed to meet again to see if the Buddhists wanted to organize themselves, for our follow-up Meetings, Rev Fujikawa kindly offered space at his Temple at 918 Bathurst Street, called the Toronto Buddhist Church. Walking into the worship area of the TBC for the first time, I found, true to its name, that it was architecturally similar to a Christian church, gabled roof and all. The congregation sat in pews with a centre aisle and sang Buddhist songs in Japanese words, to piano music that reverberated through the hall. A scroll would be hung in the centre of the stage where one would find the figure of Jesus on a Cross. The 'Minister', with the appellation 'Reverend', added to his personal name, would address the congregation standing behind a rostrum. A collection box would go round at the end of the service.

Attending first meeting of Buddhists are L to R: Fujikawa Sensei, Ven Dhammika, Fashihs Sinh Hung and Shing Chen

Establishing the first Buddhist temple in Vancouver in 1905, Japanese Buddhists, taking a lead from the US practice, had decided to follow the Christian model, employing such terms as 'Church', Reverend', 'Buddhist service', etc. displaying a scroll at centre stage but with no Buddha figure. Every inch looking like a Christian church, it reflected the early attempts at integration by a community under attack by the Christian Canadian community in the context of British Columbia.

After several meetings it was decided that we form ourselves into the Toronto Buddhist Federation (1981), to be later changed to Buddhist Federation of Toronto for reasons of branding. We would pour in hours into the finalizing of the Constitution, benefiting from the constitution of one of the earliest Buddhist centres in and around Toronto, namely, the Dharma Center in Kinmount, through the good offices of a member, George Klima. The Application for Incorporation under the Canada Corporations Act Letters Patent, that begins with the words "HOMAGE TO THE BUDDHA", comes to be signed by Suwanda H J Sugunasiri, Lok Sang Ho, J. Paul Hardman, D[arshan] Chaudhary, Noboru S Tsunoda, R[osemary] Than and Paula Fins as "the first directors of the Corporation".

It was indeed a pleasure to work with this team of committed Buddhists. Tsunoda Sensei, of course, was the Incumbent Abbot of the Toronto Buddhist Church (I would feature him later in my publication, *Thus Spake the Sangha*) and through Fujikawa Sensei, would facilitate our meetings at his temple on Bathurst, where it has been for over 50 years before moving to its new address in North

Toronto at 1011 Sheppard Ave West. On occasion, I would attend their Sunday services, and a reception or two would be held at the Temple kitchen as well.

Lok Sang Ho, of course, was representing the FaShihs Sing Hung and Sing Cheng of the Cham Shan Temple who had been present at the very first meeting of the Buddhists in 1980. Paul Hardman represented the Dharmadhatu, founded under the renowned teacher Chogyam Trungpa Rinpoche. Although farely well established in Colorado, the group was seeking to get rooted on Canadian soil where Chogyam Trungpa would eventually set up the community's Headquarters in Halifax, Nova Scotia. My friendship with Paul, though sporadic, would continue over time.

Although the number of Tibetans in Toronto was few and far between, interest on the part of white Canadians in Tibetan Buddhism meant that there came to be other Tibetan Temples. One such was Gaden Cholin, founded by Zasep Tulku Rinpoche, Rinpoche meaning a person identified in this life as a High Lama of a past birth. The community made up of Acquired Buddhists, it would be represented by Paula Fins who took a very active role particularly at the first Wesak at the Nathan Phillips Square.

The other woman signatory, Rosemary Than, I was to meet at a grocery store! Shopping with her mom, I would hear her talk when I would turn around and approach her, recognizing her to be a Burmese, and most likely a Buddhist. A temple of their own yet to make the appearance, she would turn out to be a most trusted VP of the Buddhist Council of Canada upon me becoming the President. And once the Burmese temple came to be opened, it came to be the site of many a Board meeting. She, her husband Joe and children would become family friends, enjoying a meal or so at each other's homes. Keeping up our friendship beyond the formal setting, we would spend a week or so with them as recently as 2006, in Maryland, near Wash. DC, where she has made a home.

Darshan Chaudhary, a Lawyer from India, led a small but highly devout group of Ambedkarites in Toronto. Dr. Ambedkar, Minister of Justice in the first Indian Parliament under Nehru following Independence, had embraced Buddhism, when 500,000 others had joined him. Born to an untouchable caste, he had explored the major religions of the world, including Christianity, and found Buddhism to be the most attractive. In Toronto, his group worked closely with the Toronto Mahavihara, using its premises for their activities, and offering alms to the Sinhala monks.

As for myself, even though I had been a VP at the Toronto Mahavihara, by now, I represented no one but myself. Happily, nobody seemed to have any qualms about it.

Though not a signatory, Mr. Khanh Lekim the Vietnamese Buddhist, was also one who was involved from the earliest stages. Joining later, to provide leadership, would be Dr Vansen Lee, representing the Chinese Buddhists, and John Negru and Michael Kerr on their own initiative, and Doreen Hamilton, a Minister in the Toronto Buddhist Church.

Registering ourselves, on the "20th day of July, 1982, Application for Letters Patent", under the federal Canadian Corporations Act, turning a conglomerate of interested individuals into a legal body, the objectives were listed as follows:
a) to promote the Buddha Dhamma according to the traditions of all the schools of Buddhism, and
b) to promote co-operation among Buddhist communities in Canada and elsewhere.

Historically, there had emerged two major schools, *Mahayana* 'Great Vehicle' and what had pejoratively come to be called *Hinayana* 'Lower Vehicle', a term I would change to *Adiyana* 'early vehicle'. Not occurring in the Tipitaka 'Three Baskets', the equivalent of the Bible, the labels were a fabrication of later Buddhists, in the context of India itself, partly influenced by Hinduism, but partly through internal dissension. But I was encouraged by the fact that in Toronto, none of that nonsense had raised its ugly head, and those gathered seemed comfortable with me. The signatories – drawn from Sinhala, Chinese, Tibetan, Indian and Japanese, well speak to our intent from the very beginning to work cooperatively.

Of course, looking back, there would have been good reason. Buddhism was unknown in Canada, and so everyone was interested in getting it known, including their own communities, with or without premises of their own. Only a few spoke English. Relatively new in the country, many were still adjusting to Canada. And Buddhists were all dirt poor.

By contrast, at a personal level, I had been in Canada for 13 years, had contacts with the wider Canadian community, spoke English and had a doctorate. Nationally, Sri Lanka was also well respected as the home of Buddhism when it died out in India, and also for other reasons. The Tipitaka had been committed to writing for the first time in Sri Lanka (1st c. BCE), Buddhist dates had come to be basically established on the basis of the Sinhala chronicle, *Mahavamsa* (6th. c. ACE), Buddhism had been introduced to countries like Thailand from Sri Lanka, it had given the Buddhist flag to the world (19th c. ACE), and it is the only country other than India where a branch of the Bodhi Tree under which the Buddha experienced his Awakening lives to date (in Anuradhapura). Later, it would be found, recorded in Chinese sources though not in Sinhala ones, that women's ordination, established in the country right at the time of the introduction of Buddhism to the country in the third c. BCE, had been taken to China by the Sinhala Bhikkhuni Dewasara, going by ship with a retinue of other bhikkhunis.

I was invited to be the Founding Coordinator, a position I accepted, though not without some misgivings. While I had been a Buddhist all my life, I had rarely known or met Buddhists from any other country. But just as I found that I was enjoying the opportunity, they would find that I would not disappoint them either. I well remember how I would drive over to the west end for a celebration, and drive all the way to the East end for another celebration at the appointed time, only to find that I was the first or second to arrive!

11.3 Pan-Buddhist WESAK (1981): a North American First

In the absence of any other suggestions, I would also introduce the label 'Wesak', a Sinhala term, when we decided to go public in commemorating the Buddha's Birth, Enlightenment and Final Demise. Having come to work together in the Fall of 1980, and taking quite a few months to putting the structural framework, it was a daunting task. But everybody rising to the occasion, we held the first WESAK at the Nathan Phillips Square, on **May 15, 1981**, with the participation of just about all the Buddhist groups, and attended by over a 1000 people, as reported by the *Sun*, the only newspaper to cover the event. Raining from morning, my phone was ringing off the hook, when I would joke that rain is an auspicious symbol, and in fact associated with Buddha's life.

The Vietnamese Temple, Hoa Nghiem, brought an 20 foot Buddha canvas, and festooned the area with strings of the Buddhist flag. Bishop Tsunoda, Bhante Punnaji along with Rev Fujikawa appeared on stage. I was to serve as Emcee We had also decided to refer to the ordained sangha by their cultural titles - Bhante (Theravada), Fashih (Chinese), Rinpoche (Tibetan), Sensei (Japanese), Sunim (Korean) , Thich (Vietnamese), etc.

A special feature was the Unity Song, written by Bhante Punnaji at my invitation, playing the tune on our home piano at Havenwood. A medical practitioner in his lay life before entering the robes at an advanced stage, he came up with brilliant lines, drawing upon the Teachings themselves. And we were lucky to have a veteran singer, and Buddhist, Brent Titcombe lead the crowd on the guitar, singing the words.

The service itself must have been unique. While each of the traditions had,

Author emceeing first First North American Pan-Buddhuist Wesak, (May 15, 1981). On stage are Bishop Tsunoda, Bhantes Dhammika and Punnaji, Fujikawa Sensei along with a Vietnamese representative

over the centuries, developed their own ways of paying homage to the Buddha, now we were faced with the situation of paying homage to the Buddha together. We sought to incorporate as much diversity as possible. Hori and McLellan (in *Wild Geese: Buddhism in Canada*, McGill-Queen's, 382) note how the "overall format of this public Wesak set the tone for the next thirteen years".

The poster for the first Wesak would be done by Sujata, nèe Linda Klevnick, a disciple of Samu Sunim, and a talented calligraphist.

Brent Titcombe leading the crowd on the Unity Song on guitar

By now I had also come to realize the importance of getting the ear of governments for the Buddhist cause, also for the benefit of Canada. It is in this context that I had invited the Mayor of Toronto, Art Eggleton, to be the Chief Guest at Wesak in 1982. He was kind enough to come with his graceful wife, and it was interesting to see two Catholics participating in the Buddhist practice of lighting an oil lamp.

Moving a notch higher, we would next invite Bruce McCaffrey, Minister of Multiculturalism and Citizenship of the Government of Ontario, in 1984. And with what embarrassment did I keep him, and an aide, John Nicholls, waiting until our principal players had arrived to make it possible to begin the program, punctuality not being part of the mental set-up of many an Asian community. However, I didn't know what to make of it when I realized how much the mainstream community had come to tolerate such tardiness. Arriving at an

Chart 1. Estimated number of Buddhists in the Municipality of Toronto in 1988, based on official statistics (1986) and the 'best guess' of community leaders.

Ethnocultural community	Total population, official (1986) or estimated	% of Buddhists by 'best guess' of community leaders	Estimated no. of of Buddhists
Burmese	500 (est.)	80	400
Campuchean	885	90	790
Chinese	126,340	50	63,170
Japanese	12,725	50	6,360
Korean	14,305	25	4,300[9]
Laotian	1,840	90	1,650
Punjabi	100 (est.)[10]	100	100
Sinhalese	2,000 (est.	70	1,400
Thai	1,035	90	900
Tibetan	100 (est.)	99	100
Vietnamese	10,275	70	7,200
Anglo-Saxon & other	—	—	1,000 (est.)[11]
Total			87,370

Chart 2. List of Buddhist temples and groups in Toronto, showing the school to which they belong, the country of origin and the ethnocultural background of the majority of the congregation, 1988.

School (yana)	Group	Country of origin	Ethnocultural background of major congregation
Hinayana (Theravāda)	1. Ambedkar Mission	India	Punjabi
	2. Burma Buddhist Association	Burma	Burmese-Chinese
	3. Cambodian Temple	Kampuchea	Khmer
	4. Thai Buddhist Association	Thai	Thai
	5. Toronto Vipassana Community	Non-specific[18]	Anglo-Saxon & Jewish
	6. Toronto Mahavihara	Sri Lanka	Sinhalese
	7. Wat Lao	Lao	Laotian
Mahāyāna	8. Amida Temple of Toronto	Vietnam	Vietnamese
	9. Buddhist Assoc. of Canada	China[19]	Chinese
	10. Bulgwang Sa	Korea	Korean
	11. Cham Shan Temple	China	Chinese
	12. Ching Fa Temple	China	Chinese
	13. Chua Hoa Nghiem Temple	Vietnam	Vietnamese
	14. Daekak Sa	Korea	Korean
	15. Charmadhatu	Tibet	Jewish & Anglo.
	16. Dharma Light Zen Centre	Japan	Mixed
	17. Gaden Choling	Tibet	Anglo. & Jewish
	18. Hong Fa Temple	China	Chinese
	19. Jong-Hae Zen Centre	Korea	Korean
	20. Kampo Gangra	Tibet	Anglo-Saxon
	21. Karma Kargyu Buddhist Centre	Tibet	Anglo-Saxon
	22. Linh Son	Vietnamese	Vietnamese
	23. Nam Shan Temple	China	Chinese
	24. Nichiren Shoshu	Japan	Mixed
	25. Ontario Zen Centre	Japan	Anglo. & Jewish
	26. Tai Bay Temple	China	Chinese
	27. Toronto Buddhist Church	Japan	Japanese
	28. Toronto Buddhist Society	China	Chinese
	29. Toronto Zen Centre	Japan	Anglo-Saxon
	30. Zen Buddhist Temple	Korea	Anglo. & Korean[20]

appointed time to meet a hospital Christian Chaplain on another occasion, I was almost offended to hear him remark, "Oh, ... on time"!

In addition to the annual event, and supporting each other towards growth, we also began to present Buddhism to the wider community. One of the more innovative ones was 'Meet the Teachers' program where teachers from the different temples were presented, open to the public for free, at the Friends House on Lowther Street, just North of Bloor, at St George Street, run by the Quakers. 'Buddhism on Wheels' was another when the different temples had an Open House at different times of the day for a whole week.

We also sought out the media, issuing Press Releases. Joe Serge of the *Toronto Star*, e.g., was to feature me in a column (May 8, 1989), in connection with the Wesak celebration. In the photo caption, he quotes me as saying that "if Canadians embraced Buddhism, we'd become more honest, and wiser". A reader could have been offended. But I'm also quoted as saying, "It took 2500 years for Buddhism to take hold in North America. So what's the hurry?"!

More proactively, a regular TV series of programs were presented on the Rogers community channel. They presented our diverse community, visiting teachers and Dharma topics on Buddhism. In all this, there were many a time that I was at the studio until the wee hours of the morning, working with the technical crew to finalize the program that would go on air.

Then there were the many TV programs I was invited to participate in, phone in shows, panel discussions, etc.

11.4 Buddhist Council of Canada: Traveling to form Chapters

Setting up Vision TV (as above) called for Buddhist participation at the national level. But the Buddhist Federation of Toronto, as the name suggested, was a local body. And so it was that Stanley Fefferman and I would meet one evening at Dharmadhatu, joined by John Negru, by now the Coordinator. And at this meeting it was decided that a national body, to be eventually called Buddhist Council of Canada, was to be formed so it could officially participate in the Vision TV endeavour. Thus was born the Buddhist Council of Canada, with Stanley as first President. He had it registered as a national charitable organization, and managed to keep the two levels separate, although the officials at the two levels were practically the same, except for the position of Coordinator and President.

Over time, I become the second President of the Buddhist Council of Canada.

One of the early tasks I had undertaken in my new volunteer position was to travel across Canada to meet Buddhist communities. With no funds available, I would use my travel for academic conferences to organize meetings, or pay out of my pocket when everything else failed. In the end, Buddhist Council of Canada would end up having Chapters in several cities: Vancouver, Victoria, Edmonton, Montreal, Windsor, Ottawa and Newfoundland, although I had not traveled to this last until later on a family holiday.

A letterhead shows the following line-up of the leadership, also showing

Prof. Fefferman as Past President and me as current President:

> Dr. Steven Aung (Edmonton), Vice President, Western Region.
> Louis Cormier (Montreal), Vice-président, région centrale.
> Dr Robert Kapitany (Ottawa)
> Dr. Vansen Lee (Toronto).
> Prof. Lakshman Marasinghe (Windsor)
> Glenn Mullin (Toronto) (Editor).
> Miguel Palavecino (Toronto).
> Mongkhol Salyajivin (Aurora).
> Rev. Jhampa Shaneman (Vancouver Island).
> Rosemary Than (Toronto), Vice President, Administration.
> Peter Volz (Halifax).
> Anila Carol Watt (Toronto).
> Brian Tun Winn (St John's).

Our Patrons were:
> Ven. Sing Hung Fa-shih (Toronto).
> Bishop Toshi Murakami (Vancouver).
> Ven. Geshe Khenrab (Montreal).

As can be seen, at both levels, I had sought to ensure Regional representation, and also representation of the different varieties of Buddhism present in Canada.

The 'offspring' that gave birth to the 'parent' Buddhist Council of Canada, so to speak, namely, the Buddhist Federation of Toronto would now come to be the Toronto Chapter of the Buddhist Council of Canada. Through the courtesy of Fa Shih Sing Hung, we would come to have an office at the Hong Fa Temple at 1330 Bloor West. But it was not uncustomary to have many a meeting at our own residence at 3 Ardmore Road.

We would also have our very first, and as it turned out to be, the only, Congress of BCC in 1989.

The Hong Fa was not only our Office, but also served as the 'dormitory' for the visiting delegates, for a couple of nights. The Congress provided an opportunity for us to assess the state of the art of Buddhism in Canada, although unfortunately there were no formal

On CBC Breakfast TV in Winnipeg

Congress 1989 at the Hong Fa Temple at 1330 Bloor West

presentations to be published as Proceedings.

One of the most memorable events for me during my term in office was WESAK on CBC in 1989. It was the first time a Buddhist program was telecast under its Sunday religious program, *Meeting Place*. Well attended, it was telecast across Canada. I had invited Tibetan Teacher Pema Chodron to be the Chief Guest, and lead us in Meditation, and a visiting Tibetan music group, arranged by Glenn Mullin, brought fanfare to the event. Rosemary Than, our VP administration, served as MC, while I welcomed Canadians across the land in French, respecting the bilingual nature of our country.

Another event in my memory was attending the funeral of Chogyam Trungpa in Maryland, USA, Founder of the Naropa University, in Boulder, Colorado. When he passed away, I was invited to attend the funeral. Given VIP status at the VIP Tent, I had the privilege of visiting the inner chambers (I don't remember what the building was) to view the body of the late Teacher. To my surprise, what I found was a dead body sitting upright! Covered in layers of wrapping, I couldn't see his face. It was a novel experience, for I had never seen a dead body other than in a sleeping position, face up. The exception was the Buddha figure in Polonnaruwa, Sri Lanka (and later in Thailand), lying on his right side. But seeing Trungpa's body took my mind back to something I had read in Glenn Mullin's book, *Death and Dying – the Tibetan Tradition* (1986), describing what he had seen attending a week of initiation and teaching attended by over 100,000 people.... Babies were born in this time, and several old people died.

> One night I saw an old man siting under a tree. He sat in peace and serenity, quietly saying his prayers and rejoicing in his good fortune at having made it to the holy place of Bodh Gaya at such an auspicious time. He looked over at the group I was with and beamed us an enormous smile. A few minutes later, he leaned back against the tree and, still sitting in meditation posture, passed away. His face expressed perfect

contentment.... (p. 29).

Trungpa Rinpoche was of course, a meditation Master, and so this to me explained the phenomenon of 'dying sitting'. Indeed long-term Tibetan retreatants are prohibited from stretching their legs for many a long hour.

As for my other contributions, it is with some humility that I would direct the reader to my Profile published in *Wild Geese*: Buddhism in Canada, published by McGill-Queen's University Press, 2010.

11.5 Growth and Impediments

As noted, the common event of Wesak that had its beginnings in 1981, came by its demise thirteen years later, if at least temporarily. Upon realizing that the community was holding on to me too much, and with the intent of encouraging a younger, and new, leadership, I had stepped down as Coordinator of the Buddhist Federation of Toronto. Later, after serving as President, Buddhist Council of Canada for about three years, I had stepped down from that position, too, for the same reason.

If my interest in paving the way for a younger leadership may have been the push factor here, the primary pull factor may have been a growing strength of communities, higher membership, stronger financial footing and English-speaking members. With the opening up their own temple(s) came the Teachers who may have sought to make their own personal stamp of leadership and establish the particular variety of Buddhism represented by them.

But there also came to be the flip side of the coin. Over time, leadership aspirations of some of the Sangha unfortunately seems to have developed into a personal rivalry between the lay leadership representative of the wider community and one's own leadership on the part of a given Teacher. E.g., organizing a reception for the Dalai Lama who had just been conferred the Nobel Peace Prize, the President of the Buddhist Council of Canada, Yours Truly, was not to be invited! Might it have been otherwise had the Sangha Member known that Harper Collins had sent me the Dalai Lama's Autobiography, *Freedom in Exile*, for an endorsement?

There had come to be another development in relation to the Buddhist community in Toronto around the nineties. That is the forming of the Sangha Council of Southern Ontario. While historically, the rallying crying for Buddhists had been WESAK, this in May, the Sangha Council in its wisdom had decided to hold a Walk for World Peace, but in June, making use of the better weather conditions. Successful as it was in its initial years, the outcome was that it came to kill WESAK as the common public event.

But was it also that I had come to be 'branded' as a 'Theravadin', despite the fact that I had never acted as anyone but just a Buddhist, pure and simple, with no labels? So just how is a Theravadin seen by Tibetans, and Mahayanists? I'll let a respected Tibetan Canadian Teacher himself talk about it.

In my interview with him in the eighties, under my Multicultural History Society of Ontario Project on Buddhist Sangha and laity in Toronto, which eventually came to be included in my *Thus Spake the Sangha: Early History of Buddhism in Toronto* (2008), Zasep Tulku Rinpoche was asked (as others were, too) what his attitude was towards other denominations like Theravada, Zen and other:

> Well, this is very interesting. As you know, I went to Thailand and I studied Theravadan Buddhism, and I grew up in Tibetan society, and we're Mahayanists. And I [began to] think, who is Mahayanist and who is Hinayanist ... Like some Mahayanists... they call themselves Mahayanist, but they're may be not even Hinayanist (laughs), you know. Because it is not easy to become a Hinayanist. I mean hina means 'little' [and hinayana] 'lesser vehicle'. But it's really a person trying to reach liberation, arhat, trying for self-liberation.
>
> And then there is the goal to help others. It's even harder... And they may call themselves Mahayanist. And I think, some people have the idea of Hinayanists [as being] kind of selfish. But that's absolutely wrong. I think very wrong. I went to Thailand and studied there. I found many Thai monks and teachers and lay people who are extremely generous. They have so much love. They have so much compassion. And they are not selfish people. (p. 224-5).

100 years of Buddhism in Canada celebrated at Ontario Legislature grounds at Queen's Park

Apparently that generous, and realistic, view does not seem to be shared by everyone. It was in the 1980's that the Buddhist Federation of Toronto and the Buddhist Council of Canada were formed. And Wesak was featured on CBC. Yet, the entry on Buddhism in the *Canadian Encyclopedia* makes no mention at all of any of that work, even in the 2000 Edition. Poor research? Or was it because ethnocentric Buddhism had come to raise its head.

With Univ. of Toronto Chancellor Vivienne Poy, Co-Chair, 100 years of Buddhism in Canada

Ironically then, while the Buddha's advice was for harmony, it appears to be then a case of what the laity put together, the Sangha had sought to put asunder!

Celebrating 100 Years of Buddhism in Canada in 2005, I had taken the initiative to have the Buddhist flag raised on the south lawn of the Ontario Legislature, along with the WESAK flag, in another first. But participation was low. Today, there remains neither the Peace Walk, nor WESAK as a common event in Toronto.

It is partly with the intention of re-building a common event, then, that Yours Truly took the recent initiative to revive the Buddhist Council of Canada. Helping me was Buddhist scholar and businessman Bryan Levman and Prof. Veronique Ramses who had also served on the Board of Nalanda College of Buddhist Studies (Canada). In stepping down as President, Buddhist Council of Canada, I had passed on the reins to Jhampa Shaneman of Victoria who, after two years, handed it back to me. While, since that time, there has been no active Buddhist Council of Canada, legally, I have been the de-facto 'President', receiving government communication at my residence at 3 Ardmore Road. So I am now, in supposedly my retirement years, back again as President.

While no revival took place in Toronto, except sporadically, the event happily has found a more welcoming venue in the western suburb, at the Mississauga Celebration Square, co-organized by the West End Buddhist Temple (Sri Lankan), Fo Guang Shan and Ching Kwok Buddhist Centre (both Chinese), under the leadership of Bhante Saranapala of the first temple, and with a participation of 3000 or so Buddhists of all schools and varieties, continuing the tradition and the model set up by the first Wesak of 1981.

11.6 Buddhist Literary Festival

Buddhist literature goes to the Buddha himself. The deft teacher that he was, it is no surprise to see him drawing upon parable, dialogue, poetry and the like in his teachings. The Canonical work called *Dhammapada* is exclusively in poetry as are the Psalms of the Elders, Male (*Theragatha*) and Female (*Therigatha*), expressing the joy of each one in attaining liberation. Among my favourites is the following:

Freed am I
released of the three crooked things,
the mortar, pestle, and
my crooked husband...! (Mutta)

BUDDHIST LITERARY FESTIVAL
Sunday, Sept. 24, 2017
Harbourfront Centre, Toronto (11 am – 6 pm)

PROGRAM

Our literary efforts will be guided by the language-related personal ethic, "I commit myself to true speech, not false; to healing speech, not divisive; to amiable speech, not unkind; to meaningful speech, not idle chatter."

11.00 am	**WELCOME & OPENING REMARKS:** Prof. Suwanda H J Sugunasiri: "Buddha launches Buddhist Literature"
11.30 am	**READINGS** Kelly Watt (Award-winner) *Camino Meditations: Towards jettisoning addiction*
12.30 am	**POSTER TOUR** 1. Night of Buddha's Enlightenment. 2. Buddha's Foundational Teachings. 3. Homage to the Buddha. 4. Chief Disciples of the Buddha. 5. Buddha on Economics, Social Relations, Politics and Judiciary. 6. Meditation as Empirical and Scientific Method. 7. Buddha's Enlightenment, Nibbana and Parinibbana.
2.30 pm	**TALKS & READINGS** Prof. Peter Timmerman (York University) Readings from *The Driftwood Shrine* by Roshi John Gendo Wolff Reflection: "Implosion: Learning to Live in a Finite World" Dr. Bryan Levman (University of Toronto) "Pali Buddhist Literature"
3.30 pm	**READINGS & PANEL** *Love, Kannon: Our Pilgrimage to Tokyo* Dr. Ranjini George (University of Toronto, SCS, Creative Writing). Lee Gowan, Program Director (University of Toronto, SCS Creative Writing).
4.30 pm	**READINGS (Poetry)** Suwanda Sugunasiri: from *Celestian Conversations*
5.00 pm	**FESTIVAL TOWNHALL** (4 Noble Acts: Share, Ask, Shape, Volunteer)
5.30 pm	**BUDDHIST UNITY SONG**

Please bring your own folding chairs. Thank you.

Over time, there come to be literatures in the different cultures where Buddhism takes root, from ancient times to the modern. And today, in the West, Buddhist literature can be said to have taken off. If over a century ago, it was Sir Edwin Arnold's *Light of Asia* (1879) that introduced the Buddha poetically, Herman Hesse's *Siddhartha* gives it a contemporary touch. And today, it is the novel that has come to be the highly respected literary medium in the US in particular, the Buddhist Fiction Blog seeking to capture the growth.

But yet, few, including the Buddhists themselves, know much about it, their focus understandably being Buddhism as religion. And it is to make this little known Buddhist feature its due place in world literature that I came to hold the first Buddhist Literary Festival in 2017 at the Toronto Harbourfront as part of the Word on the Street.

11.7 Buddhism on a Wider Screen

Popularity of Buddhism on the increase, Canadians were by now looking for someone knowledgeable, and willing, to help them get a handle on this intriguing religion. Word getting around that Yours Truly was more than available was enough to keep me busy.

Invited to a "Common Futures Forum" of The Pollution Probe Foundation, I present my views on "Ethics and Culture from a Buddhist Perspective" (July 1988) for which I get a letter of thanks dated July 27 from Janine Ferretti, Coordinator, Environment and Development Program.

Invited to a Medical conference in Ottawa in 1990, I present the "Buddhist View of the Dead Body". Published in the *Proceedings*. I get over 15 letters, from both East and West European countries for a copy of my paper. It also comes to be cited, among others, in an article in *J of Buddhist Ethics* "Buddhism and Medical Ethics: A Bibliographic Introduction" by James J. Hughes and Damien Keown.

Troubled by the fact that the issue of abortion was dividing Canadians, I had jotted down a 'thought piece' on it, "A Decentralized Abortion Law?" (1989/07/10), proposing that each Provincial jurisdiction be given authority to decide. It was clear that while Provinces such as Quebec and Newfoundland, with a strong Catholic presence would want to see the Catholic stance upheld, other Provinces like Ontario and British Columbia might lean towards a more liberal approach. But at the same time, I could also envision how, down the line, some smart lawyer would come to present a case law - if somebody could get away legally, killing a 'few cells' which is what constitutes a sentient being at the point of conception, then how could killing a billion or more cells that constitute an adult be a criminal activity?

My piece probably not accepted for publication, I would write a more descriptive and wider piece on the topic of abortion. I had had the opportunity to do some informal research at the Ottawa conference (above) on the topic of 'abortion', and was now, the resident 'expert' in the country on abortion in several religions - Buddhist, Hindu, Humanist, Islamic, Jewish, Sikh, Native and Zoroastrian! So I made use of the material to write a piece for the *Toronto Star*. And it was hilarious, if also frustrating, to see it bumped off from Editorial Desk to Desk. – Op Ed to Insight to Religion. It seemed related to territory! It was eventually at the intervention of Editor-in-Chief Don Sellar that it came to be published, under no particular section but as a page in the *Saturday Magazine* (p. M 19), under the title, "How Non-Christians tackle abortions" (Jan 6, 1990).

In my piece, I had said, "... the holy books of the various religions say nothing about abortion." Of course, I was referring to religions other than Christianity, as the title indicated. Yet a reader writes to me to bring to my attention how the Holy Bible does indeed make direct reference to abortion, giving the references to Exodus 21:22 and the Book of Psalm 139:16. She also thought the illustration of Philip Jones, the President of the Humanist Association of Canada, quoted in the article, of an acorn not growing into an oak, was poor.

The *Saturday Star* distribution possibly reaching around a million copies, it was no surprise that I came to be invited to a conference sponsored by North York General Hospital, on November 3, 1993, to speak about the 'Religious Attitudes Towards Childbearing and Termination', under the wider thesis, 'Multicultural Issues in Perinatal Care', covering several major religions – Buddhism, Christianity, Islam, and Judaism. For Catholics, since ensoulment begins at conception, abortion would not be acceptable at all, From the Jewish and the Islamic perspectives, it is allowed up to a certain number of weeks. Although the expectation was to publish the Proceedings, it didn't materialize.

In a *Toronto Star* column later, "Buddhists link karma to abortion" (1994.10.01), I would elaborate on the Buddhist position. There is no doubt that in Buddha's Teachings consciousness begins at conception. Abortion would therefore be tantamount to taking life, in violation of the first Training Principle to abstain from taking life. However, if a woman were to decide to go through with it, Buddhist compassion would call for us to support her in her trauma and, if possible, sit in meditation with her. But that would be after doing everything possible to discourage abortion. And this would entail talking to the woman covering the following:

a) *abortion is killing, with no if's or but's, even if it entailed the life of the mother;*

b) *the trauma experienced by the aborted life may entail possible karmic consequences, given the Buddhist teaching of Rebirth;*

c) *there are karmic consequences to herself of killing a sentient being;*

d) *the sentient being in the womb could well be a loved one in a former life;*

e) *the decision to or not to abort should be taken not in the exclusive thought 'I have a right to my body' but in consultation with, not only the medical personnel, but equally relevantly, the husband / father, parents, and the spiritual guide; and finally,*

f) in making a decision, the consequences of the individual decision on society must be considered as well.

Added to all this would be the emphasis on prevention of unwanted pregnancy.

Invited to an International Conference on 'Pastoral Care and Counseling' at OISE, Toronto (August 1995), I would speak on 'Buddhist Stories for Transition in a Strange Land', which come to be published in the Proceedings.

It was with some concern that I accepted the invitation to speak to cancer patients at Wellspring in Toronto. Here I was to talk to people who were facing possible death before long. But by way of helping them to cultivate a positive attitude towards their cancer, I would present to the 10 or 15 patients a lullaby, imagining taking the malignant cell in hand:

> *Rock-a-bye cell*
> *May you be well,*
> *May you be well...*
> *again!*
>
> *The life of my party,*
> *Let's have a hearty...*
> *Let's have a hearty*
> *hearty hearty hearty*
> *Laugh!*
> (Give a hearty laugh here.)

I also introduce some lines, to be sung along 'Jingle Bells':

> *You're me, I am you.*
> *So let's take a walk,*
> *Healing smiling*
> *Smiling healing,*
> *Healing all the way!*
>
> *Dashing through the cells*
> *In a lovingkindness sleigh*
> *What fun it is to smile the mile*
> *Healing all the way! ....*

The idea was to encourage the patients to be happy, and accept their predicament as reality, but not complaining about it, but keep making themselves happy. I don't know what lasting effect my counseling had on them, but I know that during my presentation, they seemed to enjoy!

Invited by student Vivian Lee of the Buddhist Philosophy Association of the University of Western Ontario, London, Ontario, I would speak on the topic

"Why Buddhism?" on October 12, 1995. If it was a pleasant surprise to see Room 2036 of the Social Sciences Building full, it was even more gratifying that they were having an exam the next day. I hope the students felt vindicated for the risk taken when I talked about the relevance of Buddhism to students and faculty, and to the intellectual life in North America. In particular I spoke about a morality without God, freedom of enquiry, the Noble Eightfold Path towards cultivating the spiritual life while living in the secular world, the Middle Path and the four qualities to be cultivated within oneself personally – friendliness, compassion, joy in other's joy and equanimity, and the four-fold social etiquette – sharing, pleasant speech, the social good and equalitarianism. I end with a session in meditation.

If I had been mostly introducing Buddhism within the wider Canadian community, I was also pleased to be invited to talk at the two Sinhala Buddhist temples – the Toronto Mahavihara, under Ven Ahangama Ratanasiri and the West End Vihara under Ven. Kulugammana Dhammavasa.

Another activity I would come to be engaged in was setting up a Buddhist Counseling and Consulting Services. Sharing a space at 204 St George Street with Prof. Jim Reed who had his own Counseling Service in the building, and then on rent. Sheena Sharp, an architect, and a senior member of the Humanist Association of Canada, had done a beautiful flyer for me, free of charge, using a bo-leaf I had provided her. When I look at it now, it looks as if I had sought to cover the universe. But as it turned out, most of the 'clients' came in groups, not so much for 'counseling' but just wanting to learn about Buddhism, and meditation. But I would also serve as an 'Information Centre on How to find a Buddhist Temple' in the GTA. With not enough clients, and not enough income to pay the rent, soon the Service would sure enough come to be closed. So much so for my business acumen!

Out of touch for years since leaving the Buddhist community scene in the late eighties, it was to my pleasant surprise, then, that I would get a call one day in 2009. Tony Blair, the former British Prime Minister, was looking to meet Canadian Buddhists, and would I be willing to join in. More than happy to represent Buddhism any old time, I was the only Buddhist to attend.

Organized by the Hon. Blair and the Hon. Belinda Stronach, it was a get together to deal with poverty and AIDS in Africa. Also invited to attend a Press Conference with Mr. Blair, I would also come to meet the charming Belinda. When she put

With Tony Blair, former Prime Minister of UK at Meeting in Canada

her arm around my shoulders posing for a photo, I thought she was more like a daughter than the rich millionnairess public figure. Later I would give her a copy of Swarna's *Cooking From My Heart*.

BOOK II, PART 4

SENSITIZING THE POLITICAL HEAVYWEIGHTS, LEFT, RIGHT & CENTRE

12. POLITICIANS MEET LIVING BUDDHISTS - A NOVEL EXPERIENCE

12.1 Communicating with the Provincial Heavyweights

If I saw the media as an effective medium through which to sensitize the Canadian public to multiculturalism, even before writing my first column in the *Toronto Star*, I had seen the need to sensitize the policy makers themselves, namely, the politicians. Thus, I had written my first letter to the Hon. Rueben Baetz, Minister of Multiculturalism & Recreation under the Bill Davis government (8.02.80, #1]). It was to express my "personal admiration on your foresight in appointing Dr George Bancroft to the position of Director of Culture and Recreation". A Professor at the Faculty of Education, University of Toronto, Bancroft was, as far as I knew, the first Black to be given a high level appointment in the Ontario Government. By way of both indicating that the electorate was watching, and as a form of encouragement to the government, I went on to note that the appointment will come to be seen "as another indication of your government's recognition, and appreciation of, the multicultural reality of Ontario." Sensitizing the Minister to another aspect of our multicultural society, and also not unaware that many a bureaucratic handler may read the letter on way to the Minister, I ended the letter with the line, "May I, in the best Buddhist tradition, wish you long, and healthful, life in the service of multicultural Ontario," a salutation which I would use in all my subsequent letters. A Buddhist discourse wishes everyone long life, and Buddha declares that "Health is the noblest gain".

While, as noted above, I would also next make personal contact with Bruce McCaffrey, by now Minister of Citizenship & Culture, by inviting him to WESAK 1982, it was with appreciation that I would receive two letters from the Government of Ontario. One was from Minister Bruce McCaffrey (2.22.83) himself. The other was from Premier William Davis (2.21.83), whom PM Brian Mulroney fondly refers to as "the modest and generous William Grenville Davis of Brampton, Ontario" (*Mulroney Memoirs*, p. 303). I was to encounter these same personal qualities, when, as Chair of Unicef Mississauga, I had the occasion to meet Mr. Davis, at an event highlighted by the presence of the US personality Chita Rivera. But that is not all. Sharp in his assessment of the voters of the Province "who always place their country, not their province, first when they consider public affairs and policy" (*Mulroney Memoirs*, 233), it would be during his Premiership that Ontario would become "the first provincial government to entrench human rights laws in a Human Rights Code". Ironically, I was to be reminded of this by Andrew S. Brandt, leader of the PC Party in later years, in a letter (11.02.87). Providing leadership in this area of Human Rights in particular was Attorney General Roy McMurtry who would also appoint Dr Bhausaheb Ubale to do a study on race relations relating to South Asians in particular. It was also during the Davis regime that the Ontario Advisory Council on Multiculturalism and Citizenship would come to be established. Both the Minister and the Premier wrote to congratulate me on my Order-in-Council appointment.

Thanking them, writing separately, I send each a copy of the latest issue of the *Toronto South Asian Review*, offering my expertise both on South Asia and Buddhism. In my letter to the Premier, I add, "particularly in the esthetic dimension", given my research on Literature of the Canadians of South Asian Origins which I had just completed (see above). I also make reference to a Sinhala cultural organization I had come to found, *Samskruti* 'Culture', in association with the Sinhala play *Nari Baaena* of which I was Director. I offer McCaffrey (4.11.83) my services both in the area of Buddhism as well as the South Asian community. He writes back (5.06.83) thanking me for the *Toronto South Asian Review*. Appreciating my offer of assistance "on matters relating to Buddhists and the Buddhist community", he suggests that "perhaps we take a little time at one of the meetings of the Council."

As the correspondence shows, then, in addition to making my own services available to the government, I would bring to the attention of the government two areas – Buddhism and the Literature of the Canadians of South Asian Origins. Among others who would receive copies of the new born TSAR, by my letter of 7.08.83, would be Susan Fish (Provincial Minister of Citizenship & Culture), Barbara McDougal (Federal Minister and MP for my riding, St Paul's) (her letter of thanks of 11.07.86) and Lincoln Alexander (Lieutenant Governor of Ontario) (7.06.88).

My encounters with the Provincial government had come to be so cordial and trusting that I was to have, in those good old days when terrorists had not struck, physical access to the Premier's Office in Queen's Park. I would also be one the government would turn to for advice about the community.

Congratulating the next Minister of Citizenship & Culture, Susan Fish, I also invite her to a meeting "if you consider such a meeting to be mutually beneficial". I also hint at a more common grounds: "... having arrived at the Canadian scene about the same time as you..". Fish had come from the US. In addition to a reply thanking me (8.05.83), I was to receive a letter from her a year or so later re-appointing me to the Council for a term ending March 31, 1987 (10.19.84).

I would also get an invitation from Margaret Birch, Parliamentary Asst. to the Premier of Ontario, and Chairman, Cabinet Committee on the Bicentennial, to "a celebration in recognition of Ontario's Bicentennial, on Wednesday, Dec. 14, 1983, at 12 o'clock noon Legislative building".

It was while on a family tour of the 1000 islands in the Kingston area that we had eagerly listened to the results of the Ontario election that saw the Liberal Party swept into power under the leadership of David Peterson. Thus, I would write to him (6.24.85), "Premier-Designate of Ontario", congratulating him, both on behalf of myself as well as of the Buddhist Council of Canada. By way of offering support for 'good government', I enclose pages relating to Buddha's words on good government, excerpted from Trevor Ling's book, *The Buddha*. In my usual manner, I offer my services both in my personal capacity as well as an Exec Member of Council, "to work with you in helping shape the future of Ontario". Receiving a reply, I write back outlining my background on the basis of which I supposed my appointment had been made to the Council, "consider[ing] it my responsibility to have credentials subjected to scrutiny both to allow you a free hand in appointments as well as to satisfy myself that I have confidence of the government". My appointment had been by the Conservative government.

My contacts with the Liberals, however, seem to date from Peterson's time as Leader of the Opposition, when the party was reaching out to the South Asian community. I had received a letter from a 'Special Assistant', writing on a Leader of the Opposition letterhead, seeking "to establish a permanent and ongoing communications link between the office of Mr. Peterson and the community at large." If the misspelling of my name alerted me to a potential sloppy quality of work of the emerging multicultural leadership, that was not the reason why I was not lured into the Liberal Party. In response, calling him on the phone, I invite him to my home in Mississauga, when he says it was too far for him and invites me instead to his office.

Judging from my own experience working in the Buddhist community, I didn't think that that was the way to go, in reaching out. Now, asked by the Special Assistant if I wanted to be on a 'committee', I turn it down, in the thought that it was obviously a 'party' committee. If I had wanted to be an 'insider', this would have been my opportunity. But I did pass on the name, and telephone number, of Alok Mukherjee, a former vibrant student leader at University of Toronto, and very much into politics, giving up his doctoral studies to set up the social network, Indian Immigrant Aid Society. Over time, he would become closer to the NDP, and his talents come to be recognized by being appointed to the Ontario Human Rights Commission. Most recently, having also completed his doctorate, the soft spoken negotiator comes to be the City's pick for Chair of the Police Board.

Just as the Liberal Party was wooing me, so had the PC party. But I wanted to serve Canada on the basis of my own credentials, i.e., with 'what I know' and not with 'who I know'. So I was to stick to my principle of not allying myself with any political party, a principle I had arrived at on the basis of Sri Lanka when I noted how parties had helped bring about an acrimonious society, the party system at the root of it, taking society in a direction completely opposite to the Buddha's preferred harmonious society.

But my communications with the Premier had not ended. Two years later, I would receive a letter of appreciation for the work done as member of the Ontario

Advisory Council on Multiculturalism and Citizenship. Dated May 19, 1987, it was sent to my home address, at 3 Ardmore Road in Forest Hill. It was only later that I was to discover that the house rented by the out-of-towner Premier in my own neighbourhood of Forest Hill was only four houses away, around the corner! He could have handed it to me personally! Sure!! Either I did not know my neighbourhood well enough in my rookie years at our new home, or he had moved out by the time we moved in. But did he know? Perhaps he never looked at the address as he signed the letter. In any case, I didn't run into him, the way I would with Mr. John Turner in later years, going for a walk, and talk politics.

I was also to receive a letter of thanks for my congratulatory message at his victory in the "September 10th provincial election". It was addressed to me as President, Buddhist Council of Canada, and addressed to 918 Bathurst, the location of the Toronto Buddhist Church which was also our official address.

But the more intriguing letter I was to receive from him a year later (10.06.88) related to a legal matter. A lawyer acting "for the defence of certain accused persons in the case of The Queen vs. Church of Scientology of Toronto" had apparently listed me as a person who has a "concern about this case". A copy of the Premier's letter to the lawyer had been attached. I wrote back to say that that was news to me, and said, "I am writing to categorically deny I [or "the Buddhist Council of Canada] have ever expressed such a concern, or given any indication that would lead him to arrive at such a conclusion," I added that, "It is, however, true that I have been approached by two members of the Church of Scientology.. regarding the matter". Later I was to receive a letter from Dr Wilson Head (12.30.86), basically a standard letter, in which he had urged the Premier to meet with the Church of Scientology. Again, while I had a lot of respect for Dr Head, I politely refused any involvement.

For one thing, I could hardly afford the time to get involved in a legal case which would require a colossal amount of time. Nor had I ever been convinced of the claim of the Church of Scientology that its Founder, Ron Hubbard, was the 'blonde-haired, blue-eyed' Bodhisattva (or something of that nature) said to be predicted in Buddhist scriptures. Indeed I am yet to come across any such reference, nor have I taken the trouble to get the source from the Church either.

Three years earlier, I had had correspondence with a different Exec Assistant to the Premier. In a handwritten letter dated July 25, 1985 to him, I say that I was "sorry we couldn't connect on Friday". It was regarding the issue of Prayers at the Opening of the House Sessions, beginning in September. Since the Christian, Jewish and Muslim Communities were already in place, I suggest that "at a bare minimum, we need to add three more: Hinduism and Buddhism because they are the other two world religions, and the Native Religions (for obvious reasons)". I had used the plural '(Native) Religions' to indicate that Native spirituality was as diverse as was any other such as Christianity or Buddhism. I refer to Sikhism, Zoroastrianism, Baha'i and Unitarianism as being "the other four religions mentioned in the Act", the reference being to the Cemeteries Act of Ontario, the only official document that allows us to know the legally accepted religions of Ontario. While there may have been no more than a 1000 or so adherents in the Province, Zoroastrianism, of course, is the first monotheistic religion, pre-dating Judaism. Each of Baha'i, Sikhism and Unitarianism, can be said to be 'compromise' religions, seeking to bring opposing or divergent spiritual expressions together. But I point out that "it might be a bit much to have 10 prayers, at least at the beginning." Apparently at the Exec Assistant's request, I name a Buddhist and Hindu representative, giving contact information. The latter was one "who had been invited, along with me, to be on the sanctuary at St Paul's Church with His Holiness Pope John Paul". I seem to end 'doggerely' - "Wishing you the best, and rushing out to England!". He would respond that the information will be sent to the Chief of Protocol.

Writing a column for the *Toronto Star* on multiculturalism, my suggestion to the Editor to poll the three political parties on their policy and practice of multiculturalism just before the election of 1987, had been accepted. Undertaking the work in a research capacity – unassociated with any other formal bodies I had been associated with professionally or voluntarily, I had developed a Questionnaire, "Ontario Election, 1987: Multiculturalism and Race Relations", and interviewed reps from each of the parties, perhaps a first in Canada, receiving full cooperation. After an analysis, Report submitted to the Star, nothing appeared in print .

With much embarrassment, I would write a letter to the three party leaders, apologizing for the fact that nothing appeared in print, due to circumstances "beyond the control of Sugunasiri Associates". The proposal to the *Star* was in the name of this private consultancy I had established. And "in keeping with the principles of research, and our society's sociopolitical commitment to access of information", I enclose Report, "A Tabulation of Responses...". While I would receive no response from the Liberal Premier, I would receive a response (11.02.87) from the Leader of the Ontario Progressive Conservative Party, Andrew S. Brandt, MPP, thanking me for "your recent letter and attached analysis of the responses given by three political parties to your election Questionnaire. One of the basic goals that I will be working toward .... is to reassess our policies ... [taking] into consideration our philosophical base while at the same time recognizing the realities of a constantly changing and evolving society. ... As the authors of the first human rights statute in Canada and the first provincial government to entrench human rights laws in a Human Rights Code, I can assure you that the PC Party will continue to promote racial harmony in a multicultural Ontario."

Lily Munroe, Minister of Citizenship & Culture, thanks me in a letter (7.29.85), for my congratulations (7.01.85) on her appointment as Minister, and saying, "I look forward to working with you and the Buddhist Council of Canada through your position as an Executive member of Council".

I receive another (10.02.85), a "brief note to say how nice it was to meet with you in person at the [Council] Meeting on Saturday", and also for my article, "The Literature of the Canadians of South Asian Origins" that had appeared in *Canadian Ethnic Studies*. A PhD herself, I thought she might be interested. That is, if she ever had the time!

My next letter to her was pursuant to meeting her at a Council meeting, and to her government's "expressed policy of involving people of all ethnocultural background in shaping the future of our province and country, as also stated expressly in your presentation to Council in terms of opening up 'the old boys' network'". It is to "make my services available at a higher level of responsibility [than the Council]...", specifically as a Human Rights Commissioner. I provide details of my background, 13 articles in various areas, one of them, "Rights and Responsibilities: a Buddhist Viewpoint" that had appeared in a Human Rights Commission publication, *Affirmation*. I provide several references, too – academic, interfaith and government (both federal and provincial): Prof. Margrit Eichler, OISE at University of Toronto; Whipple Steinkrauss, Ministry of Citizenship & Culture; Prof Wilson Head of York University & Founder of the Urban Alliance for Race Relations; Dr John Berthrong, Interfaith Officer, United Church of Canada; Prof. Douglas Ray, University of Western Ontario; Prof. Brenda Beck, University of British Columbia; Prof. Lionel Steiman, University of Manitoba; Prof Reshard Gool, University of PEI; Judy Young, Secretary of State for Multiculturalism, Ottawa; William P Bassel, Lawyer, and member of Council.

Dr. John Berthrong writes that I have been a "dedicated community worker", with a "profound concern for human rights in our province" and is "eminently qualified". He adds that he has found me "a most pleasant colleague to work with" and has "an excellent facility to be able to say the necessary thing in a courteous and civilized manner". William P. Bassel notes that "apart from his outstanding academic qualifications..., I have had the opportunity of observing his sincere and dedicated interest .. in public matters...". Further, "He is an intelligent, fair-minded person who also has the temperament necessary for this important work..."

This is the only time I had applied for a specific position other than to the Censor Board.

Acknowledging my "enviable credentials", she writes to say that she has taken the liberty of forwarding it to the Solicitor General, under whose jurisdiction it falls. Forwarded again to the Minister of Labour, I receive a letter from William Rye (3.24.86), that the material has been forwarded to his officials.

In my own letter of thanks to Minister Rye (12.26.86), I add the line, "*Maintenant, je me suis enrole a l'ecole Berlitz en un cours francais il ya a un ans*", foolishly showing how poor my French is, but to indicate my commitment to Canada's second language.

For all the effort, zip! My hunch: I could pull in no votes!

Sent a letter of congrats for being elected Leader of the Ontario PC Party and inheriting the role of Leader of the Opposition, Larry Grossman QC MPP of my riding St Andrew-St Patrick, writes to me (1.23.86) with thanks. But my hunch is that we had met earlier in his student days, when, the school run by students for a week, I had been invited to give a talk on Buddhism at Forest Hill Collegiate Institute.

"Thank you for your kind letter about the election. I am very much looking forward to my new role..., and it was most thoughtful of you to write," writes Bob

Rae (10.01.87), Leader, Ontario New Democrats and Leader of the Opposition. Upon becoming Premier of Ontario, I write (9.12.90) to him again. Reminding him how we had held hands together to sing "we shall overcome", at the Holy Blossom following a Seder at which I had made a presentation, I would now offer my services "to help translate that *Internationale* into praxis..'' – specifically, to serve in the capacity of "something like a Special Advisor to the Premier on Spirituality and Multiculturalism". In creating the position of "Special Advisor to the Premier on Spirituality and Multiculturalism", I was obviously pushing the envelope in conceptual thinking. But the reference to Spirituality stemmed from my interest in carrying through an advice we, invited religious leaders, had given federal Deputy Minister of Multiculturalism, Noel Kinsella, about the centrality of religion, and the need therefore to incorporate it within the concept of Multiculturalism. I was hoping to capture Rae's imagination, given his personal interfaith family background, as far as I knew - Christian-Jewish, and married to a Jewish wife. I was possibly pinning my hopes on his left leanings, which would presumably be more sympathetic to other religions, and hence spirituality that cut across religions.

I end my letter to Rae in the following words: "May I in closing, then, thank you for rejuvenating my hope in **'humanistic socialism'**, a politico-economic ideology I had argued for (though not in that name) in my doctoral thesis (with Gerry Caplan as member of committee) ....".

Further, "My Sri Lankan experience also encourages me to say, if I may venture an opinion, that wisdom lies in not making haste in bringing about change for which you have been clearly mandated. The lesson from British Columbia is also that a good thing can come to be rejected for reasons of bad management, arrogance and exclusive patronage. I am glad that there are enough people within your government with experience, of the caliber of Steven Lewis and Gerald Caplan, to make this experiment in humanistic socialism last for years, and serve as a model for Canada, and the rest of the world." The reference to Sri Lanka related to the fact that while socialism, ushered in by the Bandaranaike revolution in 1956, would find comfort in a country with a long Buddhist heritage of 2500 years, much had gone wrong in implementing policies, making an enemy out of a supportive electorate.

Whether my letter was ever read by the Premier I would never know. I never did receive a direct response from him.

Who said I was not opinionated! So, was it being too opinionated that was sending shivers down the spines of whoever read my letter(s)?

On the advice of Dr Gerry Caplan, I also write, within days, to another staff person in the Premier's Office, providing details of my background, and expanding on my offer of service "in a senior capacity, perhaps at the level of Assistant Deputy Minister, or as Director" (both Public Service positions) "or as Special Advisor, in Education, Higher Education, ComSoc, Culture and Communication, Citizenship and Multiculturalism ...". I reiterate that my offer comes as "an extension of my commitment to socialism, ... and my advocacy of 'humanistic socialism' ...". The letter is copied to Caplan. I receive a response from him, the 'Director of Administration, Transition committee', addressed to 'Ms. Sugunarsi', showing an equal lack of professionalism, and lack of sensitivity, as from the Liberal handler earlier. Noting that hiring will begin soon, it assured that my application will receive "careful consideration".

Again, zip! Perhaps I was appearing to be desperate in shifting grounds from "Advisor on Spirituality and multiculturalism" to a government position. Election called four years later, I was to write, for an intended Comment, on CBC radio, which I had come to do on occasion by now, though it was never to materialize, that we could "bet on Rae to win the next election", the punditry coming to be not even close!

Writing to me to say "[I] enjoyed your visit to my Community office" (4.22.88), Ron Kanter, my MPP, and Parliamentary Assistant to the Solicitor General, gives details of government initiatives on "multicultural policing", a topic possibly raised by me. "[O]ne of three top priorities of the Solicitor General", "multicultural policing" is explained in terms of three dimensions: a. police recruiting from a wider cross-section of society, b. better cross-cultural training of present officers and c. generally better police community relations.

He outlines four initiatives undertaken by himself, pursuant to these dimensions:

1. funding for a major symposium on multicultural policing in the fall of 1988;
2. arranging for a Staff Sergeant Syd Young, responsible for Metro Force's Employment Equity Program, to be seconded to the Ministry;
3. an internal review of recruitment practices; and
4. cross-cultural training both at police academies and in-house level.

My input, if I had any, is invited in the letter.

It is with a smile on my lips that I recall an unintended outcome of the lowering of the height and weight requirements in police recruitment. Intended to encourage immigrants who may be shorter, and possibly less strong, the police ends up recruiting shorter and fatter white police officers! Disqualifying them, of course, would have been reverse discrimination.

I had a special word for Bob Wong when I wrote to him (8.19.89) congratulating him upon his appointment as Minister of Citizenship. Noting that while some have considered the appointment a demotion, given his "excellent performance" in Energy "as noted by the independent consultants of the Cabinet", I say that "it is my considered opinion that … your appointment … has been to help raise [the Ministry's] status. I add that while for some people position brings lustre, but "others, like you, bring luster to the position".

I would also do something I had never done in my correspondence with the different levels of government. "[B]reak[ing] away from my self-imposed guidelines" not to work on a personal but only at a policy level, I nominate Sher Singh, Sikh by religion, and a lawyer who had worked on the Police Task Force and as Director of Legal Services, to be the Head of the Human Rights

Commission, first identifying the selection criteria.

Finally, in my usual manner, I also place my experience at the service of the Minister. In response, he writes to me (11.13.89) thanking me, and informing me of the appointment of Ms. Catherine Frazer as Chair.

From Ken Black, MPP for Muskoka-Georgian Bay, and Minister of Tourism and Recreation, I would receive a letter of thanks (10.19.89) for my letter of congratulations, telling me as well not to hesitate if he could be of any assistance. My interest may have been more on his other title - Minister Responsible for the Provincial Anti-Drug Strategy. It is only a vague feeling I have, and no record, that I had been invited to talk on Alcoholism from the Buddhist point of view, and perhaps I had met him there. What I appreciated more was his letter a year later, when he decided to leave politics "to seek further challenges outside of the political arena". Thanking me for my support, I was touched when he wrote that he looks forward to meeting me again, even though it may well have been a PR line. But I give him the benefit of the doubt.

In a letter dated 10.24.90 from the Speaker of the Ontario Legislative Assembly, Hugh Edighoffer, I would be invited for the "Opening of the First Session of the Thirty fifth Parliament", receiving also a Visitor's Gallery Pass.

It was "to offer to serve on the Royal Commission on Learning" that I had written to Dave Cook, MPP, Windsor-Riverside and Minister of Education and Training. Thanking me by letter (6.21.93), he encloses a press release naming the commissioners, under criteria "developed through extensive consultation." It was his invitation to "make a presentation to the commission" that irritated me. So he wants to put me to work [!] was the thought that came to me. I was good enough to be heard from, but not to be on the inside - to hear, analyze and come up with policy.

Sent my popular *Toronto Star* piece, "Who, then, is a Canadian (6.02.94), I receive a response (8.02.94) from Sergio Marchi, Minister of Citizenship & Immigration, but in the name of the Registrar of Canadian Citizenship.

Pitching for South Asian community support for Hon. Elaine Ziemba, Minister of Citizenship, Alok Mukherjee had arranged a dinner meeting with the Minister at his residence on a day in July 1993. I would write to the Minister later (7.21.93) how Canadian Buddhists have come to be "the most invisible of the Visible Minorities", pointing out that since my departure from the Ontario Advisory Council on Multiculturalism and Citizenship, there had been no Buddhist representation at any senior, decision-making levels. "So if you are looking for another pool to draw from, not forgetting votes of course, Buddhists can be of help." What Buddhists can bring, however, are "not mere academic, technocratic, business and other skills, but a morality without God, and a Middle Path outlook to matters of social policy and personal living."

I also offer Buddhist support for "the austere measures taken to tame the debt tiger. It is a Buddhist principle to live at all times within one's means." So I salute the government for standing up to interest groups, "for the welfare of the many, for the good of the many", drawing upon a famous line from the Buddha, walking the talk for a good 45 years. I end with the standard "wishing you well", but also extending it to her husband, Ed Ziemba, "who served the community before you so well..."

I also fax the *Toronto Star* featuring me, under the heading, 'Buddhist Protests God in the Constitution' (see above). Responding to my point (12.16.1993) about Buddhists being the most invisible of the Visible Minorities in Canadian society, Minister Ziemba makes the rather thin statement that "Buddhists along with members of other religious groups work for the government," adding that "within the senior management team of my Ministry is a Buddhist born in Sri Lanka. But I reiterate that he was not hired on the basis of his religion."

12.2 Communicating with the Federal Heavyweights

If my early contacts were at the Provincial level, soon my eyes were set on the federal level, receiving my first letter from David Collenette, Minister of State for multiculturalism, thanking me for "the information package left with my department..." (6.19.84). Visiting Ottawa, and as always looking for opportunity, I might have dropped off a copy of the *Toronto South Asian Review* and some other literature. Jack Murta would also receive a letter from me (9.17.1984), writing in the capacity of both member of the Ontario Advisory Council on Multiculturalism and Citizenship as well as President, Buddhist Council of Canada, congratulating him on his appointment as "the first full-fledged Minister of multiculturalism ". I offer "to serve on the Japanese Redress committee", a hot issue at the time, although I had opposed taking up the matter at the COUNCIL proceedings on the procedural basis that it was not a provincial matter. Receiving a response (11.07.1984) that he was "giving consideration to the appointment of a committee, comprised of two or three persons" and assuring me that my resume "will be kept on file for ready reference...". I respond (11.19.1984) by sending him names of ten referees, - four academic, three Religious and three Community and Multicultural. I receive a response from Chief of Staff that my offer of service "will be given every consideration". But when the Committee came to be appointed, I wasn't on it!

My next communication with the federal level was to Joe Clark, Minister of Foreign Affairs in the Mulroney government. My letter (10.10.1984) was to first, congratulate him for going beyond party lines in appointing a well-known NDP stalwart Stephen Lewis as Canada's UN Ambassador. I worded it carefully, as I try to do in all my correspondence, employing my writing skills of precision. "It shows your intention at good government is not tied to narrow party politics. As an active member of the Buddhist Council of Canada, this is a thrust I can heartily endorse because it allows for the utilization in full of our primary wealth, the people of Canada. I do hope that the direction you have taken would lead to our multicultural community as well, for they bring an expertise that Canada can hardly afford to ignore."

But if my letter was a genuine attempt at encouraging good public and political practice, it would be less than honest to pretend there was no self-interest – what I would call 'self-caring' interest. And so I continue: "In that vein, then, Sir, let me offer you my own services in the sphere of Canadian foreign policy and international development, for I bring to it an expertise and credentials that would not be readily available in Canada..".

It may sound preposterous that an immigrant with an unpronounceable name should even dare to think of himself as being up to scratch in such a critical Ministry. But as my qualifications, I list (a) my doctoral thesis in international development, (b) field experience as a volunteer in the Sarvodaya development movement in Sri Lanka, receiving part CIDA funding, too, (c) living in North America for 20 years, 17 in Canada, (d) international travel, and (e) grassroots involvement in the Canadian mainstream as well as in the multicultural stream. I end the letter with the words, "I need hardly say that my appointment would be seen as a genuine attempt on the part of your government to draw upon our multicultural community in pursuance of the policy adopted at the PC Convention on multiculturalism held in Toronto, and now recognized officially in setting up a separate [federal] Ministry of multiculturalism."

As you will have read above, but known only in the academy, 'Development' was right down my alley. Defending the thesis in the absence of my Committee Chair Prof. Joseph Farrell, he had characterized it as constituting a *new theory* of development. Writing to the Hon. Clark on my behalf at my request, Prof. Douglas Ray of University of Western Ontario, my external examiner, had observed that mine was

> *"by far the best defence that I ever witnessed. It was attended by seven or eight scholars from very different fields, each firing questions of a specialized nature. Among them was J Roby Kidd, internationally respected as an authority on adult education and development. Dr. Sugunasiri was eloquent and lucid in defence of his wholly original theoretical analysis of the international development process."*

Making reference to my offer to be a member of the advisory committee to set up "to seek public views of Canada's foreign relations and to assist … in formulating a realistic and compassionate policy that would be a credit to Canada", he comments that I would be most suitable "both because of his sensitivity for gathering public perceptions and his mature and sophisticated capacity to help shape those views into a policy that Canadians may be proud of". And his second paragraph read as follows:

> *Dr. Sugunasiri is very well read, well informed, literate, tolerant and humourous so he will be able to help the committee in their contacts with many sectors of the Canadian public that have been previously ignored. His theatrical experience enables him to win and maintain attention. His sociology helps him to understand subtle community differences. His Buddhism and ecumenical work gives him a good background for appreciating and negotiating value differences. His linguistic prowess will be valuable to the committee in some situations.*

Writing to the Minster from the University of Victoria, British Columbia, Prof. Wilson Head, a prominent Black intellectual who would later go on to found the Urban Alliance for Race Relations notes: "I ... can attest to the fact that he is a highly qualified individual of great insight and skills in areas related to development and multiculturalism. His active interest in these areas has been amply demonstrated in his many activities in the Metropolitan Toronto area." He had known me for several years.

I had also given as references John Nicholls, Special Assistant to Premier William Davis, Mavis Burke, Chair of the Council, and a Black educator, who apparently had been impressed enough by my contributions at the Councils' deliberations that she had invited me to take on the responsibility of Coordinator of the most diverse sub-committee, namely, Toronto.

Despite my own qualifications and the strong recommendations, neither Mr. Clark nor his advisors seem to have taken me seriously. I would know this when I get a letter (dated Nov. 6, 84) from a high level official of CIDA thanking me for the letter, and telling me that "[t]he Minister has asked the Agency to respond." Saying that "at this time there are no positions available at CIDA" to match my qualifications, he "suggests" that I contact the Secretary of State, Multiculturalism "which might very well be interested in a person with your experiences". He also tells me that I should "register with the PSC [Public Service Commission] if I was considering an appointment in the public service".

Upon receiving it, I write two letters. First was to the Right Honourable Joe Clark himself, referring to the CIDA letter, pointing out that "there seems to have been a misunderstanding about the intent of my letter.. Perhaps it was not clear from my letter that I was not looking for a public service appointment. Rather I was offering my expertise at a higher level - consultative or advisory." I "respectfully" urge "that my letter be looked at again ... and consider how genuine talent, untapped thus far, can be utilized in a way to maximize the quality of our Canadian life, and through it, the life of the world." Full of self-importance, you might even say, but I meant every word of it, not in a pompous sense but in the genuine understanding of my unique qualifications.

My letter to the official was scathing. Thanking him in my opener, I say "... I haven't responded to it thus far because I couldn't make up my mind whether to be insulted or angered." And I make no bones about my qualifications when I say, "I consider myself a highly knowledgeable person in the field of development, comparable to perhaps anyone in Canada, including the experts at CIDA"! Then I lambast him for the statement about there being no positions at CIDA, that it "sounds hollow if not hypocritical". And this statement was not just empty rhetoric. I knew what I was talking about, since I had, right upon graduation, and on the recommendation of my thesis examiners Roby Kidd and Douglas Ray, made a pitch to CIDA. And I was given the same answer – no positions that suits my background. It was a contact I had at CIDA that gave me the inside story – that since I had no background in economics, there was not a ghost of a chance that I would even get my toe in the door. So, the Vice President may have in fact been reflecting reality when he saw no fit.

But then, as I continue in my letter, it "doesn't suggest any attempt on the part of your agency to meet the challenge the Hon. Joe Clark has thrown at you by directing my letter to you." Regarding the advice as to how to go about getting a public service job, I say that "[i]t is as if you have tried to cover your lack of seriousness in considering my background by writing a lot to give the impression that you really care!" Regarding the suggestion about writing to the Secretary of State for multiculturalism, I say that it is "indicative... of an attempt at passing the buck".

The stinker comes in the concluding para: "You and I both know the well-known saying how women have to run twice as fast to achieve half as much. Is mine a case of a man with a non-English sounding name having to run four times as much to achieve a quarter as much?" Then I leave the matter to him "for self-search." And I don't know if he believed in my next line: "But I want to assure you that this is not an angry man writing to you but an analytical mind searching for the truth." If this was Buddhist wisdom of objectivity, my compassion was in the last line: "...this letter is sent to you personally for your soul-searching, with no copies. So you may ignore or destroy it if you so wish." But was this misplaced compassion? Should my letter have been copied to Joe Clark?

Clearly multiculturalism had not touched CIDA, I would conclude. Not Joe Clark either? Would my letter have had a better reception had it been sent to Mr. Mulroney directly? After all, he is the son of a trade union leader who had succesfully fought for the inclusion of Francophones in the affairs of Canada. But this I would know only after reading his Memoirs!

Or it may just have been a matter of timing, which is said to be 'everything'. If these early days of multiculturalism were an improvement on the pre-multicultural racism that rendered it difficult for a Black even to rent an apartment, now we seem to be at the stage of allowing Canadians of colour, but tolerating only at the lowest rungs of employment, in the public or the private sector.

Perhaps the Tory response had nothing to do with multiculturalism. Is it perchance that I was seen, correctly, to be no vote-puller for the party, Sinhala Buddhists not being numerically strong or politically active, to make a difference in any riding or seat?

Now I reach out to Stephen Lewis, Clark's surprise appointment and staunch NDP-er. After all, the left is more understanding of racism and discrimination, and rah rah rah on equality, right? So I dash off a letter to Lewis (10.18.84), congratulating him on his appointment, but now add my usual fare: "It is with a sense of obligation that I now move to offer my own services to assist you and the government in whatever way I can in the field of international development and foreign policy", pointing out again how I have an expertise that few Canadians have, and suggesting a role for me "in a consultancy capacity". I add that I am writing following a meeting with Gerry Caplan, my former professor, and NDP strategist, "who has encouraged me to make contact with you". Having met Mr. Lewis's wife, Michele Landsberg at the *Toronto Star* during my time as a columnist, I give her my regards as well.

I will only say that I am still waiting.

Re-appointed to the Council for a term ending March 31, 1987, by letter from Minister Susan Fish, and a note of thanks for my Telex congratulating her on her re-appointment as Minister (2.18.85), I continue my thrust with the federal level, next at even a closer personal level. Invited to a Public Forum on Immigration held at the Medical Science Auditorium of University of Toronto on Dec. 6, 1985, I was surprised to receive a loud ovation of hand-clapping from the multireligious gathering in audience. I had stood up to raise the issue of the Christianization of Buddhists in Canada. Apparently Buddhists were not the only targeted. Present at the event was Walter F McLean, Minister of State for Immigration, and a self-identified Christian. He had also supported my inclusive version for the preamble (see above). I would meet him, and his "enchanting wife" as I would put in my follow up letter (4.07.84) to him. In the letter, I detail out the targeted Buddhist "refugee communities" – Vietnamese, Cambodian, Laotian, Korean, and Chinese in particular. I note however that the Christianization "results more from genuine and honourable attempts at helping people in difficulty, both in Canada and overseas, than from deliberate attempts at conversion". I then elaborate upon the process that begins with such good intentions but end up with unethical conversions when a church group or representative enters the picture. "The final crunch comes when, the first Sunday after arrival, the [Christian] family takes [the refugee(s)] to 'our church' to 'meet our minister'." Then I go on to hypothesize a scenario:

> *With a view of Canada as a Christian country, with everyone assisting them seen as Christians, (2) soon internalizing the benefits of a 'Christian' society, (3) conscious of the realization of the total dependence on the sponsor-family for one's very survival, and being justifiably thankful for it, (4) being helpless, and (5) emotionally drained, it would not only be difficult to turn down the polite offer but also would most likely be seen as a welcome opportunity to return to one's spirituality [here distinguished from religion], if momentarily, even though of a different ilk. Some sponsorees may even claim to have always been Christian, and go through the motions of Christian rituals at the Church as well. The younger members of the family in particular may, in fact, even enjoy it all, attracted by the music, the refreshments, the kind words and the feeling of inclusiveness not experienced at the refugee camp or since leaving their homes. Once the first visits are made, the rest of the Christianization process is automatic. There are the social reasons now, the subtle pressure from the [host] community and the Minister, some of it perhaps unconsciously, and in other cases, the open invitation.*

Conceding that this is the 'worst case scenario', and that, despite the experience, those who have strong convictions continue to be Buddhist. "This is when and where the Christian fundamentalist enters the scene: the regular visits to the home, the literature on Christianity, the regular telephone call to remind that Sunday is around the corner!"

If this was Canada of the eighties, it is with some regret that it has come to my attention that the process had gone to high gear in Sri Lanka at the time of the Tsunami disaster when a Canadian eye-witness would see a rescued kid first receiving a cross around the neck!

I also point out a possible contributory Buddhist weakness: ".. the Buddhist community, as most other newer communities, lack the organizational base as well as human, financial and other resources to assist in the refugee process.." I also add another possible contributory factor - Buddhist scriptural freedom. The reference is to the Buddha's well-known teaching, "It is proper that you have doubt... Do not be led by reports, or tradition, or hearsay, ... the authority of religious texts, nor by mere logic or inference, nor by considering appearance, nor the delight in speculative opinions, nor by seeming possibilities, nor by the idea, 'This is our Teacher', but when you know for yourselves.." I go on to point out that "while such freedom of thought has helped ... Buddhism earn the respect and admiration of the world, Schopenhauer and Aldous Huxley included, ... it can well turn into a licence .... Particularly in times of low civilization....under conditions of war, famine, exploitation, colonialism, social oppression and so on". Thus it is understandable that "some immigrant and refugee individuals and families decide to become 'convenient Christians', often without necessarily giving up on their own convictions." About this latter, I was to have personal experience when I had happened to see an occasional Buddhist leader who would sit around the table at the Buddhist Federation of Toronto meetings wearing a cross!

The educator that I was, following the critique and analysis, I offer the Minister three proposals: (1) That the Refugee and Immigration Advisory committees .. be expanded to include Buddhist, Hindu, Islam, Sikh and Native Indian representation; (2) That all churches, church groups or other organizations involved in the immigration and refugee process be required to (a) set up interfaith (not merely [Christian] interdenominational) committees that would be involved in the process from the beginning to the end, (b) ensuring minimally that a member of the faith group of the sponsoree be present ...; (3) that Guidelines be developed to assist such groups [to include] the expression of the government ... that attempts at conversion, overt or covert, will not be condoned ..." While granting that a deeper deliberation calls for a Task Force, "the present proposals are intended to be a first step towards cultivating Canada's image, at home and abroad, as a truly multicultural, fair-minded and compassionate society". I appealed for his personal intervention in the matter, "being in the unique position of Minister of the Church and Minister of the State".

The letter, copied to Barbara McDougall, MP for my riding, and a Cabinet Minister herself, received a response from Minister McLean (5.23.86). Thanking me "for the time and considerable efforts you have given to the development of your concepts and observations on the impact of the Canadian Christian community on refugees of other faiths", it noted that my letter was "most thought provoking in its complexity of cause and effect".

Additionally noting that the problem is complex "and a hasty response may, in the long run, do more harm than good", it said that my second proposal, "to legislate the organization of the groups ... could be perceived as an unacceptable intervention by government". The same concern, it contended, would hold true for the third, about guidelines against conversion.

While the letter had every intent of dealing with the issue, neither was the matter ever dealt with nor my services called upon.

The setting up of a "Special committee on the Participation of Visible Minorities in Canadian Society" by the House of Commons in the Spring of 1984 may well have been, or seen by a skeptical and confrontational media, sociopolitical pundits and perhaps even the public as, a cynical ploy of the Liberal government of John Turner, coming as it did just prior to calling an election in the Summer. But I saw it as a small measure of victory for the many small battles waged by individuals like myself, and organizations like the Urban Alliance for Race Relations, towards a more multicultural Canada. Not one to miss an opportunity, I would thus write to Bob Daudlin, Chair of the committee, receiving a note of thanks for the letter and an article of mine enclosed, "Media and Multiculturalism: a sociopolitical view". He offered to distribute the enclosure to all members of the committee, made up of, as shown on the letterhead, Gary McCauley (Vice Chair), Norm Kelly (Scarborough), Laverne Lewycky (Dauphin – Swan River), Gus Mitges (Gary – simcoe), Steve Paproski (Edmonton North) and Miechel Veillette (Champlain). I was happy that my thoughts had gone to the hands of seven political leaders that would ordinarily not have seen, particularly as far as Edmonton and Quebec, at two opposites of the politial spectrum.

Carol Goar had written, in her National Affairs column (June 3, 86), that John Turner, Leader of the Opposition, and Liberal Leader, were "planning to hold a 'think tank' or "a policy brainstorming session" in May 1987. So I write to Mr. Turner (6.11.86), in my capacity as President, Buddhist Council of Canada, that "it would be remiss if the Buddhist community of Canada were not to offer its perspective", and offering to present it. I receive a response (8.12.86) that my letter has been forwarded to the "completely autonomous" Board for its consideration organizing the "Canada Conference". I was never to hear again. Obviously, Canada of 1987 did not include Buddhists or Buddhism! But upon running into him on my walk in the neighbourhood some years later, after his retirement – he had family, about 2 streets east of me, I did not raise the issue, although I was awed by the hunk of a man in front of me!

Having met the Minister of State for Privatization / Minister Responsible for the Status of Women, Barbara McDougal, MP, for my riding of St Paul's at her constituency office, I would receive a letter from her (11.07.86), where she adds, "I've made the *Toronto South Asian Review* a priority on my reading list". I was happy that the journal I had a hand in co-founding, with Vassanji, was in the upper echelons of power.

In a letter prior to my meeting (8.06.86), I had congratulated her on her appointment as Minister Responsible for Privatization. As a resident of the constituency, I wrote, "I am truly proud to have such an eminent daughter of Mother Canada [paralleling the common expression 'Mother Lanka'] to represent us in the highest offices of government". Adding my congratulations as President, Buddhist Council of Canada (and writing on Buddhist Council of Canada letterhead that showed the national executive), I tell that her "recent engagement with Bishop Tutu, and your involvement with your own church, tells me of the value you place on spirituality in your life and work. This is indeed comforting in a world besieged with too much materialism and too little spirituality. I, for one, would be willing to work with you in strengthening that value dimension of Canadian life, whether we label it Christian, Jewish, Buddhist or whatever".

Five years later I would write to her (12.12.91) congratulating her on her appointment as Secretary of State for External Affairs, and thanking for the St Paul's Report # 23. Since the Report is a "Special Issue on Canadian Unity", I a) enclose copy of the *Toronto Star* article on me under the heading 'Buddhist protests God..", and b) appraise her of my meeting Joe Clark on the Constitution. Having had the benefit of being kept informed of her public activities through the newsletter, I was to reciprocate and appraise her of my own work.

The Search for Meaning, my Report to the Secretary of State based on my Canada-wide survey of the Literature of the Canadians of South Asian Origins, had been handed in to Judy Young of the Department, who had given me the contract, in 1983. But it was to take another five years before it would be published officially by the Department.

Apparently impatient at the delay, however good the reasons may have been, I had written to David Crombie, Minister Responsible for multiculturalism, requesting that the English version be released without waiting for the completion of the French translation. In response, the Minister writes (11.24.86) that he will look into the question, but "only if the Official Languages Act permits exceptions". Congratulating me on "the hard work that went into [it] as well as your long-term involvement in literary and educational activities in the multiculturalism field", he ends on a touching note, with the words, "Take care", reminiscent of the affable 'tiny perfect Mayor' that he had come to be for an appreciative Toronto public.

It would be two more years before I would write to Mr. Crombie again. Attending the Heritage Day Multifaith Service (in the presence of the Queen) at Roy Thompson Hall (Feb. 14, 1988) as Buddhist Representative, I had met him, and talking about the upcoming Citizenship Act to be introduced in Parliament soon, he had said that Changes to the Multiculturalism Act, now awaiting Parliamentary approval, would still be possible at the Second Reading. I may have introduced myself as the nasty columnist who had written in my column in the Star (5.12.87) with an opening salvo, "If you expected Secretary of State David Crombie to be a multicultural Santa Claus when he presented his Canadian multiculturalism Act this week., you would be a bitterly disappointed child." Although I would qualify in my next line, "Not that he is exactly playing Scrooge, but he is delivering last year's list", he may have had every reason to be offended. I had also written a Star column (2.27.88) under the title, " 'Multi-faith' service lost a big opportunity", in which I had complained that "Only the religions that worship one God [namely, Christianity, Judaism and Islam]" were invited to the microphone. Absent at the microphone, I wrote, was "the voice of the majority, Rational Humanism". Or Hinduism, "the 6000 year old religion, whose supreme deities are at the same time one and many". "Or, of native religions", whose representatives paraded outside the hall, "hanging handwritten placards around the necks......, complaining about mistreatment by the Church". I continued: "Or, of Buddhism, which posits a morality without god", and who, unlike the Hindus, had not even been invited to the stage!

But, generous, and patient, was what I found him to be as he listened to me at the Constituency office at 65 Wellesely Street, Room 203, on March 18, 1988. I had proposed an amendment, the inclusion of a House Standing Committee Recommendation # 11: appointment of an independent Multicultural Commissioner answerable to Parliament, arguing the case. I would also take the opportunity to invite him for the Buddhist WESAK day celebration due in May. My letter (3.18.88), written the same day upon returning home, was to "put on paper, as agreed" my proposal, and it began with the line, "I want to congratulate you heartily for the candor, enthusiasm, flexibility and the warmth" he had shown. In it, I had specifically made a "Proposal – that provision be made in the Act to appoint A COMMISSIONER OF MULTICULTURAL AND RACE RELATIONS".

But how I watched all the wood I had chiselled with so much care and attention go down the stream, to adapt from a Sinhala saying, the very next day, when the news wires flashed that Minister Crombie had resigned! The tiny perfect city mayor had become the big bad politician to me. Did you not see me burning the midnight oil that day, pulling my hair, to see what on earth I had done so obnoxious to him, this time multiculturally, to make him quit right after meeting with me! Just joking! Glad I have your understanding. Ha ha ha!! Upon reflection today, I thank him for giving me another opportunity to grow, by practicing my Buddhist equanimity, coming to see reality as it has come to be, but the mind unshaken when hit by that world reality. Thank you *Dhammapada* for the wisdom!

Around that time, I had become a member of the Ontario Canada Day committee, proudly displaying my wings of Canadian nationalism, as openly as I had done expressing my Sri Lankan nationalism, a long three decades earlier. To make it clear, following the S W R D Bandaranaike socialist revolution (1956), my friends and colleagues came to be surprised, or appreciative, depending on one's political stance, one day when I showed up at work in a national attire, ditching the western attire worn all my life! To return to the Canada Day context, the next communication I was to receive from the federal level was a miniature Canada Day Poster. And it was from, no, you wouldn't guess... from none other than the very same Lucien Bouchard, who would set up, two years later, the Bloc Quebecois. Prime Minister Mulroney's political Minister for Quebec, and former

Ambassador to France, he was now Secretary of State. It was with interest, then, that I would read some 20 years later that a month before setting up BQ, he had said, "publicly, and in the House, that he would never do anything to destabilize the Conservative caucus, ... never consider setting up a separate party, and that he strongly urged everyone to support Prime Minister Mulroney, who had defended "the superior interests of Quebec". How the winds change direction! Expressing his "sincere thanks" in his letter, for my contribution "to the success of Canada Day 1988", he adds, "From all reports, Canada Day festivities continue to increase in number and in variety as Canadians come together in a demonstration of pride and celebration. Even unfavourable weather in some areas of the country did little to dampen the enthusiasm with which Canadians celebrate their national day." Indeed it was with pride I joined the celebration in front of the Ontario Legislature, wearing my 'uniform' of a white jacket with the words 'Canada Day' sewn on to the front pocket, an article of clothing I still cherish in my wardrobe, taking it out occasionally to take a look back. Enclosing the poster, he says how the "government of Canada sincerely appreciates the effort and dedication that went into the many months of planning, organizing and delivering the program".

Our work entailed encouraging communities to celebrate the Day, inviting Ontarians to apply for funds to celebrate the Day, and making decisions about who should get how much. Thanks from closer to home was the honour to be invited to the suite of the Lieutenant-governor, Lincoln Alexander, the Honorary Chair of the Ontario Canada Day Committee. The first Black to be appointed to the regal position, as Mulroney writes (p. 389), giving a personal touch his Memoir has come to be known for: "September 4, 1985, the day Nicolas was born, was also the day I appointed Ontario's first black Lieutenant-governor, Lincoln Alexander.

With Ontario Lieutenant-governor Lincoln Alexander, Chair of Canada Day Committee of which the author was a member

When I telephoned to ask him to serve as the Queen's representative to Ottawa, Linc, whose sense of humour is famous and infectious, said, "Prime Minister, this will be the best appointment you'll ever make" ". Mulroney would also appoint David Lam in British Columbia, and Yvon Dumont, a Metis, in Manitoba. I was to experience his sense of humour first hand, meeting Lieutenant-Governor Alexander in his suite. I would also receive a note from him (7.06.88) following the reception thanking me for the copy of *Toronto South Asian Review*, and my Toronto Star articles on Canada Day and Multiculturalism in Canada. The letter is addressed at Ontario Canada Day Committee, 25 St Clair East, the government building just east of Yonge where we would have our Canada Day meetings.

Working with an Advertising Executive on the Canada Day Committee, I would encourage him to turn multiculturalism into profit by using multicultural faces in advertising. As possibly the only person of colour on the committee, as far as I can remember, he would be polite, but sticks with the argument that the viewers wouldn't go for it. This was the same way that Dionne Brande was told that her books would never be published because her characters were Black, and Vassanji's first collection had to come out of UK under the Africa series, rejected by Canadian publishers. But I could only have had pity for the Exec for the money he and his company may have lost! For it was not too long after that multicultural faces and multicultural voices would appear on air.

The first letter I was to receive from Secretary of State, Gerry Weiner (6.21.89) was in appreciation of my participation as a member of an Interfaith group invited for a consultation organized by 'Multiculturalism and Citizenship Canada', with Dr. Noel Kinsela, the Deputy Minister. The issue at hand was whether religion should be included as part of multiculturalism. We had resoundingly argued that it could just not be otherwise! To the same extent that the issues in the world cannot be understood without a context of religion, Canadian multiculturalism cannot ignore religion as a driving force either. "Canada will continue to grow in freedom and strength because of the vision and openness which individuals such as you are prepared to share", he added in his letter. Following the consultation, I had attended a conference as well, organized at the St. Xavier University in New Brunswick with involvement of the Secretary of State for multiculturalism Canada, to explore the issue further.

A few months later, I was to receive another letter (8.18.89) to thank me for my "contribution to Canada Day 1989", enclosing a "mini version of this year's of Canada Day Poster, in recognition of your diligent work". A third letter (undated) was a thank you for my volunteer work again on Canada Day 1990, enclosing a Commemorative Pin.

My communication in more recent years at the Federal level was with Dr. Carolyn Bennett, MP for my riding St Paul's. As the rest of her campaign team continued on, house to house, she had stopped by to knock on our door, when I invited her in. She would spend so much time on our comfortable leather chair, chatting, that the members of her team were beginning to wonder where she indeed was. Later, she was to invite me for lunch when we went to an Indian

Swarna with Federal Cabinet Minister Carolyn Bennett, MP for St Paul's riding at our Ardmore home

restaurant on Eglinton Road at Yonge Street, when she heard my views about my anathema for party politics, for its divisive nature, and a bit about Buddhism and our family. She would later invite me to her home for a summer backyard party. Reciprocating,. I would invite her to the 100 Years of Buddhism in Canada celebration organized by Nalanda in 2005.

At a Community picnic organized by her in an earlier year at a park at St Clair and Bathurst in front of Loblaws, I was to meet Dalton McGuinty when he was Leader of the Opposition.

12.3 Encountering Municipal Politicians

I was to have some minimal contact with Municipal politicians as well. The first was when we moved to our house in Forest Hill. 'Michael Gee, QC, Executive Alderman Ward 11' as the letterhead read, wrote (3.20.86), "I understand that you have recently purchased a new home in Ward 11. I would like to take this opportunity to welcome you to the ward. As your municipal representative on City Council, I want you to know that I am here to assist you with any concerns or problems you may have. If I can be of any assistance to you, please do not hesitate to contact me." Although I have no written record of reciprocating, I must have retained some communication, since he writes to me again (6.02.86) offering to be of assistance in getting a building permit for the minor variations we were to do, which we did get.

It would be a whole decade later that I wrote to Mayor June Rowlands, having bumped into her at City Hall showing some people around. Chatting about our multicultural city, I would later enclose in my letter (12.03.91) a recent article, 'Keep the Great Experiment Going' that had appeared in the G & M (7.18.91). There was a very good reason for sending it to her – to sensitize her to the reality of multiculturalism, in Toronto in particular, while she seemed to be hiding her head in the sand. Lawyer Susan Eng had been appointed a Police Commissioner (she was to receive a piece written by me, but not published). Born and bred in Canada, Rowlands had remarked that Eng was not Canadian! She was basically saying that still, after twenty years since the introduction of multiculturalism by Trudeau, Chinese were still not Canadian. In fact, when Eng refused to swear allegiance to her Majesty upon her appointment (see my Toronto Star piece, "Challenging a Sleeping Lion over our Oath" (6.03.89), she had not made life easy for the establishment either. But, then, that was precisely the experiment Canada was engaged in. So my idea was to nudge the Mayor towards multiculturalism, allowing her to work herself into it without losing face. I was impressed, and pleased, to receive a thank you note within the week (12.09.91). Taking the time to be polite to a Canadian with a difficult sounding name, as mine was seen to be, appeared to me a sort of multicultural progress for her, sort of by osmosis.

My next letter (12.12.91) was to Howard Levine, congratulating him on his re-election as City Councillor in our Ward 14, and sending him two enclosures. One was the *Toronto Star* story, 'Buddhist Protest God in the Constitution', and the other my piece in the G & M, which, I say, "seemed to have traveled far and wide. Multiculturalism Minister Gerry Weiner responded to it as did the Monarchist League of Canada!". I would also list some of my other involvements: media, Templeton Award, Keynote in Buffalo, Buddhist Council of Canada, etc. I would further add with more relevance that Swarna was Head of English as a Second Language at Weston Collegiate Institute, located in the Ward. He writes to me (2.14.92) thanking for the letter, adding "I applaud your many accomplishments. Happy to have your family in my constituency".

But my first contact with Councillor Levine had been on a far more mundane matter – getting a building permit for an extension to our house, when the whole immediate neighbourhood had ganged up against us. Only two neighbours, both Jewish, like others, too, supported the application, one of them hinting at racism. An architect, present at the first hearing at City Hall, approaching us presenting his credentials as a university graduate *cum laude,* doing his own design to our specifications and meeting our needs, would eventually get our application, through the Committee of Adjustment on the very day that Swarna would successfully go through open heart surgery for a replacement of both the aortic and the mitral valves. I don't quite know what role Levine, also Jewish as the name had suggested to me, was to play in my getting the permit.

Just after our moving in, by way of making friendly neighbours, we had taken the initiative to invite the wife of a neighbour to visit our backyard. We were going to outline our landscape plans. Her response was to laugh it off with the words, "Oh, that'll be the day". A few years later, applying to the City Hall to put up an addition, the neighbour would spearhead the campaign against it, rounding up practically the entire neighbourhood against us. Some time later, the family was to unfortunately lose their teenage daughter in a tragic accident. I made a visit to the house, uninvited, of course, but in my usual friendly neighbourly spirit, also participating in a small religious activity that was taking place in their home. "What good neighbours we have!", I was to pleased to hear the husband say.

As an aside, would the good Councillor be perhaps intrigued by a recent poetic use of the name Levine to rhyme with 'ravine'? Here is the poem, from my third collection, *Obama Ji* (p.1):

QUESTIONS OF THE NIGHT

Answering a bell,
I open the door. Swell,
a young man, in skull cap and beard.
No, he did not look weird,
until he asked, "Are you Jewish?"
All I could put together,
"I'm a ...minion Buddhish."
"I'm looking for a Levine.
They live near this ravine.
Everyone around here Jewish."
Pity it's not British?!

Soon it was another bell.
Pizza man, oh swell!
Waiting to be paid, he summons a smile,
looks at me for a while.
Asks he, "Are you from Pakistan?"
A smiling me
confiding in m'self,
"No, only from Buddhistan."

Within half an hour! I begin to wonder.
Are these the questions that keep us asunder?

Obama Ji, 2009 (p. 1).

12.4 A Personal Reflection

Reading through the pages relating to my multiple communications with public figures, with a myriad of failures, the scrupulous reader may wonder, "Has anything been achieved from all these efforts?" Oh, very much so, I would contend. Nothing tangible perhaps, but many intangibles.

In my correspondence, or meetings, with political leaders, Federal, Provincial and Municipal, my intent has primarily been to chip away at the pre-multicultural stranglehold on the body politic, and push the envelope, to whatever extent it can be done at a personal level. This is what I had done in relation to society in general through my *Toronto Star* columns (see later), other writing, public speaking and community involvement. The chipping away was by way of educating the body politic, particularly from the vantage point of three areas: Buddhism, spirituality and the new kid on the block, Literature – multicultural and South Asian Canadian. It was also to walk the talk that I would also offer my personal services, to work informally or formally.

Self-care being a good Buddhist principle, it would have been nice if I had got a few more opportunities to serve the public good. But if that self-care was not to be an exclusive selfishness, which it needs not be nor should not be from a Buddhist point of view, it had to include other-care. And so my attempts may be seen then as seeking to serve other-care lazed with self-care.

It is my hope that my letters and personal contacts may have served the purpose of educating the polity to the existence of quality within the minority population.

I see the period 1980 to the end of 90's as a pre-paradigmatic period. Electoral successes such as of Bob Wong and Lincoln Alexander, e.g., would on the one hand say that the electorate seem to be more progressive than the politicians. But then the appointments of the likes of George Bancroft (Black), Bhausaheb Ubale (Brown) and Susan Eng (Chinese) would speak to a forward lookingness on the part of politicians on the other.

But there is no question that Canada was yet to be totally into the multicultural walk. The pages above may then be seen as walking through the pages of the pre-paradigmatic phase, with myself as the model. The fact that despite all my personal contacts, multidisciplinary academic skills and community involvement, Canada failed to draw upon my skills at a formal level is one small piece of evidence where Canada was at during these two decades. A good contrast would be the Provincial Minister Susan Fish. As noted, she had arrived at the Canadian scene, from the US, at about the same time as I had. Yet, she becomes a Minister, elected politically.

In the end, it is, of course, of no importance if, how and what I came to gain personally. What is gratifying is if, how and what Canada gained, nationally and personally.

So I can say that I consider my attempts as a praxis of the 'noble friend' (kalyana mitta) as in Buddhadhamma, never failing to call a spade a spade and giving the benefit of one's wisdom, even when one's best friend has done or said something not promotive of the good, for the self and for the others. So, given the social good that has resulted over time, I am happy to be able to say that I have been rewarded enough personally. It has brought me happiness. Mine has also been a continuing opportunity to grow in the practice of *mudita* – happiness in the happiness of others, and *upekkha* 'equanimity' in the face of realities of life. A Buddhist can ask for nothing better!

BOOK II, PART 5
BUDDHISM IN THE ACADEMY

13. SCIENCE FOR PEACE: A BUDDHIST CONTRIBUTION
13.1 Sci-Spi: Science of Spirituality

It was in 1993 when I got a call from Dr. Helmut Burkhardt a Professor of Physics at Ryerson University. Involved in Science for Peace, a movement headed by Dr. Anatole Rapaport, Professor Emeritus in Peace Studies at the University of Toronto, he wondered if I would be interested in participating. Not being a scientist I was a bit baffled. But it was to my pleasant surprise that he was to say that he was looking for religious input to the Proceedings. It was particularly so inviting, coming from a Professor of Physics, that bastion of academic materialism. What it told me was that finally, scientists were beginning to understand that science alone will neither be able to understand the totality of reality, nor resolve the problems of humanity. And so it was gladly that I accepted the invitation.

The title of the Conference seemed to capture the sentiment: *Universal Knowledge Tools and their Applications of General Science Theory*. And what was intriguing was that the 'tools' seem to include Religion, that orphan of the western Industrial Revolution and Christian-bashing. I was happy that finally it was gaining the warm embrace of academic parents.

His request to me was to be on a Panel on "Religions and their Social and Ecological Implications". Although I thought I would be the only Buddhist on it, along with representatives from the Native Canadian Cayuga Traditions, Islam, Judaism and Roman Catholicism, it was with pleasure that I found Peter Timmerman, a long-standing Buddhist, and now Professor in Environmental Studies at York University, Toronto, also on it, speaking from the perspective of 'Experiments in Truth'.

But I was to present a paper, too, titled 'Religion and the Science of Spirituality', or as I playfully called it, *Sci-Spi*! And thus, the paper gave me an opportunity to explore the concept of Spirituality in rather objective terms. The confusion around the two terms 'Religion' and 'Spirituality' had apparently been in my mind, particularly in the context of the Dynamics of Interfaith course I was teaching at Trinity. Defining *Spirituality*, to repeat, as 'the genetic potential in a given sentient being for psychophysical / biochemical harmony', I re-name religion as a *sociospirituality*, defining it as "a culture-, time- and guru- (or no-guru-) specific expression of spirituality". I argue that the suggested term "has the advantage of reminding us up-front of the sociological origins of religion". Over time, through a further division of a sociospirituality, we get *diaspiritualities*, giving the example of Orthodox, Conservative, Reform and Reconstructionist

Judaism, and Theravada and Mahayana Buddhism. But religion does indeed have an individual dimension to it. This I capture with the term *idiospirituality*, defining it as "the totality of the intrinsic spirituality of an individual at a given point in time". What I sought to capture is the idea of change within an individual from moment to moment.

The influence of Linguistics on this classification should only be obvious. What I was trying to do, then, was to provide a scientific, i.e.,. objective and analytical basis so that it could earn the respect of the scientific community. Now that the scientist has come to be open to Religion, wouldn't it be nice if they both spoke a common idiom? I end my paper with an invitation to "set up an ongoing 'Science of Spirituality' Committee", and throwing a challenge, "Should I wait for your call?" I am still waiting!

I was encouraged to see the thrust of an Interfaith input continuing at the Fourth Canadian Conference, too, held two years later, in 1995. More than 1600 scientists of 70 countries, including 100 Nobel Laureates, had signed a statement three years earlier, "warn[ing] all humanity of what is ahead. A great change in our stewardship of the earth and the life on it is required if vast human misery is to be avoided and our global home on this planet is not to be irretrievably mutilated" (Proceedings, p. III). Though conceding that "scientists have erred before", the organizers were taking the warning seriously, and were interested in a religious response, inviting me to Chair the Panel at which four presentations would be made, including one by a Cayuga Nation Writer, G A Jameison and Rabbi M Stroh of Thornhill presenting a Jewish Response.

In my opening remarks, I note how I read with great delight, words like 'caring, ethic and responsibility' contained in the Warning, since they would be the furthest away from the objectivity of the scientist. "The new attitude of the scientists seemed to be one as if people mattered! Not just microbes and high speed particles or atomic energy". Taking a crack at both Science and Religion, I continue:

> *Science was too far high up in its pedestal of objectivity to remind us religionists that human, animal and plant life were all tied in an intricate interdependency. But then, we didn't listen either! When Mr. Darwin showed us that man evolved from animal from marine life, we banned him in churches...*

And my punch-line was, "With mom of religion and dad of science, or is it the other way around, I don't know, busy taking pot shots at each other, in self-assured arrogance and rigidity, baby earth fell through the cracks, and was left unattended." I ended with the words, "Perhaps an acknowledgement by both science and religion of the 'sins' of the past, with a dash of humility, can bring the two together as well into a 'Union of Concerned Scientists and Religionists'".

Invited to present a paper as well at the same session, I speak on the topic 'Uniting People through Language and Mind Cultivation: a Buddhist Response to the World Scientists' Warning to Humanity'. The thrust of my paper was that while as a Buddhist, I have no difficulty with the message of scientists, "my critique is that by not bringing their scientific outlook to the use of language, it perpetuates... the division that already exists in society." Taking the first point of the Scientists "to restore and protect the integrity of the earth's system we depend on", I complain that this is one-sided, since the earth can be 'self-centred', too. It can "be cruel, taking a free hand in imposing its own disasters upon us humans – floods, earthquakes. Lightning.., unseasonal rains, droughts, famines, forest fires, etc."

Further, "To carry the one-sided statement to its logical conclusion, that nature must somehow be protected from us mindless omnivores and destroyers, would be to ensure human extinction. How would e.g., native people of the north survive without killing the caribou, or Newfoundland or other fishermen around the world without catching fish? How could African farmers survive without ensuring that their crops are saved from roaming elephants? How could the needs of growing cities be met without encroaching upon some farm land?"

I also critique the scientists' statement, "We must reduce and eventually eliminate poverty", pointing out that "there will never be a time or context when there will be no poverty." Continuing how the responsibility for eliminating poverty is placed in the hands of everybody else but the poor, I make the argument, "My point is that it is the poor that must make the effort, and that others could only help those who help themselves".

The point behind the criticism is a lack of recognition of reciprocity, as pointed out by the Buddha. But, given that the 'we' who are said to be mindless vis-à-vis nature includes scientists, I also urge that they themselves seriously consider purifying their own minds through Buddhist meditation by way of providing by example. I end with the point that "the emergence of a critical mass of 'spiritual scientists', both objective and compassionate, might well be the condition for ushering in that world of justice, peace and harmony envisaged by the scientists."

In 1999, I was to be invited to another conference, "Global and Local Responsibilities for a Just and Sustainable Civilization" (June 2-6). Here I developed on the concept of Human Rights (HR hereafter) on which I had written a short piece to the Ontario Human Rights Commission Publication, I began by pointing out that while HR has been hailed as a champion of the underprivileged, it "is rife with conceptual and practical problems". The first conceptual issue was that it is based in a conflictual view of the world, "possibly Darwinian reflection" [of the survival of the fittest], and thus exclusively individualistic. Thus it "goes against the very nature of reality, namely, interrelatedness", a view well captured in the Buddha's Teaching of Conditioned Co-origination, where everything rises in the context of a multiplicity of conditions, immediate and remote. Another point I made was that it places law over morality. Since it is a western view, it also entails "intellectual colonialism". For reasons such as the above, a Human Rights approach serves as a "serious impediment to building a Just and Sustainable society". But without throwing the baby out with the bathwater, I also propose a Human Rights and Responsibilities paradigm where each one gives in order to get, given that what is not given cannot be had by another.

Science for Peace Bulletin 2002 05 summarizes my paper on Justice, a Buddhist Perspective:

> *Justice is an important instrumental value that is difficult to define. Suwanda Sugunasiri, the founder of the Nalanda College of Buddhist Studies in Toronto presented a paper entitled: Justice - a Buddhist Perspective. Justice is seen as an agent that creates a dynamic social equilibrium: 'social homeostasis'. This understanding of justice is based on Buddha's notion of conditioned co-origination, which means that everything results from a multiplicity of conditions in a necessary, reciprocal, and circular relationship. Professor Sugunasiri suggests that: The goal of justice is happiness for the individual-in-society. The conditions required to achieve such a goal are at the individual level friendliness (metta), compassion (karuna), altruistic joy (mudita), and equanimity (upekkha). Conjointly are four dimensions of social-consciousness, namely, sharing (dana), pleasant speech (peyyvajja), the social good (atthacariya) and egalitarianism (samanattata). All qualities are to be understood both preventively and curatively. An approach to justice in terms of Human Rights is contrary to such principles, because it is based in selfishness, attachment, and anger.*

- *(www.scienceforpeace.ca/file_download/21/-200205.pdf)*

At a conference at York University, with participants (R to L) Professors Helmut Burkhardt, Melissa Williams , Vandra Masemann and Dr. William J. Ryan, sj. from Ottawa

13.2 You're What You Sense

Teaching Buddhist Psychology at Vidyodaya University during my two year stint in Sri Lanka in 1971-73, I had come to organize my thoughts on the Buddhist *Abhidhamma*, literally 'Higher Reality' but generally translated as 'Buddhist Metaphysics'. One of the topics that had intrigued me had been the Buddha's Teachings on the Mindbody. While, of course, there are scholarly treatments on the topic, there is not much available to the average English reader. With an emerging interest in Buddhism in the West, I thought it best to present the Buddha's mindbody analysis in a dialogue format, a technique often used by the Buddha himself. In order to capture the basic idea that there is nothing more to sentience than what is inputted through the six senses, including the mind, I came to call it, in a moment of creativity I suppose, *You're What You Sense: Buddha on Mindbody*.

I mischievously sub-titled it, A Buddhianscientific Dialogue, to capture the idea that the Buddha's discoveries constituted nothing but science, meaning that they were arrived at empirically, and after the fact, and not speculatively, and thus not qualifying under 'philosophy'. I was, of course, seeking to capture the ground lost to the west in the label 'science'. Science was not just what the west discovered under the physical microscope but what was discovered by the Buddha under the **'introscope'** (new term) of the mind as well. Analyzing the mind and the body separately, each into its 'primary features' and 'derivatives', I came to list the many 'Scientific Concepts of the Buddha' at the end. My intent at re-capturing the lost ground to Science, the Sri Lankan publisher, Buddhist Cultural Centre, showed Buddha and Einstein side by side on the cover, along with a drawing of an atom but showing the sub-title as 'a Buddhian-Scientific dialogue' as if to give the indication that this was an attempt to parallel Buddhism with science. Reportedly, the book came to be a 'best seller' at the Buddhist Cultural Centre shop at the exit lounge of the Bandaranaike International Airport.

One of the difficult Teachings of the Buddha is *anatta*, 'asoulity' as I translate it, but more popularly by western scholars as 'non-self'. The basic idea here being that there is no doer of an action, entailed in the action being only a process, I drew the analogy of the 'internet' as a modern day scientific parallel. And so it was with interest that I came to discover, while writing this Memoir, the following on the internet in the form of a letter (http://groups.yahoo.com/group/dhammastudygroup/message/14552) from one RobM to his friend, DSG. I show it below verbatim :

Hi DSG,
I was recently reading an interesting book, "You're What You Sense" by Dr. Suwanda Sugunasiri which included an Internet analogy. I expanded on the analogy and presented it to my Abhidhamma class. I think that you may find it interesting as well.

Input = visible object / audible object
Client Computer Hardware = eye base / ear base
Client Computer Software = eye consciousness / ear consciousness
Internet Service Provider = mind door
Internet = namarupa
Internet Hardware = mind base
Internet Software = nama

A person types information (input) into their computer (client hardware). The software on their computer (client software) processes the information and sends it to the Internet Service Provider, a gateway to the Internet used by a number of different clients. The Internet is made up of millions of computer servers running software which allows them to interact.

x Who Controls the Internet?
Even though the Internet is incredibly complex, there is no single entity in control.

Even though beings (namarupa) are incredibly complex, there is no "self" in control. This is the concept of anatta.

x What is the Internet?
The Internet is a concept, an aggregate of ever-changing software and hardware. None of the components are the Internet but the Internet does not exist outside of the components either.

A being is a concept, an aggregate of ever-changing nama (mind) and rupa but the being does not exist outside of the components.

x How to Describe the Internet?
Though hardware is necessary for the Internet to exist, it is best to treat hardware as a platform for software and focus on how hardware impacts the software (speed, capacity, etc.) rather than the technical details of the hardware (processors, etc.). What makes the Internet interesting and powerful is the interaction between software.

Though rupa is necessary for a being to exist, it is best to treat rupa as a platform for nama and focus on how nama experiences rupa (solidity, cohesion, temperature, motion) rather than the technical details of rupa (protons, neutrons, electrons). What makes a being interesting and powerful is the interaction of nama.

x What Makes the Internet Work?
In addition to being governed by the laws of physics (signal degradation, etc.),

the foundation of the Internet is a set of rules that define how software interacts (TCP/IP, HTTP, etc.). The Internet is almost never at rest as there are almost always inputs arriving from one of the clients.

In addition to being governed by the laws of utu-niyama (we all must age), the foundation of a being is a set of rules that define how nama interacts (citta-niyama, kamma-niyama). A being is almost never at rest as there are almost always external objects being apprehended by the five senses.

x **How to Understand the Internet?**
   One can never understand the internet looking at the macro-level (appearance of web pages, etc.). To truly understand the Internet, one must understand how the underlying hardware, software and rules work.

One can never understand a being looking at the macro-level (personality, etc.). To truly understand a being, one must understand how the underlying rupa, nama and niyama work.

Being an engineer by training, I found this analogy interesting - particularly the "Nobody controls the Internet = anatta" concept.

Enjoy!

Thanks,
Rob M

13.3 Challenging Cartesian Dualism, Defining Sentience

Still on a wider screen, it was with surprise that I received an invitation to be the Keynote speaker at "Humanity and the Cosmos Symposium" in Alphie's Trough at Brock University in St Catherines, Feb. 7, 2004. I was to speak on "Science, Spirituality, and Time: a Buddhist Perspective." As noted in a Report appearing in *Brock Press*, six years later, on Tuesday, June 15, 2010, I had been chosen "because", as organizer Keith Sudds explains, "we feel he speaks with a multi-spiritual voice". I don't quite know what was meant, but I sense that the reference is to my Buddhist co-origination approach.

In a piece on my presentation, under the title, "Western philosophy challenged in symposium", Joshua Long writes (Brock Press, 2/10/04 Section: News):

> *Western notions of the primacy of the rational mind were challenged in the keynote lecture of this year's Humanity and the Cosmos Symposium...*
> *Throughout his lecture Sugunasiri challenged the Cartesian idea that the body and soul are two separate and distinct entities. Instead he argued that they are one and the same, using the term "mind-body" to*

represent the fusion of body and soul. More specifically, he said the matter of spirituality is as "natural to us as is kicking our foot when our knee is tapped." He argued that it is ingrained in the genes which form us.

The implications of such a revelation, Sugunasiri explains, are that we have a more basic obligation to use that ability in order to better understand ourselves and the world around us. "The term is 'mind-body' and not 'body-mind' [so as to] suggest a prominence in the act of thinking," said Sugunasiri.

A recurrent theme was the dual natures of science and spirituality. He explained that science needs to respect spirituality, and vice versa. However, Sugunasiri also stresses that respect should not equal bias, nor should it affect either quest for truth.

In regard to how that idea would reflect the matter of creationism being taught in schools, Sugunasiri says "there is a difference between believing something that you have spent a good deal of time analyzing, and believing something simply because it is easier than confronting more reasonable alternatives."

He also explains that spirituality should be submitted to deep personal reflection, not simply given over to blind faith. He says that this balance between the two should be tempered with "critical compassion," where one may criticize another, yet remain respectful - just as a critic may dislike an author's work without maintaining any animosity toward that author.

Sugunasiri also tried to dispel the misconception that Buddhism is only about meditation. "Buddhism is not only about meditation, also important is self-discipline."

Not satisfied with the understanding of 'sentience' given in the Wikipedia, I make an entry from a Buddhist perspective. Picked up by the *Webster's Online Dictionary* with Multilingual Thesaurus Translation, it read as follows:

Sentience is, from a Buddhist perspective, the state of having senses (sat + ta in Pali or sat + tva in Sanskrit). And the senses are six in number, the sixth being the mind aka consciousness. Just as consciousness is in the whole body (see Sugunasiri, Suwanda H J, The Whole Body, not Heart, as 'Seat of Consciousness': the Buddha's View', Philosophy East & West, vol. 45, no. 3, pp. 409-430), sentience, then, is the ability to sense / experience pain and pleasure, make conscious choices, including not doing, not talking, not speculating, etc. Thus, while an animal qualifies as a sentient being, a computer doesn't, for at least two reasons: (a) Even if it makes intelligent decisions, it has to be programmed by an outside agent (human or even a super-computer), whereas a sentient being is self-directed, and (b) a computer must always perform using instructions in order to communicate, whereas a sentient being can still express in silence - through kinesics (body language), oculesics (eye language) and proxemics (distance).

Referring to the entire article on 'sentience', giving western scientific, Christian and other understandings, an added note says that *"This article has been cited as a source or otherwise recommended by the mainstream press. See Wikipedia: Wikipedia as a press source for details"*.

14 UNIVERSITY OF TORONTO COMES A-CALLING

14.1 Trinity Seminars on Buddhism

At the initiation of Prof Will Oxtoby, of the Faculty of Divinity, Trinity College, University of Toronto, and with support from Dean Peter Slater, I am invited to serve as a Research Associate, and also to teach. I make it an opportunity to organize a series of 'Seminars on Buddhism' beginning in 1993. The opening Fall series would offer the following:

Oct. 15, 1993 *Sweet & Sour Buddhism: North American Perceptions of Buddhism* Victor Hori, Dept for the Study of Religion, U of T; Fac of Rel Studies, McGill

Nov. 19, 1993 *Japanese Buddhist Art in the Heian Period* (lecture/slide presentation) Catherine Ludwik, Ph.D candidate, Dept for the Study of Religion, U of Toronto

Dec. 3, 1993 *Khmer Refugees in Canada: Difficulties in Establishing Belief & Practice* Janet McClellan, Dept of Anthropology, York University

Among the Professors presenting Lectures thereafter were the following: Roy Amore (U of Windsor), Julia Ching (U of Toronto), Richard Hayes (McGill),

With Prof Charles Prebish of Penn State, USA at McGill University

Victor Hori (McGill), Janet McLellan (Wilfred Laurier), Neil McMullen (U of Toronto), Charles Prebish (Penn State, USA), Leonard Priestley (U of Toronto), Robert Sharf (McMster), Peter Timmerman (York University), Narendra Wagle (U of Toronto), A K Warder (U of Toronto) and David Waterhouse (U of Toronto).

Also featured were PhD Students, such as Mavis Fenn (McMaster), Catherine Ludwik (U of Toronto), Simon Moon (U of Toronto), Terry Woo (U of Toronto). On occasion, there were subject specialists as well. Thus, e.g., Doris Dorenwend (Royal Ontario Museum) would speak on Buddhist Art at the ROM (Feb. 17.1995), Shakya Dorje, a 'practitioner of Tibetan medicine', would make a presentation on Tibetan Buddhism (Dec 9, 1994) and Eric Chen on Meditation. Meditation sometimes included at the end of a session, featured would also be ordained practitioners as well, such as, Ven Bhikkhuni Man Yi of the Buddha's Light International (Mississauga) and Ven Khenpo Sonam Rinpoche of the Riwoche Pemavajra Temple and Bhante Saranapala of the Sri Lankan temple, West End Buddhist Centre, Mississauga.

I also organize a Conference on Rita Gross' work, *Buddhism After Patriarchy*, on April 22, 1995, in association with the Department for the Study of Religion and with financial assistance from the Yehan Numata Program in Buddhist Studies, facilitated by Prof. Neil McMullen. Supporting my efforts, and commenting, "You're doing what we ought to be doing", Prof. Rhona Abramovich, of the Women's Study Centre, would pitch in financially as well.

With participation by scholars from across Canadian universities, the Conference would attract scholars from the US as well, such a s Prof. Judith-Simmer-Brown of Naropa University, Boulder, Colorado. Rita Gross (Department of Religion, U of Wisconsin-Eau Claire, USA) was to give the Opening Address, *Passion and Peril: On Being a Feminist Scholar-Practitioner* as well as a closing session, responding to the issues raised during the Conference.

I myself would present a paper under the title, "*Non-monastic Lay Buddhism-A Slippery Path to Thinning Thirsts (a Neo-Theravada Response)*".

Held at the George Ignatieff Theatre at Trinity College, the Conference would attract enough to make the house almost full.

While in general, the Trinity Seminars comprised of unrelated individual topics, it comes to be thematic, under Colloquy, in time. Among them were:
- Faces of Buddhism: Precept and Practice (4 Seminars, Fall 1996);
- Buddhist Skillful Means (Upaya): Plato, Kierkegaard & Christian Apologetics (5 Seminars, Winter 1997);
- Buddhism in North America: Historical Perspectives (5 Seminars, Fall 1997);
- Research (3 Seminars, Spring 1998);
- Engaged Buddhism (9 Seminars, Fall 1998); and
- Journeys to Sacred Buddhist Landscapes (6 presentations, Fall 1999).

The Colloquy on 'Buddhist Skillful Means (*Upaya*)' deviated from the rest in that it entailed a sort of Dialogue, or a comparative perspective, with participation of subject specialists on both Buddhism and areas other than Buddhism. If Prof. Warder would well represent Buddhist scholarship, presenting other points of view were Professors (all of University of Toronto) Graeme Nicholson (Upaya and Plato), Ivan Khan (Upaya and Kierkegaard), Will Oxtoby and Don Wiebe.

'Journeys to Sacred Buddhist Landscapes' took a different shape. They were Lecture-Video Presentations. The series presented the following:

- Buddhist Art of China; Buddhist Art of Java (David Waterhouse);
- India, the Land of Origin (Dennis Winters, freelance photographer);
- Temples of Thailand (Bill Dickinson, Royal Thai Consulate); and
- Sleepwalking in Mongolia (David Cherniak, filmmaker).

My own contribution was a slide show on "Sri Lanka: 3rd c. BCE – 13th C ACE".

In a 'Monday nights at Trinity College' series, I present the following as well:

- *Theravada Buddhism: Sinhalese as Case Study* (Fall 1996).
- *Toronto Beginnings (1980's): Buddhism in North America: Historical Perspectives* (Spring 1997).
- *Awakening of All: Ariyaratna's Sarvodaya in Sri Lanka* (Fall 1997).
- *Reviving Women's Ordination: Kabilsingh, Tsomo, Ayya Khema* (Fall 1998).

Nalanda College of Buddhist Studies (Canada) founded in 2000, the series would continue under its aegis, beginning in 2001.

14.2 Teaching Buddhism at the School of Continuing Studies

One of the most gratifying things I've been engaged in is teaching Buddhism. Be it for the University of Toronto School of Continuing Studies (SCS) or for the Learning Annex, I always came out learning a little something more of Buddhism.

Digging through my files to write these Memoirs, it was with great surprise I discovered that my earliest contact with SCS to have been way back in 1977 while I was still a finishing PhD student, and well before my years of involvement in Canadian Buddhism beginning in 1980. I write to the then Director, Dr Frank Miosi, to offer a course, "Introduction to Theravada Buddhism". At this stage of my studies, I was still 15 years or so away from earning my formal credentials in Buddhist Studies, and so I found myself to be qualified to teach only Theravada Buddhism I had been born into, studied at Sunday School, and read up on, primarily by western scholars. But in these pre-multicultural days, my letter doesn't appear to have crossed his desk or been taken seriously.

My first successful attempt comes to be 16 years later, in the Fall of 1993, teaching a course *Introduction to the Teachings of the Buddha*, offered in 10 sessions. Having by now earned an MA in the Scientific Study of Buddhism at the University of Toronto, this came to result in a joint letter written by me and my Professor, Leonard Priestley, to Prof. Alex Pathy, the new Director. Congratulating him on his new appointment, we both offer to teach for the SCS, Prof. Priestley proposing a course on *The Perfection of Wisdom*. My course shown in the general Calendar, a special flyer comes to be developed by the SCS showing a standing 'Amida Buddha – The Boundless Light'. Not only were we a decade or so into official Multiculturalism (introduced in 1979), this was also a time when courses on Buddhism at the University were at an ebb. Prof. Priestley remained as the only Buddhologist, and courses were far and few. Dr Connie Demb now being my main contact at SCS, the class enrolment was a healthy 25 or more. Offered a second year, the enrolment would continue to be healthy.

An SCS formal evaluation, through a questionnaire to be filled by the students, shows me earning a healthy 3.3 out of 4 in 1994, and a not so bad 2.9 in 1995. Among the comments given by students were:

> "The enthusiasm of the Instructor and his knowledge in Buddhism";
> "The energy and the enthusiasm the instructor brought to each class";
> "Instructor's enthusiasm gives initiative for further study..".
> ".. extremely knowledgeable not only about Buddhism....".

One referred to "the pleasant smiling Professor", with another noting that the "teacher was very pleasant". For another, the class was "Very relaxed .." "Good Handouts", noted another. What one liked best about the course were "discussions, broad range of topics", while another noted that "The content was thorough and well presented. Questions were answered in an accepting and stimulating manner. General manner of relating was open, & friendly." Some topics dealt with in class were deemed "better left for a more advanced course on Buddhism", another suggesting "A Part II".

Taking seriously a suggestion by a student of the class of 1993 to "add some time for practice", I would introduce some meditation the next year, a student noting that what he liked best about the class was "the meditation session.."

Another course, *Dynamics of Interfaith*, to be offered in the Winter of 1995, also in the same flyer as the one on Introduction to Buddhism, however, would not fly. Perhaps SCS had, like me, overestimated the interest of the Toronto population in understanding each other religiously in our multicultural society.

There would be three other Courses proposed by me, and advertised by SCS: "Buddha's Analytical Thought: an Eastern Paradigm" (Fall 1999), "Buddha's Scientific Teachings" (Fall 2000) and "Buddha's Way to Heaven" (Fall 2000). The last two were of 16 contact hours (8 sessions). My attempt in the first two was to put to rest the general notion in the west that Buddhism was only a religion, and the Buddha was nothing more than a religious teacher. By now, my book *You're What You Sense: Buddha on Mindbody*, 2001 was in the process of being published, and as the sub-title, "A Buddhianscientific Dialogue" shows, that my intent was to introduce Buddha, though undoubtedly a religious teacher, as being beyond that. The last course was intended to show the relevance of the 2500 old Teachings to contemporary life - in economics, politics, society, morality, etc. But, it appears that Canada had not matured to the level of the European understanding of the Buddha by scientists, philosophers, thinkers, poets – Einstein, Neitsche, Russell, Rhys Davids, Edwin Arnold. While over 29,000 Torontonians are said to have made it to the Rogers Centre to listen to the Dalai Lama, I know of no Canadian thinker, philosopher, Professor or any other that has said a word publicly about the Buddha, or studied him seriously. So the Buddha seems to continue to be only a religious teacher. Not getting sufficient enrolment (7 and 5 respectively for the last two), the courses came to be cancelled.

Teaching at the SCS certainly had its challenges. In the regular university courses, you can expect a certain level of academic background, intellectual preparation and serious commitment on the part of the students in the class, since the course would be part of an overall program allowing one to earn a degree, Diploma, Certificate, etc. But, in Continuing Studies, what I would find in a given class were students from an array of backgrounds – some compatible with the area of study, others not. While, e.g., one student wanted "More on Sutta", another wanted a visit to a Buddhist temple.

Given my style of teaching which encouraged raising questions throughout a lecture – "ample opportunity for questions", a student noted that there came to be situations when a basic question by a single beginning student would hold up a whole class. This was picked up by another student in his evaluation: "Too much time spent in intellectual / semantic discussion with certain individuals". A more sympathetic student would note that the classes "moved along at a speed governed by the class." A high level of absenteesism added to the challenge. Being 'interest courses', which student would turn up which day, and the total to be expected on a given day was anybody's guess.

However, teaching in Continuing Education was also vastly gratifying, despite the pittance one would get paid compared to Teaching for the regular division. For one, students were all mature learners, and mostly educated. Secondly, while there was certainly the same level of preparation to teach, there was no marking of papers!

A non-university educational organization that sought me out often was the *Learning Annex*, always on the lookout to offer courses on the latest hip topic. Seeking out the average Canadian, one of the more popular courses I would offer, beginning in March / April, 2001, would be *Buddhism for Beginners*. The classes would mostly be held in the heart of the city – Holiday Inn at King & Peter, Corporate Seminar Centre at King and York and the Faculty of Education at Bloor and St George, but with small classes rarely exceeding 15. It was a bunch of eager beavers that I would encounter, some with no background at all but some with prior exposure. The students represented a wide a variety of Torontonians, more women than men. And, judging by the fashionable attire worn by some – make up, high heels, coiffured hair, etc., they seem to come from among the young and .. possibly the restless.

But they were clearly looking for direction. Mindfulness Meditation was always a hit. One of the aspects in meditation they liked best was acknowledging whatever it was that was impinging upon the senses, and returning to watching the mind. Another they liked was the fact that the mind was always alert to self-discovery. The very process, e.g., of watching the inbreath ending up in the lungs and dissolving, and then the outbreath beginning in the lungs and dissolving at the tip of the nostrils, bring the insight of impermanence and change. And so the Buddha's first Noble Truth comes to be experienced, and not just learned from the books.

One night around 7, I would get a call from the Learning Annex wondering where I was. At home, of course! But that was not where I was supposed to be on that night at that time. So it was with a red face I would walk into a class of patient eager beavers at the Holiday Inn.

It was evident that it was time to pack in my evening and night appointments. Thus my teaching for the Annex would come to an end towards the end of 2002.

Elderhostel is a worldwide organization with more than 2500 educational establishments, "providing low-cost, short term academic programs for older adults aged 60 or better" (Coordinator's Manual). And it was from the Program Coordinator of the Wildlife Outdoor Education Centre on RR #1, Wyevale, Ontario, that I would receive a Fax inviting me to make a presentation on Buddhism (June 24, 1996), as one of a series, "Unlock the Mysteries of Each Religion". A vehicle arranged to pick me up, it was refreshing to be speaking on Buddhism in a rural setting. The three major stages relating to the Buddha's life had taken place in natural surroundings – Birth in the Lumbini Park as mother Mahamaya was on her way to her parents for the delivery of her *first* baby as was the custom, attaining Enlightenment at Buddhgaya under a tree, and attaining Parinibbana on a make-do bed between two trees in Kusinara.

The contrast in the audience, of about 30 or more, from the Holiday Inn crowd, couldn't be starker. Here were all elderly Canadians, and mostly Christian. Interestingly, however, the questions were no different. One of the specific ones I remember clearly was, "What is the purpose of life"? Many, I am sure, must have been disappointed at my answer. "There is none!". I went on to explain that that is not to say that an individual may not have a purpose in life – to succeed. Life was an abstract, and did not even have a life to ask the question!

14.3 A Few Publications

In my activities, I had met many a Buddhist leader, both ordained and lay, but I, as everybody else, knew nothing about them beyond what could be gleaned through the casual and surface encounters. Wanting to preserve for posterity the early Buddhist Sangha and the lay leadership in Toronto, I had submitted a proposal to the Multicultural History Society of Ontario in the eighties (1984-86), to conduct oral interviews with them under a 'Buddhism in Toronto' History Project. The tapes now part of the Society's multicultural collection, a quarter century later, I would bring out a publication, *Thus Spake the Sangha: Early History of Buddhism in Toronto* (2008) featuring five of the six sangha members, representing the Japanese (Tsunoda Sensei), Korean (Kwang Ok Sunim and Samu Sunim), Sinhala (Bhante Punnaji) and Tibetan (Zasep Tulku Rinpoche), the

sixth, Fashih Sing Hung, preferring not to go public. A sequel, featuring the lay leadership is awaiting completion and publication.

Sending his complementary copy, I would write to Samu Sunim how poetic I found the following description as given in his own words:

> One day, I was standing there [on the bridge on one side of the rising river], and it was getting dark, and the water was increasing. I was standing here, unable to get across, and my mother was standing there. We could see each other very clearly, but as the water level rose, we were retreating further, and further, you know. And it was getting dark. So I was there for a long time, retreating, and still trying to look at my mother on the other side.... Still I could not get close to her, and I wondered if this would happen as I grow up, you know, and that she would get old and someday, maybe, she will disappear, like I was seeing now, you know, retreating from each other, you know, from each other. And I thought maybe everything in life would be like that, that impermanent feeling. And also the change of seasons, spring flowers and summer and .. (p. 145).

An earlier publication was *Embryo as Person: Buddhism, Bioethics and Society*, 2005 (see later under chapter heading, 'A Bioethically Engaged Buddhist

Columnist'). With the knowledge gained of the community overall, I would also publish an article, "Buddhism in Metropolitan Toronto: a Preliminary Survey", in *Canadian Ethnic Studies* (1989), possibly the earliest piece of field research on the growing Buddhist community, the full length and far more comprehensive study by Janet McLellan, *Many Petals of the Lotus*, appearing in 1999. It outlines the community in terms of numbers and geographic location, both in total and by ethnic community and / school of Buddhism.

Going from sociology to psychology, I have an article published in *East West Philosophy* (1995), "Whole Body, not the Heart, the Seat of Consciousness: Buddha's View". Throughout history, all schools of Buddhism have maintained that the *heart* is the seat of consciousness. Heart Sutra thus becomes a key teaching of Mahayana Buddhism, and Buddhaghosa, the Theravada Commentator of the 5th c. even goes on to describe the 'seat' in physical terms. Tracing the description to Vedic sources, I show that the Buddha's view is that it is in the whole body, the evidence being right there for all to see – in one of the links of the Buddha's foundational Theory of Conditioned Co-origination: *conditioned by consciousness is the mindbody; conditioned by the mindbody is consciousness.*

15. NALANDA COLLEGE OF BUDDHIST STUDIES

15.1 A New Beginning in the New Millennium

One of the things that had hit me taking courses towards my Master's at the University of Toronto, with a specialization in the Scientific Study of Religion and Buddhism, was the paucity of courses on Buddhism. Once a fairly healthy component of the Program of Studies at the university, at its peak, it included visiting Professors such as Ven. Hammalawa Saddhatissa (from London, UK) and Prof. Jotiya Dhirasekara (Univesity of Peradeniya, Sri Lanka). By now though, the faculty had come to be dwindled to only two Buddhologists – Prof. A K Warder and Prof. Leonard Priestley. But even with the availability of such stalwarts, it didn't appear that Buddhism was taught in any systematic manner. I was, e.g., surprised to hear that the Four Noble Truths came to be covered in all of two sessions, in a full year overview course of about 28 sessions.

It was with the intent of ameliorating this condition that I put together, in 1993, a working group, of primarily Buddhists, among them Prof. Frank Tall of the Department of Mathematics, Peter Timmerman (now of York University) and Catherine Rathbun (later Founder of Friends of the Heart Centre).

In the expectation that a proposal for a more systematic study of the Buddhism would have the most chance of success if established as part of the University, my first approach was to the Dean of Divinity at Trinity of which I was a faculty member. Prof. Don Wiebe, ironically a self-professed atheist, was more than supportive. As Associate Director of the Centre for the Study of Religion, he had been my supervisor of my MA Studies. Prof. Thomas McIntyre, a committed Christian practitioner on the Divinity Faculty at Trinity, was equally enthusiastic. Satisfied, after several Faculty meetings, about the quality of the Program Proposal, and my own academic credentials, my proposal found approval. Going to the next level, the Divinity Council, which included representations from Alumni and the Anglican Church, it came to be approved, too, again after a long drawn process.

It was, then, with high expectations that we went to Trinity College Council, given that the proposal had been thoroughly vetted for quality. But was I in for a surprise! The Provost had a 'friendly amendment' – to come back to the Council when approval for the Proposal had been received from all the Anglican Cardinals across Canada! Not being a member of the Council, I had no speaking privileges to express my views on what I thought was an unfriendly non-amendment!

Receiving a clear verdict, my next attempt was to reach out to New College at the University, known for its innovative and forward-looking programs such as Black Studies and Women's Studies. While the Principal was personally supportive, it was not a matter within his power.

My next attempt was with the Department for the Study of Religion, the most legitimate home for our proposal. Again, while the Chair was supportive, it was not within his power.

It was at this point I wrote to the Dean of Arts and Science, within whose mandate it was to decide, after consultation, of course, on new programs. Since we didn't go with a bundle of money, a legitimate concern was continuity. Would the university want to be left with holding the bag for funding it?

In support of the thrust being made for Buddhist studies, I had begun organizing Trinity Seminars (see above) to ensure the presence of Buddhist Studies at the University. By now, six years had gone by when the writing on the wall was beginning to be visible. We were left with no choice but to go independent.

Thus it was that the doors came to be opened for Nalanda College of Buddhist Studies in 2000, under the initial name of Toronto College of Buddhist Studies. We were fortunate to be given space to hold classes at the Cham Shan Library, at 1224 Lawrence Avenue West, facilitated by Mr. Ching An Lee, an Engineer, and a Chinese Elder I had come know from the Buddhist Council of Canada days.

Given that Canada had come to be home to practically all the varieties of world Buddhism, I had successfully sought out a multicultural Board of Directors, with physician Dr. Clement Wong as Chair, and Prof. Frank Tall as Vice Chair. Kim Nguyen came to be the Treasurer. I was Secretary and President of the College.

Elder Chin An Lee.

POSITION	NAME	ETHNICITY
Chair	Dr. Clement Wong	Chinese
V. Chair	Prof. Frank Tall	Jewish
Secretary	Dr. Suwanda H J Sugunasiri	Sinhala
Treasurer	Kim Nguyen	Vietnamese
Member	Khin Hla Hla	Burmese
Member	Franz Li	Chinese
Member	Pencho Rabgey	Tibetan

Board of Directors of Nalanda College of Buddhist Studies by Position and Ethnicity

The Objects of the College, as published in the literature, were as follows:

- To provide an academic framework for the study of Buddhism.
- To meet the educational needs of Buddhism in Canada.
- To facilitate personal spiritual growth.
- To facilitate the application of Buddhist principles to everyday living.
- To increase community awareness of Buddhist principles.
- To contribute to the development of a harmonious multicultural society.

A Sri Lankan Canadian lawyer, Tilaka de Soyza, providing legal advice, and a name search done, an application was made to the Government of Ontario to register the College as a post-Secondary Institution. The Ombudsman's office satisfied with the Objects of the College and the Constitution, the registration was finalized. Meeting the requirements of Revenue Canada, the College also received charitable status, which meant donations were tax-deductible.

The literature showed the Founder's Vision in the following words:

> *The mandate of the College, in addition to imparting knowledge, can be said to help build 'a Community of Better Human Beings'. To have disciplined, mindful and wise individuals is to have such a community.*

The responsibility of becoming a 'better human being' lies within each of us – Students, Faculty, Board, Administration and Volunteers. It is a collective responsibility as well, inspired further by the Buddha's living Principle, "I do as I say; I say as I do".

I would put the words *"I do as I say; I say as I do"* as a permanent fixture on my office wall.

This vision itself was enough to signal that the College was intended to be different from the contemporary university whose educational goal was the mere transference of knowledge, if also providing practical skills (as in Medicine, Engineering, Music, etc.). Quality of life of the human being was nowhere on the

Author lighting the Oil lamp in traditional style, opening Nalanda College of Buddhist Studies in 2000. Participating are (L to R), Professors A K Warder, Victor Hori, Frank Tall, Janet McLellan, Bhante Saranapala and Swarna

horizon.

The Curriculum coming to be developed with input from Professors Priestley and Don Wiebe, as well as Frank Tall, Nalanda offered a *Diploma (later Certificate) in Buddhist Studies*, made up of as follows:

FALL
    Introduction to Buddhism.
    Buddhist Textual Study.
    Buddhist Meditation Theory.
    Buddhist Meditation Practice.
    Introduction to Pali.

WINTER
Buddhist Ethics.
Buddhist Psychology.
Buddhist Meditation Theory (cont.).
Buddhist Meditation Practice (cont.).
History of Buddhism: Asian.

The 2001-2002 Calendar introduces the program as being intended "to provide for the systematic study of Buddhism, both cognitively (i.e., theory contained in the Buddha's Teachings) as well as affectively (i.e., the experience of meditation). No prior knowledge of Buddhism is required, nor is a personal commitment to Buddhism".

In contrast to the Program of Studies at every Canadian university, which barely touched on the Buddha's Words, we wanted to make sure that students would get a solid foundation on the Buddha's Teachings, both for its intrinsic value but also as a preparation for further studies. Introducing Textual Study was intended to encourage further independent exploration.

If the courses on Meditation, Theory and Practice, were to help enhance the understanding of the Teachings from within, it was also clearly by way of setting the students on the path of the Founder's Vision. The year-long Meditation course incorporated the three major types of meditation known in the West, beginning with Insight Meditation, to be followed by Zen, and concluded with Tibetan Meditation. Evaluation of students in the Practice component, for a pass or fail grade, came to be on the basis of regular class participation and diary entries of the meditational experience. But, the Meditation Theory component was to be evaluated like any other subject.

Unlike in the US where Pali is taught in a few universities, no university

Ven. Dai Shi of Cham Shan Temple visiting Nalanda

in Canada seemed interested. It was to rectify this omission that Pali, the first language in which the Buddha's Teachings came to be committed to writing (in Sri Lanka), came to be mandatory at our College. I had studied Pali as I had done Latin: as a dead language. But my linguistics training came to whisper in my ear that the ancient language could be taught in a way to give it life. Thus over time, after centuries of neglect, it would come to be called *Pali as a Living Language,* drawing upon the Principles of Second Language Pedagogy. And it was with great satisfaction that I would watch my students – western and Chinese primarily, talk to each other in Pali, using the structures and vocabulary learned in their dialogues, though undeniably at a rudimentary level: Good morning! See you later. Did you take the bus? Or go by plane?, etc.!

The student of Buddhism is well aware how the tripartite division of the Noble Eightfold Path begins with *sila* 'discipline' (to be followed by 'concentration' (*samadhi*) and 'wisdom' (*panna*)). Hence the inclusion of the course, Buddhist Ethics.

It is an intrinsic quality of Buddhism that it would adapt to the culture of the country that it goes to. Indeed there is no Buddhism anywhere in the world today where the Buddha's Teachings have not been adapted and interpreted. Capturing these ideas, 'History of Buddhism' would later come to re-Christened, ooops!, re-Buddhianized, as **Adiyana***, Mahayana & Vajrayana: Adaptations and Interpretations.*

The student of Buddhism is also well aware how the Buddha's Teachings ended up in the form of various schools, the earliest variety coming to be disparagingly called the 'Low(ly) Vehicle', i.e., *Hina*yana,. This, as noted, was by the later Buddhists, in a self-congratulatory attempt to elevate themselves into the 'Great(er) Vehicle (*Mahayana*). It was to return early Buddhism to its due historical place, then, that I coined the term Adiyana, meaning 'Early Vehicle'.

One of the frustrations expressed to me by the Buddhist Teachers of the different temples, in my years of work in the community, was how they were unable to explain the Dhamma they knew so well to the western world. This included the younger generation of immigrant Buddhists themselves. It was to meet this need that the innovative course *English as a Second Language for Dhamma for Sangha* was offered.

Following an Open House, the Registration Days brought in a steady stream of students. With no funds, in addition to being Secretary of the Board, I was now acting in my multiple roles: President, Receptionist, Phone Answerer (getting a cell phone as the only contact), Student Advisor, Registrar, Bursar, Curriculum Builder, Publicity Coordinator, Publicist, Literature Developer, Envelope Stuffer, Stamp licker..... !

It was a hopeful opening, though, with an initial intake of 25 students. A CBC interview, done on-site, had given a good exposure. Later, I was to submit a paper, "Nalanda College for Buddhist Studies: A Canadian Experiment in Buddhist Education", Hawaii International Conference on Arts and Humanities, Hawaii, January 2003.

The initial faculty came to be, in addition to myself, Professor Warder of University of Toronto, Prof. Victor Hori of McGill, Prof. Janet McLellan of Wilfred Laurier University, Pam Dillon, a Meditation Teacher and Bhante Saranapala, a Bangla Desh monk educated in Sri Lanka and now an MA student at the University of Toronto. All of us, of course, were part-time. Prof. Priestley would join the faculty soon. Being in Canada's largest multicultural metropolis, happily, we found no difficulty recruiting younger scholars later: Jason Wong, an MA in Buddhist Studies from University of Toronto and Henry Shiu, finalizing a PhD at the University of Toronto in Buddhist studies. Teaching English as a Second Language for Dhamma was Swarna Sugunasiri, former Head of English as a Second Language at Weston Collegiate Institute.

It was an administrative decision I had made that nobody would teach for Nalanda for free, the thinking being that a professional college could not be expected to be successful without a professional faculty. At its heyday, Nalanda faculty came to be made up of up to 15 members, including a Dean.

Upon completion of the Program of Studies, students in our initial class of 2000 were head over heels:

- Nalanda *"has surpassed all my expectations. It's a joy to study with instructors who love to teach Buddhism and live by what they teach."*
- *"[It was by chance that] I fell into this course. I found it on the internet called "Meditation Theory and Practice". The weirdest thing is that recently (and I believe it's from this course), there has been a spring in my step. Suddenly, I look forward to living and I find meaning in the smallest things. Driving home from the library today, with the smell of spring in the air, I was made to stop in the middle of a road. A Canadian goose, with her four little friends had to cross the street. Before I would never have stopped and enjoyed the moment, probably even taken a different street. But I sat there and smiled at them, watching them cross the street to safely make it to the other side. Through taking this course, my eyes have been opened to a much larger, much greater purpose: LIFE! The ups, the downs, the learning and laughing, the swearing and cursing... I watch myself, and though at times I get caught up in the little things, I am now so aware of myself. I have been growing, and learning, and listening to my heart and my mind. I see how I am constantly changing and I am enjoying every step of the journey. Thanking all the Professors from the Toronto School of Buddhist Studies!"*
- *"I was able to learn more about the Dhamma in an open, stimulating environment, as well as meet interesting and enjoyable classmates, and Professors.... The College offered me an opportunity to study Buddhism from an academic perspective rather than from a specific tradition. From a practitioner's perspective, it is often difficult to discern the Buddha's Teachings apart from specific interpretations and cultural overlays...."*

- "...To learn about the Buddha's Teachings in an environment that includes all schools of Buddhist practice is most enlightening. To be able to openly discuss various perspectives and how they relate to our everyday lives is a significant learning experience. ....Having worked at my Buddhist practice for over eight years, I find that the "pieces" are now beginning to fit together..."
- "... I would like to take this opportunity to express my appreciation to the College for its effort in providing an academic and harmonious environment ....Within a short period of two months, I have benefited significantly from an intellectual perspective. Furthermore, the program has led me to apply Buddha's Teachings in comprehending my existence with deeper insights and to live my life to the fullest extent."

I couldn't have been happier that the College was delivering what it set out to do: to impart knowledge but also encourage the practice in daily living.

15.2 An Application to offer B A (Hons.) in Buddhadharma Studies

With the modest successes of the first year, and a few more challenges in the next couple of years, it was the decision of the Board that we apply to the Government to offer a 4 year program of studies leading to a B A (Hons.) in Buddhadharma Studies. Developed with the active input of Professors Leonard Priestley and Don Wiebe again, the curriculum proposed was as follows (see next page):

Bhante Punnaji of Toronto making a presentaion at Nalanda College

It will be evident looking at each of the columns how the Program, in the four areas of Doctrine, History, Language and Literature and Ethical and Social Applications, was systematic. Thus the very first comes to be the Buddha Vacana (Buddha's Words), followed by, in the Doctrine column by Tripitaka. Item 12, Special Topics ... was intended to benefit from visiting Professors with specialized knowledge, and / or student interest. The History program would begin with Adiyana... Adaptations and interpretations overview, to be followed up in detail in the next courses in order of historical development. Hence, Sinhala Buddhism, given that it is the oldest living Buddhist tradition, dating back to the 3rd c. BCE. In the third or fourth year, students studying Buddhism in the west will come to finally seek to gain an understanding of contemporary Buddhism in Canada and the West in general.

Unlike the current practice in universities in beginning with Tibetan for the historical accident and political reason of an exiled Dalai Lama, the Nalanda program seeks to begin with the first written language of Buddhism, Pali, to be followed by Sanskrit, still within an Indic context before being introduced to Chinese and Tibetan. Ethical and Social Applications beginning with Meditation Theory and Practice, ends with Buddhist Music and Dance.

The criteria laid out by the Provincial Educational Quality Assessment Board (PEQAB), the quasi-government body established to evaluate applications, required that no less than 20% of a student's program of studies over the four years be in Electives. But this again comprised of 'Linked' and 'Outside', meaning unrelated. Thus the next two charts show what came to be proposed under each of them.

The evaluation of Proposals was not only in Curriculum. The Administrative and the Financial Structure came to be scrutinized by an expert panel in business

	BUDDHADHARMA STUDIES			
	DOCTRINE	HISTORY	LANG. & LIT.	ETHICS & SOCIAL APPLICATIONS
1	Buddha Vacana	Adiyana, Mahayana & Vajrayana in India	Pali as a Living Lang. I	Buddhist Meditation Theory
2	Tripitaka	Sinhalese Buddhism	Pali ...II	Buddhist Meditation Practice (0)
3	Abhidhamma	S.E. & Central Asian Buddhism	Pali....III	Buddhist Ethics
4	Sutta	Chinese Buddhism	Pali ... IV	Bodhisattva Ideal
5	Vinaya	Korean & Japanese Buddhism	Buddhist Sanskrit I	Disciples of the Buddha
6	Madhyamaka	Tibetan Buddhism	Buddhist Sanskrit II	The Higher Lay Training
7	Yogacara	Buddhism in Canada	Buddhist Sanskrit III	Buddhist Ritual
8	The Buddha	Buddhism in the West	Chinese I	Buddhist Art & Architecture
9	Bud't Theory of Knowledge		Chinese II	Buddhist Music & Dance
10	Commentaries		Tibetan I	
11	Chinese Bud't Thought		Tibetan II	
12	Special Topics in Buddha-dharma			

ELECTIVE DISCIPLINES

LINKED

Vipassana [meditation] in health & well-being	Buddhism & Science
Transformative Education	Buddhist Critical Methodology
Buddhist Women in History	Socially Engaged Buddhism
Buddhism & Psychotherapy	Buddhist, Christian & Jewish Relations
Buddhism as Literature	The Feminine in Chinese & Tibetan Buddhism
Sarvodaya & Buddhist Models of Development	Ashoka's Righteous Kingdom
Buddhism & Bioethics	Buddhism & Jungian Psychology

ELECTIVE DISCIPLINES

OUTSIDE

Intro to Western Psychology	East Asian Literature
Introduction to Literature	Multiculturalism, Peace & Development
Introduction to Women's Studies	Commonwealth Literature
Introduction to Sociology	European Literature
Psychotherapy	Western Theories of Consciousness
Indian Aesthetic Theory	Independent Research
Sinhalese Literature	Mother in Cross-cultural Perspectives
Feminist Critique	Classical Western Literature
Western Theories of Development	Classical Indian Literature
Japanese Aesthetic Theory	Japanese, Sinhala, Korean, Thai, Vietnamese (Years 1,2)

Prof. Donald Wiebe talking to Professors Leslie Kawamura (R) & Gerald Larsen, evaluators of the proposed BA at NCBS

practice – Professor, Head of a College and a Chartered Accountant. The Proposed Administrative Structure is as seen in the next chart:

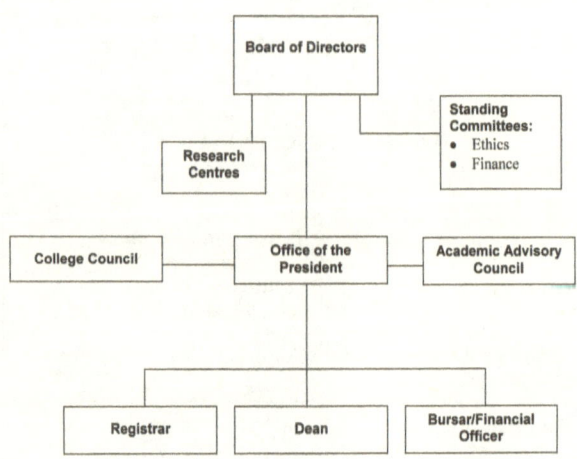

It was to our great satisfaction that our application to offer a B A (Hons.) in Buddhadharma Studies came to be successfully reviewed by the two PEQAB-appointed Panels, Curriculum and Administrative viability, on the basis of two 500-page binders as well as a site visit, though costing us $ 20,000. The Curriculum Panel, made up of Prof. Leslie Kawamura of U of Calgary saw Nalanda as being "unique" in the world. Its report, copied to us, read, among others:

> "Unique institution, designed to meet the credential standards [of the Government of Ontario] and at the same time expand the post-secondary educational opportunities to go beyond traditional western religious education."
> "The Panel believes that the greatest strength of the proposed program

> is its virtual uniqueness among undergraduate programs in Buddhist studies.... [T]here is no other program exactly like it anywhere, given its cross-cultural, interdisciplinary, and multi-faceted linguistic approach to Buddhist Studies"
> "Nalanda [is] unique in that both the faculty and the students reflect the multicultural dimension of this program and are committed to it."
> "Language training is real strength."
> "The balancing of theory and practice."
> "A competent group of experienced professionals ..."

Recommended by PEQAB, following the assessment, we waited in great anticipation. We knew that students across Canada, and Buddhist faculty members in particular, were waiting. But, after a year, it was to our great disappointment that we were to receive a letter dated Dec 22. 2006, from the Minister of Colleges and Universities, Christopher Bentley, "After considering .... relevant issues and public policy matters," that our application had been turned down! The Act that authorized the Minister to make the final decision did not require that reasons be given. It is as if the Minister had listened to, among others, the Association of Universities and Colleges of Canada, who, in a letter had expressed its opposition.

With our enrolment on a downward roll, and losing the annual grant for that very reason, it was our decision not to appeal. A lawyer kindly offered to take up the matter. But it was evident that Buddhism in Canada didn't have a stomach to fight for the serious study of the Buddhadhamma. At least not as yet.

15.3 Nalanda Research Centres of Excellence

Looking for ways other than teaching, the Board had also agreed to a proposal made by me to establish *Centres of Excellence*.

The Concept

> As an institution of higher education, Nalanda is dedicated to maintaining only the highest academic standards. In fulfilment of this imperative, Nalanda seeks to establish and maintain a research arm in furtherance of the goal of academic advancement through theory (pariyatti) in support of application (patipatti) and insight (pativedha). This tripartite division is part of the Buddhist tradition.
>
> With this philosophical/theoretical basis, Nalanda is establishing a number of Research Centres of Excellence, designed to support, disseminate and encourage ongoing research in specific areas. The Chairs of these Research Centres, along with other research staff, will eventually come to carry the bulk of the College's teaching load, thus ensuring a core faculty for the College.

The direct involvement of researchers in teaching will clearly serve to enhance the quality of teaching, and our students (and the wider learning community through research publications) will be the beneficiaries. The opposite, of course, holds as well. The quality of the research would be enhanced as classroom experience provides new insights to the researcher-instructor, opening up new vistas and directions for research. Thus the Buddha's theory of the conditioned co-origination relationship - theory augmenting practice augmenting theory – finds yet another expression.

There are pragmatic reasons for the establishment of the Research Centres of Excellence as well. The Centres will:
- allow research in under-represented areas of enquiry
- in Buddhist Studies;
- attract academics and students interested in the given areas, particularly if unavailable elsewhere.
- serve as a training ground for students to both hone their research skills and identify areas of future research, including those leading to potential employment.

Finally, there are the financial implications. In the academy, faculty members are often expected to scramble for research funds year in year out, spending valuable time competing amongst each other for meagre research dollars. In this conventional paradigm, research is an extension of teaching. In the approach advocated here, the matter is turned on its head. Teaching becomes an extension of research.

This approach will ensure every faculty member research funds as part of the appointment. Having a research-funded faculty will also mean that the faculty hiring process and course offerings will no longer be held hostage to the vagaries of enrolment.

We are confident that this initiative will allow an opportunity for funding agencies, philanthropists and other individuals to contribute to the welfare of Canadians by supporting the Nalanda Research Centres of Excellence.

The Centres to be established initially, come to be shown visually in the Campaign Lotus Literature, beginning with *Buddhism, Bioethics and Socioethics*.:
Among other Centres envisioned are Research Centre of Excellence on Sinhala Buddhist Culture and Civilization, and Korean Buddhist Culture and Civilization.

15.4 One Hundred Years of Buddhism in Canada

While our primary focus at Nalanda was academic, we had also taken some community initiatives. One was to organize the celebration of '100 Years of Buddhism in Canada', holding an academic conference as well.

Theravada monks who took part in the historic Paritta chanting. R to L: Bhantes Ahangama Rathanasiri, Udupihille Wimalabuddhi, Ashin Kawwida, Bhantes Y. Dhammarama, Hemalankara, Pannasara, Kirinde Gnanaransi, Vijitha and Buddhananda

As part of the same event was a *paritta* chanting, by nearly a dozen Theravada monks, this possibly the first time a *paritta* chanting had been done in public space in Canada.

An associated initiative was the Raising of the Buddhist flag at the South Lawn of the Ontario Legislature, probably yet again a first in Canada.

Another associated initiative, working with the Trillium Foundation, was to encourage the Buddhist community towards organ donation. To provide a visual understanding, I had developed a 'Body Chart', showing the 32 parts of the 'body meditation' (*kayanupassana*) in the Buddha's Foundations of Mindfulness (*satipatthana*) practice.

15.5 A Lecture-Meditation (*suta-bhavana*) Series

By way of a last attempt at making the College financially viable, and spiritually-relevant, I would offer a creative Lecture-Meditation series, the initial crop running as follows:

Lecture Meditation Series
Jan. 19, 08 Paul Kelly, PhD *Meditation and Psychotherapy*
Feb. 16, 08 Jack Miller, PhD *Holistic Teaching and Learning*
Mar 15, 08 Kate Partridge, PhD *Mindfulness Meditation for Stress Reduction*
Apr 19, 08 Mathieu Boisvert, PhD *Facing Death Reality Mindfully*
May 17, 08 Andrew Olendzky, PhD *The Buddhist Psychology of Experience*
June 21, 08 Mu Soeng (Dharma Teacher-Scholar) *The Great Way is not Difficult*

Intended for the professional class, we would develop a fancy flyer:
Yet, the enrolment was not encouraging.

15.6 A Few Other Initiatives

Mettā Bhāvanā
'Friendliness Meditation'

Friendliness Meditation
As another piece of public service, Nalanda Publishing Canada, an arm of the College, had also brought out, for free distribution, *Metta Bhavana Friendliness Meditation*, which I would send to the Lieutenant-Governors of all the Provinces, and to other politicians, some of them taking the time to write to me to thank.

Buddhist Youth Canada
An unsuccessful initiative was my attempt to establish Buddhist Youth Canada, with Glenn Choi, a former student of Nalanda and later Registrar, accepting my invitation to provide the leadership. This was my small way of providing a forum for Buddhist youth.

Nalanda Publishing Canada
But I would keep Nalanda Publishing Canada, the publishing arm of the College, going, showing its presence with the annual issue of the *Canadian Journal of Buddhist Studies* (see next). With funds allotted to it over the years, we had come to publish the following publications:

Embryo as Person: Buddhism, Bioethics and Society, 2005.
Multiculturalism, Peace and Development: A Buddhist Perspective, 2007
Thus Spake the Sangha: Buddhism in Toronto, 2008.

Nalanda Publishing Canada would also bring out my creative works, two collections of poetry, *Celestial Conversations* (2007) and *Obama-Ji* (2009) While it was with some hesitancy I decided to publish them through NPC, the compelling reason was that each of them had a fair amount of Buddhist content in them. So it really was an extension of the work I had been engaged in, this time adding an esthetic touch.

As publicly announced at the launch (Dec 4, 2010), 100% of sales proceeds always went to Nalanda Publishing Canada, be they my creative works, or academic work.

15.7 A Retirement

Right from the beginning, Nalanda had come to earn respect as a serious institution of academic study. However, hardly any other universities knew about us, this, despite a website. And so it was that I took the opportunity to travel across Canada, while our application for B A (Hons.) in Buddhadharma Studies was working itself through the system. I was to meet Deans, Chairs and Professors in the area of religion. And it was with a warm embrace that I was welcomed to the several universities: University of Victoria, and Simon Fraser University in British Columbia; University of Saskatchewan; University of Calgary; University of Winnipeg to Brock University, Carleton and University of Ottawa. Students were keen as well to take courses at Nalanda for credit. And the Universities expressed a willingness to exchange faculty and students, once we had approval from the government to offer the degree.

It was also my pleasure to visit the two better known Buddhist universities in the US: University of the West (formerly Hsi Lai University) in Los Angeles, founded by Master Hsin Yun, and Naropa University in Boulder, Colorado, founded by Trungpa Rinpoche.

It was not only academic recognition that we had to get but also funds. And so it was with the purpose of raising funds in particular I traveled to Asia (Hong Kong, Taiwan, Thailand and Sri Lanka).

While Dr Wong, the Chair of the Board had been able to secure some seed funding from FaShih Sing Hung, Founder of Toronto's Cham Shan Temple, at founding the College, it was a pleasant surprise when one day Henry Shiu approached to share with me the news that his Teacher, Master Tam, was offering to find funding for the College. True to their word, we were to soon to get funding from a source in Hong Kong, bringing us the first stable funding. This allowed us to have a real office, with a real Registrar.

While again every university I went to was more than happy to see a program of studies in Canada, I came empty-handed when it came to long-term funding. A Campaign Lotus launched in a home setting didn't net any funds either. So it comes

THE CONGEE POT OF THE SEVEN AANDIYAS
(*Obama-Ji*, 2009, p. 45)
(drawing upon a Sinhala folktale)
<In the face of another rejection of plea for financial support for Nalanda.>

"Any interest, in
Research Centre, Journal,
Library, College"?, in
a follow up call, for
the umpteenth meeting,
traveling across Canada
through rain, sleet and ice,
then to the far off lands
of Asia, crouched
16 hours or more
in the air, an
irritated knee complaining,
but armed with
books published,
courses offered,
seminars presented,
a faculty of MA PhD's
a unique Canadian
Journal of Buddhist Studies,
a proposed B A (Hons.)
in Buddhadhamma Studies,
Meditation of three
types mandatory, five-
year projections,
with pictorial evidence
to boot, charts and figures
to show sound financial
management, student
testimonials, of eight long years
of struggling to steady a boat,
anchored in a Vision of Cultivating
a Community of Better Human Beings,
floating like a
buoy, bumped up
by a wave
pulled down
by a wave
in an unending game of
'see if you'll last'...

"Difficult times", comes the
answer, "Perhaps next
year when the dollar
is on a par with the
Greenback."; "I've

passed it along," assures
a second, "Only I
won't be the first," offers
a third, "But why don't
you join U of T", ponders
a fourth, out loud, "We'll
get back to you," assures
a fifth, with a Golden
silence from the sixth, and
a final, "Oh, I'm sure
you'll pull through
this one, too", consoles
a seventh, a comrade, "as
in the past"!

I might as well have said
a faculty of
yemmaypiyetchdees, a
journal on abracadabra, courses
on 'dis dat and da udder', making
nary a difference in the world,
each one giving
their splendid reason
for non-support.
But why
does it take my mind
back to a folk wisdom of
seven travelers, Andiya
by tribe, spending a
night at a wayside stop
along the road, looking
forward to a warm
cup of congee but,
in the thought that
surely another would
put in his share of rice,
adding none of his own, and
goes to the pot
the next morning
after pleasant banter,
each looking to assuage
his rising hunger, only
to find an
empty pot?

to be a classic example of conditioning. Healthy soil of Canada looking for Buddhist studies and there was no single university offering a comprehensive program, a qualitative seed of Nalanda seen evaluated to be 'unique', but no watering – funds.

So what else could I do other than write a poem?

Continuing to have an empty pot, although the fires of good blessings from all around kept it hot, I wasn't seeing any light at the end of the financial tunnel. We had done everything possible to maintain excellence, academically as well as in terms of a model, and to provide programs and courses not offered anywhere else in the country. We had sought to maintain the highest academic standards. But Canada did not seem ready to dig deep into Buddhism. Going to a large arena to listen to the Dalai Lama speak, and learning to do a little meditation seem all we wanted for now. But then it seemed, nor were the Buddhists themselves! We have our own temples. What more do we need??

So it was evident that, my Buddhist educational leadership, in fifteen years of voluntary service, was not going anywhere. It was the end of the tether. Perhaps I was the obstacle. And so the best I could do was to remove that obstacle.

And so I did, to the surprise of the Board, stepping down from the positions of both Chair and President. But there were no takers. And so it was I cajoled one member, Prof. Tony Toneatto, a psychologist and Member of the Board, to take over. He loved Buddhism, he had told me. He showed it by accepting my invitation.

15.8 A Buddhist Educational Plan for Canada

On the day of my resignation (2008), I would leave with the Board *A Buddhist Educational Plan for Canada,* "Towards Excellence in learning and the social good", for implementation over 25 years:

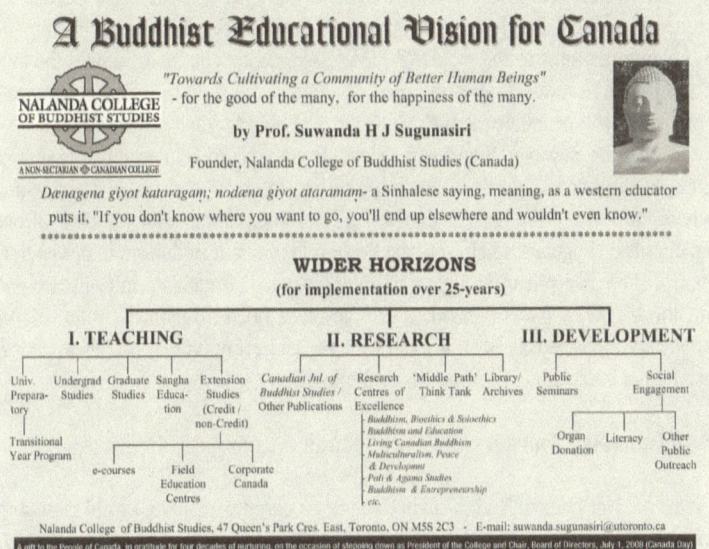

Coming up with a plan, of course, could be seen as a natural. I had come up with an Educational Plan for Sri Lanka, this for a course on Educational Planning.

But I shall leave it to the reader to figure it out. I should have guessed that it would only go to the birds since there were no educators on the Board that could have seen the value.

15.9 An Interview

Prof. Victor Hori

Following my retirement, I was to get a call from Prof. Victor Hori of McGill University. Appraising me of an upcoming book on Canadian Buddhism, he was inviting me to be interviewed. "Well, if you think I should be", was my response. Not soon after, he was to come over to Nalanda, now at 47 Queen's Park Crescent, renting space from the Toronto School Theology. Joining him was Prof. Janet McLellan, the author of *Petals of the Lotus*.

The interviews end up in a 20 page article in *Wild Geese, Buddhism in Canada*, McGill-Queen's University Press, 2010, 375-399. To share some observations: "One theme runs throughout most of the events and projects in Suwanda Sugunasiri's life – preserving the true Dharma. ... not on change and adaptation to the new cultural environment of the West. ..... This stance of preservation of the Dharma, which informs most of his career as a Buddhist leader, is strikingly different from the stance of a Western-born Buddhist leader, who is constantly trying, first, to distinguish what is authentic Buddhism from what is cultural context, and the second, to reinterpret that authentic Buddhism in a way that makes sense to a Westerner."

Asked way back in 1938 about Buddhism taking root in the West, the resident teacher of the First Zen Institute of America, Sokei-an Sasaki, likened the process to 'holding the lotus to the rock'. "So long as someone continues to hold the lotus of the Buddha's awakening to the rock, eventually the Buddha's awakening would send forth roots, penetrate the rock, and take firm hold to stand on its own." .... "Not everything that Suwanda Sugunasiri did in his attempts to help establish Buddhism had a lasting impact, but he was one of the first to go beyond his own community to hold the lotus to the rock in Canada". A two-liner captures the attempts of over two decades: "Sugunasiri helped shape the development of Buddhism in this country. His life story is a prism through which the history of Buddhism in Canada comes into focus" (397). I was pleased to see the piece titled "Buddhist", following my name, capturing the way I had worked with any and every type of Buddhist, with no sectarian or ethnocultural affiliations or preferences.

15.10 Canadian Journal of Buddhist Studies

As part of '100 Years of Buddhism in Canada' celebration in 2005, I would found the first and the only journal on Buddhism in Canada, the *Canadian Journal of Buddhist*

Studies. Because " 'Canadian Buddhism' has thus far not had an independent life of its own", I express editorially in the first issue, the hope "that the journal fills an important hiatus in Canadian Buddhist Studies." I continue:

> CJBS hopes to serve as a forum / convention floor where academics may come together to forge intellectual links by sharing their research and insights. But, going beyond academic tradition, we hope that it will serve as a spiritual forum as well, facilitating personal growth within the academy.

Thus the journal specifically comes to have a tripartite division – Theory, Praxis and Insight, the first two being refereed, and the last, as a work in progress, but primarily focusing on meditation and related dimensions – texts, case studies, personal stories, etc.

There was another reason to consciously include a meditation dimension. Buddhologists all trained in the western school of thought that separates the academy from personal practice and ethical behaviour, just about every scholar and Professor of Buddhism had come to be what may be characterized as 'a ladle in the soup' – deep inside the soup, yet not having a sense of the taste. In other words, while scholars will tell you chapter and verse of the Tipitaka and other Buddhist texts, they will not be touched by the teachings. In other words, they will not have benefited personally in cultivating the spiritual life. By including an Insight section within the same pages, it was the intention that access to spiritual practice could be facilitated, without having to necessarily go to a monastery.

Sharing my vision were three young scholars who had no compunction to be 'closet Buddhists'. They unashamedly wore their Buddhist label on their lapel. Michael Berman, a Philosopher at Brock university, was one of them. I had been invited to Brock for a Keynote earlier, and I was happy that Michael returned the favour by accepting my invitation to be Editor of the Theory section of CJBS. Henry Shiu, just completing a PhD in Chinese Buddhism at the Centre for the Study of Religion at University of Toronto, kindly agreed to be the Editor of Praxis while Angela Sumegi of Carleton University of Ottawa, with an academic background in Tibetan Buddhism agreed to provide leadership for the Insight section.

I was happy that several other scholars accepted my invitation to serve on the Editorial Board as members-at-large. Martin Adam of University of Victoria, British Columbia , Mathieu Boisvert of Universite du Quebec a Montreal, Rethi Chhem of University of Western Ontario, Victor Hori of McGill, Leslie Kawamura of the University of Calgary, Kay Koppedrayer of Wilfred Laurier University, James Mullens of the University of Saskatchewan, Noel Salmond of Carleton University, P A Saram of the University of Alberta, and three Professors from University of Toronto: Don Wiebe, Leonard Priestley and Frances Garrett.

A Call for papers sent out, it was a good omen, I thought, and beyond my wildest dreams, when I received a 50-page submission from Prof. Herbert Guenther. Here was a rookie academic journal, just trying to be born! Then appears this long paper from a respected academic, and Tibetologist, as an attachment to an e-mail. I was also happy that I was not short of papers for the inaugural issue, when the authors of the papers presented at the Academic Conference held in commemoration of 100 Years of Buddhism in Canada, agreed to being published in the first issue.

In addition to an Editorial for each of the next five issues, I also had a peer reviewed article of my own in the second annual issue 'Inherited Buddhists and Acquired Buddhists', *Canadian Journal of Buddhist Studies,* 2006, seeking to deal with an issue of practical importance. 'Ethnic Buddhist' and 'Euro Buddhist' were offensive, 'new Buddhist' and 'old Buddhist' were meaningless, and so on. I presented a more theoretical basis along which two basic types could be identified – inherited by birth or acquired later on in life. This latter criterion would allow for the inclusion of the offspring of Inherited Buddhists born in the west, who lose their Buddhism growing up in a secular western society, but discover Buddhism later in life, or lapsed Buddhists returning to the fold, etc.

Another piece I was personally happy to carry in the very issue itself of the Journal was one on Mindfulness Meditation – not the contemporary manifestation in health settings as popularized by the US Medical Practitioner Kabat-Zinn and his colleagues, but the classical formulation by the Buddha himself. If my interest was academic, it was also the guide in my personal practice. This latter giving me insight into a particular theoretical structure of the Method formulated by the Buddha, I contribute two papers on the subject in the next two issues: 'Establishing of Mindfulness Meditation: the Creative Interplay of Cognition, Praxis and Affection", (*CJBS* 4, 2008) and " 'Against Belief': Mindfulness Meditation as Empirical Method", (*CJBS* 5, 2009).

A particularly Buddhist value not forgotten by the academic journal was to give recognition to Professors who pass away – three in my time: Prof. Guenther (Issue 2006), Kawamura (Issue 2011), and Warder (Issue 2013).

15.11 A Meeting with Prof. Herbert Guenther

Taking the initiative to publish the CJBS, a Press Release had been sent out to the universities, and also posted at the Congress, the annual intellectual gathering of the Canadian academic associations along disciplinary lines. And it was indeed a great, and pleasant, surprise to receive Prof Guenther's article of over 50 pages, double the size of the standard in academic journals. Ordinarily, the size would have been reason enough to return it to the author. But this was no ordinary author. It was by one of the most renowned Buddhist scholars in the world, and who was this rookie Editor to return it? Indeed insult him? Besides, the academic respectability that would be accrued to the newly minted journal by featuring Prof. Herbert Guenther in our maiden issue would be phenomenal. And so it was that a decision was made to feature it in two Parts, the

**Prof. Herbert Guenther,
1917- 2006**

painstaking copy editing done personally by Michael, the Associate Editor.

Travelling across Canada visiting universities to make linkages for Nalanda College of Buddhist Studies (Canada) (as above), the personal highlight of my Saskatoon visit was meeting this great scholar, Prof. Herbert Guenther. Talking, by phone, to his wife, Dr. Ilse Guenther, his life-time collaborator as I would come to know later, I had been asked to come to the Senior's Care Centre where the Professor had been admitted to recently. Delighted as I walk in to see an elderly and scholarly looking gentleman in a wheelchair in the wide hall just at the entrance, I introduce myself, and very slowly and in a slow tone, begin talking pleasantries with him, thanking him also for helping to bring credibility to the *Journal* by sending his article that would adorn the opening pages. But throughout, for a full five minutes or so, there was nothing but a blank look in his eyes. A doubt creeping into me, I asked someone looking like a health worker who happened to pass by, only to be directed to Prof. Guenther's room!

Waiting to welcome me was Mrs. Guenther, who would introduce me to the Professor, sitting in his wheelchair beside his bed, with his head somewhat stooped down. Talking about Nalanda, I wasn't sure he was taking in anything, because he said nothing, although his face was not as blank as the other's. A tear from one eye dripping, his wife was to clean it with a Kleenex. Taking a galley proof of CJBS One I had taken with me, containing Part I of his article, I would hand it to him, showing him his article. When he took the copy in hand, I knew he was with me, despite the silence. And my unquestionable skills, *ahem,* in measuring facial expressions of sentient beings told me unequivocally that he seemed awfully pleased!

Even though he said nothing the total period of about half an hour as I was showing this that and the other about Nalanda, Mrs. Guenther made every attempt to make sure he was taking it in, sometimes turning to German. And I was honoured to be in the presence of this great scholar about whom I had read but had never met.

After taking a picture of the two of them, I would ask her to take a picture of the two of us. And as it turns out, it happens to be the last photo of him, since I was to hear that three days later, while I was still on tour, he would pass away.

Leaving the Nursing Home, Mrs. Guenther was kind enough to invite me to her home. The bitter cold, nor the icy roads off the main area of the city, seem to affect the steel nerve of this short built lady whose eye level was barely above the dashboard. But I can't say I was not keeping my eyes on the road for her.

It was upon entering the small living room of the Guenther residence that I came to realize that the good Professor was not only a scholar of Buddhism but a Buddhist, too. Hm! An early German Jewish Buddhist, my mind would say. At an altar beside the dining table to the right was the seated statue of the Buddha, with other items of Tibetan Buddhist veneration. At one end of the room was the small desk he had worked at all these years, and a computer. (It was an electronic version of his article that I had received.). The shelves lining the small room were all full of books, but I had really seen nothing yet.

Talking about his books, Mrs. Guenther, would invite me downstairs to see his library. Going past a tassle of beads hanging from a Tibetan design around the door frame, I was to enter a whole basement of books, and more books, stacked floor to ceiling - a collection of a lifetime that included books in Tibetan, Sanskrit, Pali, German and Russian, among others. But the most irreplaceable, and certainly priceless, were the vast collection of Tibetan manuscripts, in the traditional long and narrow binding, within hard covers, and stacked up, one on the the other. Taking a closer look, the text was written on what appeared to be traditional ola leaves used in ancient India, and in Sri Lanka. Going along aisle by aisle, for half an hour or so, I couldn't help but being impressed.

I don't know how we came to it, but now I was talking to Dr Guenther about her plans for the wonderful library. I was surprised to hear her say, in her low, soft voice, "I don't know... I just don't know." I was surprised that there had been no discussions on the matter with the University of Saskatchewan, where he had taught for half a century, lured to Canada from the Sanskrit University in India where he had been teaching. This is when I made the offer, to take care of it at Nalanda. She sighed a great big sigh of relief. "Oh, you've taken such a big burden off my shoulder, Prof. Sugunasiri", she said. I would explain, thinking through on my feet, that we would have a Guenther library where not only this huge collection would be available for public academic use, but also have a separate section with holdings of all the works of Prof. Guenther. Mrs. Guenther seemed ecstatic. She would continue to say how wonderful it would be to have such an outfit for her husband's collection and lifetime work. In the end, I would ask her to keep my offer in mind, but to do what was felt to be best, in consultation with her family and friends.

Back upstairs in the living room to the left of the front entrance, I would see a picture of Prof. & Mrs. Guenther, hanging just above the grand piano that would take quite a large area of the room. It shows a happy young couple. She tells me how they met in Austria where the Professor was doing his second doctorate to qualify to teach. She was doing her own doctorate. Asked who played the piano, she would sit at it, singing along to the tune she was playing, when I begin to record her on my movie-camera, built into my cell phone. Later, after some tea, she would drive me over to my hotel, just across the bridge.

Continuing to communicate with Dr Guenther, I would publish in the next issue of CJBS, an obituary which I had invited his wife to write. It also carried his photo, under the heading, Prof. Herbert Guenther, 1917 – 2006, adding below a typical Buddhist wording, "May he attain the peace of Nibbana!". Additionally, the issue also included his very first article on Buddhism written in English, "The Jewel of Buddhahood", reprinting from an Indian Publication, *Stepping Stones*, 1952.

Visiting Saskatoon a second time not too long after to discuss about the library, and invited home for lunch this time, I was pleasantly surprised to be served a meal of rice and curry – lentils, fish and salad. I was even more surprised, and more than a bit concerned, when I saw her taking a chair to her hutch, to take out some china to be laid on the table. Herself past her 80's, she would impress me, as stable as a strong tree. Again, playing the piano for me, she walks me through the library again, still not sure in her mind where the library should end up. While Nalanda would love to house it, I said that it was up to her to decide.

Going over the Bibliography of Prof. Guenther's publications, sent to me at my request, and posted on the Nalanda website, I was to discover to my pleasant surprise that Prof. Guenther was a scholar of Sinhala, too! One of his articles was on the 13th c. Sinhala grammar, *Sidat Sangarawa*, a text we as students of Sinhala well knew about, and the source for most of the other later grammars. "Yes, you're right…. Herbert did know Sinhalese," she would confirm, pointing out that the thesis for his second doctorate, required to teach at a German university, was a study of this classical Sinhala grammatical treatise. The only German scholar known to us in Sri Lanka that had worked on the Sinhala language and literature was, of course, Prof Wilhelm Geiger. But that was for me only a name in a book. Here I had met a German scholar of Sinhala in person and I kicked myself for not having known it when I met him in the nursing home.

The Bibliography of his works would show, in fact, not just the one paper on Sinhala grammar, but as many as 8 papers on medieval Sri Lanka, in English and German, among his earliest academic works! How it all came about came in a footnote in one of the articles: "Prof Geiger entrusted me to finish where he stopped….". In another article, agreeing with Geiger, he observes how Sinhala is not of the Dravidian group, of which Tamil is, but of the Indo-Aryan. Interested in publishing all eight articles as a Nalanda publication, Mrs. Guenther kindly accepts my invitation to translate the seven German articles into English. During my visit, she would show me the originals of the articles, which I promptly capture on my camera.

I would also come to know to my amazement, through the obituary written by their daughter, that Prof. Guenther read over ten languages other than German and English, among them French, Sanskrit, Pali, Tibetan, Chinese, Russian, and Sinhala, indeed 18 languages as I would come to know later: . A true sign of scholarship, I would say to myself, but so rare in the modern world, particularly in North America where English would hold sway to the exclusion of all others, even in Canada, founded by *deux nations*, but French becoming an official language only after a century!

Receiving all the articles translated, and putting in hours and hours and hours, I would eventually turn them into a book (2019) under the title, *Medieval Ceylon: Language, Literature and Politics*) that included a brief Preface by the 99-year old Ilse Guenther written at my request. Now in my Buddhist robes, I make a special visit to Saskatoon simply to show her the pre-final version, and to show my gratitude for her help. The Preface comes to be the last piece to be written by her, since 2-3 weeks after my meeting with her, she passes away.

BOOK II, PART 6
A MEDIA PRESENCE

16. ON THE HOT SEAT: ON CAMERA AND MICROPHONE

16.1 Hot Seat on Radio

In July 1985, national radio icon, Peter Gzowski, host of Morningside, CBC, was to interview me on the Literature of the Canadians of South Asian Origins. This was based on my research on the topic in 1979 to 1980. But it was only now that the Report had come to be formally published, with the Minister of Multiculturalism, Hon. Gerry Weiner, present at the David Mirvish Bookstore on Markham Street, Toronto at the launch. Following the interview, I write to Mr. Gzowski (July 4, 1985), thanking him, adding further, "Your disarming approach to the interview really helped give the discussion a casual touch, which I believe is what has made *Morningside* so endearing to the listeners."

One of my most memorable Radio appearances can be said to be when I was on the Ed Needham Show on CFRB at 2 St Clair West, in December 1987. My very first piece as a Columnist in the *Toronto Star* had appeared on Nov. 28, 1987, under the title, "The Final Stage – Real Change". I had outlined, making reference to Gandhi and the US psychologist Gordon Allport, how "before we accept change, we go through several stages". With clear examples, I show how Canada had now arrived at the last, i.e., the fifth stage, thanks to the initiatives of Prime Ministers Pierre Elliott Trudeau and Brian Mulroney, and Ontario Premiers William Davis and David Peterson. We now had a Black Cabinet Minister and later, first Black Lieutenant-Governor, Lincoln Alexander. We are, I wrote, "halfway up the mountain, and the top ... is visible. And more importantly, reachable", and I confidently concluded, "We are clearly at the final stage, sailing the multicultural ship with clear direction".

Returning to Toronto, having read the piece while traveling, it was with great delight that I came to accept an invitation to go on the Ed Needham show. Wow! People had read me. And, people of the establishment, for that matter, for CFRB was not known to be left-leaning. From the little I knew, it was establishment epitomized. So how wonderful it was to be invited into its belly. Wasn't that itself enough proof of my point about having reached the final stage?

Sure! But it didn't take me long to realize that I was to be given to the wolves! Being a phone-in show, the telephone appeared to go off the hook! The red button, indicating a caller waiting, was lighting up continuously. I was enjoying the experience of having to answer questions on air, something I had never done. I don't remember a single call that was supportive of the advance of Multiculturalism. And, to me, the peak experience was when a caller asked me to go back to where I came from! She spoke with a clear British accent. Perhaps taken aback, but obviously not showing it, I believe I asked where she was from and when she had come to Canada. Turns out that while I had been in Canada by now for nearly two decades, she was FOB – Fresh Off the Boat. So having come to 'my' country, she was asking me to leave! The irony seemed to have got lost even on the host of the program, who seemed to be taking sides – meaning the side of the callers. Yet, I was his guest. As I had written in my piece, "So are we now one happy family? Not by a country mile."

But I was happy to receive a letter of Dec. 21st, where the Producer of the Ed Needham show, thanks me "for appearing on the .. Show. Your contribution helped make the program both interesting and informative." I should say so! Since I would go on to appear many an other phone-in show, on radio and TV, the hot seat I had been invited to sit on can only be said to have made me steelier, if anything. We on the self-appointed multicultural leadership team had surely not taken all those pains to let a few disgruntled voices to derail the multicultural train!

Continuing my involvement on Radio, and now working with Producer Ken Wolf, I would come to do Commentary pieces on public issues on CBC's Metro Morning, beginning in 1990, perhaps the first on Meech Lake (May 25, 1990). Another was on "Cops and Blacks" (June 5, 1990) when the CBC gets 3 responses. A teacher wants the tape for students, another commenting that I point out something that is seldom said – that the police apprehends the law-breakers, not Blacks. A third was on "Putting Spirituality Centre Stage" (Jun 7, 1990). I distinguish spirituality from religion, a point of view with which a listener completely disagrees. In another, "Bet on Rae to win the Next Election" (Jan 24, 1994), I seem to have put my foot in my mouth, sorely ignoring Chinese wisdom: "It's difficult to predict, especially the future"!

I also come to be an invited guest on several other programs on CBC Radio - such as Open House, Saturday Morning and Dayshift (1989-92). On Tapestry, hosted by Peter Downey and Produced by Peter Skinner, I would talk on the symbolism of light in Buddhism (January 1995). I remember Erika Ritter being one of the hosts.

It was with great happiness I would participate in such programs, drawing upon my experience of appearing as well as an invited guest on on BBC's London Overseas Program, telecast primarily to Sri Lanka, and on Blue Danube Radio, in Vienna, Austria, both in 1985 while on my European tour. Happily, I had my experience of appearing on several programs on Radio Ceylon, too - dramas, features and panels, during the period 1960-4, prior to leaving on the Fulbright.

16.2 Tangoing with CBC TV

But my first contact with CBC was a letter dated 1980.02.22 when I write to the Producer of the TV program ACCESS, "encouraged … by your recent call for participation in your program". Referring to the Sri Lanka Canadian community, I point out that "ours is a neglected group". I give the reasons, as I saw them:

small community, small country, far from Canada, proximity to India. As if by way of impressing the then white CBC, I go on to add that "we are among the most educated immigrants.., and among us are Professors, medical doctors, psychiatrists, lawyers, teachers, accountants, civil servants, nurses, journalists, businesspersons, artists, poets, play producers, and so on." Given that, "I believe we are entitled to a program on ACCESS".

I was to receive a letter from ACCESS, dated Feb. 29, 1980, sent to my home, 1550, Boxwood Way and addressed to *Samskruti: Sri Lankan Cultural Centre*, in the name of which I had written. The attached CBC document began with the following para: "CBC ACCESS is a television program designed for groups of Canadians with something to say to a national audience, who for one reason or another, haven't ever had the chance to take their case to the nation – either because the media hasn't been interested or because only one side of the story is being told." Excellent, I thought. So we would qualify. My hopes went high when I was sent an application form, which as acknowledged "may, at first glance, appear to be a formidable document... Do not be alarmed. The most important page of the form is the blank page entitled PROGRAM CONTENT. All good program ideas will be given serious consideration."

And I would painstakingly fill out the application, by hand – computers were just making their appearance, segment by segment, going beyond the 9 suggested and going up to 12, showing the content, and the duration, for each segment. It sought to follow the suggested model to the letter, and gave the names of potential, and available participants, providing information about their backgrounds.. Among them were Educators, Professors, Dancers, Journalists, Poets and a Buddhist monk, drawn from Toronto, Ottawa and British Columbia. The "basic idea" of the proposed program was listed as presenting "the Sri Lankan community in Canada, and through them, their country of origin".

The themes that are expected to emerge through the program are fourfold:

Apparently my program ideas were not seen to be "good", since I received no further communication. One 'offence' might have been that, asked to write a program for 27 minutes, mine went double, to 55 minutes. But there was nothing that could not have been cut back on.

I had said in my initial letter that within the small Sri Lankan community is "a microcosm of all but one Major Religion (Buddhist, Hindu, Christian, Muslim), four ethnic groups (Sinhalese, Tamil, Muslim, Eurasian), and three linguistic groups: Sinhala, Tamil and English". So was it that this was too good to be believed, or too good a model that would put Canada to shame? I can only speculate.

But apparently, I continue to be on the CBC contact list. By letter of July 21, 1983, sent to the Ontario Advisory Council on Multiculturalism and Citizenship, I am invited to a consultation regarding an initiative taken by CBC to "address a major concern that you and others have expressed, namely, an opportunity to provide more on-air representation of the visual composition of our society on Canadian radio and television stations". I was delighted at the initiative, even more so since upon completion of the project, the successful trainees were free to find 'permanent positions' not just at CBC but "in any private or public broadcasting station in Canada". I thought that was truly magnanimous. And the funding was provided by the Multicultural Ministry, then under Jim Fleming. And applications called, there were to be 800, showing how much of an interest there was in going on air.

In a letter dated Oct. 21, 1983 by the Director, Province of Ontario, I am invited to a 'dialogue with community leaders' about 'CBC Radio and Television Programming here in Ontario". I believe it was at this that we were given details of the process referred to above. Of the 24 shortlisted candidates, those chosen for training could not have been more representative: George Boyd (Black loyalist descendent from Halifax), Jari Brodie (Chinese; PhD), Anthony Chan (PhD; author), Dan David (Native), David Lam (filmmaker; Winnipeg), Claire Prieto (Trinidadian-born documentary film producer) and Paul Winn (Black Canadian). Last but not least, you'll never recognize, ha ha ha, was Deepa Mehta, who would go on to make award-winning films like Water, Fire, etc.

I write a letter of congratulations (March 28, 1984) to the Manager, Regional Affairs, for the excellent choice. Having had lunch with him to discuss matters of mutual interest, I also send him a personal letter, thanking him for the lunch, and enclosing a copy of the *Toronto South Asian Review*, asking that the Librarian be encouraged to take a subscription. The Journal was new, and it could use any and every support. Two of my other articles are enclosed aa well: "Media and Multiculturalism", from the *Rikka* magazine and a *Toronto Star* piece of Jan. 21, 1984, in fact the first, "Let's Speed up the Good Work of Dialogue" (published by Religion Editor, Michael McAteer).

Receiving an acknowledgement that the enclosures have been forwarded to the Program Director, I meet with him (possibly over lunch), and follow up with a letter of April 1, 1984, enclosing "a proposal for an Interfaith Forum" for an upcoming season. I had come to be a member of the Interfaith Sub-committee of the Ontario Advisory Council on Multiculturalism and Citizenship, and I had also been working in Interfaith Relations through my association with the World Conference on Religion for Peace.

But, writing to him earlier, on Dec. 27, 1983, I congratulate him on "an excellent Christmas Eve program, From Our Family to Your Family". I added that "what my wife and I liked best was your vision to put back the family into Christmas." Further, "We're Buddhists, but yet we had no difficulty relating to 'Your Family' - toddlers, pets and all, as people."

But I would also express a concern. "It was good to include a 'touch of humanity' in the punch, but the punch landed in the wrong direction when 'humanity' came to be associated if not equated with liquor! As a family progam, many young viewers could have got the wrong message".

Reading a story in the *Globe & Mail* of May 8, 1985, I was excited about a new initiative at CBC to have "a one-hour show on religion", once a week. Writing to the Director, Performance Programming, both congratulating and wishing success. "Simply wishing you success, however, is I feel not enough. I would be failing in my responsibility if I did not offer you the benefit of my experience in the field of Interfaith Dialogue. In addition to my experience in Canada, I also offer him my 'unique perspective' that is both Eastern (birth and upbringing) and at the same time Western (living, studying and working in North America)". In a letter thanking me for my interest, I am told that they were seeking an appropriate Producer, and that my proposal will be kept on file until then. Close, but no cigars, since that was the last I was to hear about it.

While my personal appearance on air at CBC may have been limited, I am indeed gratified that Canada's leading broadcaster had come to be sensitive to such issues as Multiculturalism and Interfaith Dialogue. And I was there to add my two-cents' worth in those early days of Multiculturalism, when there were not too many multicultural leaders, never mind experts, to help, or work with, the establishment.

16.3 Still on TV

Beside CBC, there were other stations on which I appeared. One of them was the Horizon Interfaith Network on Cable 10 (1988-91). Among the public issues discussed were Interfaith relations, religious education, and religion itself.

On TVO, I would serve as a panelist on public issues, such as e.g., religion & environment, Multiculturalism, etc. (1991). What I was amused about was that on its program on Multiculturalism, I was slated as the 'anti-multiculturalist', in debate with the Chair of an official multicultural body in Ottawa! My continuing criticism of the *practice* of Multiculturalism had obviously come to be seen by some as being against Multiculturalism. Obviously they seem to have not looked into my past, nor deep enough.

Invited to appear on the Evangelical TV station, *100 Huntley Street,* beamed to 200,000 households across Canada, and asked "Who is God", I would answer, "A fiction of the human imagination"! The likeable Rev. David Mainse would tell me over lunch that while there was no doubt in his mind that Christianity was the greatest religion to appear on the face of the earth, it was to satisfy the request of his viewers to see and listen to other religions that I, and Reps of other religions had been invited. All of us other religionists had agreed to participate on the condition that what we say would be aired unedited. The good Reverend kept his word, also meeting the conditions of the CRTC license.

The long-running, and obviously popular, program had later made a successful application to go on air on a full time basis under the name CTS (Christian Televison Service). But there was the proviso that a certain percentage of the time be assigned to non-Christian programming. While this requirement could have been met just by putting films, the Station apparently decided to take up the challenge and make use of the opportunity to bring in other religious and social viewpoints. 'Faith Journal' was the result, hosted by the experienced Richard Landau, formerly of Vison TV. And I would serve as a Panelist on it on several occasions from 1999 through 2001. Among the topics were: "Is Society too Permissive?, "Divorce and Marriage", "Millennial Madness" (Dec. 16, 1999), "Grief Counsellors", "Parenting: Raising Children who are faithful". In communication with Penny Holmes, the Associate Producer, I would do two editorials, with the help of a teleprompter, which I had first used at CBC. One was "On Spanking" and another on "Human Rights: a Buddhist Critique". But I also had come to be interviewed on "Rhonda London Live" in 1999 and 2000 on Multiculturalism. I would be picked up early morning to be taken to Burlington where the Station was located, and dropped off at the end of the day. Spending practically a full day for a half hour program, I seem to have soon got tired!

Most recently, in July 2006, I was approached by OMNI TV for advice on doing a 13 part series on Buddhism that the Station itself had initiated, noting that Buddhism was underrepresented in their programming. Having met Alan Ko, Story Producer, Diversity, and Suzy Soares, Senior Producer, I was happy to provide an outline, but turning down an invitation to be Co-Producer. Working some thirty years ago on Rogers Cable as Producer on Programs on Sri Lankan Canadians, I knew what it entailed - late nights, sometimes going into the wee hours of the morning. But I was happy to nominate a replacement, Dr Veronique Ramses, of York University, and a Buddhist, who kindly agreed to take it on. Asked to help find a suitable host as well, I would recommend Glenn Choi, one time student at Nalanda College of Buddhist Studies (Canada) and by that time Registrar of the College. I also come to be interviewed by him on the same program.

Working with Meetu Khosla, an Associate Producer, I would also do other programs, such as a "3-D Dialogue on Sarvodaya", an educational-developmental program of 50 years in Sri Lanka (recorded on June 26, 2007, and aired on Dec. 3). Another in the same series was on "Marriage in Buddhism". With marriage having nothing to do with religion, the example of a "Sinhala Wedding" is presented when the mother gets a bale of cloth from the groom in gratitude for raising his future wife. The bale represents how much it takes to soak the milk breast-fed to the daughter.

17 TORONTO STAR COLUMNIST IN READER ENGAGEMENT

17.1 Introducing Multiculturalism to Canadians, Coast to Coast

"Gandhi said it. The US psychologist Gordon Allport said it. And we know from experience: Before we accept change, we go through several states. And, happily for us Canadians, we are now at the fifth and last stage of accepting Multiculturalism as a reality", wrote a confident Suwanda Sugunasiri, as noted in the earlier chapter, as a Guest Columnist on Nov. 28, 1987. The piece, titled "The final stage – real change", carried a head shot of me. As far as I know, this is the first column on Multiculturalism to appear in a major newspaper anywhere in the land.

But this was not my first of among the over forty or so Columns I would write for the *Toronto Star* over time (1984 to 1998). The very first column was in the Religion Page, at the invitation of its Editor Michael McAteer whom I may have met at a Buddhist-Christian dialogue. Titled "Let's Speed up the Good Work of Dialogue" (Jan 21, 1984), and showing a head shot of me. But the article seems to have gone largely unnoticed. Appearing in 1984, before the introduction of the Multicultural Act, interfaith dialogue was likely limited to a few interested religious leaders. This is not to say that religion had been ignored by society, given the fact that the *Star* did have a Religion Page, but that by religion was still meant only Christianity. So dialogue was likely not the interest of the pew.

Cautioned by Michael against rushing into writing more, it would be three years before the next first column would appear. With the publication of the Op Ed piece, I had returned to familiar territory, after a hiatus of nearly a quarter of a century. This was journalism. I had been a columnist, before leaving Sri Lanka, under the pseudonym *Madhupa* 'Honey-sucker', for the Sinhala daily, *Dawasa*, having also written other pieces in both newspapers and magazines. Upon leaving the shores of Sri Lanka in 1974 for the second time, my only contributions to the newspapers had been the odd letter to the Editor, a thought piece, etc., appearing in the (now defunct) *Telegram, Toronto Star, Ceylon Daily News,* etc.

Seeing a *Saturday Star* front page spread on the Dalai Lama, I was chatting with Glenn Mullin who had kindly brought out a *Journal of the Buddhist Council of Canada* when I was President. He was featured in the *Toronto Star* story. Probably sharing with him my media work back in Sri Lanka, I wondered if the *Toronto Star* might be interested if I were to write for it. "Why don't you write something and send it to them directly? That's what I do", Glenn encouraged. Working as colleagues, it would never have entered his mind that I didn't have a European name or a white skin, and that these things still did make the difference in a Canada, just coming out of the Eurocentric shell and barely flapping its first multicultural wings.

Soon, however, it was his kindness that he would introduce me to Vian Ewart, Op Ed Editor of the time. Asked to write two pieces for him to look at, I produce two (or was it three?) pieces within a short span of a day or two. "Recycling?", Vian was to ask, perhaps surprised to be told they were all original. That was when he, satisfied with my writing, published my first Column, "The Final Stage – Real Change" (Nov 28, 1987). On a visit organizing the Buddhist community, as the President, Buddhist Council of Canada,

I called him from Victoria, BC, to check. Yes, it was in.

"When the Act of 1971 is approved by Parliament, Multiculturalism will have, for the first time in our history, a legislative backing", I wrote in the next piece, "Our Multiculturalism Act: a Small Step to the Future" (Dec. 5, 1987), explaining the Act to Canadians. This again may have been the first column to appear anywhere in Canada, specifically on the Multicultural Act. This was a time when the very word 'Multiculturalism' was too much of a tongue-twister for the Anglophone mainstream, whose names were monosyllabic - Joe, Dick, Jane, Kate, etc. Ottawa bureaucrats simply reduced it to the 'multi act', and the rest of the population reduced it, as also my next seven articles, to a single act - of simply ignoring, in the certitude that Multiculturalism had nothing to do with them but was only for the minorities!

As I myself make history, "This itself makes that Act a historic one, rectifying an 18-year old omission. While in 1969 Bilingualism is legislated, Multiculturalism has remained, since 1971 when it was announced, a mere policy. [David] Crombie's Act corrects this." Then later on in the same piece, I go on to say, "What Crombie's Act does is to provide a foundation to the future. It can, we hope, help bring about a fundamental attitude change – not merely to recognize, but, more importantly, to value the changing face of Canada."

I did some national gloating as well: "The Act is no doubt a world's first." But adding an international dimension, I go on to say that "[w]hile countries such as Australia and New Zealand have been recently pursuing multicultural policies, countries such as Sri Lanka, Tanzania and Cuba have [long] included components of multiculturalism into national policy." Having pointed to the strengths and weaknesses of the Act, I end as follows: "The question, then, is not whether the minority communities are happy with the proposed Multicultural Act of 1967, but rather whether we as a nation can live with it, congratulating ourselves as a compassionate people."

Under the careful editorial hand of Vian, I would write a few more pieces over the next five years. As can be seen in the following listing, I sought to educate the readers at each critical stage of official Multiculturalism, highlighting issues such as Citizenship (3.26.88), Education (3.25.89) and the Oath (6.3.89). Two and a half years later, I write in an *Op Ed* piece that " Multiculturalism has Shaped Nations' Attitudes" (*Toronto Star*, October 29, 1990) and a year later appeal, in an *Op Ed* piece in the Globe to "Keep the Great Experiment Going" (*Globe & Mail*, July 18, 1991).

As noted above, my piece "Who, Then, is a 'Canadian?'" comes to be featured in several publications, but by two educators, too, for its intrinsic quality of language usage and precis writing.

It was when the water in the pot was beginning to boil perhaps, to draw upon a 16th century Sinhala parable, that the Canadian mainstream crabs now began to feel the heat and perhaps pay attention to my pieces. Titled, "Changing the Foundations of Our Education" (3.25.89), I had begun with the provocative line, "Is Jesus the only way?", taken from the *United Observer*, a publication of the United Church of Canada. The courts had decided that the mandatory recital of the Lord's Prayer was a violation of the rights of minority communities. And the government of Ontario had appointed a one-man commission to look into the matter, my piece noting that there already existed a *Readings and Prayers* book developed by the Toronto Board of Education, for which ironically, the Board had to fight the Ministry. I had had a hand in it, too. In my piece, I had urged input from a wide spectrum, giving the deadline and the address. I had also raised the whole issue of moral and religious education in the secondary school where a course on "World Religions" was hidden among 11 other subjects. The piece ended with thoughts to the future: "Our federal Multicultural Act has served as an international trailblazer in inter-ethnic relations. We now have yet another opportunity to provide leadership: in religious education."

I had made reference to Secular Humanism in the column, alongside Buddhism, as two spiritual orientations that had no belief in God. And thus I would hear from Philip F. Jones, in his capacity as President of the Humanist Association of Canada informing me that indeed they have already made a submission to Dr Glenn Watson, the one-man Task Force, enclosing as well a booklet published by the British Humanist Association. Sent to me was a Humanist flyer, and a letter he had already written to the *Etobicoke Guardian* a week before mine would appear. It was in response to an earlier letter by a reader urging that the court ruling be one "that should be ignored right from the start"! But the letter writer was also incensed that "a group of three people from alien cultures and alien religions have had the arrogance to demand that six million Christians ... shall be restricted in the manner we have followed for a hundred years." Added were also two other letters – one in response to Jones' response and his second response. The details I have given here seem to show that Canada was now beginning to notice Multiculturalism, ignoring being the first stage in the schema of Allport and Gandhi.

But the real reader anger was not about a column on Multiculturalism, but one on communication. Titled "If there's No Communication, it's Gobbledygook Not English" (4.29.89), I had shown how English had changed over the course of time, showing it initially through a comparison of the King James Bible of 1611 with the version of 1952. "In words, meanings and accents, in sounds and in their combinations, language changes. From place to place. Over time." As an example of 'Canajan' usage from Newfoundland, I gave the sentence, *"The bare farmer had a braffus of brews and starnaked, and went alang for a marning walk in the slob"*. And I translated it into standard English: "The broke sailor had a breakfast of hard biscuit pieces soaked ovenight, warmed in the morning and eaten with boiled codfish and butter (all this contained in the word 'brews') and tea without milk or sugar, and went along for a morning walk in the soft snow." I added, "You will see Shakespeare, Chaucer and Spencer here. Irish, Scottish and native dialects as well. But principally, you hear the speech of a fishing people cut off from the mainland." Saying that "The speakers of non-standard English may be the Johns and the Janes down the street and not the Northrop Fryes and the Pierre Elliot Trudeaus", I ask, "How is it that we never hear or read these different accents or varieties on radio, television and the newspapers?"

Of course, twenty years later, we do hear, read and see a diversity of faces and names in the media, but at that time, sending me a hand-written note, a reader notes, "... but I still maintain we must teach and speak "Queen's English", i.e., proper grammar, pronunciation, etc. Clearly, the reader errs in believing that only traditional language has a grammar, whereas the linguist in me would point out that every language and every version of a language has a grammar, without which there would be no communication. We only have to think of Medieval English and

Modern English to know that pronunciation change is only but natural.

Another reader even took the time to mark up my column in a hundred different places (exaggerating here) in red, before returning it to me, even wondering "What Star Editor passed this 'gobbledygook'?" But the point s/he makes is not without validity – "There must be a 'standard written & to some extent spoken English, or there would be no communication." In fact, it was not that I was disagreeing, but only drawing attention to the variety existing within the same sociopolity called Canada.

A next letter writer was furious. Not signing the name, I am given a piece of his / her mind: "You have the goddamn nerve, pontificating in the language of the English people – you with a name like Suwanda Sugunasiri…..". Clearly, I had touched a raw nerve – the holy cow of the venerated language of the English Founding Father. The world over – Europe, Africa, Asia, one who speaks in no more than one language is considered the village fool. But the fool in North America is the one who speaks a language other than English! Which, of course, may well explain the traditional Anglophone attitude to Francophones, as to Native People, French gaining recognition only after a hundred years after Confederation. So, being offended by writing on English by an 'alien' (as perceived by the letter writer above, in the *Etobicoke Gazette*) is understandable. The revered, and exalted position of English, seemed to be under attack. But what s/he didn't know was that I had a Master's Degree in Linguistics from the Ivy League University of Pennsylvania, studying in the very same department the renowned linguist Noam Chomsky had graduated from. I had followed up with courses in Sociolinguistics and Psycholinguistics, here in Toronto itself, at the internationally known Ontario Institute for Studies in Education of the University of Toronto. S/he wouldn't know either that I had *taught* both Linguistics and English Linguistics, at both the university and the secondary levels, and had even written on Canadian Literature, as e.g., my piece in a Canadian journal, "Step Down Shakespeare, the Stone Angel is here". Or even that all my academic qualifications were earned in the west - London, Philadelphia and Toronto. Of course, there was no way s/he could have known. The byline mentioned no academic qualifications.

A well known figure – writer, politician, academic, etc., with a European name needs only the strength of the argument in a piece to earn respectability and credibility, but not so for a Suwanda Sugunasiri. It is not unknown that, as Canadian women have pointed out more than once, that they have to run twice as fast to get half as much compared to men. It is with these thoughts of respectability / credibility in mind, then, that I had written to the publisher of the *Star*, about adding my Dr. title to my name in published material. It was pointed out to me that the journalistic tradition was that only a medical practitioner would be identified with the title 'Doctor'. While what that meant was that the readers would continue to not to have the benefit of the background of the writer, what was not said, or wasn't conscious of, was also that it was also to pay no respect for learning.

In his defence of English, the writer tells me that "apparently you ignore the fact that any country worth living in has latched on to the English language. That's why you're here and not China." Additionally, "You should know that people think in words. That's why any nation ... worth a damn has an English background," forgetting, of course, that one of the Founding Peoples of the nation of Canada is French.

The writer has other beefs, too. S/he is obviously dismayed that s/he "saw [looking through the *Star*] plenty of names like yours, but few with a true English ring to them." The writer would have been furiouser, with apologies to Alice in Wonderland, had s/he known that I would argue in my doctoral thesis that English is a counter-development force in the Post-Colonial Nations, my replacement for Two-thirds World. The outcome is that the local languages, and along with it, the culture comes to be ignored and not allowed to grow.

The next beef put me totally off balance. "You are on record as saying that if Canadians embraced Buddhism we'd become a more honest, wiser society." So the writer has obviously been watching me, which I consider a compliment, of course. These were the words in the caption of a bust-up photo of mine beside a Buddha figure in the Joe Serge column as above. And, of course, I wouldn't mind sticking my neck out even today to make the point, not with any thoughts of conversion but in terms of the quality Buddhism would add to Canadian life.

I was put in my place as well, by no less than three kind letter writers for a literary boo-boo on my part, misquoting and misinterpreting a Shakespearean line. "Imagine Juliet wooing Romeo with the words, "Where the hell are you, man?" instead of "Where art thou, Romeo?", I had written. An upset writer would put matters straight, with a mild rebuke for "perpetrating the misconception that, when Juliet says, "Wherefore art thou (no comma) Romeo?", she is not asking where he is. She is, of course, asking why his name has to be Romeo, and therefore the enemy of her family". My Editor at the *Star* asks me to check with "this lady if we can publish hers". Now I begin to see a silver lining in the critique: "… shows people are reading us." I had no reason to be unhappy.

It was a public ire I was to face when I had stepped on the toes of another sacrosanct topic. In a column titled, "Challenging a Sleeping Lion over our Oath" (June 3, 1989), I had wondered if the Citizenship Act to be introduced in Parliament soon would provide the opportunity "to move allegiance to Canada ahead of Allegiance to the Queen". As above, Susan Eng, the lawyer born and bred in Canada, sworn in as a Police Commissioner – the first visible minority appointment, had refused to say the first part of the Oath swearing allegiance to "Her Majesty Queen Elizabeth II". The British Privy Council, I had pointed out, had now been replaced by the Supreme Court of Canada, and the constitution repatriated (1982). A Quebec National Assembly committee had proposed eliminating the Oath to the Queen in 1972, and a trucker with the British Columbia Highways Ministry, Ed Price, had refused to take the oath in 1984. The idea that one person could be better than the rest of us "just by the accident of birth" was "repugnant to him". He was not alone. By1981, 74% of Canadians had thought that the importance of the monarchy was decreasing. So I had raised the issue in bold terms: "The basic question has boiled down to this: Does a monoethnic, monocultural, monoreligious and foreign monarchy mean much to a linguistically, culturally and religiously pluralistic Canada?"

Writing to the *Star* from Toronto, a reader says he "could not believe the contents of the article ... the 1982 Constitution states very clearly that Her Majesty is Head of State". Of course, I was not denying the existing reality but only wondering how relevant it was to our changing society.

Another Letter writer minces no words: "Anti-royalists living in Canada have three options: 1. Have our Constitution changed by legal means to make Canada a Republic. 2. Leave Canada. 3. Hold their noses and respect the present situation." Indeed it was the first that I was suggesting, stemming from the emerging Canadian reality. I had not disagreed with the third either, merely pointing out that such had taken place. This was not the first time the second had been suggested: crossing over to Victoria from Vancouver by ferry in the early seventies, my wife and I had heard an elderly couple mutter a similar sentiment to themselves, with us in hearing distance. As noted, over the CFRB as well, in the early eighties, I had been asked on air to go home!

But I was also to receive a surprising telephone message. The caller liked my piece, and as an Irishman, he found it difficult to swear allegiance to the Queen. The caller had obvious British (though not English) origins! I concluded that here was a first sign that what colonialism had successfully kept glued together, over 500 years, Canadian Multiculturalism had effectively put asunder, in less than 20 years! It was the 'British' who had colonized the Asian and African countries of the world, and it was the 'British' that was one of the two *deux nations* that had founded Canada. Subsumed under 'British', of course, were the English, Irish, Scottish and the Welsh, who were now breaking ranks with the dominant English. And Canada was beginning to be ripped apart at the seams.

Regardless of the conflicting positions, all of the writers above who took issue with me might have been happy to see my Letter to the Editor in the *Toronto Star* on Aug 21, 1999. The Headline captured the point I was making: "The British Population of Toronto suffers reverse racism".

Acknowledging receipt of a copy of the *Toronto South Asian Review* I had sent her, Joan M Green, Director of the Toronto Board of Education, notes that she "read with much interest" my article "Minority Ethnics build Walls of Seclusion" (Oct 29, 1990). An unexpected reader response was to my article in the *Globe and Mail* of July 18, 1991 under the title, "Keep the great experiment going". Having seen Multiculturalism policy and practice going awry, yet unable to find myself not unsupportive, the piece sought to propose some corrective measures, suggesting "a few ways our society can grow into multicultural adulthood". Among my suggestions regarding the mainstream were the following:

- o disbanding the federal Multiculturalism Secretariat;
- o disbanding the Multicultural Advisory Councils;
- o getting rid of the monarchy;
- o setting up a Ministry of Culture and Communication;

- racism to be redefined to include ethnocentrism;
- stopping funding for heritage language instruction, and instead require every student to learn a third language which would help prepare the country for international communication;
- revamping the jury system to allow for minority representation;
- including an interfaith spiritual dimension.

I also had advice for the minorities:
- stop crying racism at every turn, giving examples of racism within their own ranks;
- identify the human issues in the communities, such as wife-battering, illiteracy, alcohol and other drugs, using education as a tool;
- help the system by turning over the criminals;
- forget past injustices (something I had urged at the Ontario Advisory Council on Multiculturalism and Citizenship when the issue of Japanese compensation was successfully voted on);
- get rid of your own colonial mentality, giving here an example, as told me by Rita Deverell, host of Vision TV:
  When a Hindu sadhu was in town, the community did not want her ("a Black woman (and former Professor), ignorant of Hinduism") to interview him. They would rather have Tom Harpur ("White male (and former Professor), equally ignorant of Hinduism") do it.)
- promote intermarriage so as to rejuvenate the gene pool;
- drawing upon President Kennedy, ask not what the country can do for us, but what we can do for the country.

I ended the article with the line, "Unless we take our responsibilities seriously, and work towards multicultural maturity, one of history's great experiments in bettering the human condition will be on the rocks."

I thought I was taking no sides, seeking to strike a balance, drawing upon my vast experience, studying and living in Canada as well as overseas. A Letter writer from Ottawa wasn't impressed. He wrote to say how the article "illustrates an unfortunate misunderstanding of Canadian society." Indeed I had no difficulty agreeing with him that "If there was a 'great experiment', it was to widen our immigration access in the expectation that newcomers would join with us in a wholly new conception of nationhood". This is what I thought I was saying in so many words in addressing the minorities. Yet, to the writer, it was "highly disappointing that such persons as Dr Sugunasiri should believe that the policy of Multiculturalism, adopted by the government of Canada without any public support, with a view of enlisting the sympathies of persons from non-French or English speaking countries, for the policy of Official Bilingualism, something which equally had not secured widespread public support, implied a desire to establish this nation as a country of a number of ethnic minorities, as are found in India, where they effectively destroyed any real hope of national unity." How the writer got this idea when I had even suggested that ethnocentrism be defined as racism baffled me!

In writing a note to him, I had enclosed two of my articles on Multiculturalism that had been published in the *Star*. In a two and a half page letter, he reiterates his discomfort with Multiculturalism, taking a hit at Trudeau ("a half-educated man with strong prejudices") in the process. He points out that in contrast to the US, "we have developed a rather tolerant nationalism". He also lambasts India ("the continent from which you undoubtedly come (perhaps Shri Lanka))", as one of "the most racist countries in the world with some abominal practices…". How surprised he might have been that Buddhist Sri Lanka was a far cry from India! When he writes that "It is perhaps difficult for a person, not born and educated in Canada, to understand that both the government and the news media have become totally unrepresentative of the views of the majority of Canadians", he was again not aware, as he could not have been, that I had earned three graduate degrees right here in Toronto! Writing that "It is highly irritating to hear persons such as yourself, who were glad to come to this country, propose all sorts of changes", he attaches a "cartoon by Rodewalt of the Calgary Herald, who properly illustrates our reactions to this situation". I found it interesting in that I had made the same point in my article: "Minorities may still feel discrimination, but have they ever thought about what a hard time members of the majority have had in the past 20 years? They're even starting to call themselves TWASP's – tortured WASP's – because they feel they're forever being asked to give in".

And I found myself highly agreeing with some of his other points as well. One was about the British coming under criticism, "due to their establishment of standards of behaviour, public morals and ethics". Another was that "A truly cultured, civilized inhabitant of the world is likely to draw something good from all the world's cultures", a point I would take up at length in my book on Multiculturalism (see above for some details): "We want to breathe [in Canada] the fresh air of a global psyche brought to our borders by a hundred or more cultures, and work the landscape to its full cultural potential." *(Towards Multicultural Growth,* 1998, p. 117).

The second letter was copied to "The Hon Gerry Weiner [federal Minister of Multiculturalism], the Hon [Ed] Ziemba [the Provincial counterpart], and [Prime Minister] the Hon [Brian] Mulroney". I was in a little tizzy to see the Minister of Multiculturalism, Gerry Weiner, personally responding publicly to my column (Aug 6, 1991), although disagreeing with me.

But it was the Toronto Chairman of the Monarchist League who seemed to be particularly frazzled by my piece (Aug. 16, 1991). I had said, "the monarchy must go, because it is a racist institution. Only a white English person can occupy the throne". Picking on my unresearched claim, the writer correctly points out that "There has never been a purely white English person on the throne for at least a thousand years…", noting the mixed Asian, Arab and "part of 30 other European and world ethnicities" inherited by Her Majesty, whose "'senior' ethnicity is German". I undoubtedly stood corrected. But it was a writer from Dundas, Ontario, who took issue with the Monarchist writer: "I suggest that it is he who is "ridiculously off-base", because [the writer] argues against only one sense of the term "racist institution". Continuing, she points out that "the legacy of the British tradition is decidedly racist, in that British colonialism has a historical legacy of cruelty and degradation directed at other cultures in the name of the monarchy". I couldn't have put it better!

Here is a poem, however, that may just put the minds at ease of Monarchist League types, or perhaps confuse them, but giving nevertheless a different picture of Yours Truly:

BETWEEN WORLDS
To Elizabeth

I
*I could feel
the electricity running
down my arm
then ....*

*As I sprung
a salute, parading
loyalty, my
uniformed ego
about to explode
into a firecracker
night, as you passed by
the sea of heads
flanked
by Brown Knights.*

II
*Today
in sovereign Canada*

*we
wait
in multicultural splendour,*

*rise
as you enter
flanked by White Knights,*

*stand
to attention,
to the tune
"God save the Queen."*

*My arm that saluted
suddenly
feels sore
to the very core.*

*Every gem every
thread you wear
anointed
with blood
of a million
upon millions whipped out
in your name
en-
snaring us black brown yellow
with the promise, the
Heavenly Kingdom.*

III
*As you enter
as you depart
unaware
of the flutter
of the bird
in my heart,
you fling that charm
-ing smile, you alone
can summon
in such serene-dignity,
melting the
iceberg.*

*I salute you,
Enchanting
Lady!*

(*The Faces of Galle Face Green*, 1995, P. 29-30)

I am happy that I was able to pen these words returning from an Interfaith Service in Toronto in the presence of Her Majesty where only the monotheistic religions were allowed at the microphone on stage. The polytheistic Hinduism was invited to the stage but not allowed at the microphone and the Buddhists were relegated just to the audience! But I was happy, in pre-multicultural Canada, just to be considered worthy of being given a special guest pass!

This was published, in a slightly variant version, in *A Treasured Token,* in 1997, published by the National Library of Poetry, Maryland, USA.

In response to my piece, 'Peremptory Right' Builds in Biases to Jury Selection", based on my experience of serving on a jury, I was to receive a letter from a reader, listing his academic credentials: BA, BSc, Un Cert (Fren). He was writing from a penitentiary, "wrongly arrested and imprisoned" in 1986 and "eventually wrongly convicted to a further 12 years…". He tells me that "the prosecution was able to legally impose an all-female jury, given that I, a male, was accused of physical assault against a female." (underlining in original). He also attaches a copy of a letter sent by him to a Professor of Law.

While he was not looking for my help, what caught my attention was a line in the first paragraph: "Could it be that people like you and I more readily perceive such injustice in the legal system because our commonsense and reason are not *limited by formal legal training*?" I had written in my published piece that "the right to peremptory challenge seems to me …. a travesty of justice". I was referring to the practice of lawyers on either side (crown or defence) being able to challenge a potential juror just on a whim. No reasons have to be given. I was pointing out that the practice "takes away the fairness of the random selection process". It was indeed with no surprise that I would read in the papers (e.g., *National Post*) as I write this (in the Fall of 2009) how much more of that fairness has been wrenched away. Apparently, at least in some jurisdictions (Barrie, Ontario, was named), it seems that background checks on potential jurors have been conducted by the Police. While it didn't matter that it was for the benefit of the crown, the practice seems to confirm my argument that there was no more randomness in jury selection.

Below, then is a list of my first pieces on Multiculturalism that informed, soothed or enraged Canadians.

I would also become perhaps the earliest minority Book Reviewer in the public media, beginning with Jean Burnet's *Coming Canadians: An Introduction to the History of Canada's Peoples* ("Helping Unravel the ethnic paradox, *Saturday Magazine, Toronto Star*, Dec. 3, 1988). The next, "True Voices speak from the heart" (Aug. 19, 1989) was a review of *Harriet's Daughter* by Marlene Nourbese Philip (Women's Press) and *A Testimony of Triumph* by James W Sutton, both around the Black experience. My review of *Worlds Apart: New Immigrant Voices* edited by Millie Charon,, under the title, "The pains an pleasures of Canadian immigrants" (*Saturday Magazine, Toronto Star*, Oct 14, 1989) brought a response from Charon herself making a point that I was myself "guilty of unconscious, or perhaps conscious paranoia" in some of my observations. In a kind personal

Year	Title	Publication Info
1987	The Final Stage – Real Change	*Tor.Star,* Nov. 28
	Our Multiculturalism Act: a Small Step for the Future	*Sat. Star,* Dec. 05
	Christmas in Canada touches many faiths	*Sat.Star,* Dec. 19
1988	'Multi-faith' service lost a big opportunity	*Sat. Star,* Feb. 27
	Redrawing Roadmap to Citizenship Maze	*Tor.Star,* March 26
	Differences Okay from a Distance	*Tor.Star,* Sept. 24
	Slow Progress of Acceptance	*Tor.Star,* Dec. 24
1989	Changing the Foundations of Our Education	*Tor.Star,* March 25
	Who, then, is a Canadian?	*Tor.Star,* Feb. 04
	Challenging a Sleeping Lion over our Oath	*Tor.Star,* June 03
	Multiculturalism has Shaped Nations' Attitudes	*Tor.Star,* Nov. 7
1990	Minority Ethnics Build Walls of Seclusion	*Tor.Star,* Oct. 29 (Op Ed)
1991	Keep the Great Experiment Going	*G & M,* July 18 (Op Ed)

letter to me, she noted that I was a good writer. I would also review two works by Cyril Dabydeen, the short story collection *To Monkey Jungle* (Third Eye) and *Coastland: New Selected Poems* (Mosaic Press), under the title, "Small Incidents turned into good tales" (*Sat. Magazine, Toronto Star*, Jan. 27, 1990).

In addition to Multiculturalism, I had now been writing on and a few other topics for the *Toronto Star*, among them,

- Komagata Maru – A shameful episode in Canadian History (??.05.1988.);
- Sikhs mark 75th Anniversary of "Voyage of Shattered dreams" (22.07.1989);
- Vibrant clash of cultures enriches our literature (17.04.1993);
- 'Preremptory Right' builds in biases in jury selection (24.01.1994);
- Vison TV represent spiritual democracy (25.04.1994);
- When Science Calls Religion (17. 06.1995.);
- Steering the banks toward fairness (13.01.1996.);
- China's hunger a priority (20.12.1997).

Now I came to write my first piece on Buddhism itself, an OpEd piece, on the occasion of Wesak – the Triple celebration of Buddha's Birth, Enlightenment and Parinibbana 'Final Demise'. It appeared under the title, "Buddhist festival a sumptuous feast for hungry spirits" (May 5, 1993). I thought the Editor did very well in using the phrase 'hungry spirits' in the headline. On the one hand, there were those who were hungrily looking for spiritual heights. But there is also another category of beings specifically as in Buddhism – those born as 'hungry spirits'. They had been so stingy and miserly in one or more of their past lives that they come to be born into a form of existence where there is plenty of food, but you can't have any, thus keeping them in a perpetual state of hunger. I sought to personalize their plight in a poem, sitting at the Galle Face Hotel in Sri Lanka, watching the long Promenade where street-hawkers sell their mouth-watering savouries.

Hoping to involve more non-mainstream writers, I was happy to see Vian, now Editor of the *Saturday Star*, introduce a feature "Torontonians". I would happily share the space with Neil Bissoondath and two others.

17.2 Anatomy of a Word: Rejuvenating a Readership

I would also continue to write other pieces. But among the columns that generated the most interest was "Four Letter Words Taint Community" (*Toronto Star*, July 22, 1995). I began with the following opening paragraph:

> *Help me! I have absolutely nowhere to turn… It is everywhere … baring its ugly teeth at me, waiting to gobble me up. I can see it. It is ready. The four-letter word.*
>
> *Yes, the four-letter word .. I can't open a book, turn on the TV or walk the streets without inspiration from it…*
>
> *When and how did we lose control?*

Did the readers ever join in on the conversation! 15 of them responded by letter and one young man, of 27, as he was to tell me, via a phone message. Returning the call, the young man was intrigued by my pointing the finger to the film industry.

Writing from Bowmanville, Nancy (I drop the last names in this discussion out of respect for reader privacy), a senior, opened with the words, "I'm afraid we are to be called "prudish" or "anachronistic" or "Victorian" if we objected to the F.. word." The first two characterizations had been taken from a Letter to the Editor, attached to her letter. It opened with the line "It seems anachronistic and prudish for The *Star* to edit the word "f…" from coverage of the Bernardo trial", going on to make the point that the coverage has included "descriptions of all kinds of brutality, physical and sexual violation, psychological torture, and the dismemberment of a human body".

I had characterized the film "as a possible *first-seed spreader*" (italics added). I continued: "Not that the word wasn't there in the beginning! But that the medium cast it far and wide.." It may be these lines that prompted her to say how "ashamed" she was "at the obscene language" watching, with her granddaughter, the rented movie, '*The Paper*'. Returning it to the store, she would comment that "there would have been no dialogue" if the obscene language had been taken out.

"And for such stars as Glen Close & Michael Keaton?" she wondered. Starting a conversation with her granddaughter, she recalls how shocked they were when an actor (Rhett Butler) said to another (Scarlet), "Frankly my dear, I don't give a damn". Another was shocked by what was in *My Fair Lady* when Elga Dolittle "telling the horse to get off its arse!" Asking rhetorically "Were we wrong?" she writes parenthetically, "We were right." I was happy to see her providing some evidence for my point about the film being a 'seed-spreader'.

As if echoing my point that "the artists and the civil rightists bandied freedom of expression banners" if anyone were to protest, she adds, "The movie producers would scream "freedom of expression" or some other "rightist thing" if people said 'enough'". Adding to the words in her first line, "Well, I for one, do object v. strongly. I think it's a disgrace", she later talks about her determination to "confront it".

Agreeing with me "most emphatically" in the opening line and thanking me "for making your views public", another reader (sorry name missing) shares her experience of reading a book written by the chief psychologist at Bellvue Hospital in NY. "I can hardly believe that educated people speak to each other (and about their patients) in such crude terms". She feels that "it lowers the educative tone of a book". She attaches the same Letter to the Editor, saying that she's glad "the *Star* refrained from fully printing the word". I had myself written in the piece, "I want to be like the third monkey – not speaking it, or ever using it in my writing." The tight 750 word limit nor the secular context would allow me to say that it comes from my Buddhist upbringing and the personal discipline, guided by the 4th of the 5 Training Principles (aka Precepts) to abstain from the four types of wrongful language: lying, backbiting, foul language and gossiping.

"Thank you. Your column was a breath of fresh air", begins the letter from Mrs Muriel (appellation added to the signature), a reader in Mississauga. Noting the word's appearance even on T-shirts, she suggests that "There must be a law against" it. Extending to music, she comments on how a few years ago the host of a fine music hour had said "that the slobs were taking over". She was now wondering what he thinks "about the trash that passes for music now. And the lyrics! Very corrupting." Fearing that things will get worse, she says that "There are some very dangerous forces insidiously out to corrupt the young." "Some of the world's finest writers – Thomas Hardy, Shakespeare, John Buchan, never felt compelled to resort to abominable language, yet look what gave us – great, exciting, beautiful stories." Reading a Review of a novel she had picked up at the library, "but two pages was all I could manage. Very filthy." I can relate to the experience, when more recently, buying a celebrated novel, I returned it to the store, unable to stomach the language. Nothing had been said of the language in any of the reviews I had read either.

Thanking me for "putting into words so eloquently what I have been feeling for years". A respondent from Brampton notes that "Even gangster films seem to manage quite nicely without any swear words or nude bedroom scenes".

Karen (Mrs.), writing from Lindsay, writes that both she and her husband have been sick of the usage, and ending with the words, "I'm cutting it out [meaning my column] to keep and show".

Elizabeth (Mrs.) of Etobicoke, writing on "Your thought provoking, timely column", thanks me for not referring to the word "culture" and for saying "what I have believed all along". She also supports my "efforts for re-education 100%". She was responding to the invitation I had extended in the final line of my piece, : "Anyone who wants to join me, to confront, raise hell, or raise our consciousness, write to me at the *Star*." It must have been a bad day for me, to have been that bellicose.

Ticked off additionally at other "words", penned in their 'expletive deleted' form – ", sh.., p..... off, bas....., get off your ....., G.D. and S.O.B", Marion, from Scarborough, says she "would be glad to be the first on your list." When she asks, "Don't the TV producers think we have no imagination re what goes on 'behind closed doors'", it touches on the same point that another reader makes in relation to the language in films today – that they show "so little imagination".

Another letter comes from Doreen, a reader who seems to have read an earlier article by me. Living beside a secondary school, she finds the language she encounters "on the street and bus, offensive & inelegant." "The chord you struck with me was not this, but instead, the issue of boundaries and of discipline." She ends by saying, "Count me in on your crusade."

Calling my "stand on the use of the four-letter words admirable" Garnet, a writer from Simcoe points out that "We are not alone as we sometimes think". He refers to the issue being raised as early as 1990 and onwards by Comedian Steve Allen, a local Minister and (the well-known Catholic thinker) Jean Vanier, the Star Ombuds himself referring to the problem. He himself had already taken action against it. But his letter to the *Star*, objecting to sacrileging the name of Christ and God, didn't even get published. He signs off, "Yours for clean speech".

Ramona, a student from Etobicoke, who, as she says, was in a course I had taught at the Faculty of Education, University of Toronto, had better luck. A copy attached for my benefit, her Letter to the Editor was about "the overused fecal synonym that rhymes with it". Exposing viewers to such words "implies that we are regarded only as so much excrement." Noting that she has read, from time to time, my "wise and timely comments", she reveals that "Fearing confrontation, we tend not to speak out even to our relatives who know very well our aversion to such language." She argues with a "clever Professor of English", one of her friends, who says that these "dreaded words" are simply good old Anglo-Saxon words and as such are perfectly acceptable. Refusing to "degrade our aesthetic sensibilities and principles by succumbing to the dictates of crass, inspiration 'pop' culture and sexually explicit modern 'literature'," she has eschewed modern books, taking "refuge" in her beloved ... Austen, Bronte, Hardy and Dickens, all of whom managed quite beautifully to portray human foibles and depravities without making the sensitive reader blush." She ends by noting how it is "refreshing" to come across a point of view like mine.

Nadia, also of Scarborough, "couldn't believe that one other person out there shared this sentiment, too". Indeed, she had attempted a more direct approach than the earlier two. "Years ago, I used to express my abhorrence ... and give the user a dirty look." But not any more, "because of the growing violence. I am afraid for my life."

Less optimistic of "reversing this terrible trend" is Barbara of a reader from Scarborough. Speaking to my point that reversing the trend "has to begin with each one of us", she feels that "example alone is such a slow teacher." Of course, it is just the other day (September 2009) that the Dalai Lama had made exactly the point I had made – that peace begins from within oneself, confirming the typical Buddhist stance.

"I do not believe getting our dander up and confront[ing] ... is the answer", writes another from Hamilton, in a lengthy and entertaining letter of 5 typed 8 ½ by 11 pages. "Having had my share of confrontations, I'd rather stay clear of such collisions." But she does think that the "raising of consciousness", as also called for by me, is worthwhile to be investigated. She agrees that "it is very difficult, if not impossible, to change the direction of any, which has long ago taken on a life of its own."

She has a related beef, too. "I have come to see English as a form of cancer, aggressively gobbling up the individuality of the peoples of the earth." This struck a chord with me since in my doctoral thesis, I had argued, though not in such harsh terms, that the use of English in the Post-Colonial Nations is counter-developmental.

William, writing from Port Hope, takes a welcome critical stance toward my piece. Responding to both "Help me!" of the first sentence and "confront, raise hell or raise our consciousness" of the last, he initially points to two pieces of advice given in the *Star*, one by Miss Manners, and the other by Tom Harpur, the well-known theologian and journalist. The former is responding to the complaints of a very hospitable couple about the lack of reciprocity in the behaviour of some friends. And she advises, to quote in full:

> Since it is not possible to point out the shortcomings ... without causing them offence, you must not attempt to do so. For, if something cannot be done politely, it should be left undone.

Harpur was dealing with the topic of religious discussion and dispute. And he writes,

> Discussion of matters of faith need always to be carried on with a concern for the integrity of the other parties or they best left alone. For as was written years ago, faith is important, but not so important as love.

Finding both points of view "thoroughly convincing", he also notes that "their principal effect on my relationships with others is to move me to inaction... More completely, I should say that their effect is to focus me on the need to turn energy not outward to the correction of the world but inward upon myself." He notes this sense in my piece, too, when he then adds, "this is what you mean when you say that *the seed will bear fruit at its hour",* but that we need to begin with ourselves, "with personal restraint".

He adds another dimension. "In her parting advice, Miss Manners encouraged them simply to continue sowing the seed of hospitality, as was obviously their wont, and to be confident that the seed would bear fruit at its hour. As with all worthwhile goals, they would feel a measure of success, not when they reached it, but as they began moving in its direction. This is the kind of advice I feel is in need with respect to the four-letter word and all else..." Then he points to the seeming contradiction in my stance:

> *Through your own personally restrained action ..., you have already begun moving in the direction of your goal, and therefore, I hope, have already felt a measure of success "unimagined in common hours". Ask yourself whether such action would not draw you out of restraint into some four-letter word type of impoliteness. If so, tell yourself that your part is to sow the seed of restraint, as is obviously your wont....*

Muriel (above) was also very interested in knowing how many letters I received "that couldn't be printed." Luckily, none! Perhaps those who disagreed thought best to leave a fool, or a prude with a funny name, alone. Why waste their time defending the use, when they can get better mileage using it?

Mourning "the loss of intelligent, responsible literacy in our society today", a Toronto reader invites me to make good use in my campaign an "open forum newsletter" he publishes called *Notes at the End of a Century.*

Another also writing from Toronto, says that he read my column "with a great sense of relief", glad to see my "incisive and inspirational viewpoint in a publication as influential as the *Star.*" Noting that my "diplomatic" approach " ... has been rarely heard", he wonders, "Maybe the tide is turning?" On "Second thought, it might be a long battle, considering how easily obscenity is getting defended by others". He asks me if I saw "that disgraceful Letter to the Editor on the same day your article appeared?". He shares with me the information that he publishes an "independent magazine" called *Generation of Swine* dealing with "the fall of public propriety", available in a few select stores. The contents include attacks on music business executives, sex educators and vulgar journalists. A sample article, titled "The Day Profanity Made the Front Page", attached to the letter, talks about vulgar language used by politicians (with names named), and dutifully reported by each of *The Star, Globe and Mail* and *Sun.* An article in the publication also appears, it is footnoted, in *Humanist in Canada.*

Indeed it is from an active member of the Humanist Association of Canada, as I would come to know later, that I received the most thoughtful critical comments. Writing from Toronto, she makes the following points, writing out the word in full, not doing so "gratuitously, but because I want to look straight at the problem."

- The word [used in its usual imperative sense] does not simply mean 'sex' but means to diminish someone by having sex with them.... [giving as evidence the past participial [i.e., -ed] plus 'up' expression]. A woman's reputation rests on her sexual experience or lack thereof, while a man's does not.
- Some people seem to have only this one adjective in their vocabulary. They are in effect saying that the whole world is messed up (except for themselves).
- Western moral thought has a tradition of giving three pieces of advice relating to sex: Ignore your mind's desires, don't have sex before marriage, then get married and have sex constantly. ... For people who want to have sex, but know it is "always wrong", this has resulted in anguished hours of trying to ignore their desires, or [indulge] in surreptitions, sometimes violent, guilty sex acts, followed by anguish.
- Because of this history of moral silence, media organizations, ... act as though any criticism of a sexual message on ethical grounds is prude, or constitutional censorship. This is nonsense.
- The problem with the criticism from religious organizations is that it ... does not address the issue in detail.
- Traditional western ideas about sexual ethics are not adequate.

At the end, she identifies some principles that sexuality should be based on:

1. People want to have sex because it is enjoyable. Enjoyment is a valuable part of life. If enjoyment is achieved honourably, we should consider ourselves successful.
2. Our sexual desires often involve other people ... who have their own desires, which may or may not include ourselves. We must respect those desires.
3. Vaginal intercourse can lead to the birth of children. Having children is not a responsibility that one can walk away from...
4. Sexual acts can transmit disease. We should develop habits that safeguard us against passing along diseases.
5. Sex cannot be allowed to take over life, even enjoyable sex.. Staying in bed all day inhibits our ability to feed ourselves!

But who in society would take the time to discuss the issue as sharply as this Humanist has done? We may end by noting that the voluntary Buddhist Training Principle (aka Precept) relating to sex – one of five, that serve a Buddhist as a daily guide, only calls for abstention from 'sexual **mis**behaviour'. And as such, sex in Buddhism is considered no sin, even though it is, like any other desire or attachment (anger, hatred, love, etc.), impedes liberation, which is characterized as cutting off our attachments and graspings.

Despite the sound advice to the contrary by some of the letter writers, I go on, in my pigheadedness perhaps, to arrange a meeting, scheduled for Monday, September 25, 1995, 7 to 9 pm, at the Frankland Community Centre on Logan Avenue. Attending the meeting were only four. While I have no record of the meeting, my sense is that it simply fizzled out, the poor turnout itself being indicative of it.

Personal Reflection

I found it interesting that (a) most letters were from seniors, (b) mostly women, (c) exclusively white, and judging by the names, primarily of British origin. So where are the minorities, I wondered, whose voices are loud and clear when it comes to their rights and privileges? Is it that they are not offended, or that they don't care what happens in society as long as they are not affected personally? Or is it possibly that, cocooned in their ghettoes, they are non-participants of the mainstream culture and don't even know what is going on?

Writing a Column for the *Toronto Star*, I was overall happy that, whatever the topic, I had played a minor but wider role in rejuvenating a readership.

18 A BIOETHICALLY ENGAGED BUDDHIST COLUMNIST

18.1 A Suggestion to the *Toronto Star*

By 1994, I was happy that the *Star* had come around to working in the direction of a suggestion made by me - to make the Religious page, thus far exclusively Christian, to be more reflective of our multifaith reality. It was a continuation of a thrust that we, the Interfaith leaders, had urged federally, in the consultation with Deputy Minister Noel Kinsella. And the CRTC had thrown a challenge to the religious communities, resulting in Vision TV. And now I was happy that I had come to be a 'Buddhist Columnist', writing on contemporary bioethical issues such as, as it turned out to be, Abortion, Celibacy, Cloning, Death and Dying, Euthanasia, Homosexuality, Sex, etc.. But my topics were wider, ranging from Banks, Housing, Organ Donation, Sports, etc. In the process, there also comes to be direct topics on Buddhism itself, such as Kamma, Kindness, Meditation, Perfection, Resentment and Soul, but all in application to contemporary times and issues. And this to me was a way of helping Canadians understand the socially related teachings of the Buddha, little known even to practicing Buddhists.

18.2 Digging into Bioethical Issues in Canadian Society

In my first piece, "Let's Have Some Rules for Family" (4.16.94), in the United Nation's year of the family, I thought I was promoting the value of family. I had made the point that while women, homosexuals, humanists and children have had historical reasons to put the traditional family under fire, I maintained that

"that doesn't make the traditional heterosexual family an archaic and irrelevant institution ... It is central to civilization today as it was when primate life began... For one thing, only heterosexual sex can continue the species. Married couples are happier and healthier. A steady family is best for kids to grow in."

But a reader Frances thought that I "cannot seem to make up my mind about the definition of family". I come to be blamed as well for "... the frightening decline of society" through "popular vision writing like your own. ... and some issues which you defend are an imposition on most Canadians". Despite my defence of the traditional family, I had asked for a truce "to retain the family as the nucleus of society but transform it". As part of the terms of the truce, I had written that while adults should live in a way to earn the respect of the young, children should be respectful towards their parents, community elders and teachers, develop self-discipline, including chastity, and work diligently". I had also called on "our religious, humanist and feminist leaders [to] jettison their excesses in favour of compassion and tolerance." But what seems to have irritated the writer is that I had also said that homosexual union be recognized, and single parent families be respected. This latter is well reflected in the Buddhist understanding that marriage (at least as practiced in Sri Lanka) has nothing to do with religion, civil marriage, practically 'common law' in today's jargon, being the norm (though with exceptions), but with family and community blessing.

But it was my piece to end Public funding for Catholic schools "Time to end cash flow to RC schools" (Aug 8, 1994) that saw a letter to the Provost, Dr R H Painter, at Trinity College where I taught Christian students. "If our first level Multiculturalism was song and dance, and the second current level employment equity and the like, the third level has to be spiritual", I wrote. "This task must begin not in the secrecy of the ghetto school but in the open pastures of the public school. It is only by exposing students to each other's spirituality that they can be made to be not only sensitive to each other but to be deeply committed to their own", I added. "This is not just nice theory," I continued. "It is what my primarily Christian graduate students tell me over and over again. At the beginning of the course, the Catholics and the Uniteds and the Anglicans and the Blacks and the Asians [all Christian] find themselves quite uncomfortable, sharing their own spirituality with each other. But they leave respecting each other's differences, appreciating similarities."

A respondent Maureen saw my piece as a three-pronged attack: first against the Roman Catholic Church; secondly, against the allocation of taxpayer money, and last, against Jewish and Muslim education. She also thought, given that my association with Trinity at the University of Toronto was shown in the credit line, that meant that both Trinity and the University had approved this piece!

It was a different message I was to get from a letter writer to a piece written three months later (Nov. 26, 1994), "There's a Little Piece of Hatred in Every One of Us". A "naturalized Canadian, coming ... after the tragic events in Hungary in 1956", Miklos of North York, encloses, "as a token of my appreciation", an essay entitled, "The Open Mind". The title page showing "For Dr Suwanda Sugunasiri, with respect and friendship" seems to show that the 5-page piece reflected his thoughts as generated by my article. Beginning with a quotation, "The mind is like a parachute; it works only when it is open" – Anon, he ends in the thought, "If we keep this philosophy in mind, and practice it, I am sure that Mankind's parachute will open, and we will land safely." That certainly was re-assuring.

While his whole essay would be a good read for anyone, I will limit myself to giving some highlights. Noting "the myriad creatures on this earth, running, jumping, flying, crawling, climbing or swimming, on two legs, four legs or none at all, or on wings, bleating, roaring, barking, squeaking or singing. How many different ... manifestations of life! Yet we call them all animals." The lines could well have been inspired by the Friendliness / Lovingkindness Discourse of the Buddha. Teaching to "wish no one ill", noting here that by the Buddha's term *satta* is meant both human and animal, the wording goes as follows: "Wherever there are living beings, weak or strong or otherwise, long or fat, middling or short or strong, seen or unseen, near or far, born or yet to be born, may all beings be well...", another reference being to "two-legged, four-legged or non-legged..".

Making the same point relating to plant life and homes, the writer contrasts how we think of people as being "blacks, whites, redskins, yellow, Christians, Jews, Buddhists, Moslems, etc. – instead of just MAN, a HUMAN BEING." Having quoted Einstein, "The human mind is not capable of grasping the Universe", he ends with the words, "We need people .. who realize that no matter how many differences people may have, there is a prehistoric unifying power vibrating among mankind, beyond all colours, religions and philosophies." This is the philosophy the writer sees as Mankind's parachute that will open when man discovers other planets as well.

Included with the essay are two of his own poems, one titled "Nuclear War", with lines beginning with each of the letters of the two words.

In his covering letter, he asks me "to autograph the enclosed newspaper clipping", sending a self-addressed, stamped envelope.

My column "'Soul Myth' Propels Hatred in Us All" (11.04.95) bought two opposing responses. "....intrigued by the rather quaint idea" that the 'soul myth' propelling hatred in us all, a Christian Minister from Scarborough wondered, copying me his Letter to the Editor, how "to fit Hitler and Stalin into this theory of 'soullessness' ". He continues that "most Communists and Nazis denied that there was such a thing as an eternal soul – so they could kill people with impunity". While I did send him a note of thanks, I did not accept his invitation, in a hand-written note, to correspond with me personally concerning the topic. But had I, I might have said that while it may be true that some people may have committed crimes in denying a soul, those who believe in a soul have not been any kinder – the British, French, Portuguese, Dutch and Spaniards, e.g., in conquering lands. Wasn't a whole nation of Beotuks – 250 men, women and children, in Newfoundland, Canada, gunned down in a single day by our Canadian British soul-believers? The point, of course, is that belief or non-belief in a soul seems to make no difference for those who are looking for an excuse to act with what Buddhists call an unskillful mind.

The good Reverend also says that I don't understand "the Christian teaching that each of us has an eternal soul that can be changed from sinful to righteousness... The transforming power of Christ can then overcome the hatred and other evils in the human heart." While I can by way of a comeback say that the letter writer clearly doesn't understand the Buddhist argument for 'soullessness' (*anatta*), providing chapter and verse, suffice it to wonder where saving grace was in Newfoundland on that day.

Writer David from Toronto, by contrast, finds the piece "intriguing", but "not just because of its content, but also for its alternative thinking and analytical openness." Agreeing with the Buddha's understanding I had drawn upon, that qualities such as lust, greed, hate and delusion are intrinsic to the human condition, he makes the sharp observation that "Though perverse ... these elements have been precisely what has indulged, sustained and propelled our civilization." Had he been writing at a later date, he might even have agreed with Michal Moore, the renowned anti-establishment American moviemaker, that capitalism is, as reported, nothing but legalized greed! When the writer notes, "We humans are a perverse lot", it is as if he was taking words right out of the Buddha's mouth that "Deranged are the Masses". Noting further that the Buddha's philosophy was "not readily accepted because it wasn't dichotomously definitive enough", he hopes in his concluding para that "more articles like yours should come along to provoke and agitate our senses so as to enlist our analytical skills for the purpose of aligning any new insight with our future needs." In a page-long personal letter to the writer, I note that the best way to get more articles like mine "to provoke and agitate our senses" is to write to the Editor making the point.

"Let's Help Christians Celebrate" (12.09.95) was a piece written by a hand urged to help set right what I saw was a wrong – namely, a consistent and unrelenting attack on Christians. If earlier it was only by Humanists, now joining were all the (non-Christian) minorities that had fled intolerance in their own countries. But interestingly, it was no more the white majority that was getting hurt. Many an immigrant community, too – practically all immigrants from the West Indies and many from Africa, and substantial numbers from Asia – Chinese from Hong Kong, Koreans from S. Korea, Philipinos, to name a few. Clearly I had touched a happy nerve, several Ontarians taking the time to write to me. "Are we finally reaching new spiritual heights?' began a letter from Peggy writing from Barrie. "In our pluralistic society, and for the sake of future generations (like my grandchildren), we must learn to celebrate for each other. .. The possibilities of such a unified community could be the answer to so many of our ills, racism and ethnic cleansing.." She is kind enough to recommend a publication, *Soul of Politics* by Jan Wallis (Harper Collins). In my handwritten note to her from Trinity, I make the remark, "It is with the active participation of beings like yourself and your good friends and neighbours that we can build a spiritual Canada."

The Christian community no longer exclusively made up of the native-born Canadians, Vimal, an immigrant in Toronto, writes to thank me "on behalf of thousands of Christian immigrants and refugees, who have fled the theocratic and communist governments... These are the wounded ones in our midst. In their countries of origin...., Christmas celebrations were and are a mere dream. For these wounded people, Ontario under the NDP must have felt like another form of limitation. Many of these wounded ones may not be aware of your article. And although I am not their spokesperson, I felt that someone has to express this gratitude to you."

I consider his letter special, since it is rarely that immigrants seemed, at that time at least, to be tuned into the mainstream, i.e., even read the national dailies such as the *Toronto Star* and the *Globe and Mail*. I was also to receive blessings. "The Lord Jesus has admonished us to offer a cup of cold water to the 'little ones' (persons of little importance) in His name. He assured us that He will be their rewarder. Jesus does honour His pledge. Your reward is with Him".

Happy that, unlike for my piece on 'asouity' (my academic term for soullessness), I was speaking from the same page as Christians, something very important for me in search of a human spirituality, giving possible wings to the reader's line, "May be the pen may yet prove to be mightier than the sword."

An "appreciative" Reverend from Wellington, Ontario, wrote: "For the first time in many years I was hearing a non-Christian acknowledge some of the good things about Christianity, instead of blaming us for some form of cultural imperialism or other of the world's ills". Appreciating the "light touch to it", he also notes that my approach "was balanced".

Bringing me even more happiness was the letter from Alice, a member of the Church of the Transformation. Expressing her appreciation for my remarks in the *Star* Column, she goes on to share the good news that "some of them were quoted in my sermon the next day, and quite surprised and delighted the congregation. The goodwill generated will live long in the hearts and minds of many people." My note to her says, "Keep building bridges for an increasingly multicultural Canada."

So, all in all, while not every article generated a written response, I have every reason to believe that they were being read, one piece of evidence being that the letters came not just from Toronto but from cities as far as Barrie in the North, Hamilton in the West and Port Hope in the East. And then there was the note from the Star Editor, Susan Walker: "They seem to be reading us". Not bad, eh, I thought. Perhaps I can now breathe with some humility. Only in Canada! It was indeed a pleasure for me, an immigrant from a little known country with a Buddhist religion so removed from the mainstream spirituality - Christian and Humanist, not only to be able to communicate with Canadians, but also to learn about what ticks them. I can only be thankful to Canada for accommodating me.

My piece entitled, "Be Critical or let loose anti-social vultures" (April 27, 1996) solicits a *Letter to the Editor* by Herb Wiseman (May 4). He says he is amused by my article, "criticizing those who are uncritical." And I am said to give "Uncritical support of a deficit myth", the reference being to a statement in my piece, in relation to Premier Harris' 'Common Sense Revolution', that "we are living beyond our means". Listing several studies, he points to the observation made by The Committee for Monetary and Economic Reform (COM-ER) how the "Bank of Canada, uncritically and undemocratically, adopted an unproven monetary policy, which has caused us massive indebtedness".

My article also brings the following personal correspondence from Robert:

> *My response to your column is that the Star should be the recipient of your criticism. Star readers know and agree with every word you have written, but if you were white and dare to even mention such things, our letters will not be printed or we will be preached at and instantly labeled racist and bigoted... I am amazed that your words were ever allowed to be printed.... It has been abundantly evident that for years that the Star allows no criticism of itself or its politically correct columnists. ... The only criticism I have of your own column is when you say that we shed tears overall, making no distinction. The Star is the tear-maker, with leading headlines over criminals .., cheaters (or any attempt to track [them] down) .... I would venture to say that had your column been written by a white Canadian, it would never have been printed...*
>
> *... You mention that obedience to the law, tradition, ... religion ... are all ingredients of a mature and healthy society. Yet these are the very topics a white Canadian can never see discussed .... Perhaps now [that] you have broken new ground, they will open up their minds and pages and find out what the majority of the people of this city are truly like, and compassion which exists in the white population will be shown without mockery as in the recent Donna Mercier case. There are good and bad in all of us. The Star chooses to recognize only the good in minority groups and the bad in whites. Perhaps now a glimmer of light will penetrate to the Star's editorial offices. Congratulations, and I hope we hear from you again.*

And, in the text of the letter, the writer correctly concludes that "you must be non-white and non-Christian". The letter is signed, "Non-racist and non-bigoted white Canadian".

The Religion column shared with writers of other religions, I come to write a column about every 5 or 6 weeks. Here, then, is a list (see next page:)

18.3 'Blue Book Expert'

In retirement, I only continue to help out as an 'expert', listed in University of Toronto's *Blue Book,* the reference work for the Media. I list Buddhism, Canadian Buddhism, and Multiculturalism as my areas of expertise. But I specify that I will not be available for 30 second bites, but only for in-depth interviews and appearances. And, only if the studio comes to me.

1993	Buddhist festival a sumptuous feast for hungry spirits.	05.05.1993
1994	We all need to pay kindnesses.	06.11.1994
	Buddhists link karma to abortion.	10.01.1994
	There's a little piece of hatred in every one of us.	11.26.1994
1995	Benefiting from the essence of other faiths.	01.21.1995
	What would Buddha see at General Motors?	03.18.1995
	Celibacy doesn't guarantee liberation.	05.06.1995
	Euthanasia may be a healing well-death.	08.19.1995
	'Soul Myth' propels hatred in us all.	11.04.1995
1996	In death, we are all united.	02.17.1996
	Buddhist equinox no mere date.	03.23.1996
	Be critical or let loose antisocial vultures.	04.27.1996
	Organ donors can help end 'religious killing'.	06.01.1996
	Dharma Day message is moderation.	07.06.1996
	Meditation erases Fear of death.	08.10.1996
	It is time to include embryo as a person.	09.14.1996
	Need sex, don't want it.	10.19.1996
	An exercise to overcome resentment.	11.23.1996
	Do celebrate Buddhists' Temple Day.	12.28.1996
1997	Bare-breast image stays in memory.	02.01.1997
	Would euthanasia hinder rebirth?	03.08.1997
	Cloning not new for Buddha.	04.12.1997
	Buddha a good team player.	05.24.1997
	Honor gives MPs incentive.	07.05.1997
	Vacuum mind's over-indulgences.	08.16.1997
	Protest M-word mentality.	09.27.1997
	Buddhist story puts death in perspective.	11.08.1997
	Ten paths lead to perfection.	01.31.1998
	Buddhists keep faith in many cultures.	04.25.1998

My 'Buddhist' columns in the *Toronto Star*, 1993 to 1998

BOOK II, PART 7

A CREATIVE RENAISSANCE - POETRY, SHORT FICTION AND NOVEL

19. POEMS WITH DEEP THOUGHTS CLAD IN MUSICAL RHYTHMS
19.1 Faces of Galle Face Green, 1995

Five hours at the Schilphol Airport in Amsterdam, on the way to my father's funeral in 1982, was what prompted my *first poem*. And in English. Not my best perhaps, but here is that historic poem, when I look at death mockingly:

DISARMING DEATH

I myself not
see
in the dazzling
brilliance
of my breath-
less consciousness,
your faint image
projected
on life's screen.

Moulded,
and masked,
by the living
in a Neanderthal seizure
with the clay
of the destruction siege,
go find your prey
in warm
bodies.

(*The Faces of Galle Face Green*, 1995, p. 65)

I add a note, clearly addressed to Canadian / western audience: "The desire (*tanha*) for destruction (*vibhava*) is posited by the Buddha to be one of three desires that keep one's cycle of births going."

Clearly written from a Buddhist perspective as the note attests, we see in the first section Death, in the persona of a dead person, addressing Death, as a reality, or as personified in Buddhism, Mara, literally meaning 'death'. The former seems to be saying, "So what's the big deal. I'm dead, and I have no reason to lament. And I'm not scared of you either. So there...." In the second, the dead persona is suggesting that it is the living that makes a big issue of death. And so if Mara is looking to gain a sense of 'gotcha', then it is the living it has to work with, by making them succumb to the desire of destruction.

The poem came as a total surprise. While I had written short fiction prior to leaving for North America, the second collection published in 1963, I had never even tried my hand at poetry. While again I may have written an umpteen number of academic papers earning my several degrees in North America, I had never even dreamt of writing creatively, not even fiction. The academy can only be said to be the 'Blunter-General' (apologies!) of creativity.

But the poem seems to reflect at least two roots of my creativity, as it began to be clear over time, publishing three collections (1995; 2006, 2009). One is emotionality, which again, I'd never thought I had in any great depth. The only time I remember crying my heart out was at my mother's funeral, some twenty years earlier, as the casket was lifted from the home setting to be taken to the cemetery. But, unknown to me, it looks as if it had been lurking beneath waiting for an opportunity to make its comeback. The last time I had seen my father had been when he visited Toronto a few years earlier, and I remember both of us crying upon his departure from Pearson. We both seem to have known that that was the last time we would see each other alive. So waiting to catch a plane at Schilphol, to attend his funeral, the feelings were still probably raw. But if emotion was waiting to get the better of me, it looks as if this time I got the better of emotion. My response as reflected in the poem appears to be one of equanimity, *upekkha*, an unbiased disposition to be adopted by a serious Buddhist practitioner.

A second root of my creativity as reflected in my first poem is travel. Numbers tell the story. Of the 30 or so poems in my first collection itself, *The Faces of Galle Face Green*, about half are so inspired, written in Amsterdam, Austria, Beijing, Calgary (Canada), Colombo (Sri Lanka), Fredricton (Canada), France, London (UK), Seoul, Tokyo, Saheth Maheth (India), (better known as Savatthi in classical Buddhism) and Wales. It is perhaps because while travel is physically exhausting, it can be psychologically restful, at least for me. There is a Sinhala Buddhist concept called *citta viveka* 'restfulness in mind' that captures this. And I am also under no time pressures, having to meet deadlines, Buddha counting 'being relaxed' (*passaddhi*) as a stepping-stool (to give a common parlance term as translation of *bojjhanga*) facilitative of the Path to liberation.

And so Travel and Emotion - happy, sad or equanimous, then, seem to continue to put me in a poetic mood and a philosophical frame of mind.

A boost for my creativity prompting my first poem may have come, at a more pragmatic level, too, from my close involvement with the South Asian Canadian literary scene. My pioneering Research on the topic (see above), public presentations and academic writing seem to have energized me enough to re-generate the creativity in me. Growing up, I had read enough poetry, more in Sinhala than English, but also in Sanskrit and Pali, the popular Buddhist work *Dhammapada,* entirely in verse, that we kids would learn at the Sunday school and hear being quoted at Buddhist sermons. Here's the very first one that every Buddhist with some study of it knows by heart:

Mano pubbangamaa dhammaa, mano setthaa manomayaa
Manasaa ce padutthena, bhaasatii vaa karoti vaa
Tato nam dukkhamanveti, chakkam va vahato padam.

While the meaning is irrelevant to the point being made below, here it is for the interested:

Mind is the forerunner, mind is chief, everything mind-based;
If one were to speak or do something with a bad mind,
Suffering is assured to follow, like the wheels following the feet [of pulling animal].

If the first two end with a long *a* (shown with a double *a*), the three lines, or *paada* in Indic literary theory, represent a variation from the more standard four lines. But each line is clearly made up of two segments of four syllables each: *ma~no~pub~bam – ga~maa~dha ~maa*. But most interestingly, they seem intended to be sung to a *taala* 'tune'. Notes Prof. A K Warder, in his *Pali Metre* , "... so far from the static was the metrics recorded in the Pali Canon that we find some of its essential techniques continuing to generate new metres through many centuries, creating a vital and still popular art medium even for Hindi and other modern literatures" (vi). Prof. Warder has not been privy to the flowering of Sinhala literature for over two millennia since the introduction of Pali (along with Buddhism) to Lanka in the 3rd c. BCE by Arahant Mahinda and sister Arahant Sanghamitta. Thus, the perceptive reader may find many a poem in my three collections written to line-end rhyming.

Here's an example, from my poem, "The Knight at the Square", recapturing an experience the writer had on a visit to China in 1972 at the height of the Cultural Revolution, being chauffeured in a decorative limousine when it nearly collided in the laneless but wide Tien Mien Square with the only other limousine coming from the opposite direction:

Now here, not only did I go for a rhyming ending, I tried to arrange each verse into four lines as in a typical contemporary Sinhala verse, but succeeding only in two. But a novelty, even for me, is that I sought to give a visual picture of a 'square', though actually rectangular.

But I also had had exposure to *blankverse* in Sinhala. While G B Senanayaka and Prof. Siri Gunasinghe can be said to be the pioneers in the field in the contemporary period, it has a long history in the Sigiri Graffitti (7th to 9th c.). As deciphered by Prof. Senarath Paranavitana (*Sigiri Grafitti*, Unesco, 1956), these were poems etched by the visiting folk expressing their appreciation, on the Mirror Wall, of the painting of 500 female figures on the ceiling of King Kassapa's Sigiriya Rock.

Author with Prof. Chelva Kanaganayakam and Sri Lankan Ambassador Chitrangani Wagiswara at a literary event in Toronto (photo credit: downloaded [modified] from *The Sri Lanka Reporter*)

THE KNIGHT AT THE SQUARE

See this peasants two-wheeling   their ware
adding their flare even   at the Square!
Army trucks cart along   the Red Army hordes
Soldiers in tunic   holding on like toads.

My trimmings and curtains   as at a Ball
Waltzing to my music at our   Tien Mien Hall.
Stepping I vroom,   the armoured Knight
Roaring to sixty,   yahoo, what a sight!
The soft touch silk gloves,   the velvet cover,
Damned right you are   the key to power!

The weight is right   the passenger a delight
Ministers and Queens   in their wealth and might,
Crossing blue oceans   flying by night
All in my power-chariot   sleek and white.

In laneless Tien Mien,   I race I swerve
Where I drive   my sole preserve.
These peasants on wheels,   the baggies on trucks
Why do they stare?   Their duty to serve.
Buttoned up in uniform   creased well pressed,
My limo and me,   the Revolution at its best.

You, passenger dear,   under my good care
The panic in your eye   triggered from nowhere.
No damned rhyme,   indeed no reason,
Soon, I'm telling you,   it'd be high treason.
This, I remind you,   OUR very own Square,
Chairman Mao's   in the Chair.

(*Faces of Galle Face Green*, 1995, p. 37)

    If these classical creative spring wells have continued to feed my poetic imagination, Buddhism seems to give it direction. Indeed a whole section of the first collection is titled *Buddhism*.... And there come to be many in the next two collections, too, that are specifically on Buddhist topics. Additionally, even where the topic is not Buddhist per se, "What permeates the entire book", notes critic Chelva Kanaganayakam, University of Toronto, reviewing my first collection, in the *Toronto South Asian Review* "is a distinctly Buddhist sensibility.." He continues: "What is exciting about the collection ... is the imagination that transforms (the poet's) varied interests into moments of revelation that in turn lead to holistic vision..." He also talks of the "humor and gentle irony" in my poetry. Writing in *Canadian Literature,* Australian Professor Vijay Mishra points to "... the dominant themes ..[being] a strong political commitment alongside detached, pietistic Buddhism". And he adds, "There is much less of diasporic in his verse and much more of a straight out pleading for common sense and non-violence."

As in Mishra's comment, another hand that seems guiding me is a sense of justice. The several poems relating to women, the first section in my first collection, may be reflective of this. Another reflection of my concern for social justice comes to be seen in my poems relating to politics, that, too, being a section of the same first collection. "Cry of the Great Bird", excerpted above, expresses my frustration at the failures of political leadership.

The poem comes to be included in an Anthology edited by Cyril Dabydeen, *Another Way to Dance,* along with "The Knight at the Square", excerpted above, and two other poems, "To Fly Away", and "Light in a Hurricane", both on Buddhist themes. What is special about the last, as added in a note to the poem, is that it "avoids using finite verb forms, to reflect the Buddhist notion of action with no actor [this is the teaching of *anatta* 'asoulity']. The state of mind in the context of the poem *results* from the process itself.

With Cyril Dabydeen in Ottawa

Another is "Women on Tape", a collective title for four poems, all about women written in London (UK), Paris, Vienna and Toronto, around the lives of four married women I came to encounter visiting friends. They make into an Anthology, *Geography of Voice,* edited by Dianne McGifford of Winnipeg.

19.2 Celestial Conversations, 2007

By the time my second collection comes to be published 6 years later, while Buddhism continues to tweak my imagination, a new theme seems to have come to occupy my mind: ageing. For some odd reason you say, at age 65? Here is a sampling. In a poem titled, 'Buried at last' – you would never figure out the symbolism!, I begin with "1. A great team / you and me,/ partners / in a life-long / contract". Then I trace the different stages of my life:

BURIED AT LAST

2.
*Ignited
by youthful fire
yes, I see you
accelerating me
after
a zinging leather ball
along a the tropical green....',*

[the reference, of course,
being to cricket played in high school.]

3.
*On the platoon ground
you spring
my left foot twang,
to the Searge's command, "Forward
 march ...", two sticks,
on auto-thrust,
chin up eyes straight
right arm in salute,
in a Guard of Honour
to a visiting Queen,
earning Trophy,
Best Cadet.*

[Leapfrogging three decades,]

4.
*At Toronto's Harbourfront
on an advancing stage
a marionette
at your command, I
step in
step out
away and around,
swirling twisting
shoulders convulsing
to a drum beat crescendo....:"*

5.
*Speed
reduced to fifty five,
you get body-rub ready
for my new love,
badminton. Each spike
raising your eye-brow,
only to be lowered
by plaudits from the sidelines, ..*

6.
*By Jove, sixty five!
Now on near wobbly wheels,
wobbly knees, you rub it in.
as you begin to wear
your permanent
frown / if I jogged
if I romped
if I simply walked
beyond the neighbourhood,
throwing in for good measure
a nerve-pinch on the heel,
an ache and a collapse
of a knee, a pull on a tendon
exasperation enough
to fall in love
with a podiatrist.*

7.
*Buried
at last
under your weight,
I discover
 am...bl...ing
meditation,
getting an orthotic reprieve.*

(*Celestial Conversations*, 2007. p. 30)

So there we go!

Upon visiting Sri Lanka in 1999 after 26 years, I was not to be surprised that Sri Lanka came to be a new theme in this second collection. Touching on both Sri Lanka and Buddhism – hardly surprising, given the umbilical chord relationship that exists between the country and Buddha's Teachings, a poem I write in Sri Lanka itself (Jan 29, 1999) comes to be titled, "You Touched me".

> **YOU TOUCHED ME**
>
> *Inviting me*
> *Through the winding cavernous rocks*
> *Of Mihintalay, to the slab*
> *Where you retreated nightly*
> *Overlooking a deep cliff,*
> *You touched me,*
> *Venerable Arahant Mahinda,*
> *The flames of history re-kindled,*
> *Of two millennia and a half years*
> *When you-in-saffron robe*
> *Cut*
> *Short*
> *In his tracks*
> *King Devanampiya Tissa the Beloved of the Gods*
> *In hot pursuit of a wild deer on swift feet*
> *Sketching in bold terms the greater pursuit,*
> *The taming of the wild beast within,*
> *Offering to build*
> *A civilization,*
> *Kind*
> *To man*
> *Kind to beast.*
>
> (*Celestial Conversations*, 2007, p. 18)

Another theme that presses me forward creatively seems to be *nature*, my experience of walking along the Cedarvale Ravine in Forest Hill prompting the poem, "Tale of a Ravine Footpath" in which I see the wet shrubbery along the path as pleading to this "puny regular / going past you / religiously"… "… still recovering, / sunray by sunray", from a "cowardly attack" by the "Skylord" the night before, and thanking me "for listening, / puddles / our witness". Noting in an e-mail (of 31.5.06) that the collection itself "is a lovely work", Prof Melissa Williams of University of Toronto speaks specifically to this poem: "The poem about your conversation with the branches of Cedarvale Ravine brought an especially warm smile to my face. It is a gift to be able to make people smile".

Indeed the poem that gives the title for the book, *Celestial Conversations,* is another 'conversation' - between Sister Wind, Sun Lord and Brother Rain, when the 'Pale One' 'Moon-face' is allowed to add its two cents' worth:

TALE OF A RAVINE FOOTPATH

6.1
*At your mercy, mi-lordly Sun! But
if I may, Sister Wind,
forcing your way in,
the way you do, with a vengeance,*

*You, Brother Rain
darting sharp arrows, and
pardon me, mi-Sunly-Lord, you, too,
turning a blind eye, a mere
twelve hours, often less,
your only presence.*

*Think, all three of you,
think hard, think
deep.*

*Reprieve, you offer, I grant,
but brinkmanship is what
you seek
in your power play.*

...

*Given to extremes, you
each earn
enough hate
enough cuss
to top a Himalayan fury.*
...

6.2
*The winning recipe
back to their hearts, dear cousins,
discovered under the Tree ..*

*Moderation, Brother
Rain, the Path
Sister Wind, the Middle Path,
mi-lordly-Sun, the way
back to the hearts
of desperate humans.*

Modesty ..

A pinch of compassion ...

*Give the reason
to love you, to want you,
like with
me. Abandon your
Gods of Wrath, of
Punishment, of Vengeance.*

*Think
hard, think
deep.*

(*Celestial Conversations*, 2007. p. 36)

Enough Buddhist piety, as noted by Mishra?

Prof. Vandra Masemann, of University of Toronto comments (e-mail of 06.06.06): "Your poetry, I just loved it... so evocative.... I actually learned something about you from your poems... A celestial collection indeed." Vandra came to know me most recently in the context of Nalanda College of Buddhist Studies (Canada). It entailed exclusively academic work, and so my literary interest itself must have come as a surprise to her.

The most moving comment came from another e-mail (23.06.06) from Dr. Ilse Guenther of Saskatoon (as above). She comments: "... a book of poems with deep thoughts clad in musical rhythms, with intriguing, sometimes startling images and surprising messages... and the outlook is on the whole positive, just as I found in Buddhist Viharas in India". Upon meeting her in her home visiting Prof. Guenther, she was happy to play the piano for me. And I also know of her involvement with Choral singing. And so it was with some satisfaction I noted her reference to 'musical rhythms' in my poetry, it coming from an academic musician.

Nanda Lwin, author and educator, notes that the poems are "thought-provoking, and yet irresistibly delightful" (*Nalanda News 2*, p. 12.).

And a most surprising comment came from Wendy, a physiotherapist who had come to our home to attend to Swarna's ageing knees and I had given a copy of my *Celestial Conversations* as a token of appreciation of her professionalism. In writing "Minding Your Matter", I had only seen the poem as an expression of a dry, and esoteric, Buddhist concept, and had hardly expected a reader to even give serious thought to it. It seeks to draw attention to the Buddha's Teaching that "Mind is the forerunner", and how matter, is much, much slower than the mind, but in a mutual relationship. And in reading the last lines, "... you piggy-back on me / I on you", I was gladdened how she had come to see as the reality in life – of interdependence. "Great", I told her.

In my Preface to *Celestial Conversations,* I thank "Heidi Burkhardt for her gracious gesture of offering her artistic talents to adorn the collection and daughter Hannah for the digital graphics".

Another Poem, "Life in the Ocean", is in fact a common title for three poems: Ode to a Trigger, In Praise of a School [of Fish], The Stilt Fisherman [of Sri Lanka]: "sitting on a stilt / stuck in the water / silhoutted against the rising sun / in the glossy splendour / of the National Geographic". And it makes its way to the *Commonwealth Literature Journal*.

19.3 Obama-Ji, 2009

Writing poems only sporadically, my latest collection, *Obama-Ji*, appears in 2009. Politics not being far from my creativity, the collection includes a whole poem, "Waves of Cuba", on a whole country, Cuba, a country we watched in awe in my youthful days of social justice. Castro and Che Guevara were simply our heroes! And remain so. Not for the violence but for their heroic battle for local autonomy, and social justice for all its people. Making our first visit to the island on a tourist experience, we were to find a clean city in Varadero, although the capital city Havana continues to have its dilapidated areas. Being a beach nut, my personal interest was swimming in the hot hot tropical sun. But returning to the hotel, it was with great interest I read an information booklet published, not by Cuba, but by a British Tourist company, outlining the history of Cuba. One of the stunning points made there was that while there were 200 million women in the world who are illiterate, not one of them is Cuban! My interest piqued, out comes a poem, "Waves of Cuba". And interestingly, there are no life-size or any size photos of Castro anywhere to be seen in public, the exception being at the entrance to a hall at the University of Havana.

Adding pictures of Fidel Castro, Che Guevara, Raul Castro and Fidel with Earnest Hemingway, author of *Old Man and the Sea* (1951) said to have been written in Cuba and a few color pictures taken by Yours Truly, I publish *Waves of Cuba,* by itself, for free distribution. Our visit unknowingly coinciding with an important anniversary, I dedicate the poem 'To 50 years of the Cuban Revolution' and Fidel Castro, just as I had dedicated my study, *Towards Multicultural Growth* 'to the People of Canada'. Adding a personal touch, Swarna and I appear on the Dedication page, standing against a background of Che at the Revolutionary Square. But not taking myself too seriously, I include a picture of myself eagle-spread on a Cuban beach, penning the words, ending the poem:

> **WAVES OF CUBA**
> Waves of Cuba
> of 50 years, summoning
> youthful memories, I
> chaise-lounge
> in a capitalist doze, on
> American dollars,
> breathing the warm air
> of a Cuban Winter, feeling
> just right, in
> the full body
> of a consciousness.
> *(Obama-ji,* 2009, p. 17*)*

Sending a copy to the Canadian Ambassador in Cuba, I request that a copy be sent to President Castro. I receive a letter from the Ambassador that my gift of the poem has been forwarded, and that is about all he could do. I'm still waiting for a call from Generalissimo Castro to tell me how he was beside himself to read my poem! Good luck, Suwanda, and shame on you for your self-flagellation. Whoever has said that my poem reads well!

Not even a cousin of mine, Sonny Paranvitana, in Sri Lanka. Giving the home a name being a Sinhala custom, I knew he had named his home *Sierra Maestra,* the mountainous range where Castro and his men took cover until the final siege. But he did say something I had not known. And that is that, following the Revolution, Che Guevara had visited Sri Lanka, a point confirmed by Professor Carlos Delgado of the U of Havana I was to meet on our visit from Varadero.

But, of course, it would be hard pressed for anyone to call me a Commie for all my apparent enthusiasm about Cuba. For the poem is in a collection titled *Obama-Ji* (2009), in honour of a US President, getting its name from a poem by the same title. Perhaps an intriguing title for some, juxtaposing the East and the West, *Ji* (as in Gandhi-ji) being an honorific in Hindi, the official language of India. The US may be the historical arch enemy of Cuba, but its young and revolutionary President Obama is no patsy. Like Castro himself, he has shown to be in the business of shaking up the establishment and going against the current.

If *Obama-Ji* was inspired by the role model of President Obama, I seek to capture a Buddhist concept on the cover. Here it is to let you figure out what it is:

Like the two titles already mentioned, politics continues to inspire several poems in the collection. The themes of Buddhism, as already noted in connection with the cover, ageing, continue to appear as well, in addition to my experiences trying to raise funds for Nalanda.

Most recently, the last lines of my poem, *The Unbeatable Beat* come to be used as a sub-title to a book in honour of my Professor at OISE at whose passing away it was written: *A Tribute to David N. Wilson – Clamouring for a Better World.*

20. FICTION: SHORT AND LONG

20.1 Symbolism Galore in Short fiction

On a visit to Chicago while studying at the University of Michigan, it was my great fortune to meet Carlo Coppola of the University of Chicago. Somehow we had come to talk about literature, and the result was (as noted above) that my short story "The Ingrate" (*akrutavedi*) came to appear in translation in a journal edited by him, *Mahfil* (Vol II, no 4 (1966), a Quarterly of South Asian Literature. Originally in my Sinhala collection *Meeharak*, translated by myself, rotates around the guilty feelings of a son who loves his mother and looks after her well, but is burdened by her long, and continuing illness. The opening paragraph ends with the line, "I was re-assured – she would die soon."

Here is the ending of the story:

Feelings of guilt ran through me, as though saying, "You've wronged her!" Even to have thought that she would die! A cold chill ran through my body, numbing my limbs. Had I wronged her? Could she forgive me? I would confess everything...everything. I would ask her pardon, a pardon that would last me through eternity. Yes....

But my lips would not part. They were stitched together. I sobbed out loud.

"What is it, son?" she asked, concerned.

Clasping her, I hid my face in her bosom. I slept quietly that night. Such sleep will never return.

Under the Notes on Contributors, I am shown as "an Assistant Secretary of the Union of Ceylon Writers", which I had become, just prior to leaving Sri Lanka two years earlier, although I was never to slip into the work entailed.

It would be 16 years later my second story in translation would appear in the *Toronto South Asian Review* (1982), when I would contribute "Fellow Travellers", another story from my second collection. It rotates around three women, two of them in a servant-lady of the house relationship. While the lady is seen to act in compassion in taking in the destitute woman found walking alone along the street, apparently beaten and abandoned by an earlier household, she finds it difficult to tolerate all her idiosyncrasies - like chewing up on anything she finds on the street when going to the well for water. In the other relationship, the sister of the lady of the house, herself widowed and uncared for by her other relatives, comes to empathize with the servant who herself had no known relatives nor knew where she was from or how she got to where she now was.

Editing an Anthology of South Asian Canadian Fiction, and published under the title, *the Whistling Thorn*, the story comes to be included in it, at the invitation of the Publisher, Howard Aster. But how happy I was when I recently received the following e-mail:

> I am writing to you on behalf of the Centre for Canadian Studies, Jadavpur University, Kolkata. The Centre has been quite active in teaching courses on Canadian literature and facilitating research in the area for the last ten years. Many of our projects have been funded by the Shastri Indo-Canadian Institute. As part of a recent project undertaken by the Centre, we have plans of publishing two volumes of Bangla translations of selected Canadian short-stories. One volume would contain stories by indigenous Canadian authors while the other one would contain stories by authors of Canadian diaspora. The agenda is purely academic and non-profitable because the aim is to ensure wider dissemination of Canadian literature amongst people who are not very well-conversant in English.
>
> For the second volume we have selected your short-story entitled 'Fellow Travellers' and have got it translated into Bangla.

It was from Professors Suchorita Chattopadhyay and Swagata Bhattacharya, the Co- Editors. It was upon enquiry that I realized that Kolkata is what I had always known as Calcutta. The Editors were seeking copyright permission, which I gladly gave.

"Expectations" is another of my short fiction to appear in translation, appearing in *Toronto South Asian Review,* 2, 2. Though in prose, it comes to be published in translation, with some adaptations, as a 'poem'.

While I have scribbled a few other stories, they are yet to see the light of day, clearly showing that my priorities were elsewhere during my time of academic and professional work.

20.2 A First Novel @ 75: *Untouchable Woman's Odyssey*

"*Buddhist Pilgrim's Progress*", wrtites Rohana Wasala, Australia.

"*An extraordinary first novel*", writes Chelva Kanaganayakam, Prof. of English, U of Toronto, Canada, "by an accomplished poet".

> *Untouchable Woman's Odyssey offers a deeply insightful narrative of post colonial Sri Lanka. Beneath the placid surface lies a tale of the challenges of modernity, the deep divisions of class and caste, and the traces of the past in shaping the present. With remarkable skill, the author moves back and forth in time, linking the present to the past, demonstrating the multiple ways in which Buddhism has shaped the contours of Sri Lankan culture.*

> *An inclusive text in the best sense of the term, the novel draws together multiple traditions to explore the pathos, paradoxes and richness of modern Sri Lanka. Suwanda Sugunasiri's Untouchable Woman's Odyssey is a major contribution to both Canadian and Sri Lankan literature."*

Untouchable Woman's Odyssey, my first foray into the long fiction form, had been in the making for nearly 10 years. Here is the blurb that appears on the back cover:

> *In this engrossing first novel, Untouchable Woman's Odyssey, Suwanda Sugunasiri introduces us to two protagonists who grow in relation to each other, one of them towards spiritual heights. The work, in which the mythic pirouettes in dalliance with the historical, benefits from a structural novelty, drawing upon two Indic literary techniques: the Fable (best epitomized in the Pancatantra) and the Jataka Story (Buddha's Rebirth Stories). The linking of the Story Present to the Story Past in the latter adds an additional existential dimension to the unraveling story*
> – Frank Birbalsingh, Professor Emeritus of English, York University, Toronto, Canada

Here then are some other comments:

- Slice of life: complex or complicated?
  "... What is genius? It can be defined in variegated ways but the utmost genius in the field of writing could surface when an author manages to packet into 366 pages a 2500 saga of his country's history via a story, melodramatic yet extremely touching." - Padma Edirisinghe, Book Critic, Sunday Observer, Sri Lanka.
- ... link of 'Terroritis' with 'Englishitis' and 'Colonialitis' ....
  "..a complex novel because it is a story within a story within another story - his story, her story and the narrator's story. ...The novel's remarkable ability to portray authentic village life in rural Sri Lanka in the mid-20th century..." - Shelton Gunaratna, Prof. Emer., Mass Communication, Minnesota State Univ., Moorhead, USA.
- A Buddhist Pilgrim's Progress
  "It covers an eventful period in the island nation's recent history from the halcyon days of early post-colonial years to the tumultuous present as viewed through the author's mythopoetic imagination.... All three characters undergo a process of internal transformation, at different levels though." Untouchable Woman's Odyssey *can also be considered as an allegorical representation of the cultural-intellectual schizophrenia of the average English educated Sri Lankan scholar of the pre-1956 era hailing from a traditional Buddhist background. Conceived as religious fiction,* Untouchable Woman's Odyssey *will*

remind global readers from multicultural backgrounds of its kinship with classical English fiction of the same genre just as much as of its relation to the corresponding oriental literary traditions to which such classics as the Pancatantra and the Buddhist Jataka Stories belong. Thus John Bunyan's The Pilgrim's Progress (1678) comes to mind in this context. Probably a more interesting comparison can be made between Untouchable Woman's Odyssey and Joseph Conrad's novella Heart of Darkness (1899) in terms of their common inner-search-related themes and narrative points of view. - Rohana Ranaweera Wasala, Independent researcher, Sri Lanka, BA, Univ. of Peradeniya. Sri Lanka.

- An Unusual View of Life in a Universal and Timeless Narrative
  'The story seems to have more relevance and meaning in the new, modern globalized technocratic world, where conflicts of different kinds have their origin in a lack of understanding the other point of view. ....The author combines the mythical, historical and spiritual elements to tell an essentially human story of passion and emotion. He uses the story within a story technique of narrating his story which is reminiscent of Pancatantra and the Buddhist Jataka Tales, entailing not just this life but other rebirths as well. He also uses the cinematic technique of flash back while going back in time and place. Thus it can be said that his technique of narration is both universal and timeless. The novel shows that the writer is a scholar, steeped in the tradition of both eastern and western literary culture.' - C K Seshadri, Professor Emeritus of English, Baroda University, India.

The novel also uses verses from the Buddhist work *Dhammapada*, some sayings of the Buddha, seeking to capture the main content of a given section. The first appears on the title page:

Few are they among humans,
They who reach the shore beyond.
But these other folk, the many,
They only run along the [hither] bank.
                            - *Dhammapada,* 85

On the back cover, I would add the line, "My 75th year gift to humanity"! This pointed out to a colleague, comes a question, "But does humanity know it's coming, and want to receive it?' Good question! Only time will tell!! Reading it, a family member asks, "Where's the humility?" I still can't fathom how offering something intended to be good for the world by one at the edge of life is a haughty activity. Anyways, there it is.

21. WRITING AS ART
21.1 "You're a Great Writer"

Caution: Brag Department!
Or is it practicing mudita, as in Buddha's Teachings – taking 'joy in another's joy', here, of course, going both ways – from others to me and from me to others?

Generally speaking, when one talks of writing, the association is with a genre of writing, such as poetry, fiction, drama or film, entailing emotions such as pathos, bathos, etc., or the nine sentiments as in Indian esthetic theory – anger, lust, fear, disgust, beauty, etc. Or it is with content – life, history, politics, law, etc. Or it relates to the type of writing – analytical, philosophical, spiritual, comical, etc.

So when Sue Tennant said "*You are a great writer* (italics added) for sure..", the idea struck me, "Hm... writing as art". It is not that nobody has ever come up with the idea of writing as art, but it is that I had never consciously thought of it that way. Sue was a practicing Christian, and member of an interfaith group of which I was a member, too. She was completing her final year of study through correspondence at the New Seminary, NYC, the innovative brainchild of Dr. Rabbi Joseph Gelberman.

The Urantia Book, a particular take on the Bible, sent to me later for my edification, we had met for lunch when I had given a few pieces of my own writing as a token of friendship. In the letter sent to me following our luncheon, she writes, "[having] read through the materials", "I encourage you to maintain your sense of humour and even a healthy skepticism...". She goes on to comment on a particular piece, too: "... the preamble to the Canadian constitution (see above) was inspired! It was so moving that tears came from the depths of my soul. You expressed the best of Canada …. One day it will be appreciated by a wider audience."

My writing ego it was that was now reading the two-line in the last para sent to me by Glenn Mullen who had introduced me to Vian Ewart, the Editor of the *Saturday Star*. "By the way, you are a very good and talented writer". Indeed he had every reason to be happy about my re-discovering journalism. I had written a couple of Editorials for the *Journal of the Buddhist Council of Canada* which he had edited. So it may be that he was happy that his Buddhist friend, known in his community leadership role, has also turned out to be a writer. So here was another kind way that he had shown his regard for me.

Another recognition of my writing comes from Mary Fraser, Editor of the *Theological Digest and Outlook*, publishing my piece, "Let's Help Christians Celebrate".

Perhaps the best gift regarding my writing skills comes from Millie Charon (see above), whose book *Worlds Apart*: *New Immigrant Voices* I had reviewed (above). Writing a rebuttal to my Review, which was published in the Star, she was to send me a copy, as if to make sure I saw it. In an accompanying letter, she would write that I was a good writer, and encouraging me to keep writing. Coming in an adversarial context, the comments come to be precious, also showing Millie's quality as a person.

Responding to my column in the *Toronto Star*, Michael Bennett, Publisher of "an open forum newsletter, Notes at the end of a Century", notes creativity in my writing: "Your writing shows creativity in many ways, not least of which is your use of varying rhythm and spontaneity of emphasis, as shown by such lines as, "Caressing....necking... and finally only kissing", which is followed by, "To rave reviews!". There is poetry in your material and I hope you do not lose that in time as most published writers do. Without that poetry, a writer has no access to the heart ...." This westerner using the phrase, having "access to the heart" struck a chord with me for that is exactly how Indian writers on Esthetics describe a connoisseur of art - literature, theatre, dance, music, or whatever, literally 'one with a heart': *sa-hrd*.

Here are comments on an early version of my novel, by two Canadian literary persona (names withheld by request):

> "You have a natural writing voice, [with] the characters' voices flowing over one another as effortless as water.... The language is lush and yet not self-conscious, evocative and ... clear."

> "The novel is beautifully written and complex.... There are two protagonists in this novel, an ambitious task, and one you succeed admirably.. .

Most recently, a Sri Lanka Canadian colleague, Aloy Perera, a writer in his own right, adds his comments (e-mail of Sat 20 March 2010). I had sent him my piece, "Rebirth as Empirical Basis for the Buddha's four Noble Truths".

> *I thoroughly enjoyed reading your interesting abstract, "Rebirth as Empirical Basis for Buddha's Four Noble Truths".... It was easy reading because it was well written. No less stimulating was the novel way in which you had written it. I am sure you had the modern generation in mind.......;*
> *.. and your using modern day 'homely' similies familiar to people in this part of the world in particular, all of these, any discerning reader ought to find pretty impressive, even creative.."*

The online publisher of the article, John Negru, writes to me that since its posting, visits to his website has doubled. While there is no doubt that it is the content that has attracted the attention, re-reading it, I consider it one of my better pieces, using colloquial style to get across some heavy concepts of Buddhism, interspersed with formal language apropos to discussing the Buddha's words. Is it Shakespeare who is known for such language usage?

It occurred to me that all this was nothing but the expression of altruistic joy, *mudita*, by each of them – being happy at my happiness in writing well. Thank you all, makes me happier, to give more fodder for the practice of mudita!

21.2 Featured in 'Precise Writing'

If this was all in the private domain, I was happy to receive a bouquet in the public domain when my *Toronto Star* piece, "Who, then, is a Canadian?" comes to be excerpted in an educational publication, *Dimensions II*, edited by Glen Kirkland and Richard Davies, and characterized as "precise thought and language in the essay". It may have been for its value in terms of content, I suspect, the piece comes to be included in other anthologies.

The fact that the same piece comes to be, as noted earlier, in another anthology, *Viewpoints: Reflections in non-fiction* (ed. Christine McClaymont, Nelson Canada,1990), perhaps speaks to the same point. Other than David Suzuki, Yours Truly is the only one featured in this parade of nearly 50 pieces, all by authors with European names.

In a similar context is the piece featured in *Moving On: Reading Selections for Canadian Students* (Nelson 2003), a publication showing the Government of Ontario logo on the front cover. It, like all the other selections, comes with questions for discussion for students, before and after reading.

Writing about my writing, it now occurs to me that there had been some other writing on the wall if only I had cared to be conscious of it. It is interesting, and encouraging, that of all people, it is the examiners of my doctoral thesis that had commented on my writing, something hardly noticed at the time, but now beaming in my face. I would have expected them to talk only about the content and the theoretical arguments. But Prof. Douglas Ray, my External Examiner, points to a *"facility of expression"* in the thesis, while Prof. Joe Farrell, chair of my Thesis committee, notes how it is written *"in a lucid and novel fashion"*. He also speaks about my *"organizational competence"*, presumably an important aspect of good writing, given that the thesis is 500 pages, a point also shared by the external examiner.

21.3 A Family Bouquet

It is indeed a pleasure to note that my family – Swarna , Puta and Chutti, too, have thrown in their round of applause in appreciation of my writing in their own little way. In celebration of my 60th birthday, in 1996, they would come up with the idea of putting together 60 pieces of my writing, under the title, *Reflections*. The pieces, some published or broadcast and others not, come to be organized under 'Politics & Society', 'Language & Literature', 'Religion', 'Buddhism', Descriptive' and ' Multiculturalism '. It opens with a picture of me with Lincoln Alexander, Ontario's Lieutenant Governor, at a meeting of the Canada Day Committee, when we had been invited over to his official suite. He was ex-officio Chair of the committee.

Then there is me reading at the Harbourfront Reading Series, another standing in front of the Toronto School of Theology building with students of my Dynamics of Interfaith course, and co-instructor Paul Newman, another with my Buddhist colleagues at the Buddhist Council of Canada Congress, a fifth with my Multicultural Colleagues, all four of us holding a Certificate of Recognition given to each by the government of Ontario in recognition of our services to the shaping of Multiculturalism.

There is finally a photo of me showing a dance step to two women foreign students at the University of Pennsylvania, Philadelphia (1964).

The back cover has a photo of Swarna with me, taken by Mo Simpson when she did some filming of us for her film, "To Canada with Love – with some misgivings" (1993).

It must be a confirmation of their judgement about my writing that a lawyer niece of mine living in the US, Shanika Daluwatta, had indeed used one of the pieces in *Reflections,* "Haggling Your Way in Acapulco", to roaring laughter as a presentation at a Speaker's Bureau in Washington.

But going beyond the norm in feeding the academy, I was to not rarely jolt the western academic, when I am told to work on my English. Using the creative term Dhammexplorer, e.g., in an article sent to a western monk, I was to be told to consult a native English speaker! I guess my non-European name was fodder enough to conclude that poor I needed help.

21.4 Writing Lucidly in Sinhala

If all this relates to my writing in the English medium, I now recognize that I had been blind to the fact that my skills in writing in Sinhala, too, had been noted by critics. Reviewing my translation of Bertrand Russell's *Commonsense and Nuclear Warfare,* Jayadeva, the leading critic of the Sinhala newspaper, *Lankadeepa,* writes:

> The original of this work is written in a simple and beautiful language understandable by the average reader. Translator S H J Sugunasiri has done his job retaining this original quality. There isn't a single place in the work that goes beyond the ken of the average reader or can be understood by torturing the brain (my translation).

An anonymous Reviewer, writing to the leading Sunday Sinhala newspaper, *Silumina,* notes:

> Though the book [the original English] deals with deep concepts, the translator has been successful in putting it into Sinhala in a language that is easy and simple for the reader" (my translation).

In his Review, Ven. Haevaenpola Ratanasara, now incumbent in a temple in Los Angeles, California, writes:

> *In translating the work Commonsense and Nuclear Warfare, the translator... has served to enrich the Sinhala literature. He brings to the Sinhala reader ideas in the original unadulterated and with skill. It is a simple diction the translator adopts in this task. While there are a few difficult terms here and there, there is no evidence that the translator ever balked in rendering the concepts* (my translation).

While the language skill by itself may come to speak to the quality of writing, enhancing it can be said to be the content, too. And what comes to characterize my writing can be said to be *variety*. If in one piece, written from Toronto, I am watching in awe, on TV, Neil Armstrong landing on the moon (1969, July 21), in another, I am shedding tears, though less than my father, as I stand in the Gandha kuti, the room where the Buddha spends the last 26 years of his life in Jetavana in Saheth Maheth (now Savatthi) in India (*Riviraesa*, 1972.4.16).

21.5 Writing Skills: Genetic? Learned? Both?

Intrigued as I am that I then sort of seem to have some skill in writing, writing *qua* writing, I begin to wonder where I got it from. I have never taken any Creative Writing Courses, nor practiced the art of writing consciously. Perhaps my consciousness of language usage might have come from the exposure to several languages – in addition to Sinhala, Pali and Sanskrit, perhaps the Latin taken at junior school. And French, required for my MA in Linguistics. My formal study of Linguistics might have also made me sensitive to language usage as well.

But it might have come from the study of works - on literature, and Indian poetics, by leading critics such as Martin Wickramasinghe, and Prof. Ediriweera Saracchandra. But later, I would also read works such as the *Anatomy of Criticism* by Northrop Frye, *The Practice of Poetry* by Robin Skelton, and Prof. Warder's *Indian Kavya literature*. I have also poured over the pages of fiction, not only by Sinhala masters of the art such as, in addition to the above two, Gunadasa Amarasekara, G B Senanayaka and others, but also western writers such as Chekov, Dostoyevski and Maupassant in my early years, and American writers such as Ernest Hemingway and Arthur Miller while in the US. Sanskrit and Greek classics in translation, and English classics, too, were very much part of my reading material. In Canada, I can be said to have read just about all the great Canadian writers, from Margaret Atwood and Margaret Laurence to Michael Ondaatje, Moyez Vassanji, Rohinton Mistry, and others. Most recently, I have enjoyed the fine use of language in Canadian Prime Minister Brian Mulroney's *Memoirs*. But there were also the Buddhist Jataka (Birth) Stories themselves, very much part of the Sinhala Buddhist literary heritage, as well as the Sigiri Graffitti of the 7th & 8th c. when deciphered by Prof Paranavitana and published by the UNESCO.

But, if have internalized aspects of good writing through osmosis via reading, I have also done a thesis length analysis of the Sinhala short story, dating from the 1860's to 1960's, part of the study including observations about language usage. The material studied and analyzed includes the Sinhala versions of the Buddha's Birth Stories, to newspaper stories serialized in the 1860's, to the short stories of the formative stage, also appearing in newspapers and magazines, to contemporary works, dating from 1921 onwards. Training my mind in writing my thesis on the Sinhala Short Story was also Martin Wickremasinghe's *Buddhist Jataka Stories and the Russian Novel*.

But as in any craft, there is nothing to beat the practice itself. So whatever little skills I may have had in writing, no doubt, came to be sharpened in the process of engaging in the practice of writing itself. First the short fiction in Sinhala. It was Chekov's advice to his brother who had submitted a literary piece – "Cut more than half", and this must have weighed heavily on me. Then there were the translations which demanded precise language to capture the essence but also to convey it in a different language. This is not to mention the myriad of pieces written for the media and magazines. Then there were the two Master's Thesis, and a bulky doctoral thesis, which must have certainly tapped mightily into, and at the same time further sharpened, my skills. Boy, do the Professors have sharp scissors and sharp intellects! But there is little doubt that writing for the *Toronto Star* gave me a most precise training in the art of writing, as good as I would get from any excellent school of journalism. 750 words, and only 750 please. So, thank you, Vian Ewart, for putting me into a journalistic straightjacket. Tight, and no room for maoeuvring. Then there were the Commentaries on CBC and Vision TV and CTS.

But if all this relates to the latter day, I can't help but think of the hand of my father, in two specific ways. One was his upward mobile foresight of enrolling me, along with my two sisters, in the only English-medium local school, Christ Church College. And this was at least at the age of 10, for I remember being in Grade V. A second possible hand of my dad could be genetic. He was not only a Principal, but a writer as well, joining a leading Sinhala daily, *Lankadeepa*, in his retirement years. And as I was to discover recently, he was a poet, too. So perhaps I have some writing genes from him.

As well, did I bring my own from a past life, too? So who was I? Or ... oh, please don't come for autographs, but was I Kalidasa, the great Sanskrit dramatist, or perhaps the great bard Shakespeare himself? No no, I wrote the first novel in Japanese, *Genji Monogatari,* didn't I? So Kurasawa? Why go that far? Perhaps I was the Great Sinhala King Parakramabahu who wrote the Crest Gem of Poetry (*Kavsilumina*) in the 13th c.! Just hallucinating!!

Who was it that said Dr Ego sees no bounds? OK, alright. I'll go humble.... I was the Sinhala poet who, writing on the Mirror Wall at Sigiriya, in Sri Lanka, in the 8th c. , got away with the lines

Budal am I.
Got here alone.
Lookin' aroun',
since many a one wrote,
didn't write!

I just don't know. The jury is still out. Might be for ever! But all I know is that I enjoy writing, switching between and among genres, and subject areas, and between formal and popular writing. I hope I have succeeded in capturing some of that dexterity to a small measure in writing these Memoirs. Hope you have joined me at the delectable table of reading, savouring at least some of it! Ask Swarna. She'll tell you that I've never been seen by her without a book in hand.

BOOK II, PART 8
SHRINKING & EXPANDING THE WORLD

22. OUR TRAVELS
22.1 Travel In Canada: From Sea to Shining Sea

It will be remembered that our first travel in Canada was on the very day we entered the country as immigrants, coming from Ann Arbor, Michigan, past the Detroit River to Windsor in our rambling Rambler, pulling all our worldly belongings in a U-Haul. And that was on Sept 1, 1967. We were smiling ear to ear!

Ending up in Kingston welcomed by a Sri Lankan Professor friend, soon we were on our way to see the Expo in Montreal, celebrating 100 years of Confederation. On another occasion, too, the Olympics were to summon us there. It was with great interest that we made it a point to visit the more historical Quebec City, walking along its narrow streets, lined with curio shops, boutiques, restaurants, and the like, and where only French was spoken. I had studied French at Michigan alright, but that was basically reading French. So it was with enthusiasm that I sought to draw upon my book French to speak to the Quebecois. But my broken French was only met by a Quebecois broken English! No, I would not be allowed to murder their holy language. But I was not the only one to have the experience. Coming from French-speaking New Brunswick, Louis Cormier, a native born Canadian, as he would tell me, fared only a bit better. He spoke no Joual, the local variety of French spoken by the people! Over the years I have traveled to Montreal many a time Academic Conferences and Buddhist meetings. But my most recent was in 2010, at the kind invitation of Prof. Vandra Maseman, to read my poem, at a session of the Congress, that gave the title to a work in honour of Prof. David Wilson of OISE.

In a visit to Montreal during the summer of 1997, going by car with the family, it was our quick decision just to continue, when we ended up in New Brunswick. Welcomed by a bagpiper or two on the way, we would hit the Cabot Trail, ending up at the Bay of Fundy. And it was with trepidation we watched the water rise several feet high, exactly where we had been walking a few hours earlier! Another attraction was the Magnetic Hill, which tricks our eye into the illusion of water going upstream, the upward slope clearly visible.

Continuing, we were welcomed in Prince Edward Islands by our friend, Prof. Reshard Gool of South African origins, and author of the novel, *Nemesis Casket* and the short story collection, *Price*. Following directions, we thought we had come to the right place, but looking around there were no houses to be seen. Did I say, "to be seen"? Exactly! The home was surrounded by the bush, and going around, we all of a sudden found ourselves in front of the house. Voila! Walking in, we were to meet his Curator wife, Hilda Woolnough, just back from a skin dip in the stream just flowing past their closeted, I mean, bushed-up, home! Spending a few days, nature lovers all, it was with delight they would show us around. Visiting a crab factory, we would watch the processing of newly caught crabs on their way to a sealed can. One night, the dinner was a delightful treat of mussels and steamed rice, baked in a blanket of herbs from her own garden, as Swarna reminds me. And it was with surprise that we would see dirt roads for the first time in Canada! All we had seen were well paved ones.

It was our luck that we happened to be in Prince Edward Islands when the Tall Ships were in town. Majestic and comely as several of them were, their popularity meant disaster for a returning us! I had to spend the whole night at the wheel on our trip way back. Every hotel was booked solid for miles and miles.

Missing out on Newfoundland on that impromptu trip, we would make it to St John's a few years later. What we couldn't immediate help but feel was the difference in air quality. It was so fresh, and being at the beach was a qualitatively different pleasure, even when compared to the Waikiki Beach in Hawai'i. Another unique experience we had was going to Cape Spear, "the most easterly point in North America". And we still cherish a document signed by the powers that be at the Lighthouse on Aug 20, 1997, certifying that "Chutti, Swarna and Suwanda Sugunasiri has turned his / her back to the Atlantic Ocean at Cape Spear National Historic Park, Newfoundland, thus having the special privilege of facing every other person in the continent of North America". Now imagine!

While we had heard jokes about Newfies, what we found was a friendly, and unassuming, people. It was with great interest I listened to them speaking. In a piece that appeared in the *Toronto Star* on April 29, 1989, under the title, "If There's No Communication It's Gobbledygook, Not English", I had talked about 'Canajan', giving an example from Newfie English as well (as above). This, as you will remember, infuriated a reader.

You will well remember that my first trip *across* Canada, and the only one by train, was in 1979, on my research trip on S Asian Canadian literature for the Secretary of State. It is not a trip I can easily forget. If the vastness cannot help but make its imprint traveling three nights and four days, the variety of scenery was another. The flat land of the prairies, the Rockies, Fraser Valley carrying the lumber downriver, and the city of Vancouver. Though not by train, it has been our pleasure in later years to have been able to visit Vancouver, from where we would either take the ferry or the 20 minute flight to Victoria. It was our privilege to be welcomed with open arms by our friends, Prof. Siri Gunasinghe and his wife, Hemamali, herself a PhD in Linguistics, teaching at a College in the island. But it was as a student at Anula Vidyalaya in Sri Lanka I had first met her, visiting the school as Secretary of the Literary Association at Ananda College to arrange, or attend, a debate. She was also the Maname Princess on the very first night of the popular play which remains a hit after 50 years. Siri himself I had come to know through my involvement in Maname. He was in charge of stage set up and costumes. But it was before I came to personally meet him that I as a student had come to know him as the one who (re)introduced *blankverse* to Sinhala literature, after its first appearance on the Sigiriya rock in 7-9th centuries ACE (see above). In my work as President of Buddhist Council of Canada, I've had the occasion to visit several other cities in western Canada, including Winnipeg, Calgary and Edmonton.

Ottawa would become another favourite city of ours, visiting the Parliament or the Museum of Civilization in Hull, Quebec, just across the river from Ottawa, or watch skaters along Rideau Canal on a wintry morning, or to take in the view during the Tulip Festival. I would also take the play I produced in Toronto, Nari Bena, for a Sinhala audience. Then, there have been many a conference, meeting, consultation, etc. in which I have taken part by invitation. My most public participation was addressing the nation from the Ottawa Press Gallery, urging Canadians to support the new Constitution that was going to have – or as we were made to think, an Interfaith Component in the Preamble (see above for the fiasco).

So then, during our four decades or more, we can say with nostalgic pleasure that we have indeed seen this vast country of ours, 'From Sea to Shining Sea', *'de la mer jusqu'à la mer'* (or, if you prefer the more classical version in Latin, *A Mari usque ad Mare*) - Victoria to Newfoundland. But it is with regret that I have to say that we have never braved ourselves into the True North free, of the cold belly.

22.2 Over to Hawai'i & the Caribbean

At the end of my Fulbright term in the US, we had travelled in our Rambling Rambler to San Francisco, Los Angeles and back to Ann Arbor, Michigan, through the 100-mile Salt Lake Desert, the Grand Canyon and Colorado. On that trip it was with a sort of revulsion that we came past Las Vegas, at the thought of how the gambling mecca was ruining people's lives. But then should you be surprised that once settled in Canada, Swarna and I have been to this 'sin city' many a time, once our children were out on their own? No, it was not to gamble, but to get away from the Canadian cold winters, benefiting from the cheap flights, grand but cheap hotels and the good food. And the many attractions that can be had only in Las Vegas. Even having to go past the ubiquitous slot machines, as we enter and exit hotels and shows, the gambling rope seems not to have been able to ensnare us to its bosom. And it was later I was to hear about the many Buddhist temples that had come to spring up in locale.

While we had gone to Philadelphia, New York and Washington DC that last year in the US, we were to make it to Florida, too, on many a trip, to enjoy the warm waters, and taking the kids to the Walt Disney duplicate. They seem to enjoy it as much as they did at the original one in Los Angeles.

In addition to the cruise we would take (see below), Swarna and I would do the standard March and Winter Break getaways to the Caribbean and the Latin American resorts. Traveling with our daughter Chutti and a niece to the Dominican Republic, it was a lot of fun we had, driving a doon-buggy, with the kids sitting on the ledge and the vehicle going at no more than 10 mph. A few weeks after our return, it was with a chill that we were to read that there had been intruders at the very hotel we were at, when a tourist lost his life in the very room we ourselves had slept!

Our experience in Acapulco wasn't that excruciating, but facing the vengeance of Montezouma meant being imprisoned in the hotel for the whole two weeks we were there! Wanting to experience the 'real' Acapulco, away from the tourist centre, Swarna and I had gone for a stroll in a neighbourhood not too far from the hotel. Walking under the hot sun, and thirsty, we could not resist trying out what we had seen the locals enjoyed – drinking cool something with a straw, off a plastic bag. Sure enough we enjoyed it, having a bite, too, at a wayside food stop. But Revenge was waiting for us the next day. Both purging heavily, we had to summon a doctor. And, for the rest of the time, our room was our hospital, with one or two other visits from the doctor, who was also not very cheap. Luckily, we had health insurance.

But at least I am happy that this was the visit that prompted me to write the piece, "Haggle Your Way In Acapulco For $ 349 A Week" (April 2, 1989) that niece Shanika would later use to entertain a crowd (as above).

Visiting Hawai'i as we had been wanting to do for a long time, our old time friend, Prof. David Kalupahana, of the University of Hawai'i, would find us accommodation at the University for a reasonable price. It was thanks to the kindness of Indrani, his wife and a Hall-mate of Swarna's at Peradeniya, that we had pots and pans to cook our food. The supermarket was a short bus ride, and the Kalus would often surprise us with cooked food and fresh fruit as well.

The very first morning I remember waking up to the singing of birds. Looking out the window, what do we see? A whole family, or flock, of birds, of varying colours, just hopping around singing as if with nary a care in the world! I even remember recording the music which I'm sure I have somewhere.

Making our trips out of the university, one thing we could not miss was the variety of fauna and flora, ever fresh and green, watered by the skies, many days of the year. And it was to our pleasant surprise that we would read later that some of them had their roots in the Botanical Gardens of Peradeniya, from Sri Lanka. Apparently during the colonial era, an enthusiast had brought them over to give a new home, one in which they have, over time, multiplied.

Although we have probably seen some of the best of the beaches of the world, it was not difficult to be impressed by the Waikiki Beach. Stretching almost as far as the eye would go, the vast expanse of water can only be characterized as irresistibly inviting. Walking along the beach was as pleasurable as along any beach, watching the breaking waves kiss our feet, and recede to the bosom of the ocean, if only to return with another *haava bhaava* sensuous gait of a damsel!

But the one that impressed me most was a human damsel. Taking the bus around the island on a whole dollar, and good for the whole day, too, allowing the benefits of hopping on and off the bus, as long as the break was no more than hour or so. But on his first ride, this visiting Canuck was not to have the exact change. And so, here's the poem I wrote capturing the moving experience that followed:

> **HAWAI'IAN MEMOIRS**
>
> *When you, native*
> *of the soil, patience*
> *tested by*
> *two little-uns, one*
> *on your lap,*
> *the other tugging,*
> *offered a dollar,*
> *a US dollar,*
> *saving face*
> *for the Canuck*
> *carrying*
> *no exact change,*
> *you built for me*
> *a brazen*
> *palace,*
> *brick by civilizing*
> *Aloha brick,*
> *pushing the bottom line*
> *into hiding shame*
> *beneath your caring shade.*
>
> *Dark glasses, long-worn,*
> *skittled out*
> *watching the new*
> *Yankee face*
> *come into view,*
> *the tourist ponders*
> *a matching move,*
> *when, noting movement*
> *as the bus eases to a halt,*
> *he shoves a bill,*
> *a five-fold bill,*
> *into an open tote-bag.*
>
> *Smiles cross,*
> *along a pathway*
> *of humanity,*
> *momentary*
> *but momentous.*
>
> *Aloha!*
>
> (On way to the Waikiki beach in Honolulu, Hawai'i, January 2001).
> (*Celestial Conversations*, 2007, p. 10):

Making the same bus tour several times, enjoying the different scenery, it was with great satisfaction that we saw that seemingly poor locals were not deprived of enjoying the waters. Packing a lunch, they would take the bus, and get off at one of the many beaches. One of the stops we noted was at Hotel Hilton, where the locals would mingle with the world's richest, the tourists.

22.3 Driving One-Eyed Through European Tunnels

If my visit to the UK, Denmark and the Eastern bloc countries, including the Soviet Union, in 1971, was a solo trip (see above), our daughter Chutti going to England for her education in 1981 – at the James Allen Girls' High School, seems to have given us the excuse to go on a family European tour. It was also a wonderful opportunity to spend some time together with my school-time buddy, and fellow fiction writer, Namel Weeramuni, and his family. Now a lawyer practicing in London, he would rent a Benz van that would pack in us, and his family – wife Malini, son Heshan and daughter Slushna, as well.

This was, of course, not our first trip to the Mother of the Commonwealth.

We had many a time visited with my cousin Padmini, husband Dougie and their family, Dr Buddhadasa and Karuni Bodhinayaka, cultural friends Hemendra and Lanka Bandara and many an other friend over the years. I had gone to watch tennis at Wimbledon with their children, nearly got run down in front of Buckingham Palace crossing the street when the motorists reign, and stood gazing at the Thames. But this was to be the Mother of Tours, covering France, Italy, Germany, Austria and Switzerland!

With Swarna at the Rexall Tennis Court Centre at York University, Toronto

Namel had lent his car for us to make a tour of the countryside, taking us to Wales that welcomed us with a single word

Llanfairpwllgwyngyllgogerychwyrndrobwllllantysiliogogogoch

which translates as "The church of St. Mary in the hollow of white hazel trees near the rapid whirlpool by St. Tysilio's of the red cave". It is recorded on the internet as the world's longest single word. We looked in disbelief at the two hills from which the Highlanders and Lowlanders are said to have taken aim at each other in their ongoing battles over the centuries. Checking in to a Bed & Breakfast in a Welsh Farm Home, I must have been irate enough at the farmer to write the poem, "Another Link" (in *Faces of Galle Face Green*).

In and out of Wales, the meandering topography and the fauna and the flora was a delight to the eye, but now I was driving on the left side of the British road – right was wrong and left was right!

Driving the two families across the English Channel to Calais, France, I may not have even been sure any more which side of the street to drive on! In Canada, I had driven on the right side of the road, but in the UK on the left, and across the bridge, too, the next day. The left was still right. But, reaching Calais, left came to be wrong, and right was the right! Oh, enough, the confusion. But now I was feeling right at home, again driving on the right, as in Canada.

The Eiffel Tower was probably our first stop, and the Louvre – the Museum of Art, proudly displaying the Mona Lisa, taking a whole day, was no surprise. And this was just the first of many a Museum we would go to. Going out to take a look at Paris by night, it didn't take us long to notice the far too many one-way streets to our liking, and to discover how horribly lit the streets were and how horribly small the street signs were. We could see the street we wanted to go to on our right or left, and we knew, from our map, which street would take us there; but we just couldn't read the names. But what forced our eyes away as we drove along a red-light district not too far from the Arc d'Triumph were street women, gaudily made-up as they were, baring themselves in glass boxes!

We also had the occasion to visit with our mutual friend Dr Sarath Amunugama, on assignment with the UNESCO, and his wife. He and I had shared a rooming house at Regal Flats in the Fort in Colombo with two others – Kulanatha Senadheera and Chandrasekara, way back in the fifties, and he was Namel's university buddy in the Sociology Department.

Our first experience into Italy was a touch scary, though as it turned out to be pleasant. Looking for the Hotel we had booked outside of Rome, and arriving in the city somewhat close to night, we were lost, not knowing if we were headed in the right direction. Just then, two or three hunky youth on their swanky motorbikes, appeared on the scene when we ask them, in English, of course, how to get to our hotel. It was with our hearts pounding, as we would all confess later, that we followed the young riders, given an indication to follow them. It was miles and miles, and was this the notorious Italian Mafia, the thought came to us. But after driving quite a distance, the young men pointed to the hotel, and with a cheery goodbye, took off on their bikes. We didn't even get to say, Gee, thanks.

The next day, the Papal Square was waiting. I tried to visualize the smoke coming out of the Papal Palace, along with the words, '*Habemus Papa*', announcing to the world "We have [the new] Pope". Walking across the stone paving, it was with interest we noticed how women in short dress, and men in short pants, were barred from entering the holy site Basilica, by formally-dressed guards. Going past the pews in the different Prayer Halls, two or three smaller ones in addition to the main one, we probably lit a candle or two, or perhaps made a donation towards a light or candle. But needless to say, it was the art work on the ceiling of the Cystine Chapel by Michaelangelo that took our breath away. We tried to visualize how he would have hung himself on his back doing all the intricate art work. It was with interest that I would read later that when he took off his shoes and socks for the first time in months, his skin would peel off. Apparently he washed up not very often, and the skin had been starved of oxygen. And it appeared then that he spent most of his time doing the artwork, hung up way high, food probably being sent up to him.

Doing a tour of the Stadium in Rome, it was not without some anguish that I reflected on the dour consequences for the man who, earning the wrath of the Emperor, was thrown to the lions to the rah rah rah of an obedient citizenry. The Leaning Tower of Pisa was still leaning, I can assure you, when we climbed it. Not even the weight of the seven of us had moved it a millionth of a cm! So it is still safe, and you will enjoy the view from the top. But getting there, it was through single lane streets, with houses lining both sides, and kids playing on the street, that we had to drive through. An occasional horn brought smiles from an elderly Italian lady.

Visiting downtown Rome one afternoon, just past noon, it was to our puzzlement that we found store after store after store closed. It was later we would learn that summer was a time for Italians to be at the beach, explaining the deserted town. For the rest of the year, it was the siesta time, as in many a European city, when afternoon work begins after a long noon hour break. But making up for the disappointment of being robbed of a shopping spree, especially for the ladies in our team, was the Lait-Minta, a drink of fresh and cooling mint-flavoured, green coloured milk. It was in vain we would look for it in Little Italy upon returning to Toronto.

But the highlight of our Italian trip was our visit to the water-surrounded city of Venice. We began at the Square where pigeons had made a conference centre, as at London's Hyde Park. We walked through its narrow streets while our daughter Chutti and Namel's daughter Slushna took a Gondola ride to a nearby island where glass-blowing was the main industry. But it was the night out on Swarna's birthday at the Rio Grande that was the most enjoyable, the wandering minstrels serenading us throughout.

Leaving behind Italy, it was to our surprise that we would encounter many a tunnel. There might not have been anything particularly special about it had I not had to drive with one eye. As luck would have it, one of my glass lenses had dropped. Having no spare glasses, it was not occasionally that I had to drive with one hand, covering the eye with the other!

But if this was not challenge enough, it was a steep slope with many a sharp elbow bend that I found myself driving along, headed to Monte Carlo. On one side was a precipice beyond which was the Mediterranean Ocean! With dusk approaching, it was not rare that the eye would be blinded by the head-beam of an approaching vehicle, young fun-seekers, or locals, zooming in their racing cars. Adding to the tension was a near-empty gas tank. Not until later would I hear how panicky just about everyone had been, sitting at the back in the jeep!

Leaving Monte Carlo, we decided to take the mountainous route back to France. Driving through Switzerland, our stop was at a Swiss Chalet – not the folksy eatery in North America, but a real Hotel in the Swiss Alps. And what a surprise it was to see snow-peaked mountains all around us at the height of summer. But the greater surprise was when, crossing on to France, our ladies wanted to use the toilet facilities at a gas station just across the border. We needed no gas, and so the curt answer was, 'No! Customers only'!

Having seen just about every piece of Art and Architecture, in Paris and Rome, by the time we reached Vienna, another cultural Mecca, we wanted to have nothing to do with art or culture. They were coming out of our ears, and eyes! Except that our imagination was captured by the layout of the Palace of King Francis Joseph, with rows of trees on either side of continuing small pools. Surprisingly, it had a sense of familiarity. It was then that it occurred to us that it was exactly the same design of King Kassapa's Sigiriya Rock Castle of the 6th, 7th centuries in Sri Lanka. The only difference was that all four approaches – north south east west, to the Castle had been similarly designed. It was later that I would read a suggestion that the Austrian design may have had its origins at Sigiriya. The spot would inspire the poem "Palaces" (in *Faces of Galle Face Green*, 1995).

I was also inspired enough to write a poem about a toilet in Austria, tripped by a laser beam. The electronic gadgetry may be oh so common today, but way back in 1986, it was an original, and a novelty. Submitted to the University of Toronto Alumni Magazine, *Graduate*, Editor John Aitken found it interesting enough to publish it under 'Openers'. And so, here it is (1986, Vol XIII, No. 5):

ON TOILETS (OR IS IT 'TOILETTES'?)

In how many ways can you flush
   a toilet?
You can press a lever
   as in Canada,
   press it on the left
or reach up and
   tug at a chain
   as in London,
press it at the top of the tank
   as in Paris,
push a button on the wall
   as in Rome,

step on it
   as in Basel,
or
gem of gems
   trip a laser beam
   as in Pass Thurn, Austria!

Fascinating
   come to think of it
   how man / technology responds
   in non-standard ways
to a standard situation!.

22.4 Asia and the Pacific Rim

C. W. Siriwardhena, my colleague at Ananda College, and the former Director of Immigration who had facilitated getting my Passport within a day to help me get on the Fulbright plane at short notice, had now come to reside in Australia. The country itself was of fascination to me, from the time I was a cricketer at Nalanda at the age of 16. High scoring batsman Don Bradman, and fast opening bowler Keith Miller were our heroes, and going to the Oval cricket ground to watch a Test Match between Australia and Sri Lanka, it was a thrill for us youngsters to touch, just to touch, a visiting cricket legend, and his team mates.

But while all that was a long past memory, Siri had now given us the excuse to visit the country, specifically Melbourne. I had worn a jacket to the airport on the day we left Toronto on a Fall day in 2002. But the weather was still Summery that I decided to leave my jacket behind. After all, it was Australia we were going to, a warm country of all-year cricket, or so I thought. So why carry unnecessary clothing? How wrong I was. It turned out that it was already 'Winter' in Melbourne, Australia! Though very mild in nature compared to the frigid weather back in Canada, it was cold enough to have to wear a sweater. But our discomfort was a surprise to Siri. Had we not, after all, come from a cold country where we had lived for three decades or more? What he didn't know was that native-born Canadians would feel the cold just the same, but knew how to weather the weather with the better kind of cover, leather or other. And also, that we also had central heating in our homes.

But what surprised us during our stay in the city was the number of old friends and colleagues we would meet. Apparently, Australia had become a popular haven for would be emigrants. Though even the Burghers of Sri Lanka, of mixed European and Sinhala / Tamil blood, had been rejected in the early days of immigration for not being 'pure' enough, there had come to be an apparent softening of attitudes.

One of those who I would meet in Melbourne was Mr. Baldwin Kuruppu, my teacher at Ananda, who had taken me under his tutelage (see above). Another was my Cricket Captain at Ananda, Dhanasiri Weerasinghe. Yet another was Shyamon Jayasinghe, the narrator of the epoch-making drama, Maname. A real surprise was Satischandra Wimalajeeva who had been one of my best friends at Nalanda, but had completely lost touch with after leaving College. This is not to mention several relatives on both sides – Swarna's and mine. Indeed we were to discover that Nalini, Siri's wife had been at Peradeniya University with Swarna.

But I was also to have an embarrassment. Mr. Kuruppu had taken me to a gathering of Sinhala Seniors, and I was asked to talk about Canada. No problem, I thought. But there was a problem! I was to speak in Sinhala! Since I had left Sri Lanka in 1964, and especially after 1973 leaving for good, I had had no contact with Sinhala in any formal sense except in the very early years (see above). True my Master's Thesis at University of Pennsylvania was a linguistic analysis of the spoken verb in Sinhala, but it was in English. And living in a Sea of English all around, our language of communication at home had come to be in English. Our children only spoke English, and each of us, Swarna and I were both English professionals – teaching English or English Linguistics or Linguistics at University level In Canada, whatever contact we had had with Sinhala was limited to social banter, but that too to a limited extent. It was the habit of English-speaking Sinhalas to speak in English when we get together. So here then was this once-upon-a-time Sinhala writer, Yours Truly, – columnist, critic and fiction writer who had even written a thesis on the Sinhala short story in Sinhala, who was now unable to give a formal lecture in Sinhala! My my my.. My teacher Mr. Kuruppu, under whom I had learned Sinhala, could hardly believe it! However, given the informality of the situation, I was happy to be able to pull in together a speech in Sinhala, begging for pardon for any errors, and so with help from the audience, and, of course, my teacher and others around.

On our final night, Siri had brought together a few friends to bid us good bye, when we had a good time. But the dinner at Shyamon's was perhaps the most memorable. This was when, meeting after nearly four decades, it was as if we were in olden times, when, returning by bus from a Maname show we would sing to our heart's content all the way back. And on this night in Melbourne, we were to go through practically the entire play Maname! All in song, Shyamon not having lost his mellifluous voice. Something those at the meal liked appeared to be me doing the steps and the dance of the Maname Princess as Shyamon and others sang! There was a repeat request on the final night at Siri's house. Did I oblige? I don't remember.

Our visit to nearby New Zealand was to visit Slushna, Namel's daughter, and now a doctor practicing in Auckland. The last time we had met, during our European tour (see above), she was just a teenager. But now she was a professional, and a mother. But I was indeed happy to see the same old humble Slushna waiting for us at the Airport.

What we had come to note immediately upon arriving at her house outside of Auckland was the rich, green vegetation. While the constant raining made human lives a little uncomfortable, the fauna and the flora seemed to enjoy every bit of the humidity and every drop from the sky. The rain and the green lush also meant an air so fresh that it was a pleasure to do a breathing in and out meditation (although I must confess, I don't know if I did it). Not since our time in Newfoundland had we breathed such fresh, and healthy air.

Our visit to Rotarua by Choo-choo train was the only outing we did outside of Auckland. It was to see the phosphorous wells oozing out the stuff from time to time. We were also treated to a cultural program presented by Australian native people.

22.5 A Cruise on the *Sovereign of the Seas*

Indeed our first and only cruise came at the initiative of Mr. Rogers, a Cruise veteran, and Swarna's boss, the Principal at Weston Collegiate Institute. The year was 1989. It was a Caribbean tour lasting a week, and it was an experience of a lifetime. Though the price of a cruise has, happily, come down today, as in the case of electronics, at that time, it would only be the select few who were able to go on a cruise. Our experience was made all the more pleasurable since the Sovereign of the Seas was the biggest ship at the time to ride the oceans. A 14-floor luxury, we could only afford a room at the sea-level. While the three higher levels gave even a better view of the ocean, we were happy we were not below sea-level during the week. A floating city, the Cruise provided luxury at its best. And viewing water, through the window of our room going past us at eye level was a visual treat!

Food can only be characterized as conspicuous consumption! There were first the three formal meals at the restaurant when both customers and the waiters were formally dressed. These three-course meals provided any and every kind of food you could ever imagine. We enjoyed the meals, as if sitting in a water pool, since as in the room, the water was passing by just by the window. If that were not enough, there was always a buffet meal available right up to midnight and beyond. It was no less in the entertainment department, with a different show each night.

The Captain's night was another occasion when we were all seen walking along the decks formally dressed. Delicious and entertaining as the food and the entertainment were, it was a recipe for putting on weight! There was, of course, a track, a swimming pool, jacuzzi, and even aerobics classes, but by and large, they were sparsely made use of. There just wasn't the keep-fit environment.

Then there were a few stores that carried jewellery and other expensive items like scents and brand name clothing.

But we also had a scare when at one meal time, the ship started to wobble and rock from side to side, as we watched the rolling billows throwing the ship up and down, as if holding it on their finger tips. The sea was so rough that one of the landings on our way had to be cancelled. But the landing at St Thomas was the most popular for the women tourists. They couldn't wait to check out the jewellery sold at kiosks as if at a flea market.

23. A CULTURAL RETURN TO 'GOOD OLE SRI LANKA'

23.1 A Return After 26 years!

Leaving Sri Lanka in 1973, our life in Canada had been busy, and fulfilling – with my own studies, Swarna's and my employment, children's education and my own multifarious social activities, speaking, writing and making media appearances on a range of topics from literature to Buddhism to Interfaith to Multiculturalism. Sri Lanka had been the furthest from our thoughts. With technology not as advanced as now, the flow of communication had not been regular either.

But 1998 made a dramatic change. There came to be stirrings within us about paying a visit to the country we had left 26 years earlier. We were mostly curious, but frankly, apprehensive, too. No, it was not the war the government was waging against the terrorists that was at the back of our minds. Just what kind of society might we encounter? How will our friends and relatives receive us? Swarna in particular had concerns about the heat. It was on a holiday in Acapulco, Mexico, that I had seen her walking in pain across from the hotel on the hot sand to reach the beach. Having had open heart surgery, and now on a lifetime medication of Coumadine, it would render her highly sensitive to hot weather. And she wondered as well: what about health and hospital facilities?

Around this time, we had a visitor from the UK. Karuni Bodhinayaka, a dear friend of several years. Always in contact with Sri Lanka, she would egg us on, offering whatever help needed, the President Chandrika Kumaratunga, whom the Bodhinayakas had known from their youthful days, a telephone call away. As she went on to tell the story, they have been personal friends for a long time. Husband Bodhi had been the President of the Youth wing of the Sri Lanka Freedom Party, and Mrs. Sirimavo Bandaranaike, Chandrika's mother and then Prime Minister, was a regular visitor to their home whenever she was in London.

However, the Canadian winter was reason enough, we convinced ourselves, to take the plunge and make the trip to Sri Lanka.

Traveling in business class luxury on Sri Lankan airlines, with blessings from the Buddha who teaches the 'happiness of enjoying' (*bhoga sukha*) the wealth justly earned, gone were any thoughts of discomfort. The food was great, and the service of young smiling stewardesses seemed to take our minds back to the smiling people we had long forgotten. And the comfort of the lounge seats took the sting out of the 12 hour long flight.

Arriving at the Bandaranaike International Airport, in the wee hours of the morning, the standard time of arrival for many a European flight, my poetic pen would capture the moment later.

Having lived most of our lives overseas, Sri Lanka was now no more than just another country, albeit one closer than any other beside Canada. Visiting it as part of our world travel, after 26 years since becoming a Canadian, we are met by Somalatha Subasingha, known to me in school days but more recently in Toronto when she was invited to a conference of Women Play Directors from around the world at York University. It was a pleasure to see her husband, Lionel Fernando, also a friend from my Maname days, and by then an Ambassador, accompanying her. But it was a sense of ambivalence I had, seeing soldiers, fully armed in those war-torn days. The title of a poem I would write to mark the occasion, "The Twilight Zone" (*Celestial Conversations*, 2007. p. 8) speaks to this ambivalence.

It was with the eye of tourists that we watched the trees, shops and houses go by as we were driven along from the airport. Later only would we know that the two Canadians were travelling on the 'Canada Highway', a gift of the Canadian government, linking the Katunayaka Airport to Colombo. Though sunrise was a good hour or so away, we could see that the vicinity of Colombo was coming to life, as people were beginning to take the early bus to work. The capital area had changed so much in their road structure since we had left that I didn't have a clue how we got to the hotel as the sun was sending its first rays over the horizon.

True to her word, Karuni would arrange for us, for a special rate, Mt. Lavinia Hotel, a few miles from Colombo. Included in the package was a shuttle pick up at the Katunayaka Airport.

Once the official residence of the British Governor, Mt. Lavinia Hotel overlooked the vast expanse of the Indian ocean, lapping the shores a mere few feet away from our room as I looked out of the room next morning. Tired after nearly a day of travel, we were still in our room until hunger pangs pushed us out. Leaving the room, we were walking along the marble floor of what we would later come to know as the Visitor's Lounge where we would meet the few close relatives who would come to see us.

A few steps up, and to the left was the swimming pool, empty at this noon hour, when our nostrils took us towards the wafting aroma coming from the right. What a pleasant surprise it was to see the dining room décor reflecting the local culture, and the favourite local dishes on bold display! What struck our eye immediately was the local preparation called 'sambol' displayed, not in a dish, but on the *miris gala* itself. Literally meaning 'hot pepper [grinding] stone', this was the implement upon which the spicy sambol would be prepared, by crushing the hot peppers, maldive fish, onions and mixed with freshly grated coconut. A favourite dish – indeed a 'rice puller', in any Sinhala menu, it would be later featured in Swarna's cookbook, *Cooking from my Heart*. The dish, along with other dishes such as milkrice, and a host of local greens, not to mention fish, pappadam chips and fried hot peppers, were all under a roof like structure of a hut thatched with green and yellow coconut leaves. Wow! And the serving ladies were dressed in a green sari. This certainly wasn't the Sri Lanka we had left, when the mantra of the middle class, to which we ourselves had belonged, in imitation of the 'Brown Sahibs', to use that apt label of journalist Tarzie Wittacchi, was to hold in disdain any and everything local. The British had done an excellent job of colonizing the Sinhala minds, so much so that Professor Smith, of the University of Pennsylvania, my *alma mater*, is said to have come to characterize the Sinhalas as the example *par excellence* of the colonized mind! And, as if to serve as a reminder that this was a grand hotel with a history, the concierges wore a tunic buttoned coat with top hat! And I capture the experience: in the poem 'Knick-Knacks at a Hotel' (*Celestial Conversations*, 2007. p. 33).

What I don't say in the poem is how, in our post-High school years, I would, accompanied by a friend, ride six miles on my bike every Sunday, and take on the rolling waves near this very Mt Lavinia Hotel. For all the hours we would spend in full view of the Hotel, there was no way we would even think of stepping in, nor were the chances of two youngsters being allowed an inch into the marble floor better than zip!

Indeed the country had changed. Having seen, the cultural and the value differences both in Sri Lanka and the West, and lived in both, I must confess being not too happy. It was not that, as a Buddhist, I was averse to change. It is identified by the Buddha as one of the three characteristics of sentience – impermanance, suffering and asoulity, or more commonlym 'non-self'. But it was that I was not for any and every change. And having done a doctoral study on development, I wasn't convinced that the western models were all that necessarily applicable to every country. I would express my misgivings in a poem: A People and the IMF (*Celestial Conversations*, 2007. p 31).

But whatever the ills of tourism, the return to the culture was one of the better results. And Swarna and I couldn't have been happier.

If we had had any concerns how we would be received, they were soon put to rest when my sister Sunanda came to see us at the hotel with her teenaged daughter, Rasangi, who would later go on to be a teacher at my old school, Ananda College, as had my sister, too. And then there was my favourite cousin (mother's younger sister's daughter), Pearl, *sudu akka* 'fair older sister' who once again would retell her family that had accompanied her how I, as a kid, had enjoyed her tube of toothpaste when they first came to stay with us upon her marriage. I had also, in my working years, helped a couple of her children educationally by buying the books needed for school.

And then there were my long-standing friend Punchihewa, or Punchi as we fondly call him, and his lovely wife Anoma whom we had met in Canada itself

With Sujata Wijetunga and Swarna at Toronto Nathan Phillips Square

several times on their visits to her brother in Toronto and sister in the US, married to a Sinhala Heart Specialist practicing in the US. Then there was Wije(tunga) and Suja(ta), whom we also had met in Toronto on a tour of North America when serving as Registrar at the University of Manoa, New Guinea, after a stint as Registrar at Peradeniya University.

Towards the end of our stay, it was the Galle Face Hotel we had picked, the other grand old hotel, and the only one of a colonial era in Colombo, where the royalty had dined and wined in days of yore. I remembered the first time I had been there - as a clerk in the Official language department which had some kind of exhibition. And I remember stepping on to the wide foyer up a few steps with my heart ticking faster. Standing tall, and wide, beside a stretch of the Indian ocean, it was awesome, and this was clearly not clerk territory.

But now, walking along the promenade beside the green, this is how I enjoyed the moments:

IN THE REALM OF HUNGRY GHOSTS

Let me,
please,
oh man,
touch 'em
feel 'em
only.

Kadala dhal
dressed in Sunday best
in white coconut bites
and red hot chillies,

Mango thins
green and peeled,
coat glistening
in stars of salt,

My taste buds
all agog
for a night on the town
along the promenade,
receive gentle reminder
puree water bottle
pressing the palm.

....

Oh here, the paper-thin face
of manioc chips,
flooding my mouth,
tooth after tooth
a-tinkling, but alas
no crunch crunch crunch
for me.....

....

Fingers, drooling in pocket, oh man,
...
But when
under the kerosene lamp
bare sweaty hands
arrange the pile,
my fingers
beat a hasty retreat
out of the pocket, memory
jogged by a Mexican Odyssey,
the Revenge of Montezouma,
felling us
purging
with an appetizing juiceful
on the sidewalk
along the Puerto Vallarta outback....

(*Celestial Conversations*, 2007, p. 48-50.)

Later in Canada, I would title my first collection of poetry, *Faces of Galle Face Green,* the theme poem well reflecting my experience on the vast green lawn facing the hotel. It was in1956 when we attended the final rally of the coalition put together by S W R D Bandaranaike, with the help of the political left, bringing together the 'five pillars' of the country, the dispossessed under colonialism – the sangha (Buddhist monks), native physicians, native-language teachers, farmers and workers. I was among the 100,000 people clamouring for change, and an end to the leadership of the horse-back riding D S Senanayaka, the first PM of Independent Ceylon. It was with difficulty we followed the hoarse voice of Mr.. B., punished by a long campaign. I had recalled how as kids flew kites on the green while lovers walked down the promenade under the gaze of the moon.

Walking to the Registration desk of the hotel one day, after a delicious breakfast of hoppers and tropical fruits listening to the roaring waves and soothed by the wind warding off the heat, I was accosted by a clerk. "Sir, there is an envelope for you... from the Minister."

"Oh, two tickets for tonight's show", I said turning to Swarna. It was for a 'multicultural show', with participation from India, Malaysia and a couple of other Asian countries, in addition to Sri Lanka. The previous day, I had been to the office of the Deputy Minister of Culture, an elected MP unlike in the Canadian system of a civil servant holding the position. Prof A V Suraweera had taken a leave of absence, and winning a Parliamentary seat, had been appointed to the Cabinet. A few years earlier, the two of us had co-authored a special issue of the *Toronto South Asian Review* on Sri Lankan literature, bringing out, for the first time, works in all three languages – Sinhala, Tamil and English. And during the present visit, I had gone to see him in his new role when in casual conversation he said what a pity it was that there were no more tickets for a show that was to be held the next day at the Bandaranaike International Memorial Hall. However, he said he would try to see what he could do. It must have been our lucky day that the Minister had been able to find the tickets.

The culture vulture that I had been in Sri Lanka, of course, I was no stranger to Sinhala song, dance and music. However, Swarna and I were eager to see just where the country had come to be culturally after a quarter century. What I saw blew my mind! Over the years we had seen the very best in the west, of dance and mime Canadian ballets like Cinderella or Swan Lake, dance and mime of Cirque du Soleil quality, classical concerts at Toronto's Roy Thompson Hall, fantasies like the Phantom of the Opera, etc. I had also been at the Bolshoi in the Soviet Union. And so judged by any standard, the musical show combining dance, song and music here was second to none. After our time, there had now come to be a Faculty of Fine Arts at the university, and this performance was presented by these students. Was I happy I didn't have my movie camera in hand! I pleaded with the organizers to make a video of it for international consumption, but there has been no signs that it had fallen on deaf ears. Insularity?

I had had similar luck with the country's foremost musical maestro Amaradeva, trying to get his CV to be given to the *Harbourfront Centre*. I had been trying to arrange a performance of this artist who, studying at Shantiniketan, had come first on the violin in an all-India competition. Becoming Music Director at Radio Ceylon, he had carried a whole Sinhala nation over the last 50 years creating and helping to mature a Sinhala music, so much absent from the Buddhist culture. On his visits to Toronto, he would perform to packed houses, and I was looking to give the Canadian cultural aficionados a rich evening of entertainment, like Ravi Shankar, with whom he had played, from time to time. Despite letters and phone calls, no was CV received, and my contacts at Harbourfront couldn't move forward. But I would still write a piece on him, to be published in Sri Lanka in the leading *Sunday Observer*. Invited by the BBC London service for a piece on his 80th birthday, but not used, I would publish a second on the internet. And I would hammer the point again and again, whenever I could, that while the Sinhala people have a wonderful culture, only but they themselves knew about it. Going beyond the borders seems to be too much for them. At the end of the show, I would pose with my friend Somalatha and the Tamil singer who sang melodiously.

Having also been invited to the very first play directed by Somalatha's daughter, Kaushalya, our minds had come to be profused with the culture that we had left behind. Particularly so, since after checking out from Mt Lavinia Hotel, the first thing we had done was to rent a vehicle for a couple of weeks and go on a tour. It was to become more and more nostalgic. While both Swarna and I had read and studied about the ancient Sinhala Buddhist culture and civilization as part of going to school and post-secondary education, I had actually seen only one or two places of historic importance. Travel not being a pastime of the Sinhala culture of my time, some fifty years ago, whatever I had seen of Sri Lanka before coming overseas in 1964 was thanks to the play Maname in which I had two minor roles. A popular hit, it would be taken around the country, and time permitting, the cast would go on tour of local places of interest. But our focus was certainly not seeing the country but to have a good time together off stage. Swarna had seen even less of the country, in the traditional thought that such fun was to be had only once married and not while in the care of your family. However, in fairness to her, she had had the occassion to visit Adam's Peak – a holy place for Buddhists, Christians and Muslims, this as a kid on the shoulders of hired labour! So it was really a case of two Canadians on a Sri Lankan tour!

23.2 Two Old Tourists

As part of my job as a Labour Officer (1960-62), I did get to see the Tea Estate areas, going on my rounds to ensure labour standards for the imported Tamil Labourers on the Estates.

I had also seen a bit of the hill country traveling past Badulla to Koslanda, visiting my sister Chitra. While I had, as a cadet, managed to take a cold shower at 5 in the morning in Diyatalawa, also in the upcountry, it was rarely that I would join my brother-in-law Nimaldas under the rushing waters off a waterway up high, fed by a waterfall.

Being entitled to, as a government servant in Sri Lanka, a certain number of free passes for travel by train, I remember taking the train to Jaffna with Swarna soon after we had got married. Having had a short posting there as an Assistant Assessor trying to collect revenue for the government from recalcitrant importers, I don't remember seeing anything other than the dry land and the palmyrah trees. A specific memory is the high fences people would have around their compounds.

Our first visit upon our return after these many years was to Anuradhapura, where the southern branch of the Bodhi Tree under which the Buddha attained Enlightenment still stands, tall and majestic. Having paid homage as in Buddhist fashion, I sat cross-legged on the sandy surrounding, and spent a few moments. Opening my eyes, I would catch a bo leaf falling off its stem, yellowed and showing signs of age, a reminder, I thought of my own immortality, and the truth of Buddha's teaching of impermanence. Taking it with us, it would be donated to an elderly relative who begged to have it. Today I have at our home altar a bo leaf showing only the ribs, but with a Buddha figure stamped on it, in a usual Chinese initiative.

Leaving the Bo tree, we were now headed, almost at noon hour under the blazing sun in this dry zone where rainfall is a rare gift of nature, along a pathway towards two stupas, or reliquaries, touching the sky in the distance. Just then, we were caught almost unawares when a kid of ten or so would stop on his bike just beside us. "Hundred rupees," he would say, unfolding a set of tourist postcards strung together. Yes, capitalism had eaten into the holy land! A few women a short distance away, with mammoties in hand, stood chatting. Chatting on the job? We wondered.

The first thing to catch our eye as we approached the first reliquary,

Ruvanvelisaeya, of circa the 3rd c. BCE, was the 'Elephant Wall' (*aet pauwra*), a row of white elephant heads with two long tusks on either side, forming a wall three other plain walls joining to make a square, of about 4 to 8 city blocks. At the centre was the historical reliquary, each side of the platform supporting the bell-shaped 'belly'. The relics of the Buddha in its 'relic chamber' had been placed there with great reverence, as the *Mahavamsa*, the national Chronicle tells us, by King Dutugemunu himself who had just rid the country of south Indian rule of 40 years. So it was not without a sense of awe and reverence that we entered the compound in the presence of both history and piety. Paying homage again, offering the flowers Swarna had bought on our way, at one of the four altars facing the four directions, we did a perambulation, keeping our right shoulder to the reliquary following tradition.

What the next reliquary, Abhayagiriya, half a mile or so away, lost esthetically, and in size, was to make up from a longer antiquity. It was the very first to be built in Anuradhapura, or anywhere in the country. Brick-workers, several of them, balancing on tall scaffolds, were busy doing repair work, paying no attention to the two tourists. All around were to be seen loosened bricks giving way down the slopes.

On the way out, we stopped by an area where huge rock pillars, ten or so feet each side, stood at different angles, only a few straight. I tried to visualize how this nine storey building, called Brazen Palace, would have looked like in its ancient glory. Built in 3rd c. BCE by King Devanampiya Tissa, as a residence for the monks, the most senior occupying the uppermost level. It had earned its name because the roof was made of brass.

Exhausted by the heat, we soon headed to the Kandalama Hotel, a reservation facilitated, and paid for by my nephew Upul Arunajith in Toronto. Himself a former Hotel Executive, he still had his contacts.

Before we knew, Kandalama stood before our eyes, surrounded by greenery all around. Designed by the well-known architect Jeffrey Bawa, it had been built into a stone slab, in the thick of the jungle. There had been protests by the Sangha who had feared that the jungle tourist hotel would become a bikini jungle, but the concerns had been addressed. Like many an area of the hotel, our room was also rendered cool and trendy with glass walls showing at many angles. Dinner was again a feast, with even more local dishes.

Back in our room, how could we resist stepping on to the room balcony in the moonlit night, when our eyes began to dance over the glistening water of a lake that seem to extend to the horizon? No less were our ears treated to a chorus of music generated by birds as well as frogs in the lake. But soon, we were fast asleep.

It was the next day that we were to discover the pool. Built at the edge of the hotel, beyond it was only the sky, above the great big lake we had seen the night before from our room. There appeared to be no pool wall on that further side as the water flowed over the ledge. It was too tempting for me to not get in. Swimming to the ledge, I toyed with the water as it flowed over the ledge, looking down to see the overflowing water collected at a lower level, and presumably recycled to maintain the water level.

As the evening gave way to another moonlit night, there was yet another treat – the mellifluous sounds of a flute, played by a musician sitting atop an elevated rock. Clad in white, it was only a disbelief in mythology that saved us from seeing a heavenly angel in the lofty company of *gandharvas* 'heavenly musicians' in the orchestral chamber of literary imagination. Later in the night, we were to be dragged deeper into the culture as we were entertained by a virile show of low- and up-country dancing. Adding to the flavour was, as we were to find out later, that the dancers were themselves none other than the hotel staff itself in this remote part of the country not served by a regular bus service. Performing music and dance constituted part of the training the young men and women would receive at the hotel upon been hired.

But before the evening entertainment, Polonnaruwa, the other archeological centre, was calling. No more than an hour from the hotel, it was the capital city beginning in the thirteenth century when the ruler had moved further south in the face of invasions, abandoning Anuradhapura which had served as the Capital for 1500 long years. Here we were to see the reclining Buddha we had seen in pictures for so long, at close range for the first time. Measuring 46 feet, I looked for the one foot which is said to have moved at the point of his last breath. The sculptor had caught it alright. Next was the standing figure, a tear in the eye indicating it to be of Ananda, the Personal Attendant of the Buddha for 26 years who began lamenting at the impending death of his Master, and getting a stern reminder from him, "Have I not told you, Ananda, many a time, that whatever comes to be, passes away?" Ananda, not yet an Arahant who has cut off the very last blemishes, might have wanted to cry out and say, "Yes, Master, but not easy to take in the reality with dispassion".

Author at King Parakramabahu statue in Polonnaruwa, Sri Lanka

But my favourite was another statue about which theories abound as to who it stands for. Holding a book in hand, my favourite theory is that it is of King Parakramabahu, a poet himself, who revived Sinhala literature following the Hindu invasion of a century or more earlier.

Torontonian, the late Kirthie Abeysekara would report about our visit, under a headline, 'Nothing like Ole Sri Lanka':

> *When I touched the soil at the Ruwanweli Seya, I had the feeling, 'This is my soil', an emotionally charged Swarna said. It was a trip she should have made many years ago, she says, although "I did make many mental trips". Swarna was also impressed, the article continues, "by the school uniforms of boys and girls, even in rural Sri Lanka. In Canadian schools, anything goes...". Elsewhere, "Gazing at the Parakrama Samudra [a massive lake so big and hence called 'Parakrama ocean'] and the reclining Buddha statue of Polonnaruwa, revived fond memories of their early years in the Homeland, and thoughts of the engineering feats of the ancient 'Sinhalayas'.*

Swarna at Bentota Beach, Sri Lanka

BOOK III
A CREATIVE GRATITUDINAL CLOSING

24 A CRINTFREETH IN THE ACADEMY

24.1 Introduction

Let me begin by noting that this item, as well as the next, finds a home in the Memoir as beneficiaries of the several years of delay in publishing this. As seen above, much of my early contributions in Canadian Buddhism had been in the field, at the community level. But, joining the Trinity Divinity Faculty in the 1990's, I begin to focus on the academic side, although the community needs were not totally ignored. Setting up Nalanda College of Buddhist Studies and later *Canadian Journal of Buddhist Studies*, can then be said to be my attempts to widen the academic contribution.

Now when it came to writing scholarly articles, I was still following the traditional methods of scholarship as I had adopted earning my PhD at University of Toronto, earning the accolades 'extraordinary'. This is the same standard I sought to maintain at the peer-reviewed *Canadian Journal of Buddhist Studies*.

However, I was beginning to see the constraints to knowledge when there was more focus on the methodology than on the content. Has the latest research been taken into account, has all the commentarial literature being covered, has the case been made beyond a measure of doubt, etc. While these are all legitimate issues in academic study, I was now beginning to be creative, shunning the traditional methodology. I was no more interested in quoting and citing every other scholar in the field, leaving that to the younger or the traditional scholars. My focus was now on the content, drawing upon my interdisciplinary background, a rarity in the academy, the demand on academics being on knowing more and more of less and less, i.e., specialists. My thinking can be said to have been influenced more by Max Wertheimer's concept of "'productive' (insightful) ... thought processes". So now I was beginning to be more like a Commentator of the early era, free thinker– simply seeking to establish my views arrived at independently, and not in relation to what others had said. And so literally, I was beginning to think of myself as a CRINTFREETH: creative, interdisciplinary free thinker! And so in this section, I present you some of my research, four book length and two articles.

24.2 Books
24.2.1 Night of the Buddha's Enlightenment

Here then, is a chart showing what happened on that critical night when the Buddha attains Enlightenment:

RECONSTRUCTION
A Canonically-based Intuitive Reconstruction of the Process of Samana Gotama becoming Buddha, through the Three Watches of the Night, attaining both Nibbana and Buddhahood
© 2009, Suwanda H J Sugunasiri suwanda.sugunasiri@utoronto.ca

WATCH	TIME PERIOD	KNOWLEDGE TYPE	WATCH DETAIL	CONTENT	DETAILED CONTENT	SPRITUAL STATUS
3	6 AM ↑ 2 AM	III 'Knowledge of getting rid of flows' (āsavakkhaya nāṇa) **(END OF (RE) BIRTH (ajāta); END OF DEATH (amata))**	5 – 6 AM ↑	Path (magga) ↑	EXCELLENT SAMMĀ: Concentration *samādhi* Mindfulness *sati* Exercise *vāyāma* Livelihood *ājīva* Conduct *kammanta* Language *vācā* Conceptualization *samkappa* View *diṭṭhi*	Buddha theorizing on the Path ↕ in the Bliss of Emancipation
			4 – 5 AM	'Cessation' (nirodha)		Attaining Buddhahood Attaining Nibbana
			3 – 4 AM ↑ 2 – 3 AM ↑	'Arising' (samudaya) ↑ 'Suffering' (dukkha) ↑		'Emerging Buddha' ↕
2	2 AM ↑ 10 PM	II 'Knowledge of exiting and Re-appearing' (cutūpapāta nāṇa) **(REBIRTH)**		"…according to their actions, bad .. leading to misery and good .. to a good destiny"		Samana Gotama
1	10 PM ↑ 6 PM	I 'Knowledge of former lives' (pubbenivāsa-nānussati nāṇa) **(REBIRTH)**		"seeing how he himself was born in several life-times"		Samana Gotama

24.2.2 Dhamma Aboard Evolution: Buddha Unfolding the Universe

Agganna Sutta of the Buddha has been one of the more difficult Discourses (Sutta) studied by western scholars. The pioneer who introduced the Canon to the west a century ago, Prof. Rhys Davids, saw it as "a "good-humored irony". A century later, Prof *Steven Collins* of the University of Chicago, sees it as nothing more than "a satire". Prof. Richard Gombrich of Cambridge University in the UK sees it as a 'parody' of the ancient Vedic 'aetiological myth' of Creation.

Not convinced, I was to do a close reading of the few short paragraphs in Pali. And what I discovered was the Buddha doing nothing but unfolding the universe! And this with very much parallel to modern day science which is why my study came to be titled, *Dhamma Aboard Evolution: A Canonical Study of the Agganna Sutta in relation to Science..* In this view, an Evolutionary period is followed by a Devolutionary period, followed by a next @Evolutionary period to be followed by another..... This means that there is no first cause of a creator, or a beginning. This means that the Big Bang in Westernscience which is said to be the beginning of the universe is nothing but the end of a given devolutionary process when everything goes up in flames under the heat of seven scorching suns!

Here then is a comparative chart:

1	2	3	4	5
ERA	SUB-ERA	TIME IN YEARS	WESTERN SCIENCE	THE BUDDHA
PRE-CAMBRIAN	1	13.5 + **bya**	Big Bang	End of Devolutionary Phase; Presence of Ābhassara Beings in the sky
	2	9 bya	---	Beginnings of Evolutionary Phase / Ābhassara Beings continuing
	3		---	Formation of Water
	4	4.55 bya	Formation of Earth	Formation of Earth
	5	4.4 bya	Condensation of water into oceans	
	6	3.8 bya	Earliest chemical evidence of Life	
	7	2.7 bya	Earliest Chemical Evidence of Eukaryotes	
	8	2.6 bya	Bacteria living on land	
	9	1.8 bya	Oldest multicellular fossils	
CAMBRIAN	10	575 **mya**	Oldest animals (Ediacarans)	
	11	500 mya	Plants evolve	Plants evolving
	12	450 mya	Insects and other vertebrates move on land	Plants variegating; Insects evolving
	13	360 mya	Four-limbed vertebrates move on land	
	14	225 mya	Mammals and dinosaurs	
	15	5 mya	Ancestors of humans and chimps diverge	
PLIO-CENE	16	150 **kya**	Anatomically modern humans	Anatomically modern humans

Benchmarks identified by the Buddha as against the Benchmarks of Evolution in Western Science

I shall leave it up to you to go over it on your own time. But here are some of the comments on the study:

- Prof. Victor Bruce Mathews, Dean of Arts, Acadia University, Canada:
  ... a novel perspective on this ancient text. ...[The author] urges us to see how the Buddha's views on cosmological and evolutionary topics are not contradictory to what he calls 'Western science'... - in other words, Buddhist teachings traveling compatibly alongside of modern evolutionary concepts.
- Ven. Ajahn Punnadhammo Mahathero, Canada:
  ... The approach in this book is .... to guide the reader along the way to the same vision as the Buddha's listeners twenty-five centuries ago. Paradoxically, the result more often than not seems surprisingly modern. ... a bold opening to a new area of investigation.
- Rupert Sheldrake, PhD, British Evolutionary Biologist and author of *Science Set Free*:
  ... Your research on this Buddhist text goes into areas I've never seen explored before in Buddhist scholarship.

24.2.3 Triune Mind, Triune Brain: Map of the Mind through the Eyes of Buddhianscience and Westernscience

The Buddha uses three terms to refer to consciousness – *Citta, Mano* and *Vinnana*. Sometimes they are taken to mean the same, but other times, they are clearly distinguished in terms of function. I had published an article seeking to clarify the usages, in both ways – i.e., same and different. And the article was titled, "Triune Mind in Buddhism: a Textual exploration".

It is around that time I had come to encounter the concept of a *Triune Brain*, by the American evolutionary Biologist Paul MacLean. So is there any compatibility, or relationship between the Triune Mind in the mind dimension of the mindbody, to use the Buddha's terms, and the Triune Brain in the body dimension? The book then is the result of that inquiry, basically a neuroanatomical study seeking to establish a physical home in the brain for the three aspects of the mind.

To quote the excerpt on the back page:

> This is an interdisciplinary study of mind and body, embryonic level included, relating to Buddhianscience and Westernscience. It draws upon Sutta and Abhidhamma [Discourses and Metaphysics], and Neuroscience, Anthropology, Linguistics and Embryology. The three terms used by the Buddha are analyzed against the 17 mindmoments making up a stream of consciousness, labelling them Triune Mind collectively. Analysis extended to a neuron and the ear, it is paralleled with Triune Brain... Reinterpreted under the Buddha's phylogenetic concept of *satta* 'sentient beings', covering both humans and animals, Citta, Mano and Vinnana are shown to find a home in the re-branded Proto-, Paleo- and Neo-sentient brains. Evolution in the West is a process of species change. Showing it as a cumulative outcome of changes at the individual (phenotype) level

within a given species (genotype). Citta is identified as the mind that carries the 'folkloric memories' life to life, this in the form of peptides as in neuronal communication, through mitochondrial-DNA. The study ends in an ironic twist – that there is indeed nothing called 'brain' or 'mind', both being processes!

Here then, is that Figure:

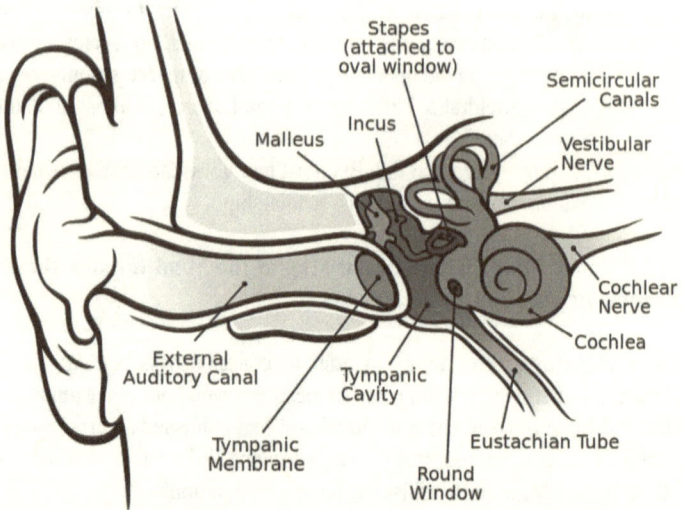

24.2.4 *Swarna Sugunasiri: Born Streamentrant, Next Life Nibbana* (forthcoming).

This relates to the spiritual life of Swarna, discovered only after her passing away. And the discovery is that she had indeed been a born-streamwinner' (*jati-Sotapanna*), the first stage towards liberation, and now on her way to Nibbana. In figuring out the many complexities, another discovery that emerges relates to her past life. And that is that she may well have been the controversial Madame Blavatsky, the comparative data relating to the two lives seeming to suggest the strong possibility. Co-Founder of the American Theosophical Society along with Col. Henry Steel Olcott of New Jersey, USA, having read a Report on a Buddhist-Christian Debate held in Ceylon, both were to become Buddhist on their own while in the US itself. But visiting Ceylon in 1882, and embracing Buddhism formally, they were to visit the site of the debate, in the city called Panadura. Seemingly conditioned kammically, a concept central to Buddhism, Panadura also happens to be the birthplace of Swarna! Another intriguing characteristic of Swarna was that, growing up in a family where meat-eating was not eschewed, in a Buddhist society where vegetarianism was not a key feature as per the

Buddha's stance, she comes to have the 'idiosyncrasy' of not touching meat. In the words of Blavatsky herself in answer to the specific issue, the stance at the Theosophical Society was one of going vegetarian. Speculative as the hypothesis may be, there is other material in the book that seems to go in that direction.

24.2.5 Sauris Silva... : in the Eyes of Himself and Others

This is a *Chapbook*, as I call it, on my father, Sauris Silva. What prompted my hand was the discovery, after five or more decades, of a 25 page Bio, handwritten by himself. It was on his parents, his wife and on himself. The piece on my mother ends with the words, "for the children, me and my wife and the house became a school for behavior and morals, learnedness and handicrafts training" (p. 26).

School Principal for three decades, he was also the principal dancer of his father's exorcistic Tovil dance troupe, a performance not rarely taking a whole night. So it was a case of a Dr. Jekyll, Mr Hyde act. He was also the first to commit to writing the oral tradition of Low Country Dancing, also developing a curriculum on it, currently used at the newly founded University of Visual and Performing Arts.

But I was also to be impressed by the many areas of social services he had been engaged in - education, cooperatives, rural development, temperance, health, religion, among others, ranging over ten. Another surprise was that he was a poet. And so it was with no surprise that I read his words at the end, "Sauris Silva, the one who put to the lie the words, 'One in the world excels in one'".

For all his social, educational, cultural and other engagements, he was also the model Buddhist, of solid ethical conduct, never smoking or drinking in his life.

And this wide engagement had not gone unnoticed in the media, generating an umpteen number of pieces on him, including the time when his dance costumes came to be donated to the Museum. There was no shortage of celebratory publications and events in his honour either.

Now all this was too much to be left alone on my shelf. I learned much from it, both personal and social. And so it was my decision to publish it, 10,000 miles and five decades away from it all! The bilingual Chapbook, in Sinhala and English, was then published as a gift for future generations, to etch into history a model of the ideal human being in both a self-care and other-care.

State honored *Kalaguru* 'Maestro of the Arts, more recently, a street has been named after him, Sauris Silva Mawata [Street]. A statue to be put up in his birth town of Tangalla in recognition of all his services is currently in the works.

24.3 Articles
24.3.1 Gandhabba, the Celestian Pro-mom Pheromone chaser

For conception to take place, the Buddha posits a third partner, in addition to the parents:

> "Bhikkhus, the descent to the uterus takes place through the union of three things. Here ...when there is the union of mother and father, and the mother is in season, and the gandhabba is present, through the union of this threesome, the descent to the uterus takes place."

Thus does the Buddha posit the three conditions for conception, the third being the **Gandhabba**. This paper seeks to understand what or who 'gandhabba' is and its role in conception, something that has baffled scholars.

Perhaps in an extended methodology, the paper also happily benefits from Westernscience when the Canon is not helpful enough to explain and/or help understand a given dimension of the process under discussion.

While there may be much interesting detail, one point of particular interest might be the study suggesting that it is *not the father who determines the gender* of the spring, as in contemporary wisdom, *but the incoming sentient being itself – i.e., you and me*! Did I receive a knock on my head? Patriarchal did you say, ha ha ha!!

24.3.2 Sarabhañña: An Esthetic Buddhist Chanting Style

This paper seeks to understand a style of reciting the Dhamma (= Teachings) authorized by the Buddha, called *Sarabhañña*. In contrast is a style known as *Geetassara,* disapproved. We explore the two concepts in relation to both 'speech' and the '7-note diatonic scale', this comparatively - '*saptak'* (*sa ri ga ma pa dha ni*) as in Indian Aesthetics and '*septet'* (*do re mi fa sol la ti*) as in Western music.

To make the paper accessible to the non-specialist reader, the paper draws upon the western movie, The Sound of Music, using the song sung by Julie Andrews, to explain the septet:

      DO - a deer, a female deer
      RE - a drop of golden sun
      MI - a name, I call myself,
      FA – a long long way to run....
      SO – a needing pulling thread
      LA – a note to follow SO
      TI – a drink with jam and bread
      That will bring back to do
      DO – RE – MI – FA – SO - LA - TI - DO! – S0 – DO!

Later on it is shown how the Paritta chanting in Sinhala Theravada Buddhism serves as the example par excellence of the style approved by the Buddha.

24.3.3 ESP: Reality Turned Myth in Westernscience (*Mindfield* [Bulletin], 13.1, May 2021).

In Westernscience, a human being is seen to be constituted of only the five physical senses. In the Buddha's analysis, however, a sentient being, this including animals, is made up of six senses, adding the mind sense. In another analysis, a mindbody is shown to be constituted of the Four Great Elements – water, heat, wind and earth, plus space (meaning as e.g., in the nose, ears, mouth, etc.) plus consciousness (under the term Viññāṇa). And consciousness is not only the sixth sense, but the primary one behind each of the senses, including the mind itself. And so, the separation of Viññāṇa from the physical component is what constitutes death. This then means that, under the Westernscientific view, every human being or animal living on earth come to be dead, since by definition, they are said to have only the five physical senses, and no consciousness!

To cover the shortfall in Westernscience, ninety years ago, the Duke University psychologist J. B. Rhine introduced the concept and term ESP (Extra-Sensory Perception). And this helped Physicists to get away with their flawed thinking, since now, somebody else was taking care of what was left out by them. And there then emerges the Discipline called Para-psychology, happy that they now had a place on the podium of Science.

My paper "ESP: Reality Turned Myth in Westernscience" is then my small attempt to highlight this and point to how it has led to confusion in the public as to who is right – physicists or parapsychologists? It not only explains the reality of the mind as the sixth sense, but also points out that the ultra psychological skills possessed by some, such as Telepathy, Psychokinesics, etc., are based in the mind, and not something outside, or *extra*, as suggested by the label Extra-Sensory Perception, and that they are indeed biologically rooted. So I replace Extra-Sensory Perception with ***MSUP – Mind-Sensory Ultra Perception***.

While there are other books, and articles, the sampling above hopefully shows the writer in his new creative academic mischief and other articles.

25 HAPPY BUT STRIVING: REFLECTIONS AND A FINAL STRIVING

25.1 Minimum Expectations

Looking back over the years, I can say that I was never one who had any long term aspirations, or ambitions, like, for example, wanting to be somebody, or get somewhere. I guess I was happy to be whoever that I had come to be at any given time and enjoy whatever that had come my way.

At school in Colombo, I did cadetting because I enjoyed being smart. I played cricket I guess because everybody did it, just as I took part in athletics because it was so much fun to be out there. Being Secretary of the Literary Association allowed me to meet other students, and I guess allowing me to enjoy what seems to have come naturally - providing leadership. Looking after mom in her illness gave me personal satisfaction. Writing stories gave me excitement just as translating Bertrand Russell (*Commonsense and Nuclear Warfare*) did.

I kept bulging my academic profile not towards any specific job or profession, but simply because I seemed to have loved knowledge. In Canada, working for the cause of Multiculturalism and Buddhism in particular, brought me happiness, each of them calling for leadership.

This is not to say that I did not have my eye on things, or that I was freed of greed. But if I were greedy, they were mostly of immediate relevance, not too far out and within easy reach, and in a stepwise fashion. This then was both happiness and the striving.

And, happy to say, I have achieved whatever little expectations I have had. All but one. I know you can't wait to hear. But ... you won't be disappointed.

25.2 What's in a Name? A Parental Projection

Indeed my parents seem to have projected all this happiness and striving into the screen of life at the point of my birth in picking for me the personal names *Sugunasiri Jayasumana*.

We can begin with an exploration of them, first with the first: *Sugunasiri (su + guna + siri)*. If '*guna*' means virtue, *su-*, interestingly also the first syllable of 'su-perior', indicates the superlative. *Suguna-* then means 'of super virtue'. From a Buddhist perspective, it is being virtuous that brings happiness. This is not to say that as a Sentient Being, I don't have my share of blemishes, but that to the extent that 'to name is to guide', as the American linguist Edward Sapir and the Indian linguist Bharthrhari would have it, it serves as a constant reminder to me, as if to say, 'Hey, there's a candid camera on you'. Great! Thanks.

Now *Siri* means 'prosperous', as in Sri Lanka (or *Siri Lanka*, as in Sinhala), as in Sirimavo Bandaranailke, the world's first woman Prime Minister. '*Shri*' Nehru, to think about India's first post-Independent Prime Minister, adds another meaning in its Sanskrit rendition. Literally 'Sir', it is honorific, as we have in Shrimati Gandhi for Indira Gandhi, his daughter and Prime Minister to be later. By adding such a syllable to my name, it is as if my parents intended and portended that my life be on the honorific roll.

So it is that Sugunasiri captures the notions of *virtue* and *prosperity*, the latter also, needless to say, bringing happinesss.

To look at my other, little known name, *Jayasumana*, it appears that it may have something to do with the striving dimension. *Sumana* literally means 'of good mind', *su*, as noted, being the superlative. Thus it could be taken to mean 'of superior mind'.

Jaya- literally means 'victorious'. So *Jayasumana* then means 'Victorious in good / superior mind'. And so the victory is over my own mind, calling for a constant striving

So the mouthful *Sugunasiri Jayasumana* may be taken to mean 'super virtue and prosperity, victorious through good mind'. Sorry, the sounds are spilling off the sides of my mouth! Both names then can be said to be not unrelated to happiness and striving.

So it looks as if my parents seem to have had a vision as to my future, by choosing for me the names Sugunasiri Jayasumana.

But have I lived up to my parents' expectations? Before answering that, let's listen to our local Bard telling us, in a poem titled, 'the Many Names of the One', how the wider world has come to playfully give many a twist and turn to my parents' vision, as if asking 'What's in a name?'.

THE MANY NAMES OF THE ONE

"For my different names & identities.
This is a poem written from the point of view of the name." -

(*Obama-Ji,* 2009, p. 29-42)

How It Begins

When in that first rush of fresh air
into the lungs, swooshing its way
back past the vibrating vocal chords, he
my future body-buddy, screamed
his lungs off, to
announce, to give notice,
to this world, "Watch out.
I've arrived", I did not hear,
nor feel the sonant vibrations,
being yet to be strung, of
my phonemic cells, enriching
meanings and sonorous cadences.

Upon arrival, he had
but one name -
mindbody, known
to itself alone, getting
the nod from the Buddha, the
scientist smiling, every cell
of his body just loving it, the
cellular but nameless it.

Meeting him
face to face, on that historic day
not much later, when,
keeping the soothsayer happy,
parents had invited kith and kin
to a naming party, I loiter
in apprehension, yet hope.

Looking for his daily bread, the
soothsayer did his cheerleading.
"Give me an S", and
"Give me a J", moving
his checkerboard pieces
House to House
of the zodiac chart,
me now feeling the stirrings
in my groin, of an imminent
birth, waiting in the wings,
to be catapulted
into a namely existence.

Seeking the virtuous,
the punctilious soothsayer
strung a *guna*, giving me my
first morphophonemic existence
for virtue, gluing on a *siri*, for
prosperity, pre-positioning
a syllable '*Su*', jacking up
virtue to an nth degree,
ballooning my buddy's ego, the
kite of his hopes, up up
and away, to a soothsayer smile.

Guiding the kite,
the soothsayer next,
deftly brands a
second string, *Jaya*,
the 'victor', yoking
su-mana of the 'good mind',
now summoning a pride
in his mom
in his dad.

The demands of S,
the demands of J
met, his mom, oops,
dad, turning the pages
of the *tombu mitiya*
family annals, makes the
ancestral link, *ge* 'of
the house of', linking
my story to his-tory,
of a house renowned
for fetching (*aedi*)
perfumed waters *suwanda
saen,*
titillating the royal noses
into an aromatic frenzy.

Marching me now
to the tune of
Dutch drums, in the heels
of a modernizing dad
in-step with the times,
a *Silva* strung, the final
    thread
meaning nothing,
giving nothing, only
ensuring my place
in the march of history.

Me, now in full regalia, in
the lofty company of this
name-form, minted in a
less-than-run-of-the-mill,
count the many names of the
one, but in no holy company
of Zarathustra Yahweh
Brahma God Allah,
my laurels resting on
Good Smelling **Suwanda**, of the
Scent Delivering House **Hennedige**, a
Super Prosperous **Sugunasiri**, joined by
a Victorious Minded **Jayasumana**,
delighting in resting my ego
on a Dutch *Silva* platter*!*

Now I know what to call'im,
and I myself, not just
'Hey you, name-form' but
SuwandaHennedigeSugunasiriJayasumanaSilva,
Passport confirming the branding.

A Shrinkage

Floating way up high,
carried by the winds of
a distant royal touch
wagging a Dutch tail,
I suddenly nosedive, shattered,
to see my well minted
virtue, prosperity, and
victory of the mind,
heartlessly crowded into
four single letters, in
a classroom, S and H
taking the lead, S and J
the rear, only a Silva
keeping its full
phonemic regalia,
in full English regimen,
initials surname,
five syllables demanding
too much space too much time
for the teacher tongue,
end up in an **shsjsilva**,
though now in the elite
company, *swrdbandaranaike,*
an Oxford-returned.

Sinhala Grandeur

S W R D anointing
to its rightful place, Sinhala,
stolen by a cruel history,
Dutch name receives its
last rites, on a bonfire of
long disdain, the nameform
and I, returning to a
11th century Hela-hauvla of
Puritanical Sinhala vintage,
to appear now, in
an Op Ed piece, here,
there and everywhere, of
the national Sinhala media,
a de-Anglicized *Su Hae Ja, in*
true Sinhala grandeur, of a
first *ge-* family name, personal
name ***Sugunasiri*** showing up
last, alone hoisting
a multisyllabic pedantry, with an
occasional additional flamboyancy
of an expanded *Ja* into
its full feathers of
Jayasumana.

An Ordination!

Writing a Letter
to the Editor, my buddy,
in the name of the solo
multisyllabic pedantry,
adding in front the
place of birth, the editor,
talked into by a *sangha*
tradition, upgrades him
to ordained status, Venerable
tangalle sugunasiri swamin vahanse*,*
giving me the
highest kick ever!

A Wife's Choice of a "Most virtuous radiance"

Disrobing back
into secular life,
wifely-lover of my
bosom buddy life-long pal,
making the personal the familial,
I sign on to a repositioning,
Swarna now threading my
multisyllabic pedantry, into
her personal fabric, of
a family name, giving
me a new pride, an entry
to a lineage, with children,
and their children inheriting
me in my new
Knight's Armour, a Scholar,
Canadian, wondering if
this 'family name' is
"Sanskrit-derived", meaning
"most excellent Sir" or
"most-virtuous radiance/
splendour", propelling me
to the stratosphere!

Warming to Pals

In a multiple-variation
of a theme, how close
to my buddy's friends
I felt, welcomed into a
shortened *Sugune,* the
warmth of friendliness
wrapped in a final /e/, to
last a lifetime of friendship,
a more recent friendship
from native Sri Lanka
emerging with the drop of
even the final /e/, ending me
in a *Sugun* dynamic.

A Friendly Twist

Crossing the oceans, in
Fulbright regalia, funny I
thought 'twas, trudging along
a Philadelphian winter, in
thick boots, when buddy's
first fellow-student buddy
in a new city, and buddy's
children's Uncle Lionel, a
Canadian to boot, twisting
a tongue around a long
name too painful,
does surgery on me, changing
vowels, axing meaning,
the new version *Suji*, first
hard to gulp, but becoming
or so very or'nary, hearing it
over and over again, for a full year,
helping cement a life-long friendship.

Professor Discretion

Traveling across oceans,
the double-double
family name, double-double
personal name not within
a western psyche, buddy's
Professor, Canadian, answering
to a cultural imperative, pick
the first partner of the
family double, to be
buddy's personal tag, heralding,
a *SuwandaSugunasiri*,
sending the doubles partners
to the waste bin of
disuse, national identity of a
suhaejasugunasiri pushed
to the backwaters of history
in a new Canadian identity.

Wedging

Looking to earn
academic respectability,
my buddy wedges in
the occasional HJ
between the first and the
last name, the variation
finding comfort in one
or the other, and
most meaningfully
in a Nalanda College
Founder-Presidency.

Techno Cut-back

University UTORDIAL, tolerating
no nonsense of
more than 8 letters, I am soon
reduced, to a *sugunasi*, semantics
out of sight, feelings
in flight, the proud
Capital S now in company
of a lower case ignominy
joining the rest.

A Marketing Move

Buddy's *Toronto Star* readers
complementing him,
tearing him apart, though
not knowing, from my
Suwanda name if
I am male or female, the
Marketplace, looking
for clients, makes a
definitive move, when,
in feminist hey days, I am
crowned, in a successful
sex change operation,
news announced via mail
to a *Ms.*, to a
Mrs. Suwanda.

Time taking it in stride,
now I undergo plastic surgery,
performed with a savvy
business hutzpah, on
the surgical bed of yet
another market survey, the
change again announced
by mail to a *Sue Wanda,*
wow, a dainty lass!

Dion D'or Parfum, Lexus, and
Suzy's Zecret Lingerie, now
showering buddy's home
with a torrent of Mail,
bringing a smile upon me,
heaving a sigh
of relief
I was
not taming animals
as Zoo Wanda!
Or being tamed
a Zoo Panda!!

Security Risk

Calling a Credit Card Company, on
business, the 'routine' questions
asked, but hearing a 'first
name' Suwanda, my buddy
promptly transferred to 'security',
to a battery of questions, to be
explained, with apologies,
the name is *female* in
routine questioner's
culture, 'Indian',
David taking a
Goliath hit!

Followed with a GUN!

Struggling to jiggle
the syllables of my name
over the phone,
selling soliciting and
everything else in between, I
soon come to be
pushed into a
membership of a
dubious club, populist
in Ranch country
in the Bible Belt, when
Su- comes to be followed
with a **GUN,** my buddy's lips
quickly moving to
begin to own up
my true self, not letting
to vandalize me anymore,
to trample upon the
the rest of the
mortified syllables,
returning **Sugunasiri**
to its rightful origins
recouping its
challenged dignity.

Continuing the Walk

In competition
with his mindbody cells
as they struggled
to be born, live and die,
I took to every trick
in the book, with
panic in my eye,
oh my, if you only knew,
hoping to make it
stick, the phonemic sounds
in the meaningful pattern
as moulded by loving parents
by a soothsayer's dextrous hand,
uncut unbutchered, but alas,
in vain ... all.

Having now lived the reality of *anicca* change, for a full life time, should I now yearn for a rebirth, looking to be truly blessed, to get into high company of the Great Ones, gaining an unchanging Name, like Atman of the Vedas? "You dummy", I hear a voice, my thoughts deciphered, "Why be a fool when you have gained wisdom of the reality of change?"	Brought to my senses, I put my hands around the shoulders of my Mindbody buddy, to continue the walk of our lifetime together. Hurrah!! *NOTE: Buddha teaches that the idea of an unchanging mindbody, a soul, is a fiction of the human imagination.* - Obama-Ji (2009, 29-42)

In an e-mail dated 24, 2010, Pat Weldon, a former colleague of Swarna's, writes from British Columbia:

> *I particularly enjoyed THE MANY NAMES OF THE ONE. It was the piece in which you seemed most at home with yourself and your poetic muse -- it was zany, spiritual, imaginative, fast paced and charming. I laughed out loud at the sex change.... followed by the name change... but I think I know what you're getting at there... very clever.*

Thank you, Pat, very encouraging.

Having listened to the Bard and taken a name tour, let us now see if and to what extent I have lived up to the parental projection. My sense is that the best way to do that would be to place my history against the hand that has guided it. And so, what would this be? It would undoubtedly be the Buddhadhamma, meaning the Teachings of the Buddha.

25.3 *Buddhadhamma* as the Source of Happiness and Striving

Writing a chapter-length article on my work in Canadian Buddhism (in *Wild Geese, Buddhism in Canada* ((2010), Professors Victor Hori and Janet McLellan title it: 'Suwanda H J Sugunasiri: Buddhist'. Intrigued as I was with the characterization 'Buddhist' when I first read it in print, upon closer reflection, it appears that they have been sharp to capture me in my very essence, even though it is only now as I write this Memoir that I myself am coming to see it consciously.

If Buddhism in Canada is the context and the case study that have provided the basis for their observation, I hope that my life story has shown no less - that it is my upbringing as a Buddhist, born to Buddhist parents in a country with a history of Buddhism of over two millennia, that have helped me to be happy and striving; and that I have not failed to live up to my parents' vision.

Leaving it to the reader to decide as to how helpful it is, let me make a beginning with the Buddha's words, 'The one with wisdom, based in self-discipline' (*sile patitthaaya naro sapañño*). A critical term here is *wisdom*. So what does it mean? I take it to mean understanding reality experientially in its interrelatedness.

A resident of Greek Town in Toronto, having never left the neighbourhood will conclude, "Oh, Toronto is made up of Greeks". One honed in Chinatown likewise might conclude, "Oh, Toronto is made up of Chinese". Another in Little India might conclude that all Torontonians to be South Asian. Living in Forest Hill, one might take Toronto to be a city of Jews, with our family as a single exception, as one living in Rosedale might decide it to be all Anglo-Saxon. But an Anthropologist taking a survey of the city will say how multicultural Toronto is! Here then is the wisdom – understanding reality in its interrelatedness, particularistics giving way to universals.

The point then is wisdom comes through not knowing more and more of less and less, as in the academic world of specialization, where the thumb specialist knowing every little detail of the thumb but nothing of the hand of which the thumb is part.

Directing my lens on interdisciplinary areas of knowledge such as Buddhism, the languages of Buddhism – Pali, Sanskrit and Sinhala, Moral Philosophy, Linguistics, Education, National development, Language Planning, Educational Planning, Language Pedagogy, Psychology, Literature, Sociology, etc., may then be said to be my routes to wisdom, my academic work as a Crintfreeth in later years reflecting the outcome. While growing in each discipline made me happy, it needs hardly be said how it also entailed a striving.

Going through the pages of this Memoir, the reader would have not failed to see how I have been more than happy to be of help in many a diverse field. Clearly, then, *other-care* has also been the clarion call for me in all these years of involvement. The Buddha talks of four types of individuals: One who cares not for others but be obsessed just with oneself; one who cares only for others, ignoring oneself; a third that cares neither for oneself nor the other; and finally, one who cares for both oneself and in equal measure for others. The last, of course, is the Buddha's ideal type. Should I, in my contributions in diverse fields, see myself as fitting the bill of the Buddha's choice character type?

Once the Buddha was asked, "Sir, your disciples take only one meal a day, yet they are always all smiles. How come?" Says the Buddha: "My disciples don't spend their time on the past, nor on the future. They keep their mind on the present." So perhaps, then, could my happiness have also come from the very fact that I had no great future expectations, nor lamented the past, but kept on going with whatever I had at a given moment in time, with contentment, enjoying the lemonade that has come to be in my hands? The Buddha's words are "Contentment is the greatest wealth"!

So am I in contentment? I am happy to say, "Yes, indeed". For one, there is my general attitude of 'little wanting', *appiccha* in Buddhian terms. "I can be easily satisfied with the very best", Churchill is reported to have said. I can say that I can be satisfied with the very least! E.g., returning to Lanka after seven years of luxury in the West, at a Sarvodaya rural work camp helping dig a canal to divert waters to the fields, I eat off a banana leaf and drink off a coconut shell! This then also speaks to a *flexibility* of mind. And 'little wanting' is not just living within one's means but perhaps living even below par – perhaps be happy with even less than what one could afford, as a matter of principle.

But contentment in mind is not to play dead with what we have, but simply to savour what we have while at the same time striving for the better. It is in fact the calm that contentment brings to the mind that allows one to withstand the calamities in the face of the inevitabilities of public life - success and failure, fame and infamy, blame and compliment, happiness and unhappiness. Withstanding them like a rock in the wind would be, as in the Buddha's words, what brings peace and calm, and contentment. To put it in colloquial terms, taking them with a pinch of salt, or in Buddhian terms, equanimity, also allowing for that striving for the better. Letting go of things, if only for the moment, and/or in expectation of perhaps returning to it at a more appropriate time, seem to have been for me a part method of maintaining that contentment.

My life, as with everyone else, has been both a bed of roses and a bench of thorns, from time to time, both self-inflicted and other-inflicted. I failed in Grade V, and then also at University entrance. You've seen in this Memoir the many contexts of 'Apply, apply, no reply', and my qualifications and offers of service turned down or ignored many time. But my happiness is that I was able to take the pain *sans* the suffering, consciously or unconsciously. Pain is a physical reality. But suffering is the psychological counterpart. While we have no control over the former, the latter is very much within our control. So what is it that allowed me to smile even when pricked? To be unshaken by the winds blowing from the four quarters, taking it all in stride, in equanimity, and without attachment. So it is this walking the talk perhaps that can be said to have helped me through the thick and thin, though perhaps not always successfully, to not let pain turn into suffering. And not allow myself to be waylaid by the failures, but go on to strive, in diligence and happiness.

Equanimity calls for a letting go of things, if only for the moment, and/or in expectation of perhaps returning to it at a more appropriate time.

Alongside 'equanimity' in the face of realities of life, mine has also been a continuing opportunity to grow in the practice of *mudita* – happiness in the happiness of others, one of the four Noble Abidings. Combined with the other three – lovingkindness, compassionate action and equanimity, what I experience is happiness in others' happiness, but also still striving to do better.

While we generally don't think of it, I know that I would not have been able to get anywhere near what I have been engaged in without the loving arm of good health around my shoulders. In Buddha's reckoning, 'good health is the primary gain', me thus engaging in a regular health regimen, rain or shine. The addition in my e-mail signature 'life-long teetotaler and non-smoker' may speak to a self-discipline dimension of the health regimen.

Of most direct bearing on my conduct in mind, body and word, may be the Buddha's last words, "Strive with diligence". Need I say more?

In summation, the basis of my happiness then is that I have tried to *live* my life as a 'Buddhist', in particular adapting the Buddha's motto: "I do as I say; I say as I do". What that means is seeking to live my life as closely as possible guided by Buddhist values. As the Buddha says in the *Dhammapada*, winning over oneself is the greatest victory.

My contribution to the social good may not perhaps be of gargantuan proportions, but I am happy to say that I have been rewarded enough personally in the thought of the social good that may have resulted from whatever little effort I may have put in, through striving.

Sorry, perhaps I may not have made a convincing argument as to how it is the Buddhadhamma that has helped me in my happiness and striving. But I know that it is. And that is all that matters. For, convincing others has not been the focus of the Memoir but telling it as it is, allowing the reader to make their own judgements.

It is not, of course, that I was conscious of a particular teaching of the Buddha at any particular given time, and actively sought to live by it. But it was a super-virtuous and prosperous (sugunasiri) mind on auto-gear coming to be victorious over itself (jayasumana), in an unconscious striving to live up to the expectations of my parents.

As for prosperity, the –siri part of the name, I can happily say that I have never been short of the essentials of life – food, clothing and shelter. We may not qualify for the DINK – double income no kids Trophy, but indeed I can make a claim for half the trophy, my better half bringing me a life-long dowry!

25.4 Visible Conditioning - Other Sources of Happiness

While Buddhadhamma has certainly been my richest resource for being happy but striving, there are some others that can be said to have contributed. The first are my parents. And then there is Swarna in particular, and the two children in their own silent way. Then there are the Three Countries – Sri Lanka, USA and Canada. While this would be obvious, I am making it by way of expressing my gratitude.

These three combined, I call it *visible conditioning*, to be contrasted with the *invisible conditioning* next.

25.4.1. Family

Would you say I am filled with wisdom if I were to say that I didn't just drop from the sky? Ha Ha Ha!

Says the Buddha, in a seeming word play, 'Parents are [your] Brahma', this in an Indian Hindu context where Brahma is the mythological Creator. My parents are clearly the primary human resource for my happiness and striving. First it may be because of their personal qualities, such as my mom's compassion. And my father's upright moral character such as life-time non-smoker and teetotaler and his fiery social conscience, love of learning and multidimensionality - school Principal but also Principal dancer in his father's dance troupe, social worker, journalist, writer, poet and more. Inspirational enough for me to spread my wings?

It was, as noted elsewhere in the Memoir as well, also my upward mobile father's meticulous care in guiding my educational life. Beginning with the Sinhala school at the primary grade, I, along with my sisters, was sent to the Catholic school where the medium of instruction was English. Completing Grade 5, now well versed in English, the three of us were to be sent to Colombo, when I attended the leading Buddhist schools – Nalanda and Ananda, in which the medium of instruction was English, too. If not for this systematic training, my English would have been nowhere close to where it is now. And if I were to get an entry level understanding of Latin at Nalanda, the solid background gained in Pali and Sanskrit at Ananda is what has allowed my systematic study of Buddhadhamma in the original texts. But, even before that was his thoughtfulness to send me to the local temple to introduce me to Sanskrit while still in Tangalla.

But it was much more than the specifics. It was that they were the iconic symbols, the living reminder, of Buddhist values. While certainly it was our practice growing up to do a daily Homage to the Buddha (and Homage to mom and dad, too, at the end), it was to be a hit and miss in later years. Schooling and working in the capital city Colombo, it was hardly part of my life, the religious dimension practically distant in my professional, cultural and literary involvements. Coming to N America, it was not any sooner than the early years of the the two children that it returned as a regular home habit, this by way of initiating them.

Yet, the values imparted by my parents were never far from me in whatever I did. Taking the fellow actresses home in my car after a rehearsal or play, when my home was in the opposite direction, may have been in the confidence that it would be what mom would have liked to see me do in compassion. The inspiration for working in the diverse fields in Canada was indubitably dad as was the search for learning. And, since their lives were also guided by Buddhadhamma, my parents can be said to be the medium, the visible and the living, condition, that kept me in a Buddhist life.

If the sources of inspiration and guidance in my early life were my parents, the shining beam lighting up my happiness and striving for the next five decades, of course, was Swarna. But it is going beyond the familial relationship that I find the real source. It is her spiritual life, discovered only after her passing away. that she had indeed been a born-streamwinner' (*jati-Sotapanna*), the first stage towards liberation.

As in the Buddhadhamma, experiencing Nibbana constitutes liberation. And, while one may experience it within one's lifetime, the not so diligent might take up more lifetimes, going through three stages, Stream-winner being the first. And if one has been successful in coming by it in the preceding lifetime, then in the immediate next life-time, one can be said to be a 'born-sotapanna'. While this is not the place to argue for the view, or explain in detail, we can defer to the Buddha to see what characteristics would be seen in a given individual of sotapanna vintage. While there are more in the Canon, a few stand out in relation to Swarna – moral uprightness, generosity, learnedness, leadership, comfortable life, longevity and beauty.

'Learnedness' calls for no clarification, this being formally and / or informally. 'Generosity' and 'Leadership' are clear, too, again, formally or informally. A 'comfortable life' does not mean being totally free from illness and the average complexities of life, but only speaking in relative terms, in the context of a given sociological context. 'Longevity' again needs to be understood in relative terms. While today, octogenarians may not be rare in a western context, it may be rare in other contexts. Beauty again is not easy to measure, but again only in general terms. Even though such qualities were not known while alive, there is little doubt they contributed to the quality of life in her, impacting on me as well.

Then there are the two children. Puta and Chutti. They can be seen as resources for my happiness but striving because of their own personal qualities - obedience, self-discipline, and cheery disposition in their childhood. And their own love of learning, earning their academic multi-credentials in later years, not to mention their professional success, and needless to say, their own happy family life.

So what can be said is that the family served as a visible condition for my happiness, though perhaps not always deciphered in time, for striving in my own way, throughout my life.

25.4.2 Three Countries: Sri Lanka, USA, Canada

If my parents and family are the direct human resources that have helped keep me happy and striving, there are the three countries who provided the supportive visible conditions as well – Sri Lanka, USA and Canada.

25.4.2.1 Sri Lanka

To begin with, Sri Lanka has been the home of Buddhism, the earliest variety, for 2500 years, when in the land of its origin, India, it died out. And if my parents are the primary human resource for my personal qualities, it is because of their own birth in this Buddhist land. It is also the Sinhala society I was born into and grew up in that also served as the model for living the good life.

I can talk about the high rankings of the country under National Indices such as literacy, longevity, infant mortality, etc., in contrast to other South Asian countries, or women's equality as noted by the 16th the British prisoner Robert Knox, women getting the franchise in the 1930's at a time when in Canada women were not even 'persons', the high standards of irrigation engineering as by R L Brohier, historicity of records by Wilhelm Geiger or literary quality in the medieval period by Herbert Guenther. Or I could point to the free education K to U, free health care, official recognition of all four religions – Buddhism, Hinduism, Christianity and Islam, and a host of other features in modern day society such as the richness in literature and the arts – theatre, ballet, film, etc.

This then is the quality of life that can be said to have served as conditions for my own striving for a life of quality. But also the values for everyday living. A folk poem provides an insider clue:

> *By every pretense of going to school,*
> *My small-older brother always in the bush.*
> *Just wait until I get to the Teacher's house*
> *And see the bellyful you'll get!*

First in the poem to be noted is that a younger brother has a concern for his older brother's well-being. Upon hearing that the youngster has not been kept away by some home need, or due to the distance to get to school, the Teacher is sure to let the parents know, so there would be no repeats. This care for the other also inherent of the term 'small-older brother', the reference to 'small' being the younger of two older brothers. But it is not the detail that tells the story. The 'brother' here may not necessarily mean one's own sibling, but any kid of the same age anywhere in the village. This is just as mother, father, auntie, uncle, grandpa, grandma, etc. may refer to not only your own personal relatives but anyone of a given generation. The incipient value in the Sinhala usage is how every member of a given the community is treated as a member of the family. So if everyone is related, as sentient beings, how could one have anger, hatred or enmity towards any other, or do harm?

Now to give an example of practice in my own life, when my father arrived at the Pearson Airport in Toronto for a visit, after been separated from the culture for a few years, I fell prostrate at his feet in a five-point touch – knees, elbows and forehead, in the usual Buddhist way of paying respects. Accompanying my father was the father of Swarna's sister-in-law. And I would do the five-point-touch at his feet, too, although Swarna or I had never met him. And he was to write to me later how comforting he had come to be that his daughter was in the care of good hands in a far away land.

My answer to a question by June Callwood on her National Treasure program on Vision TV (as above), gives another example of an internalized value. Arriving in Canada, one brings one's own cultural norms and behavior patterns. But they may conflict with Canadian norms and patterns. So how do you deal with it? My answer was that I would first ask, "Is what I have brought beneficial to me?" If the answer is yes, I would ask the next question: "Is it beneficial to others?" If the answer is yes, I would continue to hold on to it, but if the answer is 'no', then I would take another look, and even abandon it.

To come to the other inherent meaning in the poem is how everyone keeps an eye on every other as if to make sure that everybody toes the values line. To give an example from my own life, Tangalla is a fishing village, and pulling the net is a daily routine. While going anywhere near the ocean was a no-no to every youngster, one day, I had walked my way to the shore and was in hearing distance from the net-pullers. But soon, one of them was to approach me and ask me to head right back home. As I was to come to know later, using foul language was not unknown in the process of pulling the net heavy with fish! So it was that the villager would not want me to hear bad language.

Another value in the community is respect for learning, Buddha, of course, meaning the 'Enlightened One'. My father being a school Principal, and mom respected as well with the title 'school madame', our home was assured of a free share of the daily fish catch.

Another feature of Sinhala society, as I remember from my own Tangalla Medaketiya example, is how even the poorest of the poor with no regular income had their own piece of land to put up their own house, wattle and daub as many of them were, the gap between the rich and the poor being minimal. This kind of equality was actually something I was to see in Mao's China, as noted.

It is for the quality of social life, then, that my hometown Tangalla, symptomatic as it of the country in general, too, can then be seen as sources for my own happiness and striving, taking it to be symptomatic, though with no research. But that was not all.

This is where the first pavers were laid for my later academic path. First, it was at the Temple named Gotama Vidyalaya where I had my introduction to Sanskrit. Then there was the Catholic Christ Church College that initiated me into English, continuing at the two Buddhist schools in Colombo, Nalanda and Ananda. It was English that has facilitated my swimming in the multidisciplinary waters.

If the English language has helped me to not only earn my academic credentials, from BA to PhD, but gave the communicative skills, too, so critical did it make me accessible to Canada, making Canada accessible to me, in a reciprocity.

But most meaningfully, it was Sri Lanka that offered me the Fulbright that has made an ocean of difference for me in terms of my grasping at many an academic branch, both in the US and Canada.

So it is with much gratitude then that I can say how, although I have been away from the land of my birth for over five decades, Ceylon / Sri Lanka is the first country that provided the grounding for my happiness in my life, my striving.

So then, it looks as if what goes around has come around. But, sorry, not "Around the world in 80 days" as in French writer Jules Verne's adventure novel, but, clearly far less creative, in 80 plus years!

25.4.2.2 USA

USA is the second country resource that can be said to have contributed to my happiness and striving. First, it is the far-reaching wisdom of Senator J W Fulbright, the source of inspiration for the Fulbright-Smith Mundt scholarship program. So my initial happiness was that the scholarship was all inclusive, covering everything from travel to tuition fees to book allowance to a personal allowance, providing me a highly supportive life in an unknown land.

Then there is Dr Richard Arndt, Chair of the Fulbright selection committee, who, in my eyes, exemplifies the line, "Beauty lies in the eye of the beholder". Seeing the beauty of my background, and the potential flowering, then was the condition that provided me the basis for my later happiness.

Then there were the many caring professors, at both Penn and University of Michigan, providing the supportive conditions for building upon my interest in learning, helping towards my interdisciplinary interests

While my original scholarship was for only 10 months, facilitating my stay up to three years could be said to have been a monumental striving, bringing monumental happiness as well. The extension allowing Swarna and Puta to join me, there comes to be a return to my family happiness as well.

It is thus then the USA comes to be my second source of happiness and striving.

25.4.2.3 Canada

I need hardly argue for how Canada comes to be the third country resource, given that the Memoir is primarily about it. So the first basis for recognizing Canada as a valuable resource is again the Buddhist value of gratitude.

First it was the multicultural policy that opened up the doors to me and my family, on a points system. Both Swarna and I speaking English, and with academic credentials, and me with the additional credential of French, our family may have been among the earliest to benefit. Once in the country, it opened the doors to pursuing studies, guiding me towards an increased interdisciplinary wisdom. And allowing for opportunities for Swarna would add financial comfort for the family. Going beyond these were the wonderful opportunities offered to make my contribution to the good of the totality of the country.

When it came to my role in Buddhist leadership, after the seeds were sown, the fear, suspicion and ignorance on the way out, the quality of Buddhadhamma itself was enough for Canada to be attracted, allowing me to be the ideal social worker – one who replaces oneself to give way to a new leadership. Then, of course, were my other diverse contributions. All this can then be said to be the conditions that encouraged me in my striving as well as bring happiness.

At a surface level, many of the points made in relation to Sri Lanka, USA and Canada as above may appear to be run of the mill opportunities, but in Buddhian terms, they can be understood only in terms of conditionality, nothing in the universe being unconditioned. And so, what is outlined above, be it in relation to either or all of the three countries needs to be seen as 'visible conditions' supportive of both my happiness and striving.

'So thank you, Mother Lanka, USA and Canada!

25.5 Invisible Conditioning?

In the context of understanding reality, a treatment of the visible conditions should end the story. But a Buddhist perspective calls for going beyond, taking us to 'invisible conditions'. It is, of course, entirely possible that they may be laughed off even before we begin to look at them. Leaving that decision to the reader, it is my resoponsibility to not fail presenting them - Kammaic conditioning, leaving aside for now, past-life conditioning.

25.5.1 Watch out, Kamma Policeman on Duty 24/7!

Taking you first to Lanka, I end up in a lucrative prestigious government job that would be the envy of any, but I give it up simply to take to writing on an unstable pauperish handout. Happy as I was, just then opens up the Fulbright opportunity! It is coming to the US then that brings us to Canada.

But then, how did we end up in Canada as our long-term home, and not the US which had opened the doors to us initially? Having earned one degree at a most prestigious Ivy League university, I could well have earned any number of other degrees in the US as I did in Canada, and found employment, too. And, already with a BA in hand, and well versed in English, opportunities for Swarna would have been no less. But we end up in Canada.

Swarna now getting her credentials of Teacher training in Canada, we return to Sri Lanka, "never to return". Yet, within the year, we are back in Canada, 're-entry casualty' Award in hand.

Upon coming to Canada, it was to Montreal we were headed to, our Visa application made to a Quebec office. Going past Toronto, we make a first stop in Kingston. But, guess what, soon we were soon heading back to Toronto.

It is not as if I hadn't heard the lines,

Turn back Whittington
Lord Mayor of London.

But perhaps a variation of it was what must have made me turn around and make it to the lane in the opposite direction. So what were the lyrics that must have resonated in my ears?

Turn back, silly goose, Sugunasiri.
Toronto's where the action is, so hurry!

Where in Canada did you say I got embroiled in the action?

In Toronto, upon returning to Canada the second time, basically penniless, my doctorate comes to be funded by a graduate scholarship. Doctorate completed in 1978, and looking around in a striving, to see what next, was I to hear two newly minted poetic voices, one in each ear?

> *Can you not see the tender child of Multiculturalism*
> *Kneeling away in slow pace from Mother Colonialism,*
> *Crying for your deft hands to till the soil with professionalism*
> *Adding nourishing water, too, in needed measure, sans regionalism.*

What I mean by 'Regionalism' here is both the geographic / provincial and / or the ethnocentric particularism.

And what do I hear in the other ear?

The words of the Buddha, dinchya know, are waiting at the merry ferry,
To make multicultural Canada, coast to coast, healthy, wealthy and sans worry!

Is this then not what allowed me to till the soil and plant the seeds of Buddhism in Canada and fertilize the soil for Multiculturalism in its diverse fields?

While the multicultural seed had been planted by the Prime Minister, Hon. Pierre Elliott Trudeau in 1971, I had completed my doctorate (1978) when the multicultural policy had received legal standing (1979). But there were no 'experts', or locals, in the field - government or non- governmental, white or non-white, academic or non-academic, to spread the seeds, i.e., introduce multiculturalism to Canadians, if also to water. So how it is that my hands came to be free just in the nick of time?

Then there was the opening up of an opportunity to write a column for *Toronto Star,* with a million plus readers, to spread the seeds, my membership at the Advisory Council allowing the opportunity to help water.

Could you please then tell me how all these happened the way they did? The sceptic's standard words would be, "Oh, just coincidence"! Oh, thank you. I now have an additional student in my English Linguistics course at the Faculty of Education, University of Toronto. "Dear students, 'coincidence' is a fancy way of saying 'happened at the same time' (-incidence + co-). It is no 'explanation' but a mere linguistic 'register' variant – High English (or Queen's English, if in a British context), to replace the phrase 'something happening at the same time' in colloquial jargon!" But saying something in a different register is surely not to provide an explanation.

So, unless someone can kindly come up with a better explanation, what I see captured in the poems then is 'invisible conditioning'. In more Buddhian terms, 'kammaic conditioning', kamma meaning both action and result.

You can laugh all the way...., but my answer is kamma kamma kamma – the principle of kamma. Or the Policeman Kamma on 24/7 duty!!

To give you even a heartier laugh, it is what both Swarna and I had brought from our past lives. But let's stop it right there while you're still enjoying....!

But can I be kindly allowed a re-visit to my parents' expectations? Do all of the above show how my life has been one of happiness but yet striving?

Now it is important that while I have in these pages looked to flush out reasons for my happiness encouraging striving, it is not that I had consciously sought them out at the point of any particular conduct. It was simply that a given value or norm was embedded in me to generate the particular thought and action. Also, while I have dragged on the words '[and] striving' in talking about happiness, it is not that the sources were themselves behind the striving, but rather that the striving was a natural response to the happiness.

25.6 A Final Striving

In a letter of the early 1980's, my father tells me that the horoscope I have had is in error! Gee, thanks! If that brings to question this entire business of horoscopes, and horoscope readings, let me hasten to add that it has never ever had any bearing on my life. Certainly not in my marriage either, when it has been very much so among my own friends. It has never had a role in any of the decisions or a course of action or a direction taken by me.

But apparently it was important to my dad. In the same letter, he says that, on the basis of a re-writing and a re-reading of my horoscope, he exults that I have come upon this birth from a *deva loka*, the world of deities, and that I will be headed there again.

This brings me more than a fair share of happiness since, as noted, Prince Siddhartha the future Buddha had descended from heaven. And the mother Queen herself ends in heaven. So, in good company in both directions, should I be happy?

But this is still to be on the 'Path to Heaven' (*sagga magga*), as in the Buddha's characterization. I ended the first section of this chapter by saying that I have achieved all but one of my aspirations, holding you in suspense as to just what that 'but one' might be. I hope your patience will not have been in vain when the secret comes out of its place of hiding. Ready then?

Throughout my life, my striving has been for the social good, the personal good never far behind. In my sunset years, it is no disrespect to my father that my final aspiration is not to be reborn in Heaven as a Deva, but **TO BE NOT BORN AT ALL**! In other words, my goal is liberation from *samsara*, the cycle of birth-death-birth.... So what I have yet to achieve is that *summum bonum* – Nibbana, an end to the cycle of life, the *unborn* (or 'not born') as it has been characterized. So there! You're now privy to the secret!

Now in many a place in this Memoir, you may see what could be seen as shades of attachment on my part, from zip to hip. My parents, Swarna and children, and the three countries – Sri Lanka, the US and Canada. But I can say in all honesty that all that is by way of reporting on historical fact, and presenting an objective description. I am certainly grateful to all those who have made my life happy, and kept me in my striving gear. But I want to say that my predilection is to have nary an attachment, this, of course, for the reason that experiencing Nibbana results from eliminating all attachment.

So, at the end of writing these Memoirs I can say I am indeed happy but still striving for that ultimate goal. But with no attachment even to come by it, that itself being taint enough to stymie any chance of success!

25.7 A Final Bow

Thank you, dear reader, for your patience, and for your company through the pages. Hope you have enjoyed the ride, benefiting from the happiness of a fellow human being, always up to the mischief of striving! I hope you have enjoyed reading it as I have enjoyed writing it. If the poems added a touch of lightness and entertainment, that would make me even happier.

This Memoir has been called *Happy But Striving: Memoirs of a Buddhist Canadian.* Hope it is clear why it has been slated as the Memoir of a *Buddhist* Canadian. What you will have seen in this tome is a Buddhist in action, giving an insight into what is entailed in being Buddhist. You will have seen that it is not to spend all of one's time at a temple, or being engaged in ritual or sit in meditation. While they all have their own intrinsic value, it is not to stop living a normal lay life, living in a way that is good for the many, for the well-being of the many, but never ever forgetting myself. This is equally a way of living a 'Buddhist' life, making sure as well to critically maintain a regular health regimen. What was also critical to be kept in mind at all times was that the reins were always in my hands, in the full knowledge that the Buddha is only the teacher. It was also to be confident that I and I alone was to reap the benefits or suffer the consequnces of my own conduct in mind, body and word. And I could also vouch that the benefits or the sufferings of my conduct were experienced in this very life, short term and long term.

If this Memoir then serves as an encouragement and inspiration to be your best at all times, Buddhist or other, facing the vicissitudes of life with a smile, then all my efforts will have been well worth it.

Thank you again, and the best in health and happiness!

Thank you my family. Thank you Lanka, thank you USA, thank you Canada.

Thank you Tangalla, Thank you Colombo, Thank you Philadelphia, Thank you Ann Arbour and Thank you Toronto!

In Metta friendliness!

-

NEW TERMS

Adiyana 159, 219, 221
Autosociobiography XVIII
Buddhadhamma 40, 327, 330, 331, 335
Buddhian 329, 335, 337
Buddhianized 40
Buddhianscience 315
Buddhianscientific 203, 211
Buddhistan 197
Colonialitis 281
Crintfreeth 312, 328
Dhammexplorer 286
Englishitis 281
Idiospirituality 200
Introscope 203
Linguality 151
Mom of Religion and Dad of Science 200
MSUP – Mind-Sensory Ultra Perception 319
Multireligism 152
Religioscape (cf landscape) 153
Scientificity
Sci-Spi (Science of Spirituality) 199
Sociospirituality 199
Spirituality 199
Spirituometer 153
Sponsoree 188, 189
Terroritis 281
Westernscience 314, 315, 318, 319

POEMS INDEX

Livin' w'm'n 48

An Ode to a Golden One 61

The unbeatable beat 66

Cry of the great bird 136

Deck the halls 139

Rock-a-bye cell 172

Questions of the night 197

The congee pot of the seven aandiyas 230

Between worlds 252

Disarming death 268

The knight at the square 271

Buried at last 273

You touched me 274

Tale of a ravine footpath 275

Waves of cuba 278

Hawai'ian memoirs 294

On toilets (or is it 'toilettes'?) 298

In the realm of hungry ghosts 305

The many names of the one 321

PLACE INDEX

A
Acapulco 286, 293, 301
Adam's Peak 307
Africa 6, 6, 52, 66, 67, 98, 104, 106, 107, 135, 150, 173, 194, 247, 264
Ajanta 39
Alberta 74, 99, 233
Amsterdam 268, 269
Ann Arbor 11, 13, 14, 15, 17, 20, 25, 27, 43, 290, 292
Anuradhapura 159, 307, 309, 310
Ashbridges Bay 54
Auckland 300
Aurora 164
Austen 257
Australia 245, 280, 298, 299
Austria 48, 236, 239, 269, 295, 298

B
Badulla 307
Banff 104, 105
Barrie 253, 264, 265
Beijing 49, 50, 269
Benarese 40
Berkeley 134
Boston 133, 136
Boulder 99, 133, 165, 208, 229
Bowmanville 255
British Columbia 30, 89, 99, 108, 157, 170, 180, 181, 186, 194, 229, 233, 240, 248, 327
Brock 205, 229, 233
Buddhgaya 39, 212
Buffalo 153, 196
Bulgaria 38
Burlington 243
Burma 80, 81, 134

C
Calais 295
Calcutta 280
Calgary 99, 224, 229, 233, 251, 269, 292
California 3, 17, 19, 23, 141, 286

Cape Canavarel 26
Cape Spear 291
Caribbean 61, 66, 292, 300
Champlain 190
Chicago 3, 24, 138, 139, 279, 313
China 44, 46, 48, 49, 50, 51, 53, 80, 96, 97, 159, 209, 237, 248, 270, 334
Cocoa Beach 25
Colombo 43, 56, 73, 78, 269, 296, 302, 304, 320, 331, 334, 339
Colorado 25, 133, 158, 165, 208, 229, 292
Cuba 245, 276, 277, 278
Czechoslovakia 36, 38

D
Denmark 35, 36, 294
Detroit 27, 290
Dominican Republic 292

E
Edmonton 99, 132, 163, 164, 190, 292
Ellora 39
England 6, 126, 179, 294
Etobicoke 246, 247, 257
Europe 35, 44, 103, 247

F
Florida 23, 25, 292
Forest Hill 15, 57, 178, 180, 195, 274, 328
France 193, 269, 295, 297
Fraser Valley 99, 291
Fredricton 269

G
Georgian Bay 183
Germany 295
Grand Canyon 25, 292
Greece 37, 80
Guelph 107
Guyana 80, 107

H
Haight-Ashbury 24, 141
Halifax 73, 158, 164, 241

Place Index

Hamilton 140, 141, 158, 258, 265
Havana 276, 278
Hawai'i 65, 292, 293
Hong Kong 47, 49, 51, 80, 99, 99, 134, 229, 229, 264
Hull 292

I
India 16, 37, 39, 42, 45, 47, 69, 80, 82, 85, 90, 91, 95, 98, 106, 107, 109, 110, 158, 159, 209, 236, 240, 250, 251, 269, 275, 278, 282, 287, 306, 328, 332
Ireland 90, 107
Isipatana 40
Italy 295, 296, 297

J
Jaffna 100, 307
Japan 22, 24, 44, 45, 134
Jeta Grove 41

K
Katunayaka 42, 42, 302, 302
Kenya 101
Kingston 27, 28, 138, 149, 176, 290, 336
Kinmount 157
Kolkata 280
Korea 22, 134, 136, 264
Kusinagar 42
Kusinara 40, 42, 212

L
La Guardia 53
Las Vegas 292
Latin America 65, 64, 66
Laverne 190
Lindsay 256
London 1, 4, 6, 17, 37, 99, 149, 172, 214, 239, 243, 247, 269, 272, 294, 298, 301, 306
Los Angeles 23, 24, 229, 286, 292, 292
Lumbini Park 212

M
Malabe 2
Malaysia 85, 306
Manitoba 66, 180, 194

Manoa 304
Markham 117, 238
Maryland 158, 165, 253
Meech Lake 239
Melbourne 298, 299
Mexico 301
Michigan 11, 13, 16, 17, 29, 73, 80, 96, 98, 279, 290, 292, 335
Mihintale 40
Mississauga 54, 84, 86, 90, 91, 111, 147, 168, 175, 177, 208, 256
Monte Carlo 297
Montreal 4, 19, 28, 30, 46, 99, 113, 163, 164, 233, 290, 336
Moorhead 281
Moscow 38, 53, 136
Mt. Lavinia 2, 302
Muskoka 183

N
Naramata 137
Netherlands 126
New Brunswick 194, 290
Newfoundland 151, 163, 170, 201, 246, 263, 264, 291, 292, 300
New Guinea 304
New York 6, 12, 25, 53, 153, 292
New Zealand 245, 300
Nigeria 69
North York 65, 82, 117, 148, 171, 262
Norway 35, 36
Nova Scotia 73, 127, 158

O
Ottawa 46, 83, 85, 98, 101, 106, 143, 144, 163, 164, 170, 180, 184, 194, 202, 229, 233, 240, 242, 244, 250, 272, 292

P
Pacific Coast 23
Panadura 2, 43, 316
Paris 5, 6, 272, 295, 297, 298
Peel 111, 296
Pennsylvania 2, 3, 4, 11, 12, 13, 71, 72, 96, 247, 286, 299, 303
Peradeniya 30, 38, 72, 214, 282, 293, 299, 304

Peterborough 116
Philadelpia 2
Polonnaruwa 165, 310, 311
Port Hope 258, 265
Prince Edward Islands 107, 290, 291
Punjab 99
Q
Quang Dung 49
Quebec 170, 190, 192, 193, 233, 248, 290, 292, 336
R
Rockies 99, 291
Rome 296, 297, 298
Rotarua 300
Roumania 38
S
S. Korea 264
Saheth Maheth 41, 269, 287
Salt Lake Desert 292
San Francisco 18, 19, 21, 22, 23, 27, 141, 292,
Saranath 39
Saskatchewan 229, 233, 236
Saskatoon 235, 236, 237, 275
Savatthi 39, 41, 269, 287
Scarborough 190, 257, 258, 263
Seoul 134, 269
Shantiniketan 306
Sierra Leone 22
Sigiriya 39, 270, 288, 292, 297, 298
Simcoe 190, 257
South India 82
Soviet 1, 26, 36, 37, 38, 39, 294, 306
Sripada 137
St Catherines 205
St John's 291
Sudbury 99
Swan River 190
Switzerland 295, 297
T
Taiwan 49, 229
Tangalla 23, 317, 331, 334, 339
Tanzania 245
Thailand 69, 134, 139, 159, 165, 167, 229

Tokyo 45, 49, 269
Trent 116
U
UK 4, 6, 17, 34, 35, 72, 76, 105, 124, 148, 149, 173, 194, 214, 269, 272, 294, 295, 301, 313
V
Vancouver 99, 100, 101, 134, 148, 157, 163, 164, 249, 291
Vancouver Island 164
Varadero 276, 278
Varanasi 40
Vatican City 136
Venice 297
Victoria 6, 89, 163, 168, 186, 229, 233, 244, 249, 291, 292
Vienna 239, 272, 297
Vietnam 16, 80
W
Waikiki Beach 291, 293, 294
Wales 269, 295
Washington 5, 25, 86, 107, 136, 286, 292
Washington DC 5, 25, 292
Waterloo 88, 141
Wellington 265
Western Ontario 67, 73, 125, 172, 180, 185, 233
Windsor 27, 73, 163, 164, 183, 207, 290
Windsor-Riverside 183
Winnipeg 10, 98, 99, 107, 122, 164, 229, 241, 272, 292
Woodbine Beach 54
Y
Yugoslavia 38, 48, 80

NAME INDEX

A

Abramovich, Rhona 208
Adachi, Ken 105
Adam, Martin 233
Ahmad, Iqbal 106
Aitken, John 298
Ajhan, Viradhammo 85
Aklujkar, Ashok 99
Aldrin, Buzz 26
Alexander, Lincoln 73, 176, 193, 198, 238, 285
Alexander the Great 37
Alice 6, 7, 248, 265
Allen, Steve 257
Allport, Gordon 238, 243
Almeida, Douglas 6
Amaradeva, W D 4, 89, 90, 306
Amarasekara, Gunadasa 4, 89, 287
Amore, Roy 207
Amunugama, Sarath 296
Andrew, Prince 73,
Angelou, Maya 128
Arahant Mahinda 5, 40, 270, 274
Arahant Sanghamitta 40, 270
Ariyarajah, Wesley 135
Ariyaratna, A T 70, 77
Armstrong, Neil 26, 147, 287
Arndt, Richard 2, 335
Arnold, Edwin 211
Arunajith, Upul 309
Ashraf, Muhammed 143
Aster, Howard 106, 280
Atwood, Margaret 108, 126, 132, 287
Aung, Steven 132, 133, 164
Aunt Edna 22
Aw, William 81
Aziz, Nurjehan 102

B

Baetz, Rueben 175
Bancroft, George 122, 175, 198
Bandara, Lanka 295
Bandaranaike, Sirimavo 56, 70, 301
Bandaranaike, S W R D 106, 192, 305
Barbara 176, 189, 190, 258
Bassel, William P 180
Bawa, Jeffrey 309
Beaman, Nancy 93
Beaudoin-Dobbie 143, 144
Beck, Brenda 99, 180
Beck, Clive 32
Bellana, Indrani 83, 84
Bennett, Carolyn 194, 195
Bennett, Michael 284
Bentley, Christopher 225
Berman, Michael 233
Berry, Thomas 150
Berthrong, John 133, 137, 180
Bhaggiyadatta, Krishanta Sri 89, 106
Bharthrhari 320
Bhattacharya, Swagata 280
Bhikkhu Ananda 95, 96
Bhikkhu Nagasena 37
Bhikkhuni Dewasara 159
Bhikkhuni Man Yi 208
Birbalsingh, Frank 101, 122, 123, 281
Birch, Margaret 176
Bissoondath, Neil 101, 105, 106, 119, 131, 255
Black, Ken 183
Blair, Tony 173
Blatchford, Christie 128
Blavatsky, Madame Helena 43, 316
Bodhinayaka, Karuni 295, 301
Boisvert, Mathieu 228, 233
Bondar, Roberta 128
Bopearacchi 37
Borovilos, John 91
Bouchard, Lucien 192
Boucher, Sandy 134
Boyagoda, Randy 101, 106
Boyd, George 241
Bradman, Don 298
Brande, Dionne 194

Brandt, Andrew S. 176, 179
Brief, Fredelle 140, 141
Brieger, Tracey 116
Brodie, Jari 241
Brohier, R L 333
Brown, Ian 128
Brown, Rosemary 132
Brown, Stuart 143
Brundage, Donald 69
Buchan, John 256
Buddha 5, 37, 37, 40, 41, 42, 45, 55, 70, 79, 94, 95, 132, 138, 142, 147, 153, 154, 157, 159, 160, 161, 165, 169, 170, 175, 177, 183, 201, 203, 210, 211, 221, 234, 235, 248, 261, 263, 267, 268, 269, 282, 287, 302, 303, 307, 308, 310, 311, 313, 315, 318, 318, 322, 327, 328, 330, 331, 332, 334, 337, 338, 339
Buddhadasa 295
Buddhaghosa 214
Buddhiprabha, Prapart 69
Burke, Mavis 115, 129, 186
Burkhardt, Heidi 276
Burkhardt, Helmut 54, 199, 202
Burstinzky, Ed 31
Butler, Rhett 256
Butovsky, Lillian 58

C

Caccia, Charles 127
Cairney, Jim 141
Callwood, June 122, 128, 131, 333
Caplan, Gerald/Gerry 63, 64, 181, 187
Cardona, George 9
Carr, William 12
Case, Fredrick 67
Castro, Fidel 276, 277
Castro, Raul 276
Chandrasekharan, Shan 84
Charon, Millie 253, 283
Chattopadhyay, Suchorita 280
Chaudhary, Darshan 157, 158
Chaudron, Craig 69
Che Guevara 276, 278

Chen, Eric 208
Cherniak, David 209
Chhem, Rethi 233
Chilton, David 128
Ching, Julia 207
Chitra 73, 74, 307
Chodron, Pema 165
Choi, Glenn 228, 243
Chomsky, Noam 2, 247
Chretien, Jean 146
Clark, Joe 73, 112, 143, 145, 184, 186, 187, 187, 191
Clarke, Austin 102
Clarkson, Adrienne 95
Clayden, Marie 128
Close, Glen 256
Collenette, David 184
Collins, Steven 313
Collure, Palita 33
Cook, Dave 183
Cook, Suzanne 70
Coppola, Carlo 279
Cormier, Louis 164, 290
Craig, Ian 28,
Crombie, David 191
Crusz, Rienzie 88, 89, 106, 107
Cuthbert, Linda 119

D

Dabydeen, Cyril 106, 254, 272
Dai Shi 218
Daluwatta, Shanika 286
Dassanayaka, Ari 34
Daudlin, Bob 190
David, Dan 241
Davids, Rhys 211, 313
Davies, Richard 128, 285
Davis, William/ Bill 94, 114, 175, 186, 238
Day, Rene A 126
Dei, George 150
Delgado, Carlos 278
Demb, Connie 210
de Santana, Hubert 90, 106
de Silva, Edward 33, 76

de Silva, Lakshmi 89
de Silva, Sugatapala 2, 17
de Soyza, Tilaka 216
Deverell, Rita 130, 131, 250
Dhammavasa, Ven. Kulugammana 173
Dhanjal 107
Dharmapala, Anagarika 24, 42, 138
Dhirasekara, Jotiya 35, 214
Dickinson, Bill 209
Diefenbaker, John 95
DiGiovanni, Caroline 143
Dillon, Pam 220
Dodge, Alice 6
Dolittle, Elga 256
Donyol 22
Doobay, Bhudendra 143
Dorenwend, Doris 208
Dorje, Shakya 208
Downey, Peter 239
Draper, James 64
Dresden, Prof. 10
Dumont, Yvon 194
Dunphy, Bill 117
D'Sousa, Philip 107

E

Edighoffer, Hugh 183
Edirisinghe, Padma 281
Eggleton, Art 161
Eichler, Margrit 74, 150, 180
Ekanayaka, Stanley 29
Elizabeth 252, 257
Elliston, Inez 75
Eng, Susan 196, 198, 248
Enros, Prajna 101
Ewart, Vian 118

F

Faiz, Andrew 107
Farquarson, Walter 134
Farrell, Joe 64, 66, 285
Fefferman, Stanley 130, 133, 163
Fenn, Mavis 208
Fenner, Dianne 128
Fernando, Lionel 302

Ferretti, Janine 170
Fields, Rick 122,
Fins, Paula 157, 158
Fish, Susan 176, 188, 198,
Fleming, Jim 241
Flemington, Peter 130
Fontaine, Phil 132
Forrester, Maureen 132
Fox, Matthew 150
Franklin, Ursula 150
Fraser, Mary 140, 283
Frazer, Catherine 183
Frye, Northrop 287
Fujikawa, Sensei 157, 160
Fulbright, J. W. 5

G

Gagarin, Yuri 26
Galbraith, John Kenneth 46,
Gamalath, Sucarita 89
Garnet 257
Garrett, Frances 233
Gee, Michael 195
Geiger, Wilhelm 9, 237, 333
Gelberman, Rabbi Joseph 283
Ghiz, Joe 127
Gill, Laksmi 107
Ginkle, Eileen Van 143
Goar, Carol 190
Goliath 326
Gombrich, Richard 313
Goodman, Harvey 117
Gool, Reshard 104, 107, 180, 290
Gotlieb, Rabbi D. 143
Green, Joan M 249
Greer, Germaine 29
Gross, Rita 30, 208
Grossman, Larry 180
Guenther, Herbert 9, 233, 234, 235, 236, 333
Guenther, Ilse 235, 237, 275
Gunananda, Ven. Migettuwatte 43
Gunaratana, Bhante 86
Gunaratna, Shelton 281
Gunasinghe, Hemamali 89

Gunasinghe, Siri 89, 270, 291
Gunatunga, Sunil 83
Gunawardhana, Dayananda 83
Gunawardhana, Phillip 36
Guruge, Ananda 3
Gzowski, Peter 128, 138,

H

Hamilton, Doreen 158
Harbaugh, Christine 18
Hardman, Paul 133, 157, 158
Hardy, Thomas 256
Harney, Robert 87
Harnwel, Gaylord P 17
Harpur, Tom 130, 250, 258
Harris, Mike 265
Hassam, Cathy 102
Hayes, Richard 207
Head, Wilson 178, 180, 186
Heisig, James 135
Henderson, Jim 95
Hewage, L. 70
Hill, Daniel 73
Hitchcock, Peter 133
Hla Hla, Khin 216
Hnatishin, Ray 146
Ho, Lok Sang 157, 158
Hoenigswald, M. 11
Holmes, Penny 243
hooks, bell 150
Hori, Victor 4, 207, 208, 217, 220, 232, 233, 327
Hubbard, Ron 178
Hughes, James J. 170
Humber, Charles J 73, 130
Hutt, William 132
Huxley, Aldous 189
Hyatt, Corinne 93

I

Ianuzzi, Dan 84
Ijaz, Helene 117
Ituen, Sam 69
Itwaru, Arnold 107

J

Jameison, G A 200
James, William 24
Jantzen, William 143
Jayadeva 2, 38, 286
Jayanta 6
Jayasinghe, Shyamon 299
Jayasumana 320, 321, 323, 324, 330
Jennings, Sir Ivor 1
Jones, Philip F. 171, 246
Joseph, Francis 297
Juliet 248

K

Kabat-Zinn, Jon 234
Kabilsingh, Chatsumarn 139, 209
Kalsey, Surjeet 101, 102, 107
Kalupahana, David 293
Kanaganayakam, Chelva 89, 100, 270, 271, 280
Kanter, Ron 182
Kapitany, Robert 164
Karen (Mrs.) 150, 256
Karunesh 83
Kate 228, 244
Kawamura, Leslie 224, 233, 234
Kawwida, Ashin 227
Keast, Ron 130
Keaton, Michael 256
Keith, A B 4
Kekulawala, Sumana Lal 71
Kelly, Norm 190
Kelly, Paul 228
Kennedy John F. 46
Kendall, Ronald 93
Kernahan, Deo 130, 131
Kerr, Michael 158
Keuneman, Peiter 37
Khanh, Lekim 158
Khenrab, Ven. Geshe 164
Kher, Inder Nath 99
Khosla, Meetu 243
Kidd, Roby 63, 67, 77, 79, 185, 186
King Asoka 40
King Devanampiya Tissa 274, 309

King Dutugemunu 308
King James 246
King Kassapa 39, 137, 138
King Menander 37
King Parakramabahu 110, 288, 310
King Suddhodana 40
Kinsela, Noel 194
Kirkland, Glen 128, 285
Klevnick, Linda 161
Klima, George 157
Knox, Robert 333
Ko, Alan 243
Kogawa, Joy 95, 128
Kohl, Rabbi Frydman 142
Koppedrrayer, Kay 233
Kostash, Myrna 128
Kumaratunga, Chandrika 301
Kurasawa 288
Kuruppu, Baldwin 78, 299

L

Lam, David 194, 241
Lamont, Corliss 152
Landau, Richard 132, 133, 242
Lao Tzu 152
Laurence, Margaret 105, 108, 287
Layton, Irving 127
Leacock, Stephen 128
Leary, Timothy 24
Lee, Ching An 215
Lee, Vansen 158, 164
Lee, Vivian 172
Lerner, Michael 150
Levine, Howard 196
Levman, Bryan 168
Lewis, David 112
Lewis, Stephen 184, 187
Lewis, Steven 181
Lewycky, Laverne 190
Li, Franz 216
Ling, Trevor 177
Lisker, Prof. 8, 9
Livingstone, David 64, 74
Lockhead, David 134
Logan, Madge 117

London, Rhonda 243
Long, Joshua 205
Lowe, Keith 150
Ludwik, Catherine 207, 208
Lwin, Nanda 276

M

MacLean, Paul 315
Mahamaya 40, 212
Mahapajapati Gotami 40
Mainse, David 242
Maiterth, Karlheinz 125
Majhanovich, Suzanne 125
Malini 28, 294
Mandela, Nelson 128
Manning, Steve 124
Mao Tes-Tung 113
Marasinghe, Lakshman 164
Marchi, Sergio 183
Marcus, Paul 117
Marion 257
Marmur, Rabbi 141
Maseman, Vandra 150, 290
Masi, Ralph 149
Master Tam 229
Mathews, Bruce 86, 315
Maupassant 287
Maureen 112, 132, 262
McAdam, Christine 128
McAteer, Maureen 112
McAteer, Michael 138, 139, 145, 241, 244
McAvity, Charles 148
McCaffrey, Bruce 114, 161, 175, 176
McCauley, Gary 190
McClaymont, Christine 128, 285
McDougal, Barbara 176, 190
McFarlane, Mrs. 2
McGifford, Dianne 272
McGuinty, Dalton 195
McIntyre, Thomas 215
McIvor, Mrs. 15, 21, 27
McKay, William 93
McLaughlin, Audrey 144
McLean, Walter F 144, 188, 189

McLellan, Janet 4, 208, 214, 217, 220, 232, 327
McLeod, Keith 75
McMullen, Neil 208,
McMurtry, Roy 94, 114, 176
Mehran, Toni 140, 141
Mehta, Deepa 241
Mendis, Tyrell 89
Mercier, Donna 266
Miklos 262
Miller, Arthur 287
Miller, Keith 298
Miosi, Frank 209
Mishra, Vijay 272
Missinona 74
Mistry, Rohinton 101, 106, 287
Mock, Karen 150
Mohideen, Alavi 85
Moon, Simon 208
Moore, Michal 264
Morson, Aldo 81
Mougeon, Raymond 64, 70
Mowat, Farley 128, 132
Mowat, Susan 28
Muinuddin, Muin 130
Mukherjee, Alok 90, 177, 183
Mukherjee, Arun 102, 106
Mullens, James 233
Muller, Helmfried 133
Mullin, Glen 164, 165, 244
Mulroney, Brian 143, 146, 175, 238, 251
Munroe, Lily 115, 116, 179
Murakami, Toshi 164
Muriel 259
Muriel, Mrs 256
Murta, Jack 184

N
Nadia 257
Nalini 299
Nancy 93, 255
Needham, Ed 238, 239
Negru, John 158, 163, 284
Nehru 42, 158, 320

New, William H. 108
Newman, Paul 136, 137, 150, 286
Ng, Roxana 150
Nguyen, Kim 216
Nicholls, John 114, 161, 186
Nicholson, Graeme 209
Nimaldas, W S P 307
Norton, Tom 32
Nostbakken, David 130

O
Obama 60, 66, 197, 229, 230, 276, 278, 321, 327
Olcott, Henry Steele 43, 316
Olendzky, Andrew 228
Ondaatje, Christopher 88
Ondaatje, Michael 89, 101, 106, 287
Orchard, Tom 88
Oxtoby, Will 134, 207, 209

P
Padmini 6, 295
Painter, R H 262
Palavecino, Miguel 164
Paproski, Steve 190
Parameswaran, Uma 98, 99, 107, 122
Paranavitana, Senarath 270, 287
Paranvitana, Sonny 278
Partridge, Kate 228
Patel, Sheriyar 125
Pathy, Alex 210
Paul, Pauline 126
Pearl 303
Perera, Aloy 82, 85, 284
Perera, Hema 82, 83
Perera, Nimal 83, 85
Perera, Ranjini 149
Persaud, Sasenerine 107
Peterson, David 115, 116, 177, 238
Phillips, Marlene Nourbese 124
Piper, John 90,
Plautt, Rabbi Guenther143
Pope 148, 179, 296
Poy, Vivienne 168
Pratt, E. J. 128
Prebish, Charles 207, 208

Name Index

Preuter, Ken 69
Price, Ed 248
Priestley, Leonard 34, 71, 208, 210, 214, 221, 233
Prieto, Claire 241
Probyn, Jean 93
Punchihewa, P. G. 32, 303
Punnadhammo, Ajahn 315
Punnaji, Bhante 85, 160, 213
Purdy, Al 108

Q

Queen Elizabeth 248
Queen Mahamaya 40
Qureshi, M H K 102,

R

Rabgey, Pencho 216
Rae, Bob 73, 143
Rahula 40, 44
Rainsbury, Fred 64
Rajanayagam, Solomon 29
Rajanayagam, Rosalind 29
Rajapaksa, Deepthi 83
Ramona 257
Ramses, Veronique 168, 243
Rapaport, Anatole 199
Ratanasara, Ven. Haevaenpola 286
Rathanasiri, Ven. Ahangama 227
Rathbun, Catherine 215
Ray, Douglas 63, 67, 180, 185, 186, 285
Reed, Jim 173
Rhine, J. B 319
Richards, Gerry 69
Rinpoche, Khenpo Sonam 208
Ritter, Erika 128, 239
Rivera, Chita 175
Roach, Charles 111, 112, 113
Robert 87, 112, 149, 164, 208, 266, 333
Rodewalt 251
Rogers, Larry 57
Romeo 248
Rowlands, June 195, 196
Russell, Bertrand 38, 128, 320

Ryan, William P. 202
Rye, William 180
Ryerson, Egerton 94,

S

Saddhatissa, Ven. Hammalawa 34, 35, 214
Sainte-Marie, Buffy 132
Salmond, Noel 233
Salyajivin, Mongkhol 164
Sandler, Mark 117
Sapir, Edward 320
Saracchandra, Ediriweera 4, 38, 39, 45, 89, 287
Sarah 22
Saram, P A 233
Saranapala, Bhante 168, 208, 217, 220
Sarwana, Ahmad 10
Sathasivam 12
Sauve, Jeanne 127
Saylor, Randy 81
Scarlet 256
Schopenhauer 189
Scott, E. W. 143
Sellar, Don 171
Selvadurai, Shyam 83, 101, 106
Selvadurai, Steven 83
Sen, Joya 69
Senanayaka, D S 05
Senanayaka, G B 270, 287
Serge, Joe 162, 248
Seshadri, C K 69, 282
Shakespeare 39, 91, 246, 247, 256, 284, 288
Shaneman, Jhampa 164, 168
Shanti 6
Sharf, Robert 208
Sharp, Sheena 123, 173
Sheldrake, Rupert 315
Sheriff, Hassan 85, 86
Shields, Carol 128
Shiu, Henry 220, 229, 233
Shiva, Vandana 150
Siddhartha, Prince 5, 40, 338
Sigmund, Sternberg 149

Silva, Nihal 83
Silva, Sauris 55, 74, 317
Simmer-Brown, Judith 208
Simpson, Mo 286
Singh, Manohar 143
Singh, Sher 182
Singh, Vara 128, 129
Sing Hung, Fa-shih 158, 164, 213, 229
Sirisena, K M 38
Siriwardhena, C. W. 298
Sister Benedetta 132, 133, 134
Skelton, Robin 287
Skinner, Peter 239
Slater, Peter 207
Smith 5, 303, 335
Soares, Suzy 243
Soeng, Mu 228
Sokei-an Sasaki 232
Southworth, Franklin 9, 15
Stanfield, Robert 112
Steiman, Lionel 10, 14, 66, 99, 180
Steinkrauss, Whipple 180
Sternberg, Sir Sigmund 149
Stiller, Brian 143, 145
Strauss, Christine 128
Stroh, Rabbi M. 200
Stronach, Belinda 173
Subasingha, Somalatha 302
Sudds, Keith 205
Sue Wanda 326
Sugathadasa 6
Sugune 14, 324
Su Hae Ja 324
Sujata 139, 161, 304
Suji 10, 11, 325
Sullivan, Edmund 150
Sumegi, Angela 233
Sunanda 73, 74, 303
Sunim, Kwang Ok 135, 213
Sunim, Samu 141, 161, 213
Suraweera, A V 88, 89, 306
Surendra, Rathi 85
Sutherland, Roland 105, 108,
Sutherland, Wilber 143

Sutton, James W. 253
Suzanne 7, 70, 125
Suzuki, David 127, 128, 285
Swarna [Sugunasiri] 58, 62, 220, 316

T

Taché, Father Alexander 143
Tall, Frank 215, 216, 217
Tennant, Sue 283
Terpstra, John 80
Than, Rosemary 141, 158, 164, 165
Thorpe, Michael 108
Tilakaratne, Sirisena 28
Timmerman, Peter 199, 208, 215
Titcombe, Brent 160, 161
Tito 38
Toneatto, Tony 231
Trieger, Seymour 28
Trudeau, Justin 128
Trudeau, Pierre Elliot 238, 337
Trungpa, Chogyam 133, 158, 165,
Trungpa, Rinpoche 166, 229
Tsiolkovsky 26
Tsomo 209
Tsubouchi, David 117
Tsunoda, Sensei 157, 213
Tun Winn, Brian 164
Turner, John 111, 178, 190
Tutu, Bishop 191

U

Ubale, Bhausaheb 176, 198
Uncle Cy 22

V

Vajitkova, Eva 36
Vandezande, Gerald 143
Vanier, Jean 257
Vasheeharan 12
Vassanji, M G 101, 103
Veillette, Miechel 190
Vennen, Robert Vander 149
Verne, Jules 334
Vimal 264
Vinnels, Dick 146
Visser, Margaret 128
Volz, Peter 164

W

Wagle, Narendra 208
Walker, Susan 265
Wallis, Jan 264
Warder, A K 34, 71, 208, 214, 217, 270
Wasala, Rohana Ranaweera 280, 282
Waterhouse, David 134, 208, 209
Watson, Glenn 246
Weeramuni, Malini 28, 294
Weeramuni, Namel 294
Weeramuni, Slushna 194, 294, 297, 300
Weerasingha, Asoka 106
Weerasinghe, Dhanasiri 89, 299
Wees, Wilfred 33
Weiner, Gerry 147, 194, 196, 238, 251
Weldon, Pat 123, 327
Wendy 276
Wertheimer, Max 312
Wickramasinghe, Martin 4, 39, 287
Wiebe, Don 71, 149, 209, 215, 217, 221, 233
Wije(tunga) 304
Wilbur, Ken 33
Williams, Beverly 126,
Williams, Melissa 202, 274
Wilson, David 33, 65, 66, 290
Wimalabuddhi, Ven. Udupihille 227
Winn, Paul 241
Winters, Dennis 209
Wirasinghe, Chandana 99
Wiseman, Herb 265
Wittacchi, Tarzie 303
Wolf, Ken 239
Wong, Bob 182, 198
Wong, Clement 216
Wong, Jan 46
Wong, Jason 220
Woo, Terry 208
Woolnough, Hilda 290
Wright, Grace 69

Y

Yeramian, Jake 32
Young, Judy 98, 180, 191
Young, Lyle 149
Young, Syd 182
Yun, Hsin 229

Z

Zachariah, Mathew 99
Zasep Tulku Rinpoche 158, 167, 213
Ziemba, Ed 184, 251
Ziemba, Elaine 183

WORKS BY THE AUTHOR (Selected)

A. ARTICLES

The author has published over 300 articles, academic and popular, both in English and Sinhala. Among them are:

Toronto Star Columnist, 1980's (introducing Multiculturalism to Canadians) and & 1990's (looking at contemporary bioethical issues from a Buddhist perspective). See *Embryo as Person: Buddhism, Bioethics and Society*, and *Reflections*, in the list below).

Dawasa Columnist, under the pseudonym *Madhupa* 'honey-sucker', 1960's, prior to leaving for overseas on his US Fulbright Scholarship.

B. BOOKS

I THESES
Doctoral
    1. *Humanistic Nationism: a Language- and Ideology-based Model of National Development, with Special Reference to Post-Colonial Nations*, Ontario Institute of Studies in Education, University of Toronto, Canada (1978).

Master's
    2. *The Sinhala Short Story: Origins and Development (1860-1960)* (in Sinhala), Vidyalankara University, Sri Lanka (1964).

    3. *Morphological Analysis of the Finite Verb in Sinhala*, University of Pennsylvania, Philadelphia, USA (1966).

II ACADEMIC
Buddhism
    4. Sugunasiri, Suwanda H. J., 2001, *You're What You Sense: Buddha on Mondbody*
- Sinhala translation: *oba yanu hudek induran maey*!, Dehiwala, Sri Lanka: Buddhist Cultural Centre (forthcoming).
- Spanish translation: Tu eres lo que sientes.
- Russian translation: ТЫ — ТО, ЧТО ТЫ ЧУВСТВУЕШЬ "Ty-to chto ty chuvsbuyesh" (forthcoming)

    5. *Embyo as Person.: Buddhism, Bioethics and Society*, Toronto: Nalanda Publishing Canada (2005).

    6. *Arahant Mahinda as Redactor of the Buddhapujava in Sinhala Buddhism* (with Pali text, translation and analysis), Colombo, Sri Lanka: Godage International Publishing (2012).

7. *Dhamma Aboard Evolution: a Canonical Study of Aggñña Sutta in relation to Science*, Toronto, Canada: Nalanda Publishing Canada (2014).

8. *Night of the Buddha's Enlightenment*, Sumeru Canada (2016).

9. *Triune Mind, Triune Brain: Map of the Mind through the Eyes of Buddhianscience and Westernscience*, Lambert Academic Publishing (2017).

10. *Swarna Sugunasiri: Born-Sreamwinner, Next Life Nibbana* (forthcoming).

11. *Death, Heavenly Sky-Rebecoming and Rebirth: Life Cycle of the Meritorious* (forthcoming).

12. *Ethics is for the Mind as Food is for the Body* (forthcoming).

Literature

13. *Step Down Shakespeare, the Stone Angel is Here: Essays on Literature, Canadian and Sri Lankan*, Toronto: Nalanda Publishing Canada (2007).

14. *Sinhala Short Story: Origins and Development of the* (1860 – 1960), Colombo, Sri Lanka: Godage International Publishing (2021) (forthcoming).

III POPULAR

15. *Reflections* (60 Collection of articles), Family (1996).

16. *Towards Multicultural Growth: A Look at Canada from Classical Racism to Neo-multiculturalism*, Toronto: Village Publishing House (2001).

Children's Books

17. *Two Palm Bow*, 2012
    - *Die Verbeugung* (German Edition), 2014
    - *La Venia de Dos Palmas* (Spanish Edition) 2014

IV EDITED WORKS

18. *Search for Meaning: The Literature of Canadians of South Asian Origins*, Ottawa, Canada: Secretary of State, Department of Multiculturalism, Government of Canada (1983 (1988)).

19. *Sri Lankan Literature* (*Toronto South Asian Review* Special issue.. (co-edited with A. V. Suraweera) (1983/4)

20. *The Literature of Canadians of South Asian Origins*, Centre for South Asian Studies, University of Toronto, Canada; Multicultural History Society of Ontario (1987).

21. *The Whistling Thorn: An Anthology of South Asian Canadian Fiction*, Oakville, Ontario, Canada: Mosaic Press (1996).

22. *Thus Spake the Sangha: Early Buddhist [Sangha] Leadership in Toronto*, Toronto: Nalanda Publishing Canada (2008).

23. *Sauris Silva of Tangalla, in the Eyes of Himself and Others*, Colombo: Godage International Publishing (2016).

24. *Medieval Ceylon: Language, Literature and Politics* (a collection of Articles by Prof. Herbert Guenther, written in the 1940's), Colombo, Sri Lanka, Royal Asiatic Society (2021).

V CREATIVE WRITING
Poetry
25. *Faces of Galle Face Green,* Toronto: TSAR Publishing (1995); Reprint, Colombo, Sri Lanka: Sarasavi (2007).

26. *Celestial Conversations,* Toronto: Nalanda Publishing Canada (2006).

27. *Obama-Ji,* Toronto: Nalanda Publishing Canada (2009).

28. *Waves of Cuba,* Toronto: Nalanda Publishing Canada (2010).

Novel
29. *Untouchable Woman's Odyssey,* Toronto: Nalanda Publishing Canada 2012).

VI WORKS IN SINHALA
Translations
30. Bertrand Russel, *Commonsense and Nuclear Warfare*, Gunasena Publishing (1963).

31. A B Keith, *Classical Sanskrit Literature*, Department of National Languages, Government of Ceylon (1965).

Creative Writing
32. *Nonagate* 'Inauspicious Hour' (with P. G. Punchihewa), Gampaha: Sarasavi (1960).

33. *Yamayudde* 'Life Struggle', Colombo: Gunasena Publishing (1961).

34. *Meeharak* 'Idiots', Colombo: Gunasena Publishing (1963).

FEATURED IN

Canadian Who's Who;
June Callwood's *'National Treasure'* on Vision TV;
Canada at the Millennium;
Canadian Encyclopedia of Literature;
Wild Geese, Buddhism in Canada.

COMMENTS

"An extraordinary thesis" (Doctoral: *Humanistic Nationism* ....)
- 'Prof. Roby Kidd, Internal Appraiser, OISE, U of Toronto.

"An extraordinary first novel" (*Untouchable Woman's Odyssey*)
- Prof. Chelva Kanaganayakam, Dept. of English, Trinity. College, U of Toronto.

"The dominant themes of Sugunasiri's verse is a strong political commitment alongside detached, pietic Buddhism.. There is much less of diasporic ..and much more of a straight out pleading for Commonsense and non-violence".
- Prof. Vijay Mishra, Australia (Canadian Literature).

"Sugunasiri helped shape the development of Buddhism in this country. His life story is a prism through which the history of Buddhism in Canada comes into focus."
- Professors Victor Hori, McGill University and Janet McLellan, Wilfrid Laurier University, *Wild Geese: Buddhism in Canada*

MEDIA
Toronto Star Columnist.
CBC, CTV, TVO, Vision TV, CTS, OMNI, CFRB, BBC

PRINT
Christine McClaymont (ed), 1990, *Viewpoints: Reflections in non-fiction*, Toronto: Nelson Canada (essay).

Diane McGifford (ed), 1992, *The Geography of Voice*, Toronto: TSAR (poetry).

Glen Kirkland & Richard Davies (ed.), 1996, *Dimensions II: Precise thought and language in the essay*, Toronto: Gage (essay).

Cyril Dabydeen (ed), 1997, *Another Way to Dance*, Toronto: TSAR (poetry)

Suwanda H. J. Sugunasiri is a US Fulbright scholar (1964-7), in Canada for over five decades. Formerly on Trinity Divinity, University of Toronto, and now in retirement, he continues with his research and writing. His five academic degrees – London, Pennsylvania and Toronto (3), are in diverse fields: Oriental Languages, Linguistics, Moral Philosophy, National Development and Buddhism.

Long-standing Fieldworker in diverse fields - Multiculturalism, Education, Literature and Interfaith Relations, among others, he served as advocate, advisor, promoter and activist, serving also on several bodies - Ontario Canada Day Committee, Ontario Advisory Council on Multiculturalism and Citizenship and the Ontario Provincial Interfaith Committee on Chaplaincy. Buddhist spokesman since the 1980's, he is the Founder of Nalanda College of Buddhist Studies and Founding Editor of *Canadian Journal of Buddhist Studies*.

Pioneering *Toronto Star* Columnist introducing Multiculturalism to Canadians, his later columns on Buddhism were on contemporary bioethical issues – abortion, euthanasia, homosexuality, cloning, etc. Author of over 300 articles and over 30 books, including three collections of poetry and a novel, *Untouchable Woman's Odyssey,* critiqued in the context of John Bunyan, Joseph Conrad and Mark Twain.

www.ingramcontent.com/pod-product-compliance
Lightning Source LLC
Chambersburg PA
CBHW032015230426
43671CB00005B/95